EDUCATIONAL LEADERSHIP AND PLANNING FOR TECHNOLOGY

Anthony G. Picciano

Hunter College and Graduate Center
City University of New York

PEARSON

Boston   Columbus   Indianapolis   New York   San Francisco   Upper Saddle River
Amsterdam   Cape Town   Dubai   London   Madrid   Milan   Munich   Paris   Montreal   Toronto
Delhi   Mexico City   São Paulo   Sydney   Hong Kong   Seoul   Singapore   Taipei   Tokyo

Vice President and Editor in Chief: Jeffery W. Johnston
Executive Editor and Publisher: Stephen D. Dragin
Vice President, Director of Marketing: Quinn Perkson
Marketing Manager: Christopher Barry
Project Manager: Holly Shufeldt
Editorial Assistant: Jamie Bushell
Senior Art Director: Jayne Conte
Cover Designer: Suzanne Duda
Cover Photo: Fotolia
Full-Service Project Management and Composition: Saraswathi Muralidhar/GGS Higher Education Resources,
    A Division of PreMedia Global Inc.
Printer/Binder and Cover Printer: R. R. Donnelley & Sons Company
Text Font: Minion

Every effort has been made to provide accurate and current Internet information in this book. However, the Internet and information posted on it are constantly changing, so it is inevitable that some of the Internet addresses listed in this textbook will change.

Photo Credits: Ann Bancroft/yourexpedition.com, p. 2; Jupiter Unlimited, pp. 14, 52, 68, 267; Katelyn Metzger/Merrill, p. 35; iStockphoto.com, pp. 91, 133, 214, 248; Bob Daemmrich Photography, Inc., p. 115; David Mager/Pearson Learning Photo Studio, p. 159; Pearson Learning Photo Studio, p. 186, Masterfile Royalty Free Division, p. 228.

Library of Congress Cataloging-in-Publication Data
Picciano, Anthony G.
    Educational leadership and planning for technology / Anthony G. Picciano.—5th ed.
        p. cm.
    Includes index.
    ISBN-13: 978-0-13-705822-8
    ISBN-10: 0-13-705822-5
    1. Education–Data processing–Planning.   2. Computer managed instruction–Planning.   3. Computer-assisted instruction–Planning.   4. School management and organization–Data processing–Planning.   I. Title.
    LB1028.43.P536 2011
    370.285–dc22

                                                                                                2010006096

www.pearsonhighered.com

ISBN 13: 978-0-13-705822-8
ISBN 10:   0-13-705822-5

26 2022

Fifth Edition

EDUCATIONAL LEADERSHIP AND PLANNING FOR TECHNOLOGY

To Sister Anne O'Driscoll
and Sister Genevieve Love

ABOUT THE AUTHOR

Anthony G. Picciano is the author of nine books in the fields of educational leadership, technology, and research methods. *Educational Leadership and Planning for Technology* is the fifth edition of an earlier work, *Computers in the Schools: A Guide to Planning and Administration.* In 2007, Dr. Picciano was a co-editor of *Blended Learning: Research Perspectives* (Sloan Consortium), the first book devoted entirely to research on the then new and growing area of blended or hybrid learning environments. In 2004, Dr. Picciano published the *Educational Research Primer* (Continuum). In 2000, Dr. Picciano published *Distance Learning: Making Connections across Virtual Space and Time* (Merrill/Prentice Hall), which extensively covered the field of online learning.

Dr. Picciano is a professor in the Education Administration and Supervision Program in the School of Education at Hunter College. He is also a member of the faculty in the Ph.D. Program in Urban Education where he is currently serving as the Executive Officer, the doctoral program in Interactive Pedagogy and Technology, and the CUNY Online BA Program in Communication and Culture at the City University of New York Graduate Center. His teaching specialties include educational technology, organization theory, policy, and research methods. From 1994 through 2002, he was a faculty fellow at the City University of New York Open Systems Laboratory, a facility dedicated to experimenting with advanced uses of instructional technology and to providing staff development programs for organizations including public schools, colleges, and private businesses. In 1997, he cofounded CUNY Online, the administrative and faculty development facility for providing online courses for students in the colleges in the City University.

Dr. Picciano has served as a consultant for a variety of public and private organizations, including the Commission on Higher Education/Middle States Association of Colleges and Universities, the New York City Board of Education, the New York State Department of Education, New Leaders for New Schools, the U.S. Coast Guard, and Citicorp. He has received numerous grants and awards from the Alfred P. Sloan Foundation, the National Science Foundation, the U.S. Department of Education, and IBM. His articles have appeared in journals such as *The Teachers College Record, The Urban Review, Equity and Choice, Journal of Asynchronous Learning Networks, Journal of Educational Multimedia and Hypermedia, Computers in the Schools,* and *EDUCOM Review.* He lives with his wife, Elaine, in Pocantico Hills, New York.

Visit Dr. Picciano's Web site at: anthonypicciano.com

BRIEF CONTENTS

CONTENTS

PREFACE

This book provides educators with both the theoretical and practical considerations for planning and implementing technology in schools. Basic concepts of technology and planning that use systems theory are presented. Emphasis is placed on the importance of the total application of technology as opposed to any individual component, be it hardware, software, facilities, personnel, or finances. The book forms a foundation from which educators will provide leadership and become agents for realizing the powerful potential of technology in their schools.

The material is designed for practicing administrators and other educators such as teachers, technology coordinators, and media specialists who are involved in initiating and supporting technology in their schools. This book is most appropriate as a text in a preservice or in-service course on planning technology applications designed primarily for school administrators.

NEW TO THIS EDITION

When I started to write the first edition of this book in 1992, the world of educational technology was quite different than it is now. Technology in schools has evolved from the predominance of stand-alone computers to a blend of computer, media, communications, and other forms of technology dominated by the ubiquitous Internet and World Wide Web. In addition, K–12 education has evolved into a much more outcomes-driven enterprise that depends on technology and data to perform many of its basic functions. This fifth edition has been updated mainly to reflect the expansion and integration of technology and its derivative activities, specifically:

- All chapters and case studies have been updated to reflect current thinking and advances in technology as applied to education including 63 new citations.
- An entire new chapter on data-driven decision making has been added.
- The separate chapters on evaluating hardware and software in the fourth edition have been combined in this edition to reflect the increasing integration of these two components of technology planning.
- New material has been added on social networking, distance learning, blended learning, open source software, eBooks, multimedia, electronic whiteboards, and wireless local area networks.

ORGANIZATION

This book is divided into three sections: I, Basic Concepts and Foundations; II, Technology in Action; and III, Planning and Implementation. Although each chapter can be read independently, it should be taught in sequence. Several supplemental sections are presented for reference: Appendix A reviews basic technology concepts and terminology; Appendix B lists educational leader competencies; Appendix C is a sample checklist to help educators evaluate instructional software; and the Glossary provides a quick reference for technical terms used in the text.

Section I: Basic Concepts and Foundations

Section I provides the basic concepts and foundation for an overall understanding of the themes and major issues related to planning for technology in schools and school systems. It is directed specifically to those who are or will be leading their schools in planning for technology. This section concludes with a chapter on pedagogical and social issues related to technology that should be considered as part of the planning process. Readers who are not familiar with basic technology—especially computer concepts or terminology—should review Appendix A before proceeding beyond this section.

Section II: Technology in Action

Section II provides six chapters on the nature of technology applications used for both administration and instruction. Although similar in some respects, enough differences exist in the nature, design, and policies associated with administrative and instructional applications that they require separate treatments. A chapter on data-driven decision making has been added and is new to this edition. Three separate chapters discuss technologies related to multimedia, and the Internet, and distance learning conclude this section.

Section III: Planning and Implementation

Section III presents the primary components of planning for and developing technology applications in schools and provides practical information on evaluating and implementing these components. Entire chapters are devoted to hardware and software evaluation; people, technology, and professional development; facilities, policies, and procedures; and financial planning for technology.

End-of-Chapter Elements

Each chapter concludes with key concepts and questions, suggested activities, and/or case studies to stimulate thought and discussion on the material presented. They also relate the material to situations that exist in schools. The case studies, although having some basis in fact, are fictitious and designed to put the reader in the position of leaders having to make decisions about technology and related issues. Reference lists are also provided at the end of each chapter.

Epilogue

The Epilogue re-emphasizes the need for school leaders to look to the future and to integrate technology into their visions for their schools.

Definition of Terms

Technology is a general term applied to various administrative and instructional applications involving calculators, overhead projectors, telephones, television, and so forth. In this book, technology refers primarily to computer as well as other technologies such as data communications, video, and multimedia.

School districts sometimes are referred to as small, medium, or large, depending on their enrollment:

Small: fewer than 600 students

Medium: at least 600 but fewer than 25,000 students

Large: more than 25,000 students

School districts in the United States generally are governed by independently elected or appointed boards of education with the power to raise taxes and issue bonds. Some districts, particularly those in urban areas, are governed by other governmental entities such as a municipality, from which they receive an operating budget. Unless otherwise noted, references to school districts include all school districts. In some cases, the term *municipally governed* is used to refer specifically to those school districts described earlier.

ACKNOWLEDGMENTS

I gratefully acknowledge the guidance and assistance provided by the Pearson staff, especially Steve Dragin, without whom this fifth edition might never have been written. I thank the production staff at GGS Higher Education Resources especially Saraswathi Muralidhar.

I am most grateful to a distinguished group of reviewers who took the time to read the previous edition and made many fine suggestions for this fifth edition: Patrick Durow, Creighton University; Jim Jeffery, Andrews University; and Steven B. Smith, Northern Kentucky University.

In addition, I have benefited significantly from my professional associations with a number of colleagues, specifically the faculty in the Department of Curriculum and Teaching at Hunter College, the faculty and staff in the Ph.D. Program in Urban Education at the CUNY Graduate Center, colleagues at the Alfred P. Sloan Consortium, and all of the school administrators who provided source material and who are truly leading their schools in creative uses of technology.

Especially important to my efforts were the students in the Administration and Supervision Program at Hunter College and the students in the Urban Education Program at the CUNY Graduate Center. They are an industrious group of individuals who will make many fine contributions to education for years to come.

Lastly, my gratitude to Michael and Dawn Marie, Michael Anthony, Isabella, Ali, and Grace Sophia, who have helped me to be a better person, and Elaine, my wife, companion, and friend who always supports me in everything I do.

Anthony G. Picciano

Section I

BASIC CONCEPTS AND FOUNDATIONS

Chapter 1

Introduction to Technology and Planning

On February 11, 2001, Ann Bancroft and Liv Arnesen became the first women to cross Antarctica on foot. It took 94 days of walking, skiing, and ski-sailing to complete the 1,700-mile trip in temperatures as low as −35°F. Although the expedition itself will go down in history as a great feat of woman against nature, there are other elements of the Ann and Liv story that are of particular interest to educators.

Ann is from Minnesota and was a former physical education and special education teacher; Liv, a Norwegian, was a former literature and physical education teacher. A significant aspect of their efforts was to share their journey with others—especially schoolchildren. As part of the meticulous planning, they developed curriculum materials that could be shared with children throughout the world. In addition to all of the basic survival equipment (fuel, food, tents, clothes, skiing equipment, stoves) needed to exist on the frozen continent for 3 months, Ann and Liv also carried a good deal of computer and communications equipment that would be used not only to keep contact with their base camp but also to tell their story to children in classrooms. They chose not simply to log their day-to-day activities in a journal but to share them through audio and video files that could be downloaded to Web sites anywhere in the world where children had access to the Internet. When asked why they devoted so much energy and effort to sharing their experience with the world's children, Ann and Liv responded: "to inspire and to touch kids' lives."

Anyone who has had the privilege of being a teacher knows that at one level, teaching is about information, child development, social maturation, and so forth, but at its highest level, to teach is to inspire. The best teachers understand that their most important goal is to be an inspiration to children to learn, to dream, and to try to accomplish. Ann and Liv accomplished their goal well. More than 3 million students in 116 countries learned, followed, and participated (virtually) in their journey.

The story of Ann and Liv is provocative spiritually but also serves as an apt introduction to the main topic of this book: technology in schools. Once on Antarctica, they relied solely on their human strength and endurance to complete their journey; however, to touch children's lives, they were totally dependent upon technology including an Apple laptop computer, a satellite phone, and digital cameras. They used the Internet extensively for communicating with schools literally around the world. Most of their equipment with the exception of their energy packs could be purchased at a local computer store. The Internet of Ann and Liv is the same Internet that most children use to send e-mail, to share bits of themselves on social networking Web sites, to look up information, and to do schoolwork. The Internet—which has reshaped much of humankind's social, professional, and educational activities—can connect people even in the most isolated places.

Liv, while resting one night in her tent on the ice of Antarctica, reflected:

> It was funny to think that the rest of the world was so accessible to us through this modern technology, and yet, if Ann and I were to be injured in this area, no plane could land here to save us. The terrain was too rough. We were completely connected and completely isolated at the same time. (Arnesen & Bancroft, 2003, p. 8)

Liv's observation is an important one because increasingly it is the nature of digital communications technology to bring people together even when they are miles apart. An important aspect of this book is to present the benefits of technology to connect teaching and learning, to connect students to knowledge, and to connect educators to the powerful potential of modern digital communications, computers, and media equipment for the betterment of schools and schooling.

Ann and Liv's accomplishment was the culmination of years of planning. The key to success was the fact that they had a vision of something they wanted to do and were able to lead and persuade others to help them accomplish it. Thousands of educators in schools around the country are in positions similar to that of Ann and Liv. They are in positions to lead others in developing and implementing projects and programs that will surely touch children's lives. They need vision and resources—but, most importantly, they need the will to share and accomplish their goals with others.

PURPOSE

Explaining the purpose of this book requires a discussion of the purposes of schools and schooling. Educational technology, to be successful, must be integrated into the main functions of schools. Technology for technology's sake is an expensive and generally futile endeavor. However, when integrated into an educator's vision of what children and young adults need to learn about the world and themselves, then technology can be an effective tool in achieving that vision.

Views differ among educators and communities regarding the purposes of schools and schooling. For some, education should focus on the intellectual and emotional needs of children. For others, the focus may be a society's social and economic needs. Fundamental to most of these views is a sense that children, as a result of education, will come away with a desire to learn more about themselves, others, and the world about them. Drawing from experiential theories, a basic assumption is that children are born with a natural curiosity about the world, and the main function of schooling should be to stimulate that curiosity. Once the desire to learn has been instilled, children will learn a great deal on their own. Schooling succeeds when children begin to learn through experiences, and by learning they are motivated to experience more, so that a cycle of lifelong learning and experiencing evolves. Seymour Sarason (1995) describes this concept most succinctly:

> If when a child is motivated to learn more about self and the world, then I would say that schooling has achieved its overarching purpose. . . . The student knows that the more you know the more you need to know. . . . To want to continue to explore, to find answers to personally meaningful questions, issues, and possibilities is the most important purpose of schooling. (p. 135)

The role of technology in achieving this purpose can be made evident by briefly describing its relationship to education. For much of the 20th century, technology in education centered upon print media. Paper, pens, books, and chalk were critical for communicating ideas, accessing information, and learning about the world. In the latter part of the 20th century, electronic media began to replace print media. Word processing, e-mail, fax modems, CD-ROMs, DVDs, multimedia, teleconferencing, videoconferencing, and the Internet have become the common tools for communicating ideas and accessing information. The morning newspaper is now read either in paper form or at a Web site to provide additional insight into what was already seen and heard on the nightly news broadcast. The linearity of the sentence, paragraph, and page is used in conjunction with hypertext branching and searching. The one-dimensionality of the lecture achieves depth and perspective as it is integrated into multiple, interactive dialogues and small-group discussions on local and international data communications networks. Technology is becoming the tool of choice for communicating in, accessing, and learning about our world. It should be integrated with any educational vision or plan that attempts to help individuals, including children, understand this world.

The purpose of this book is to provide educators with both the theoretical framework and the practical considerations for planning and implementing technology in schools. Basic concepts of technology and planning that use systems theory are presented. The book emphasizes the importance of the total application of technology in the educational enterprise more so than any individual component, be it hardware, software, facilities, or staff. This book is meant to form the foundation from which educators will look ahead and become the agents for realizing the powerful potential of technology in their schools.

THE POTENTIAL IN PRIMARY AND SECONDARY SCHOOLS

"For many firms, using computers . . . is an absolute necessity." So said James O'Brien (1989, p. 33) about the use of computers in business organizations. His readers would have accepted this statement with little reservation. In the latter part of the 20th century, computer (or digital) technology became an integral part of most business operations, as fundamental as accounting, finance, marketing, and management. Architects, engineers, bankers, and salespersons routinely used computers for various aspects of their jobs.

The same was true for many organizations in the public sector. High-technology agencies such as the Department of Defense, NASA, and the Federal Aviation Administration have become totally dependent on computers for all aspects of their operations. Weapons systems, the space shuttle missions, and air traffic are controlled almost exclusively by computer technology. Most other public agencies, such as the Internal Revenue Service and the Social Security Administration, also rely on sophisticated information retrieval systems to conduct their operations. Take a walk through a hospital, a library, or a college, and you will likely see technology routinely used to monitor a patient's heartbeat, to borrow a book, or to conduct research.

Those who have studied and observed the use of computers in primary and secondary education see a substantially different picture. Educators are surely interested in the potential of the technology but also express reservations in its implementation.

In June 1997, the journal *Technological Horizons in Education* celebrated its 25th anniversary with a special edition that looked back at educational technology milestones over the preceding 25 years. Articles by major contributors to the field of educational technology celebrated achievements and lamented obstacles. Technology luminaries such as Andrew Molnar, Director for Applications of Advanced Technologies, National Science Foundation; Seymour Papert, developer of Logo and professor at the Media Laboratory, Massachusetts Institute of Technology; and Alfred Bork, Professor Emeritus, Information and Computer Science, University of California, Irvine, all agreed that technology in education had grown since the 1970s from an object of study to an indispensable tool. However, they also agreed that the potential had yet to be realized and that education was not as far along as other endeavors in its use of technology. Molnar summed up the situation well:

> "The world of education has changed from an orderly world of disciplines . . . to an infosphere in which communication technologies are increasingly important. While education is changing, it is not changing fast enough." (Molnar, 1997, p.68)

In the provocatively titled book *Oversold and Underused* (2001), Larry Cuban, a professor at Stanford University and a respected voice in American education, saw as the major problem the lack of involvement of teachers in decisions regarding the implementation of technology. He argued that in too many schools teachers were not given a say in how the technology might reshape their instruction and, as a result, computers functioned basically as high-speed typewriters and that classrooms continue to run much as they did generations ago. In his studies of early childhood, high school, and university classrooms in Silicon Valley, Cuban also found that students and teachers use the new technologies far less in the classroom than they do at home and that teachers who use computers for instruction do so infrequently and unimaginatively. Cuban further points out that historical and organizational economic contexts influence how teachers use technical innovations. Computers can be useful when teachers sufficiently understand the technology themselves, believe it will enhance learning, and have the power to shape their own curricula.

Recent research tends to support the above observations. In 2007, the National Center for Education Statistics (see Dynarski et al., 2007) issued a report based on a series of experimental and quasi-experimental studies on the use of a number of different reading and mathematics educational software products by 439 teachers in 132 schools in 33 districts. The major findings indicated that test scores in treatment classrooms that were randomly assigned to use the software products did not differ from test scores in control classrooms that used traditional instructional methods. This study was followed up 2 years later and essentially made the same findings (see Campuzano et al., 2009).

The conclusion here is that although schools continue to invest significant resources in technology, educators are still cautious and concerned about its impact and that much instruction relies heavily on traditional people-intensive modes of instruction. In sum, we can make airline reservations, buy lottery tickets, withdraw money, or tally a cart of groceries electronically at the push of a button or the wave of a wand. Yet, the vast majority of primary and secondary schools continue to rely on intensive manual efforts to conduct one of our most important "businesses"—that is, the education of children. Why this has occurred is an important starting point for the study of planning and administering technology in primary and secondary schools.

THE BEGINNING YEARS

Primary and secondary schools were effectively excluded in the early years of the computer revolution (1960s and 1970s) for a variety of reasons. Much of the earliest software provided for computers was designed for data processing applications rather than for educational purposes. The exceptions were several scientific software languages and packages that were useful in organized research activities and major military-industrial and space exploration projects. International Business Machines (IBM), which dominated the entire computer industry and provided much of the leadership, developed products for organizations that were already part of an office machine customer base, such as users of typewriters and punch card equipment. Although extremely active in higher-education markets (to familiarize future business leaders and engineers with its products), IBM was not as active in marketing to primary and secondary schools. In a 1988 article in *Think*, an IBM publication, Jim Dezell, the general manager of IBM's Educational Systems, was quoted as saying, "We were way behind, way behind. . . . As recently as three years ago, the only IBM software in education . . . the company was offering was Writing to Read. . . . We had no installed base or customer references" (Grimm, 1988, p. 5).

Schools have a long tradition of being people oriented rather than machine oriented. In addition to teaching, schools provide nourishment, health, recreation, and other social services to their students. A fundamental concept of teacher education is to nurture children and to take care of the "whole" child. As a result, in their earliest courses teachers are trained to be child oriented. Many of them considered most of the earlier computer technology as an impersonal approach to teaching, particularly in the primary grades, and did not embrace it. Furthermore, teachers who received their training prior to 1990 likely did not receive formal training in computer technology in their undergraduate programs. As a result, this technology did not become a routine part of their repertoire of teaching tools.

When major advances in computer technology were being made in the 1960s and 1970s, schools were also going through significant changes. No other organizations in this country were affected as much by the major social issues of the times as were the primary and secondary schools. Racial integration, bilingual education, and the rights of persons with disabling conditions have affected all aspects of society. However, it was the schools that were called on to spearhead changes in the way the United States would resolve these issues. While private businesses and many governmental agencies were gradually changing, major and sudden changes were occurring in the nation's schools. These changes rightfully dominated much of the planning that school administrators and education policy makers did and became the major priorities for improving the schools and their instructional programs.

Although some larger school districts could afford it, most of the 15,000-plus school districts in the nation did not have adequate financial resources to invest in the new computer technology. Businesses were willing to invest resources in designing and developing computer applications, but schools used their available resources for other priorities. Smaller school districts could afford neither the hardware nor the expensive support staff that the large mainframe computer systems of the 1960s and early 1970s required. Some districts made pioneering attempts to use time-sharing systems provided by universities, state and local agencies, and educational consortia, but these efforts did not affect the vast majority of teachers and students in the schools. As late as 1980, after reviewing the results of several national surveys, H. J. Becker (1991, 1994) estimated that no more than 50,000 microcomputers or computer terminals were available in the nation's primary and secondary schools. With more than 40 million students and a student-to-computer ratio of 800:1, this technology was surely not a part of their educational experiences.

Without hardware, software, or training and with other more important and pressing priorities, primary and secondary schools did not enter the technology revolution that occurred in the 1960s and 1970s. However, the situation changed in the late 1970s and early 1980s with the introduction of microcomputers. Major new computer manufacturers such as Apple, Commodore, Tandy, and Atari were genuinely interested in marketing their products to schools. They were also interested in the children's market in general and provided hardware and software that could be used in the home for playing electronic games. Teachers and school administrators began to observe that more and more children were becoming computer literate at home. Parents were also becoming more familiar with computer technology as their workplaces began to require them to use it. New software companies such as Sunburst, Broderbund, Tom Snyder Productions, and Scholastic appeared almost overnight with educational software that was more appealing and pedagogically more interesting than any developed in the previous 20 years. As a result, schools finally began to make meaningful investments in computer technology in the 1980s. With the advent of the Internet in the 1990s, schools accelerated their involvement with and investment in technology (as did all segments of society) as they attempted to connect to the communications and data resources of the information superhighway.

At the beginning of the 21st century, helped by a reduction in hardware prices combined with federal subsidy programs such as E-Rate, school districts have begun to aggressively purchase hardware and software to support administrative and instructional activities. Although unquestionably behind other American enterprises, schools have begun to make significant strides. The time has come for administrators and teachers to take control and harness the power of the technology at their disposal. This task involves engaging in thoughtful evaluation, discarding or improving what does not work, accepting and building on what does, and carefully planning for new applications.

STEADY PROGRESS IN ADMINISTRATIVE SYSTEMS

Technology applications in education can be divided into two major categories: administrative and instructional. Administrative applications support the administrative functions of a district or school. Examples include database management and transaction-processing systems such as student demographics, grading, budgeting, payroll, personnel, scheduling, and inventory control, all of which are designed for and used primarily by administrative staff. Instructional applications support teaching and learning activities that are designed for and used mainly by teachers, school library media specialists, and students. The background, implementation, and planning for these two major categories of applications are different and need to be distinguished.

Administrative systems have progressed more steadily than instructional applications because they are similar to the data processing applications in private industry and public agencies. Customer and product database management systems in private businesses resemble student and course systems in schools; personnel, payroll, and financial database systems designed for public agencies are identical to those used in schools. As a result, schools were able to draw on the expertise and software products developed for general data processing applications for their own administrative operations. Computer manufacturers, software developers, and data processing service bureaus could market many of the same products to schools, private industry, and government agencies. Many of the larger school districts were able to afford and use the benefits of these data processing applications. For example, school districts governed by local municipalities generally were required to follow the same administrative procedures established for all the other agencies under the municipality's jurisdiction. This was especially true for financial applications such as budgeting, payroll, and purchasing. As municipalities began to computerize these applications, so did the school districts.

In the late 1960s and 1970s, state education departments became much more active in data collection and evaluation activities, partly because of the reporting requirements of the federal government regarding entitlement programs and partly because of a desire and need to better understand what the schools were doing. Schools were increasingly required to provide data on student demographics, performance, and expenditures. To streamline these data collection activities, some states (e.g., Florida, Minnesota, Texas) established statewide computer networks to assist the school districts. Administrators soon were able to use these networks not only to fulfill the reporting requirements but also to meet their own informational and other administrative needs.

By the 1970s and 1980s, as microcomputers became available, many school districts were converting existing applications or developing new ones to meet their administrative needs. Even districts with very little access to computing before this period were able to draw on the experiences of other districts and utilize established software products.

In the late 1990s and the early part of the 21st century, as federal, state, and local governing bodies required schools to become more accountable, school districts have invested significantly in data-driven decision-making systems designed to monitor carefully student outcomes and to provide parents and the public, in general, with "report cards" for each school. In addition to meeting reporting requirements, these systems can also aid in designing and developing intervention strategies that can improve student performance.

INSTRUCTIONAL SYSTEMS SHOW PROMISE

The comments in The Beginning Years section of this chapter that referred to the potential of computer technology, reflect the thinking of educators regarding the instructional rather than the administrative uses of computers in schools. Practically all schools have begun to invest in technology, but many are struggling with it for various reasons in terms of a teaching philosophy, the benefits, and problems in implementation.

Most of the early research and development that went into software development was directed to improving data processing applications that were prevalent in businesses and many public agencies. Such research concentrated on data and information flow and was primarily concerned with improving speed and other transaction-processing features. Although critical to high-volume, service-oriented organizations such as banks, insurance companies, stock broker-age houses, and many governmental agencies, these features were of minimal value to teaching and learning. Several of the early attempts at developing packages for schools consisted of copies and conversions of software developed primarily for businesses and other organizations. For example, the Bank Street College of Education, which enjoyed an excellent reputation for having developed a variety of interesting educational software packages, started by converting standard word processing (Bank Street Writer) and database management (Bank Street Filer) software for use in primary and secondary schools.

Many of the earliest instructional software applications developed in primary and secondary schools in the 1960s and 1970s were of the drill-and-practice variety and concentrated on providing repetitive exercises for learning basic skills. Although drill and practice is widely used by teachers using flash cards and other manual techniques, when delivered electronically on computers it became the topic of much debate (Gagné, 1977; Trumbull, 1986; Yates, 1983). Although drill and practice has proponents, many teachers were not receptive to the early software developed in the 1960s and 1970s. Some, in fact, were turned off to computing technology in general and viewed it as an impersonal, "Big Brother is watching" approach. Even if schools wanted to use software before 1980, they still had to overcome financial and other technical hurdles. To deliver computing power to the classroom using a large mainframe or even a mini-computer system required a significant organizational commitment. Hardware costs alone made it prohibitive for many school districts. Other problems (e.g., establishing data communications networks to allow student access, attracting and training highly paid technicians, building environmentally controlled facilities) made it impossible for all but some of the larger districts.

In the early 1980s, with the proliferation of microcomputers, some of these problems were overcome. Hardware costs decreased dramatically. Software began to be designed for children. Although intended more for entertainment than education, video games were effective in breaking down the first barriers that prevented children from using computer technology. In addition, video games such as *Pac-Man* and *Space Invaders* relied heavily on motion and graphics that significantly added to their appeal to children. As a result, a good deal of software research and development in the 1980s was devoted to improving graphics, not just for children but for adult and business applications also. Thousands of titles of software packages now exist that were designed for children and are very appropriate for use in primary and secondary schools. Video gaming is growing in popularity as the software for developing games becomes easier to use. Howe (2008) describes the popularity of summer cyber camps where high schoolers learn how to design and develop their own video games.

According to data collected in a national survey by Quality Education Data (1996), 98% of all public schools had acquired some form of computer technology by 1990. By 1999, the vast majority of all classrooms were connected to the Internet and schools had an average ratio of one instructional computer for every 5.7 students (Fatemi, 1999). By 2008, the ratio had dropped to as little as one instructional computer for every three students with some states (e.g., Maine and South Dakota) and as low as one computer for every two students in other states (Bausell, 2008). Presently, school districts have begun to introduce "laptop for every child" policies wherein laptops are purchased for all children. The software applications on these laptops are integrated with instructional activities, serve as textbooks, and are used as communications devices among teachers and students during and after school hours.

THE NEED FOR PLANNING

One of the major issues impeding the establishment of successful technology programs in schools is the lack of careful and effective planning. Although some schools and districts have shown progress, others appear to be struggling. Cuban (2006, 2001, 1993) and others lament that even though technology is widely being acquired in American schools, its successful impact on learning tends to be more the exception than the rule. For instance, the November 2003 issue of *Education Week* included an article titled "Budget Crises May Undercut Laptop Efforts" (Trotter, 2003). It described a number of school districts throughout the country that were having second thoughts about participating in "laptop for every student" initiatives. School districts in Maine, Michigan, Washington, and South Carolina had decided not to participate in state-sponsored programs or to withdraw from programs they had already started. The fundamental problem presented was that educational policy makers had invested significant resources on initial funding for the laptop program without considering future costs. It has been well documented that for many technology programs, ongoing costs for staff support, training, repairs, and upgrades frequently equal if not exceed the start-up costs.

Problems of hardware cost and software development and acquisition are being resolved, but other problems such as curricular integration and staff development remain. Careful planning at both the district and school building levels would more clearly define these problems and provide alternatives for their resolution. Planning for technology requires concentrating on a total application. By choosing an application and asking what is needed to make it successful, educators will naturally have to consider questions regarding obvious components such as hardware and software as well as other less obvious components such as staff development, curricular integration, facilities, and ongoing maintenance. To emphasize further the importance of planning, the U.S. federal government now requires school districts to have approved technology plans to participate in the Universal Service Fund program, commonly known as the E-Rate program. Most states have also established a similar requirement in order to apply for technology grant programs funded by the No Child Left Behind Act of 2002.

Another important aspect of planning is evaluation and feedback. Although schools have implemented computer applications, few have evaluated them in terms of achieving intended goals or objectives. Evaluation in education is not easy, given the variability of human conditions and skills. However, because they are dealing with new approaches, administrators need to assess what works or does not work in their schools. What is successful in one school or district may not be successful in another. Why this happens is the essence of evaluation, a process that identifies strengths and weaknesses in all the various components of an application within a specific operating environment. For example, excellent hardware with poor software will likely not result in a successful application, nor will excellent hardware and software ensure success without teachers and other staff members who know how to use them properly. All components depend on each other, and a weakness in one affects all the others. By the same token, a particular strength in one component may disguise or make up for weaknesses in another component. For instance, some of the early successes of computer applications in the schools involved teachers and administrators who were most interested in and enthused about using technology. Their basic interests and enthusiasm were strengths that made for apparent successful applications even in cases in which software was mediocre or facilities were inadequate. However, as administrators attempted to replicate these applications with less interested or less knowledgeable staff in other settings, the weaknesses frequently became more apparent and the applications failed.

Planning for technology also requires involvement of the people who will ultimately use a computer application, be they administrators, teachers, or clerical staff. For the many reasons already discussed, educators have been cautious and in some cases even antagonistic regarding computer technology. Top–down implementation of computer applications without consultation and involvement will likely increase resistance among staff and may possibly doom entire undertakings. Involvement is critical—particularly in identifying training and curricular needs and other less obvious components of a computer application, to say nothing of securing the commitment of those who will ultimately influence its success or failure. In private industry, public agencies, and other segments of society that have been using computer technology for many years, the concept of planning has become widely accepted. For many organizations, planning resulted from trial and error, like some schools are experiencing today. For others, planning resulted from a gradual change in thinking that evolved as their organizations became more dependent on computer technology. At the same time, systems analysts, software engineers, and information specialists became managers who were increasingly involved in the overall operations. Their prior training in systematic problem solving and analysis allowed them to adapt their analytical skills to broader organizational issues that required planning and evaluation methods and tools.

Conversely, in school systems, with the exception of some larger school districts, systems analysts and designers generally are not present in the administrative hierarchy. As a result, school administrators and teachers must assume the responsibility for planning for technology.

THE SYSTEMS APPROACH

In presenting any topic, a basic framework for study needs to be established. Systems theory is most appropriate for the major topics of this book: technology in primary and secondary schools and the need for planning for successful implementation of technology applications. The basic systems concepts of "input, process, and output" and their interrelationship are generally accepted as fundamental to all aspects of computer technology. For example, the basic configuration of a computer hardware system consists of one input device, a central processor, and one output device. All other hardware configurations are variations of this, whether with multiple input, processor, or output devices or with multiple hardware systems and subsystems working together.

The systems approach is also appropriate for studying schools and school processes, including planning. Many social scientists and sociologists would describe and analyze schools as social systems. Basic concepts of input, process, and output are regularly applied to communities, students, teaching, curriculum, and outcomes in describing school systems. Using systems theory for presenting the technical aspects of computing technology and the planning aspects of school administration makes for a consistent, integrated approach for presenting the material in this book. It would be difficult and perhaps impossible to identify another framework that would work as well.

ORGANIZATION

This book is organized into three major sections. Section I provides the basic concepts and foundation material for an overall understanding of the themes and major issues related to planning for technology in schools and school systems. The foundation of sound planning is conceived as the total application of the technology. Important policy issues in planning for technology are also presented.

Section II presents major applications of technology as used in schools today. A variety of administrative and instructional applications are examined in terms of planning implications.

Section III develops the implementation of each of the major components of successful technology applications: hardware, software, people, facilities, policies, procedures, and finances. The objective is to relate each of these components to an overall application.

The book concludes with appendices and a glossary of technical terms. Appendix A is designed to provide a review of basic computer concepts. Appendix B identifies the competencies required for educational administrators to be leaders in planning, developing, and implementing technology in their schools and districts. Appendix C serves as a checklist to help educators evaluate instructional software. The Glossary is a quick reference for providing definitions of technical terms.

Summary

This book offers a foundation that educators can use to become the agents for realizing the potential of technology in their schools. The current state of the uses of computer technology for administrative and instructional applications has been briefly described in this chapter. Administrative applications have progressed steadily, but opinions vary as to the benefits of technology in regard to instructional applications. Administrators need to plan and carefully evaluate the implementation of computer technology in their schools. The chapter also establishes systems theory as an appropriate framework for examining technology and planning its implementation.

Key Concepts and Questions

1. Schools have not evolved as other organizations have in the use of computer technology. Why?

2. Administrative computer applications are different in design and purpose from instructional or academic applications. Are there counterparts to administrative applications in organizations other than schools? How are they similar or dissimilar? Are there counterparts to instructional applications in noneducational organizations? How are they similar or dissimilar?

3. Administrative applications have progressed more steadily than instructional applications. Why? Is this changing? Will it change in the future? Explain.

4. Planning for computer technology should center on the application rather than on only hardware, software, or other individual components. How and where in a district or school should this planning occur? Who should be the major participants in planning for technology? Explain.

5. Systems theory is appropriate for technology applications in schools. What is the systems approach? Does it apply only to technology such as computer systems? Identify nontechnical environments in which the systems approach is an appropriate framework for describing and analyzing processes.

Suggested Activities

1. Consider a school district or school with which you are familiar. When did it first become involved with computer technology? What were the first types of applications that were implemented? How advanced is the school or district now in terms of its use of computer technology? Visit the Web sites of several school districts and schools; compare how they are using technology to communicate who and what they are.

2. Compare a school to a local private business or a public agency in terms of reliance on computer technology for

conducting daily operations. Which relies more heavily on technology? If computers were suddenly eliminated, would classes and other activities be conducted as usual in the school? What would happen in a private business or public agency?

3. For students who are unfamiliar with computers or who need a review of computer technology, Appendix A (at the end of the textbook) provides an introduction to basic computer concepts.

References

Arnesen, L., & Bancroft, A. (2003). *No horizon is so far.* Cambridge, MA: Da Capo Press.

Bausell, C. V. (2008). Tracking U.S. trends. *Education Week, 27*(30). Retrieved February 23, 2009, from http://www.edweek.org/ew/articles/2008/03/27/30trends.h2.html?qs=Technology+Counts

Becker, H. J. (1991). How computers are used in United States schools: Basic data from the 1989 I.E.A. Computers in Education survey. *Journal of Educational Computing Research, 7*(4), 385–406.

Becker, H. J. (1994). *Analysis and trends of school use of new information technologies.* Irvine: Department of Education, University of California.

Bork, A. (1997). The future of computers and learning. *Technological Horizons in Education Journal, 24*(11), 69–77.

Campuzano, L., Dynarski, M., Agodini, R., & Rall, K. (2009). Effectiveness of reading and mathematics software products: Findings from two cohorts. Washington, D.C.: U.S. Department of Education, Institute of Education Sciences - NCEE 2009-4041.

Cuban, L. (1993). Computers meet classroom: Classroom wins. *Teachers College Record, 95*(2), 185-210.

Cuban, L. (2001). *Oversold and underused.* Cambridge, MA: Harvard University Press.

Cuban, L. (2006, October 31). 1:1 Laptops transforming classrooms: Yeah, sure! *Teachers College Record.* Retrieved February 16, 2009, from http://www.tcrecord.org (ID Number: 12818).

Dynarski, M., Agodini, R., Heaviside, S., Novak, T., Carey, T., Campuzano, L., Means, B., Murphy, R., Penuel, W., Javitz, H., Emery, D., & Sussex, W. (2007).

Effectiveness of reading and mathematics software products: Findings from the first student cohort. Washington, DC: U.S. Department of Education, Institute of Education Sciences.

Fatemi, E. (1999). Building the digital curriculum. *Education Week, 19*(4), 5–8.

Gagné, R. M. (1977). *The conditions of learning.* New York: Holt, Rinehart & Winston.

Grimm, E. (1988). Coming on fast in the classroom. *Think: The IBM Magazine, 54*(6), 5–8.

Howe, J. (2008). *Crowdsourcing.* New York: Crown Business.

Molnar, A. R. (1997). Computers in education: A brief history. *Technological Horizons in Education Journal, 24*(11), 63–68.

O'Brien, J. A. (1989). *Computer concepts and applications with an introduction to software and BASIC.* Homewood, IL: Irwin.

Papert, S. (1997). Educational computing: How are we doing? *Technological Horizons in Education Journal, 24*(11), 78–80.

Quality Education Data. (1996). *Education market guide and mailing list catalog 1996–97.* Denver: Author.

Sarason, S. (1995). *Parental involvement and the political principle: Why the existing governance structure of schools should be abolished.* San Francisco: Jossey-Bass.

Trotter, A. (2003, November 5). Budget crises may undercut laptop efforts [Electronic version]. *Education Week, 23*(10), 1, 21.

Trumbull, D. J. (1986). Games children play: A cautionary tale. *Educational Leadership, 43*(6), 18–21.

Yates, D. S. (1983). In defense of CAI: Is drill and practice a dirty word? *Curriculum Review, 22*(5), 55–57.

Chapter 2

Basic Concepts of Planning

Jeff Howe, a journalist and contributing editor for *Wired* magazine, published a book in 2008 entitled *Crowdsourcing: Why the Power of the Crowd Is Driving the Future of New Business.* Crowdsourcing is a process by which the power of the many can be leveraged to accomplish feats such as designing a new product, performing a service, or solving a problem that were once the province of a specialized few. Critical to crowdsourcing is the presence of online communities, the availability of open source software, and most importantly, the rise of an amateur class that contributes opinions and ideas to a host of endeavors; each of these spawned during the evolution of the Internet. Howe provides a number of examples in which businesses have used crowdsourcing to achieve some objective that in years past might have been assigned to a department or group of individuals within the organization. In one such case, Howe described Procter & Gamble's strategy using scientists and researchers from around the world to help develop new products for the company. Although Procter & Gamble employs about 8,500 staff in its Research and Development operations, it also uses InnoCentive, a Web site that allows 140,000 scientists worldwide to work on product development problems on a part-time basis. The part-time scientists opt to work on the problem or not and are paid only if they come up with a solution. An important and perhaps surprising aspect of the crowdsourcing process is that these scientists share what they are doing with other scientists on the InnoCentive Web site. Howe describes further variations of the crowdsourcing model that have helped companies such as iStockphoto and Threadless tap into the collective wisdom created by large numbers of individuals engaged in some endeavor or working on a problem. Howe mentions that the popular Wikipedia is a variation of the crowdsourcing model minus the payment for one's contribution.

In Chapter 5 of his book, Howe describes the work of the Austrian economist, Friedrich A. Hayek, who wrote a paper with the simple, straightforward title, *The Use of Knowledge in Society,* the central thesis in this paper being that not all knowledge resides in academies, businesses, or government agencies. Hayek emphasized that large organizations have failed to recognize and appreciate a category of knowledge that resides "locally" and is situated in specific times and places. He posited that nearly every individual has some private information that might have beneficial use and that, furthermore, civilization would benefit if it could figure out ways to utilize the knowledge that is widely dispersed among individuals. Hayek's theory forms the conceptual basis for the crowdsourcing phenomenon. It is interesting to note, as Howe reminds the reader, that Hayek wrote his paper in 1945. He subsequently went on to become a world-class economist, received the Nobel Prize in Economics in 1974 in part for his work on social or collective knowledge, and died in 1992. Hayek never saw the entity we now call the Internet evolve into the most efficient vehicle to date for utilizing the collective knowledge of individuals.

Many of the concepts that form the basis for planning in complex organizations, including schools and school districts, have been around for quite a long time. Some of these concepts have been reintroduced and frequently repackaged as "old wine in new bottles," but they are fundamentally sound and important starting points for a discussion on planning.

PLANNING FUNDAMENTALS

One of the most fully treated topics in educational administration is planning. Numerous books, articles, and guides have been written on how to plan and whom to involve in educational planning. Journals devoted entirely to issues of planning are available to enable administrators to keep up-to-date with the most current thinking. Consultants abound at conferences where sessions are routinely dedicated to planning, its theories, and practices. On the other hand, skepticism exists regarding the value of planning in education, particularly during periods of fiscal constraint and "tight budgets" (Engvall, 1995). The major purpose of this chapter is not to review this extensive literature but to provide a framework for educational planning as related to technology.

First, a generally accepted definition of planning is elusive. In one extensive review of the literature, Adams (1987) provided at least seven different definitions, all of which he considered incomplete. An obvious reason for his conclusion is that planning means different things to different people and is done for different purposes. However, common elements of a definition involve individuals thinking about and developing strategies to prepare their organizations for the future.

Second, planning goes on in all organizations, including schools and school systems, and takes on different characteristics. Planning can be structured, formal, top–down, and nonparticipatory in some cases, or it can be unstructured, informal, bottom–up, and highly participatory in others. It can involve complex social and administrative phenomena such as economics, personalities, and individual needs.

Third, schools are social systems that in the course of their activities, including planning, consider the social needs of students, teachers, administrators, and communities within the context of the school and the larger social environment.

These assumptions form the basis for constructing a framework to define and describe planning in educational organizations. They may be considered oversimplifications of a very complex topic; however, because this book is written for all who are involved in school administration and technology, these assumptions recognize and respect a variety of existing situations. The implementation of this framework is left to the judgment of superintendents, principals, assistant principals, and other administrators, most of whom know best what will work in their schools. Educational leaders must be aware of the differences that exist within a community and among individual constituents if planning is to be successful in their schools (Engvall, 1995).

SCHOOLS AS SOCIAL SYSTEMS

Various theories and models have been developed to describe and explain the way schools operate in our society. Most of them stem from general organization theory and development. The writings of organizational theorists such as Chester Barnard (1964), Herbert Simon (1945, 1957, 1960), Talcott Parsons (1951, 1958), and Amitai Etzioni (1961) are cited in basic administration courses and form the foundation of much of our knowledge in this area. More current literature on organization, such as that by Senge (1990), Bennis (1997), Wenger (1999), Kanter (1999), and Fullan (2001), has expanded on earlier theories and applied them to modern organizations that have had to deal with changes emanating from societal and cultural shifts, globalization, and technology. Likewise, the more recent literature in educational administration deals with topics such as organizational culture, strategic planning, environmental scanning, transformational leadership, and shared decision making. The common thread throughout this material is the assumption that schools operate, as do most organizations, as part of their larger societies. Teachers, students, and administrators interact with each other in a place called school and also interact individually and collectively with their communities and larger societies.

Figure 2.1 is a simplified version of a social process model developed by Getzels and Guba (1957) that is applicable to any social system and easily adaptable to a school. In this model, a school functions as a subsystem (institution) that interacts with the larger environmental social system. The needs of individuals as well as the expectations (roles) of the school (institution) operating within and responding to the values of the culture of the larger environment (community) are the essential elements. Processes related to teaching, administering, and planning

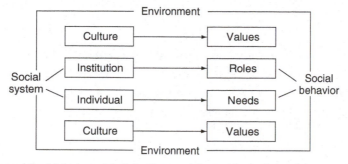

FIGURE 2.1 General Social Systems Model. *Source:* Adapted from the social process model cited by Getzels and Guba (1957).

that operate within the schools are social processes involving people and social interactions. This concept provides an important fundamental assumption for understanding educational planning processes.

Using this model, administrators would plan and make decisions based on the human needs of people both inside and outside the school—including students, teachers, parents, and taxpayers. The model also supports the practice of allowing others to participate in administrative processes. At one time or another, many school systems (e.g., Chicago, Denver, New York, and Miami) have implemented school-based management and shared decision making in their schools; their policies are based on this concept.

As with most theories or models, this one is not perfect. One common criticism is that a social system model is not the most efficient approach for administering complex organizations. Involving many people in administrative processes is time consuming and leads to more decisions based on consensus and sharing of resources rather than on optimization of resources. Furthermore, people do not always operate in a purely rational manner. They may be focused too much on individual needs and issues and not necessarily on the needs of the school or society as a whole. Indeed, we would be naive to expect a social system model to provide a perfect explanation of how such a complex organization operates. The best way to use this or any other model is to assume that it provides direction focused on a "big picture," that it will not fit perfectly, and that conceptually it exists on a continuum.

EVALUATING THE BOTTOM LINE: THE SOCIAL PROCESS AND RATIONAL MODELS

Figure 2.2 represents a continuum with the social process model on the right and its opposite, the purely economic (or rational) model, on the left. The economic/rational model posits that schools operate similarly to private businesses, with an emphasis on bottom-line profits. In practice, it is a problem to administer schools and other nonprofit social agencies strictly according to this model. Unlike businesses, in which one can compare earnings and costs with a common evaluation measure (the dollar), a school's "earnings" are very difficult to define. "Earnings" in education are imperfect. Evaluation measures such as student academic achievement (as a function of student potential), social development, and other student outcomes do not compare or measure well with their costs. Universally accepted measures for student achievement do not exist. Standardized tests have been the subject of intense debate regarding their validity, reliability, cultural bias, and poor administration, and leading education

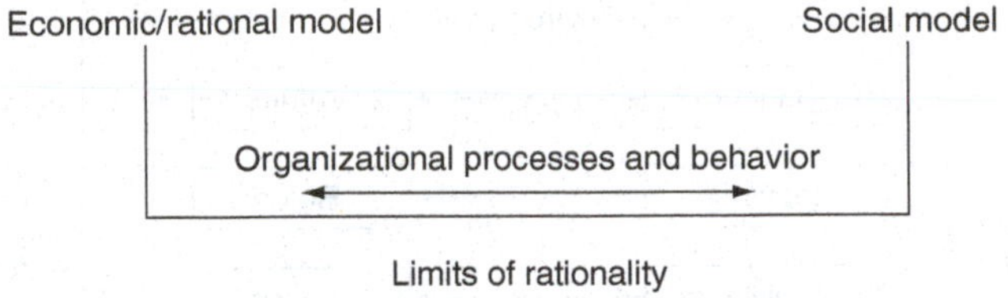

Economic/rational model   Social model

Organizational processes and behavior

Limits of rationality

FIGURE 2.2 Continuum of Economic/Rational and Social Process Models of Organizational Behavior. *Source:* Adapted from Luthans (1981).

researchers have expressed concerns about their misuse (Darling-Hammond, 2007). Other techniques for measuring student achievement—such as portfolios and outcomes-based education—are also difficult to compare with costs.

Human talents and abilities are very diverse. One child may be a poor reader with a talent for mathematics. Another child may perform poorly in mathematics but be a gifted writer. Experienced administrators and teachers would probably agree that the most desirable outcome would be for these children to achieve their potential in all subjects while recognizing that they will probably achieve much more in their strengths than their weaknesses. However, attempting to measure these outcomes becomes an almost impossible task given existing achievement measures and assessment techniques.

The wide disparity in school district spending even within the same states and counties, municipalities, communities, and boards of education clearly shows that school districts have very different ideas regarding appropriate costs for their children's education. This further complicates the problem of establishing evaluation measures and attempting to understand and administer school programs according to the economic/rational model.

Instead, what schools do is attempt to serve their children as best they can by offering variety in their curricula and by hiring trained teachers who understand children's diverse needs and talents and can interact with them appropriately. In managing and coordinating schools, administrators interact with teachers and other staff as well as with parents, school board members, state education departments, colleges, and local businesses to try to understand the environment in which these children will eventually use their talents and abilities. However, administrators and teachers will admit that their understanding of this environment is imperfect. Social interaction helps improve our understanding of educational goals and outcomes and the problems in achieving them, but it does not perfect this understanding.

These concepts stem from the foundations of organizational theory. An individual commonly associated with them and whose work is highly recommended for further reference is Herbert Simon (1945, 1957, 1960, 1979, 1982). Simon was awarded the Nobel Prize for Economics in 1978 for his research on decision making in organizations. His theory on the limits of rationality—later renamed *bounded rationality*—posits as its main principle that organizations operate along a continuum of rational and social behaviors mainly because the knowledge necessary to function strictly according to a rational model is beyond what is available to administrators and managers. Although first developed in the 1940s, this theory has withstood the test of time and is widely recognized as a fundamental assumption in understanding organizational processes such as decision making and planning (Carlson & Awkerman, 1991; Luthans, 1981; Peters & Waterman, 1982; Senge, 1990; Tyson, 2002). Simon (1991) devoted a good deal of effort to examining the role that computer technology can play in expanding the knowledge necessary for administrators to be more effective planners and decision makers.

COMMON ELEMENTS OF EDUCATIONAL PLANNING

In a review of planning processes, Sheathelm (1991) identified four major elements of successful planning as the four Cs:

- Comprehensiveness
- Collaboration
- Commitment
- Continuity

They are very much worth exploring for developing a framework in planning for technology.

Comprehensiveness

Planning needs to be comprehensive. A total view of a school and what it is supposed to accomplish for students and the community is an essential element. An important distinction here is the difference between having a total view and necessarily having solutions for everything. Part of planning is examining and understanding both the school and the environment as much as possible with the caveat that they cannot be understood entirely. Likewise, providing solutions for problems that are not fully understood is an imperfect, if not impossible, way of operating. Administrators need to be aware of the needs of individuals (e.g., students, teachers, other administrators, board members) that may be specific and at times very unique. These needs can frequently be converted into goals and objectives on which a plan is formulated. On the other hand, teachers and staff frequently need to have a better understanding of the total enterprise, including objectives and resource availability. The essence of a comprehensive plan links individual needs and objectives to overall institutional goals.

Collaboration

Planning needs to be collaborative (Bennis, 1997). Although administrators generally have a good deal of expertise in education, they need to rely on others to help improve their understanding. Specialists such as science teachers or speech therapists know their subjects better than administrators. Business managers, librarians, counselors, school nurses, and other staff have specific expertise that frequently is more complete and more current than that of a general administrator such as a principal or superintendent. This vast pool of knowledge, expertise, and experience should become a vital part of any planning process.

In addition to the exchange of knowledge, collaboration also allows for greater appreciation of several perspectives of a goal, objective, or need. As Deborah Meier—the nationally recognized school reformer and founder of Central Park East elementary and secondary schools—states, educators need to develop "the capacity to see the world as others might" (1995, p. 40).

Commitment

Through collaboration, securing the commitment of those who are vital in carrying out a plan becomes easier. Commitment is critical because the best plan will not be realized if the people who are expected to implement it are not committed to the task. Commitment comes from being involved with formulating overall goals and objectives and with developing specific courses of action. Collaboration also allows others to understand a plan, a goal, or a course of action and the purposes behind it. Greater understanding generally fosters higher levels of commitment.

The commitment of administrative leaders, such as principals and superintendents, to planning is also critical. Commitment from teachers, staff, or parents will only come if there is a sense on their part that the administrative leadership is committed to a plan. Administrators must exercise their leadership skills in securing commitment by offering themselves as examples in sharing knowledge, formulating goals, developing objectives, and implementing courses of action.

Continuity

Every planning process is continuous and never-ending. Societies, schools, and people are constantly changing, and plans must change with them (Kanter, 1999). An organization is like a living organism that continually responds and adjusts to environmental stimuli. As the values of a society change, so must the way schools prepare students to live and function in that society. As new tools and technologies are developed, so should our methods of training students to use these tools and technologies.

Planning usually involves developing a written plan as a result of a series of meetings and committee work. However, planning does not begin with these activities and end with the production of the written plan. On the contrary, the written plan is a guideline for everyday activities. Administrators, teachers, and staff follow this guideline and accumulate information on how well the objectives of the plan are being implemented. This new information (including adjustments to the plan) then becomes input for further planning activity.

PLANNING FOR TECHNOLOGY

An overall model for planning for technology in a school district is shown in Figure 2.3, which is derived from the social process model. This model attempts to show planning for technology as proceeding from values defined by the environment toward goals and objectives formulated primarily at the school district level. To achieve these goals and objectives, computer applications are identified as the main courses of action that in turn require hardware and software, staff needs, facilities, and finances to be implemented or provided for at the school building level. Once

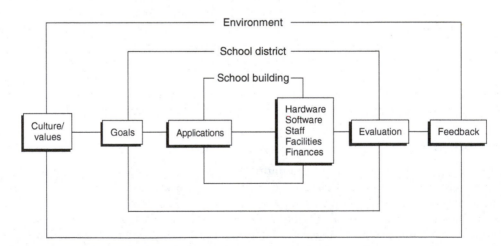

FIGURE 2.3 Model for Planning for Technology.

implemented, they are subsequently evaluated, and feedback is provided to the planning process for establishing new goals, objectives, and applications and for revising existing ones. Information flows both ways in this process, from left to right as well as from right to left. School district policies such as equipment acquisition, software evaluation, or collective bargaining agreements for staff development and evaluation may also need to be considered and addressed.

The model requires a good deal of information gathering and idea sharing, which may be done formally through committees as well as informally through ad hoc discussions, observations, visits, and reading the literature. This model fits well and should be integrated with other planning activities in the school district.

An important feature of this model is that it incorporates external *environmental scanning*, which simply means engaging in activities to provide information on the community, state, and society for planning purposes. In addition to understanding societal and community values, environmental scanning is critical for comprehending changes in technology. The fundamental nature of technology includes change and, in the field of digital electronics and computers, rapid change. In a global, high-tech world, organizations need to be "more fluid, inclusive, and responsive" (Kanter, 1999). For many people involved with technology, this is frustrating but also invigorating. Developing an understanding of trends in hardware and software is important and enables planners to avoid technology that will quickly become obsolete. Successful environmental scanning involves establishing and developing contacts with experts in the community, local colleges, and private businesses. District-wide committees for planning for technology are becoming common and can be used effectively as the bridges between school districts and the communities they serve.

A basic assumption of this model is that an administrator, most likely at the district level, provides the necessary leadership in converting environmental values and conditions into district-wide goals and objectives. Committees may be necessary for specific areas such as administrative applications or instructional applications, which allow for participation on the part of administrative staff and teachers. Identifying courses of action and technology applications, in particular, should also allow for input from sources at the building level. In a study of the progress of a technology committee headed by a principal at an elementary school in Idaho, Keeler (1996) concluded that cooperation and collaboration were enhanced and the principal was viewed more as "a leader and model of lifelong learning than as a manager of a school" (p. 342). A technology coordinator, a teacher, or a library media specialist can also function as a facilitator who leads a building-level committee for identifying applications that coincide with district-wide goals and objectives. In large high schools with several thousand students, several such committees might exist, representing different subject areas or grade levels.

By allowing teachers, parents, and others in a school to participate, those responsible for planning become more knowledgeable about the alternative courses of action and applications that a district might support. It is thus important to include at various levels the input of a school district's business officer or manager who can provide information on available financial resources. Naturally, planning is easier if the available financial resources can support all the various proposals that are being considered. However, if these resources are not available, then administrators will need to draw on their leadership abilities in bringing committees to agreement on which proposals to include and which to exclude. If true participation has been effected, then priorities should become more evident to all participants.

A plan covers a period of time, frequently from 3 to 5 years, which can allow for more inclusion than exclusion. Administrators should attempt to be equitable and to distribute resources among competing participants. If resources are severely limited, then a major goal of the planning participants should be securing more funds rather than developing applications. In this case, the participation of community representatives may help identify and develop financial support from various sources, including governmental (federal, state, local) and private agencies.

A pivotal step in a planning process using the technology planning model depicted in Figure 2.3 is the development of a written plan. The purpose here is to provide understanding of the plan to all participants. Just as information flow is critical in the formative stages of planning, a written summary of what has been discussed or agreed on is essential for implementing the plan. Participants and others such as board members, administrators, and teachers need to understand what the goals are and what their responsibilities are in achieving them. School districts, in fact, can be creative in presenting and communicating their goals and objectives. Such creativity is desirable and not only helps participants and constituents understand the plan but also builds interest in it. Written summaries also form the basis for the next cycle of planning activities. Figure 2.4 and Figure 2.5 are excerpts from state and school district educational technology plans.

Evaluation and feedback are critical for continuing planning activities from year to year or from planning cycle to planning cycle. Planning participants need information on how well computer applications are achieving objectives. This can only be provided if mechanisms are established for evaluating applications and generating feedback to the planning participants.

TAKING A POSITIVE ATTITUDE TO EVALUATION

Undertaking evaluation with a positive attitude is desirable for all involved in the planning process. Unfortunately, educators approach evaluation with caution or reluctance, especially when it is conducted or administered by others or "outsiders." For decades, school and governmental officials have used formal measures such as SAT scores, state competency testing, and other standardized instruments to evaluate school performance. The 21st century ushered in another era of school standards in which testing is used to monitor student achievement and progress. And once again, many view testing as unjustified pressure brought on teachers and children to perform. On the other hand, testing is viewed as the mechanism needed to hold schools accountable for the enormous investment that has been made in public education in this country. The entire issue of standardized testing has and will continue to be hotly debated for years to come among educators, politicians, and government officials.

Educators must not abandon evaluation in their planning but instead should attempt to develop evaluation criteria on which participants (administrators, teachers, and parents) can agree. This is especially true for technology planning because resources will be scrutinized even in the most financially able school districts. Large expenditures for equipment, staffing, and facilities are common when implementing technology and justifiably should be evaluated carefully.

In developing evaluation criteria for technology planning, the measures should be appropriate to the goals. Goals for administrative applications frequently require summative evaluation criteria and the establishment of timetables and milestones for accomplishing certain events. Goals for instructional applications may or may not require standardized measures. However, if an instructional goal is directed to student achievement, then testing or other performance measures are appropriate evaluation criteria and should be considered.

For instructional applications involving student achievement, multiple evaluation criteria are highly recommended. As an example, Rock and Cummings (1994) described a project designed to evaluate the implementation of interactive video technology in 15 schools in California, Illinois, Missouri, New York, Pennsylvania, Oregon, Texas, and West Virginia. In every

Washington State's education system must prepare students for their futures, not this generation's past. Reflection on the driver for educational restructuring nationally brings a recognition of tension between an education system designed for the industrial age and the reality of an information age.

Technology has changed the very fabric of today's society. It has been a driver of change in such areas as global communications, economics, the arts, politics, and environmental issues. Education must analyze the changing fiber of today's society and weave the reality of the information age into the education system.

Technology is key to learners' achievement of world-class standards. First and foremost is the critical need for students to be able to access information, manipulate data, synthesize concepts, and creatively express ideas to others using video, text, and audio media.

Technology can virtually bring the world to the child, providing a depth and richness of instructional approaches to reach children of all learning modalities. The child becomes a "knowledge architect" using the rich resources at his/her fingertips through technology to bring personal meaning and expression to knowledge.

Secondly, technology is an administrative tool which can bring efficiency to the management and assessment realms of education. This is especially important as teachers begin to use performance-based assessment to continuously improve the students' learning. The power of the technology allows easy tracking of student work enabling teachers to develop and maintain individual learning profiles for all learners.

Our changing society and workplace demand citizens who can take responsibility for their own learning and well being. Educational reforms which can develop these citizens are dependent on the adequate and appropriate infusion of technology to support the new education system.

Washington State educators have identified seven roles learners will play as they use technology in order to achieve the essential academic learning requirements:

1. The student as information navigator
2. The student as critical thinker and analyzer using technology
3. The student as creator of knowledge using technology, media, and telecommunications
4. The student as effective communicator through a variety of appropriate technologies/media
5. The student as a discriminating selector of appropriate technology for specific purposes
6. The student as technician
7. The student as a responsible citizen, worker, learner, community member, and family member in a technological age

FIGURE 2.4 Excerpt of a State's Educational Technology Planning Guidelines. *Source:* From the Quincy (Washington) Public Schools Technology Plan. Retrieved February 26, 2009, from http://www.qsd.wednet.edu/qsdtechplan.htm

school, a standardized test—such as the Iowa Test of Basic Skills, the Missouri Master Achievement Test, or the New York State Regents Examination—was used in conjunction with some other measure, such as a student attitude questionnaire, portfolio assessment, or classroom observation. Of the 15 schools, 7 used two evaluation criteria, 2 used three criteria, and 6 used four or more criteria. Teachers and administrators reported that the use of videotape to observe and record student involvement and interactivity with lessons was particularly helpful because

Benchmark 2–Technology Integration and Literacy

The Palmer Public School District encourages all staff to utilize technology integration in the course of their teaching. The Palmer Public School District encourages both staff and students to use district and school technology resources on a daily basis.

A. Technology Integration

1. Outside Teaching Time–At least 85% of teachers use technology every day, including some of the following areas: lesson planning, administrative tasks, communications, and collaboration. Teachers share information about technology uses with their colleagues.

The Palmer Public School District has 100% of teachers use technology every day, including some of the following areas: lesson planning, administrative tasks, communications, and collaboration.

Teachers share information about technology uses with their colleagues.

2. For Teaching and Learning–At least 85% of teachers use technology appropriately with students every day to improve student learning of the curriculum. Activities include some of the following: research, multimedia, simulations, data interpretation, communications, and collaboration (see the Massachusetts Recommended K–12 Instructional Technology Standards).

The Palmer Public School District has at least 85% of teachers use technology appropriately with students each week, including some of the following areas: research, multimedia, simulations, data interpretation, communications, and collaboration.

B. Technology Literacy

1. At least 85% of eighth grade students show proficiency in all the Massachusetts Recommended PreK–12 Instructional Technology Standards for grade 8.

The Palmer Public School District strives for 85% of students from grade 8 to show proficiency in all the Massachusetts Recommended PreK–12 Instructional Technology Standards.

2. 100% of teachers are working to meet the proficiency level in technology, and by the school year 2010–2011, 60% of teachers will have reached the proficiency level as defined by the Massachusetts Technology Self-Assessment Tool (TSAT).

The Palmer Public School District teachers are working to meet the proficiency level in technology, and by the school year 2010–2011, 60% of teachers will have reached the proficiency level as defined by the Massachusetts Technology Self-Assessment Tool (TSAT).

C. Staffing

1. The district has a district-level technology director/coordinator.

The Palmer Public School District has a full-time equivalent (FTE) district-level technology director.

2. The district provides one FTE instructional technology teacher per 60–120 instructional staff.

The Palmer Public School District provides one third time instructional technology teacher per 40–80 instructional staff at the high school only.

3. The district has staff dedicated to data management and assessment.

The Palmer Public School District does not have one FTE person dedicated to data management and assessment due to fiscal budget constraints.

FIGURE 2.5   Excerpt of a School District's Educational Technology Plan.   *Source:* From the Palmer Public School District Technology Plan. Retrieved February 28, 2009, from http://www.palmerschools.org/Technology/Palmer%20Public%20Schools%20Local%20Technology%20Plan%20Outline%202009-11.pdf

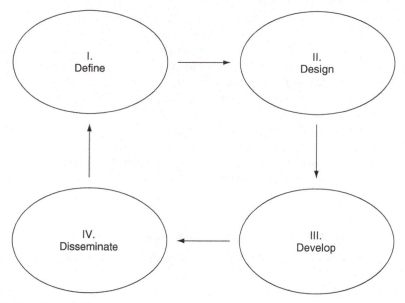

FIGURE 2.6   Four-D Model for Instructional Development.

significant differences were consistently observed between classes using the interactive video technology and those not using it.

Educators and policy makers must also prepare for the reality that not every plan and implementation will be successful. However, good technology planning will minimize risks by establishing basic evaluation criteria early in the process. This is especially important for major technology initiatives involving an entire district. Dick and Carey (1985), Thigarajan, Semmel, and Semmel (1974), and Willis (1993) propose an instructional development research model (see Figure 2.6) that is appropriate for this type of evaluation. This model essentially recommends defining, designing, developing, and disseminating technology in small incremental stages until satisfied that the technology is meeting expected goals on a limited basis before implementing it on a larger scale. Such an approach reduces the risk of making a large investment in technology that may not be beneficial.

ADMINISTRATIVE AND INSTRUCTIONAL APPLICATIONS

The most important characteristic of the framework for planning, in Figure 2.3, is the concentration on technology applications as the fundamental courses of action. Applications simply refer to applying technology to the goals and objectives of the plan.

Planning for Administrative Applications

Planning for administrative applications is different in several ways from planning for instructional applications. The goals, nature of the applications, participants, and evaluation are different. Environmental scanning is helpful in formulating goals, especially for identifying appropriate technology. State education departments, local governmental agencies, accreditation associations, and professional organizations are valuable resources for helping school districts determine the types of administrative applications that are being used in other school districts. Local businesses such as banks or insurance companies, which frequently use current information technology such as database management systems (DBMS), can be helpful in identifying appropriate software for establishing and maintaining computer-based information systems. School districts that are part of larger local or state governmental jurisdictions also need to make sure that they understand the information or administrative system requirements of these governing entities. For example, urban school districts frequently have certain administrative systems such as budgeting, payroll, and purchasing provided to them by municipal agencies. Any planning involving these systems should provide for participation by the municipal agents familiar with the future development of these systems.

In planning administrative applications, the goals of a district can be stated in many different ways, and planners are encouraged to be creative to generate interest in a plan. However, administrative applications frequently relate to common themes such as the following:

- To develop/improve information resources
- To provide/improve new administrative services
- To improve/increase administrative productivity and efficiency

These themes can be stated in many different ways as goals, objectives, and applications in actual planning documents.

Information resources are all aspects of the data collection, storage, and retrieval processes and procedures needed by school administrators to monitor, report, and understand what is going on in their schools. The major data collection and record-keeping applications in most schools pertain to students, curriculum, finances, personnel, and facilities. They typically use database management software systems that are maintained centrally at the district level and that can be distributed to the individual schools.

Providing new administrative services is a broad goal with an emphasis on doing or improving that which is not being done or not being done well. Examples include expanding student grade reports to provide prescriptive information, automating substitute teacher lists, improving general communications to parents and residents, or establishing an online student guidance system. These services may use database, office automation, e-mail, Internet, electronic spreadsheet, or desktop publishing software, and they can be developed centrally at the district level or locally at the building level.

Increasing productivity and efficiency in administrative operations is frequently associated with computer technology and refers to improving information and communication flow. For example, database management systems have been particularly effective in improving reporting and reducing redundant data gathering activities (e.g., having two or more offices collecting the same information). Providing administrative staff with office automation software, such as word processing, e-mail, and electronic spreadsheet programs, has also been widely accepted because it helps them become much more efficient in presenting, communicating, and assembling all types of text- and number-based materials.

The major leadership in planning for administrative applications exists centrally at the district level, because applications involving information flow and data management typically are directed and controlled centrally. Building-level administrators and staff should understand and accept the need for central administrative information systems. However, in planning administrative systems, staff at the building level should be involved. They are important resource people who begin the information cycle by collecting source data on students, families, personnel, payrolls, and so on. They will do a better job of data collection if they understand the purposes of their efforts. They will do a spectacular job if they personally can realize some benefits such as less paperwork or less need to do repetitive periodic reports. They can also help planners determine staff development and training needs that are as important for secretaries and administrative assistants as they are for teachers and instructional staff.

Developing evaluation criteria as part of the planning process is usually straightforward for administrative applications. Initially, it involves determining whether certain milestones in developing an application are being met, culminating with the application becoming operational. For example, the evaluation criteria for the development of a new computer-based financial information system might be to establish dates by which certain modules or subsystems are to be operational. When the system is established, additional evaluation criteria might involve comparing the timeliness and accuracy of critical reports before and after the system became operational.

Figure 2.7 provides a partial example of a school district's plan for implementing a new integrated financial management system. The plan is organized with goals relating well to

---

Background

The following is excerpted from a planning document for implementing an integrated financial management system in a large urban school district. The need for this system occurred because of changes in the way funds were provided by external agencies (i.e., state aid), which increasingly were being allocated later in the school year, requiring the school district to make allocations and adjustments to allocations even later. In addition, demands for fiscal data and accountability had increased significantly from both external funding agencies and internal departments. This application was designed to replace several nonintegrated computer applications that were implemented in the district office in the late 1980s.

North Central School District No. 1
Five-Year Technology Plan (2004–2008)

Goals (from district's long-range plan)
Improve financial reporting capabilities to external funding agencies.
Improve financial record keeping within the district.
Improve fiscal accountability within each of the schools in the district.

-
-
-

Objectives (2004)
Design the requirements of a new, integrated financial management system (FMS).

-
-
-

Objectives (2005)
Evaluate computer software products that can meet the design requirements of FMS.
Procure a computer software product that meets the design requirements of FMS.
Evaluate hardware requirements of the central office and schools for implementing FMS.
Evaluate the data communications facilities required to implement FMS in the schools.

-
-
-

(continued)

FIGURE 2.7 Samples of Planning Goals and Objectives for an Administrative Technology Application.

Objectives (2005–2006)
Acquire the necessary computer hardware in the central office to implement FMS.
Implement the financial accounting and budget modules of FMS in the central office.
Train all central office staff in the use of FMS.
Acquire the necessary data communications facilities to implement FMS in all the schools.

-
-
-

Objectives (2006–2007)
Acquire the necessary computer hardware to implement FMS in the schools.
Implement the financial accounting and budget modules of FMS in the schools.
Train all school staff in the use of FMS.
Implement the purchasing and accounts payable modules of FMS in the central office.
Continue training staff in the central office in the use of FMS.

-
-
-

Objectives (2007–2008)
Implement the purchasing and accounts payable modules of FMS in the schools.
Implement the payroll and personnel modules of FMS in the central office.
Continue training staff in the central office and in the schools in the use of FMS.

-
-
-

Objectives (2008)
Implement the payroll and personnel modules of FMS in the schools.
Continue training staff in the central office and in the schools in the use of FMS.
Conduct an in-depth evaluation of the benefits of FMS to the school district.

-
-
-

FIGURE 2.7   *(continued)*

objectives and the application, and it also shows how planning goals respond to needs emanating from both outside and inside the district. Objectives are clearly stated, and appropriate time frames are established for design, implementation, and evaluation. Focusing on the financial management application, the plan also provides for various components such as hardware, software, and staff development.

Chapter 4 is dedicated exclusively to an examination of the major administrative applications that can exist in a school. There you will find additional information related to planning for these applications.

Planning for Instructional Applications

Planning instructional applications is similar to planning administrative applications, but several differences do exist. Environmental scanning is just as important, and many of the same agencies—such as state education departments, accreditation associations, and professional organizations—can be excellent resources for information and ideas. In addition, professional organizations such as the National Education Association and the Association for Supervision and Curriculum Development are active in presenting issues on the instructional uses of technology. Local colleges, especially those with teacher education programs, may also possess valuable expertise in developing planning goals and applications.

A school district's goals and objectives regarding instructional applications can be diverse; however, they frequently relate to one or more of the following themes:

- Preparing students to participate in a technology-oriented society
- Enhancing/improving learning by using technological tools
- Enhancing/improving teaching by using technological tools
- Providing technology-based curricula for students with special aptitudes or interests in technology

As with administrative applications, these instructional application themes may be stated in many different ways in actual planning documents.

The first theme—preparing students to participate in a technology-oriented society—recognizes that all types of jobs, professions, and everyday routines increasingly use technology. Students should develop basic competency, literacy, or fluency in using technology during their primary and secondary school programs. Accomplishing this may involve taking specific, dedicated courses in computer software applications or more likely integrating technology with other courses (such as using databases to conduct research in social studies), or a combination of both. In recent years, Internet-related activities such as the use of e-mail and searching for information on the World Wide Web have become important objectives of this theme.

The second theme—enhancing learning by employing technology—refers to students' use of technology in general curricular areas. Examples include how to use Internet resources to conduct research, word processing software to teach writing, electronic spreadsheet programs to teach accounting or business subjects, and World Wide Web social networking tools to share information. The list of possibilities is almost endless. Increasingly, integrating technology into the curriculum has become a major goal for many school districts in planning instructional applications.

Enhancing teaching by making use of technology refers to teachers incorporating technology in classroom presentations and other teaching activities. Specific examples are the use of interactive whiteboards, large-screen monitors, and other multimedia in the classroom. The emphasis here is on the use of technology by teachers for teaching, more so than by students for learning. A popular element of this theme is staff development and the training of teachers to use technology in the classroom.

Providing technology-based curricula for students with special talents or interests in technology is a rapidly expanding theme for many school districts. This includes special vocational programs such as computer operations, computer maintenance, and data communications. These programs can be designed to prepare students seeking employment immediately upon graduation from high school as well as to prepare them for 2-year community college programs. High school programs that offer electives in computer programming for students who are considering a computer science or engineering career can also be included.

The leadership for planning instructional applications should be shared at the district level and at the building level with the teaching staff who possess expertise in the various subject areas. Diverse subject areas and grade levels require different computer hardware and software or specialized staff training. Tens of thousands of instructional software packages are available, which make it increasingly more difficult for central office staff to keep current and maintain a level of expertise. As a result, planning for these applications more frequently allows individual teachers, academic departments, and grade-level coordinators to make specific proposals that might fit an overall planning goal. This process may also involve establishing an ongoing budget and approval mechanism for evaluating, funding, and acquiring instructional software at the building level. In addition to drawing on the expertise of many of the professional staff members, this approach also allows teachers to use technology best suited to their own teaching styles and philosophies. It should also encourage a greater commitment to its successful utilization.

Evaluating the implementation of instructional applications should include a formal assessment. In addition to establishing milestones for implementing instructional applications, a district that uses standardized tests can incorporate these into the overall evaluation criteria. A good student record-keeping system in a district should easily provide these and other student achievement data, such as grades and graduation rates, for evaluating an application's instructional effectiveness. Other evaluation techniques that should be considered include portfolios, student and teacher attitude surveys, and classroom observations.

Figure 2.5 is a partial example of a school district's plan for integrating technology into the instructional program; it illustrates several characteristics of a good instructional technology plan. It sets clear goals and objectives, some of which are quantifiable. It provides for multiple evaluation criteria. It also identifies certain fiscal constraints that exist in the district.

Chapter 6 is dedicated exclusively to a review of instructional applications and also presents additional information related to planning for these applications.

CASE STUDY

Place: Lotusville   Year: 2007

Lotusville is a suburban school district in the Southwest with an enrollment of 5,000 students distributed among one high school, three middle schools, and six primary schools. The population has been increasing by approximately 2% per year. The district's tax base has also been rising because of recent commercial development. A formal planning process was implemented in 1985 by the board of education. A district-wide Planning Committee was established and has continued to be active in establishing goals and objectives. The membership of the Planning Committee is as follows:

- Three parents, one of whom is the president of the PTA
- Two school board members
- The manager of the local bank, who is a former school board member
- A teacher who represents the teachers' union and who teaches high school mathematics
- The district superintendent
- The director of pupil personnel services for the district

The district superintendent also acts as a resource person for the Planning Committee and has established formal processes for gathering information for the committee's planning activities.

In 1995, at the suggestion of two of the parents, the Planning Committee established an Advisory Committee for Instructional Technology. Although the Planning Committee had always been supportive of technology in the instructional programs, the resources devoted to it were increasing significantly. The perception was that a need existed to review more carefully the district's future resource allocation. The Advisory Committee has the following membership:

- Two parents
- The manager of a local computer hardware distributing company
- One school board member
- A teacher who represents the teachers' union and who teaches science in the high school and was a former part-time technology coordinator
- The assistant superintendent for instruction
- The principal of one of the middle schools

The Advisory Committee has worked well with the Planning Committee and has been effective in expanding instructional technology in the district.

In the entire district in 1991, there were 80 microcomputers in three computer laboratories in the high school. These were supervised by one science teacher who was released from half of his teaching responsibilities. Pascal, BASIC, word processing, and electronic spreadsheets were taught in elective courses within the high school mathematics program. An instructional technology plan was developed in 1996 that called for a significant increase in the number of microcomputers being used for instructional purposes at all grade levels and the hiring of at least one technology teacher for each school by 1999. By 2000, the district had installed 700 microcomputers, primarily in central laboratories and open access areas in school libraries. Increasingly more units were being distributed to individual classrooms, especially in the high school.

Currently [2007], each school has at least one full-time technology teacher who supervises the laboratories and teaches technology courses. A full-time technician has also been hired who maintains the equipment for the entire district. A wide variety of computer software packages is available for all grade levels, including simulation programs, desktop publishing, word processing, spreadsheet, database, Visual BASIC, and Microsoft PowerPoint. All the schools are connected to the Internet including the computer laboratories, libraries, and classrooms. All classrooms were wired by 2001. The Advisory Committee has established a technology replacement policy that maintains the number of computers at approximately 650 to 700 units throughout the district.

A major issue facing the district's Planning Committee is whether the expansion in instructional computing has been worth the investment in equipment and personnel. Annual standardized test scores indicate that academic achievement increased modestly from 1999 to 2005 but decreased slightly in the past 2 years. The teachers' representative on the Planning Committee has stated that many of the primary school teachers would like to see more microcomputers placed in the regular classrooms. The district superintendent has been advised by the assistant superintendent for instruction that locating equipment in the regular classrooms would require a major increase in the number of microcomputers and an extensive new staff development program because a number of teachers, especially in the primary schools, needed more training to use the technology effectively.

Discussion Questions

1. Analyze the preceding case study. What observations can you make regarding the effectiveness of the planning process in the Lotusville school district? Do you have any suggestions for improving it? Consider especially the structure, membership of the committees, evaluation, and feedback.

2. Compared with your own environment, does Lotusville appear to be more or less effective in the way it plans for technology?

3. Finally, if you were the district superintendent, what courses of action might you consider or recommend to the Planning Committee to help resolve some of the recent issues identified regarding instructional computing?

Summary

This chapter describes several basic assumptions and concepts regarding educational planning for technology. A great deal of literature exists on educational planning, much of which has its roots in organization theory and development. One of the more important concepts is the idea that schools operate as social systems and are part of larger social systems. Individuals (teachers, students), organizations (schools), and larger environments (communities, towns, cities) interact with one another through social processes. One way of describing and understanding organizations is to understand that social processes provide the foundation for how they operate.

In applying the social process model, four common elements are identified as important to effective educational planning. Planning needs to be comprehensive, collaborative, and continuous. In addition, it needs to have the commitment of all involved: administrators, teachers, parents, and other community representatives.

Planning for technology can be incorporated into other educational planning activities and processes, following a social process model that involves individuals, the school, the community, and the larger environment. It should allow for the participation of administrators, teachers, and staff at the district, school building, and departmental levels. Because of the dynamic and changing nature of technology, planning should extensively use environmental scanning and data gathering on technological trends and developments. Evaluation is critical to meeting objectives, and educators should adopt a positive attitude to using it in planning processes.

In the development of objectives and courses of action, applications become the fundamental building blocks on which hardware, software, staff development, facilities, and financial components depend. Administrative applications are different from instructional applications, and writing applications are different from science applications, which are different from music applications, and so on. Microcomputer technology has matured to the point where specific solutions identified as applications can be provided to meet specific goals and objectives.

Key Concepts and Questions

1. Planning is a frequently used term among individuals, schools, organizations, and government agencies. How do you define planning? What are its common elements?

2. Much has been written and said regarding what is needed for successful planning to take place in complex organizations such as schools. What are the essential elements of an organizational planning process? Are these elements evident in your organizational environment? Explain.

3. Private businesses and governmental agencies use planning processes. Are processes developed for these organizations appropriate for schools? Why or why not?

4. Schools can be described and analyzed as social systems. How do you define a social system? Who are the major participants in this system? What are their roles, if any, in planning?

5. Planning involves the establishment of goals and objectives. In planning for technology, meeting these goals and objectives should center on technology applications

rather than on individual application components. What do you consider the essential components of technology applications? Are some components more important than others? Explain.

6. Planning for administrative applications and planning for instructional applications have similarities and

differences. Compare the two in relation to objectives, participants, and evaluation.

7. Environmental scanning has become a frequently used term in planning processes. Why is it particularly important when planning for technology?

Suggested Activities

1. Identify how planning is accomplished in a school district with which you are familiar. Who are the main participants in the planning process? What suggestions can you propose for improving the planning process at the district level?

2. Identify how planning is accomplished in a school. How does the school process integrate with the district planning process? Who are the main participants? What suggestions can you propose for improving the planning process at the school level?

References

Adams, D. (1987). Paradigmatic contexts of models of educational planning and decision making. *Educational Planning, 6*(1), 36–47.

Barnard, C. I. (1964). *The functions of the executive.* Cambridge, MA: Harvard University Press.

Bennis, W. (1997). The secrets of great groups. *Leader to Leader, 3*(Winter), 29–33.

Carlson, R. V., & Awkerman, G. (Eds.). (1991). *Educational planning: Concepts, strategies, and practices.* New York: Longman.

Darling-Hammond, L. (2007, May 2). Evaluating 'No Child Left Behind'. *The Nation.* Retrieved February 28, 2009, from http://www.thenation.com/doc/20070521/darling-hammond

Dick, W., & Carey, L. (1985). *The systematic design of instruction* (2nd ed.). Glenview, IL: Scott, Foresman.

Engvall, R. P. (1995). The limited value of planning in education: Getting back to basics isn't all about curriculum. *Urban Review, 27*(3), 251–262.

Etzioni, A. (1961). *A comparative analysis of complex organizations.* New York: Free Press.

Fullan, M. (2001). *Leading in a culture of change.* San Francisco: Jossey-Bass.

Getzels, J. W., & Guba, E. G. (1957). Social behavior and the administrative process. *School Review, 65*, 423–441.

Hayek, F. A. (1945). The use of knowledge in society. *American Economic Review, 35*(4), 519–530.

Howe, J. (2008). *Crowdsourcing: Why the power of the crowd is driving the future of business.* New York: Crown Publishing Group.

Kanter, R. M. (1999). The enduring skills of change leaders. *Leader to Leader, 13*(Summer), 15–22.

Keeler, C. M. (1996). Networked instructional computers in the elementary classroom and their effect on the learning environment: A qualitative evaluation. *Journal of Research on Computing in Education, 28*(3), 329–345.

Luthans, F. (1981). *Organizational behavior.* New York: McGraw-Hill.

Meier, D. (1995). *The power of their ideas: Lessons for America from a small school in Harlem.* Boston: Beacon.

Parsons, T. (1951). *The social system.* New York: Free Press.

Parsons, T. (1958). Some ingredients of a general theory of formal organization. In A. W. Halpin (Ed.), *Administrative theory in education* (pp. 40–72). Chicago: University of Chicago Press.

Peters, T. J., & Waterman, R. (1982). *In search of excellence.* New York: Harper & Row.

Rock, H. M., & Cummings, A. (1994). Can videodiscs improve student outcomes? *Educational Leadership, 51*(7), 46–50.

Senge, P. (1990). *The fifth discipline: The art and practice of the learning organization.* New York: Doubleday.

Sheathelm, H. H. (1991). Common elements in the planning process. In R. V. Carlson & G. Awkerman (Eds.), *Educational planning: Concepts, strategies, and practices* (pp. 267–278). New York: Longman.

Simon, H. A. (1945). *Administrative behavior.* New York: Macmillan.

Simon, H. A. (1957). *Administrative behavior* (2nd ed.). New York: Macmillan.

Simon, H. A. (1960). *The new science of management decision.* New York: Harper & Row.

Simon, H. A. (1979). Rational decision making in business organizations. *American Economic Review, 69,* 493–513.

Simon, H. A. (1982). *Models of bounded rationality.* Cambridge, MA: MIT Press.

Simon, H. A. (1991). *Models of my life.* New York: Basic Books.

Thigarajan, S., Semmel, D., & Semmel, M. (1974). *Instructional development for training teachers of exceptional children: A sourcebook.* Reston, VA: Council for Exceptional Children.

Tyson, C. (2002). *The foundations of imperfect decision making.* Stanford, CA: Stanford Graduate School of Business Research Paper Series. Retrieved January 20, 2004, from http://www.gsb.stanford.edu/facseminars/events/economics/pdfs/101002.pdf

Wenger, E. (1999). *Communities of practice: Learning, meaning, and identity.* Cambridge: Cambridge University Press.

Willis, J. (1993). Technology in teacher education: A research and development agenda. In H. C. Waxman & G. W. Bright (Eds.), *Approaches to research on teacher education and technology* (pp. 35–50). Charlottesville, VA: Association for the Advancement of Computing in Education.

Chapter 3

Technology, Learning, and Equity Issues

As technology continues to expand in the nation's schools, a variety of associated issues are developing with which administrators should be familiar. Some of these derive from the larger issue of the effectiveness of technology in instruction and learning. Others are equity issues, perhaps involving gender or race, that derive from larger societal or educational policy issues. Administrators in all environments should be sensitive to these issues as they plan for and implement technology in their schools. This chapter reviews some of the critical issues emerging as technology expands in the schools. Knowledge and understanding of these issues are particularly important during planning activities.

TECHNOCENTRIC EDUCATION

Seymour Papert has made significant contributions to the decades-old debate on the effective uses of technology in K–12 education. In *Mindstorms: Children, Computers, and Powerful Ideas,* Papert (1980) revealed his philosophy regarding the beneficial effects of computer technology on learning. This was one of the first major works to weave an educational philosophy into the development of a computer programming language (Logo). In what is perhaps one of the more controversial passages, Papert says, "I am optimistic—some might say utopian—about the effect of computers on society" (p. 26). He then described the benefits of the Logo programming language on children's learning and cognitive development. For many educators, Papert's theories generated unbridled enthusiasm for the use of computing technology in the classroom. Throughout the 1980s and 1990s, Papert's work and philosophy were the subject of great debate and discussion (Becker, 1987; Davy, 1984; Maddux, 1989; Maddux & Johnson, 1997; Papert, 1987; Pea, 1983, 1987; Walker, 1987). The debate revolved around a technocentric approach to teaching and learning in which computers would become the vehicles for solving many of the problems in education. Although several educators have since called for a more cautious and deliberate approach in the use of computers in education, the issue remains open.

Lewis Perelman (1992), the author of a very successful book titled *School's Out: Hyperlearning, the New Technology, and the End of Education,* called for policy makers to seize an opportunity that was presenting itself in American education. He described classroom teachers as approaching "rapid obsolescence" and stated that their jobs could be done better by technology. He called for a major overhaul of the nation's schools that would transform teaching and learning from the traditional, human interactive activity into a machine-intensive activity. He claimed that computers could replace teachers and that the only reason this had not yet occurred was because the academic establishment and "educrats" were not allowing it to happen. Frank Levy, Rose Professor of Urban Economics at Massachusetts Institute of Technology, and Richard J. Murname, Thompson Professor of Education at Harvard University, disagreed with Perelman and posited that teaching and learning involve complex communication processes and expert thinking that computers are not yet able to duplicate. For example, a student can download a lesson on calculus from a Web site—but although the student has access to the information, there is no guarantee that he or she will learn it. To the contrary, the student needs the help of a teacher to translate the information about calculus into usable knowledge (Levy & Murname, 2004). Helen Mele Robinson (2008), in a study of how young children used computers in their homes, cautions that parents should be available to their children should they need help and guidance. She also applies her study's findings to classroom situations, stressing the importance of the teacher in guiding what children are doing with the technology. Although many educators consider Perelman's viewpoint extreme, it nonetheless continues to exist and should not be ignored. The use of technology is expanding, and as schools advance, questions are emerging as to how much technology should be employed in the schools. Is more technology better? Can technology replace teachers? Is it more cost-effective?

To provide further insight into this issue, an examination of integrated learning systems (ILSs) would be helpful. These systems represent the most intensive uses of technology in teaching and learning available. They integrate hardware, software, and curriculum and also usually provide sophisticated computer-managed instructional techniques that are able to customize or individualize material for each student using the system. They were designed not to be an adjunct to teaching but actually to perform the teaching function. Two examples of an ILS are Computer Curriculum Corporation's SuccessMaker, which has several reading and writing applications, and the Waterford Early Reading Program, which focuses specifically on young readers.

In schools with ILSs, teachers' roles have been transformed to a certain degree from those of instructors to managers of instruction. However, in the vast majority of these schools, instruction is provided on the ILS for a limited period each week.

The Educational Products Information Exchange (EPIE) Institute conducted one of the most extensive studies of these systems (Sherry, 1990). Field visits were made to 24 schools using ILSs, and eight different ILSs were evaluated. In general, administrators, teachers, and students supported the use of these systems. For example, 96% of the teachers and administrators interviewed in these schools recommended that other schools install similar systems, and 99% of the students interviewed indicated that they too would recommend these systems for other schools. Longitudinal student performance data based on grades or standardized tests were not collected. The researchers contemplated collecting the data, but they concluded that the outcomes of ILS use were "too difficult or impossible to measure" at the time. The overwhelming support for the ILSs in these schools indicated their general acceptance. The major benefits of ILSs most often cited by teachers and administrators in this study were the individualization of instruction, the extensive reporting capabilities, and the completeness of content.

Should all schools acquire such systems, and should schools with these systems expand their use? Because technology is good, is more technology better? The answer to both these questions is probably no. In addition to careful planning, EPIE recommended caution in investing in ILSs. Administrators, teachers, and students, all supported and endorsed their use, but their enthusiasm for such systems would not likely endure if ILSs were the primary (or only) teaching delivery system employed in their schools. Although ILSs can be important tools when integrated properly with a district's curriculum, they should not replace that curriculum entirely. Furthermore, teachers must be well trained to use these systems and to integrate them with other teaching activities.

More recently, technocentric education has centered on making laptop computers available to all students. "One laptop per child" initiatives are on the rise, and some states such as Maine have provided funding for schools and school districts adopting such policies. Nicholas Negroponte, founder and chairman of the One Laptop per Child Foundation and co-founder and director of the MIT Media Laboratory, has been a major figure in promoting this program worldwide and especially in developing nations.

These laptop initiatives concentrate on making a wide range of software tools available to both students and teachers. Perhaps the greatest benefit of "one laptop per child" programs is that they ensure that all students have access to technology both in school and at home. However, these initiatives are not without cost, and careful planning and decision making needs to be undertaken to make sure that the benefits are worth the investment. Trotter (2003), for example, reported that some school districts in Maine opted not to participate in one-laptop initiatives. He observed that if given a choice between funding more technology or reducing class size, a number of school district policy makers would choose the latter. He concluded that district officials' negative reaction to the laptop initiatives reflected a more mature understanding of the costs of technology than in years past. The issue here was not simply the use and benefits of the technology, but whether the costs would be worth the educational benefits and whether other options such as the reduction of class size would be more worthwhile. Warschauer (2007) concluded in a review of the research and his own study of 10 schools in California and Maine that "one laptop per child" programs are not the magic bullets that will solve all of our educational challenges. He also stated that they do offer important affordances for promoting information literacy and research skills but that socioeconomic context, visions, values, and beliefs all play a critical role in shaping how laptop programs are implemented and what benefits are thus achieved.

Papert's observation from *Mindstorms,* cited earlier, gave the impression that technology is a utopia for learning and education. However, later in this same passage, he referred to the computer as "a useful educational tool" (1980, p. 27). Like all tools, the value of computers and other forms of technology can vary depending on who uses them and how they are used. Administrators should adopt this "tool" mentality as opposed to a "technocentric" mentality when implementing technology. Though continuing to improve and advance, technology has not yet reached the point of replacing teachers. Administrators should be supporting and developing teachers to capture and harness the power of technology so as to integrate it with other teaching and learning activities.

WHEN SHOULD COMPUTER EDUCATION BEGIN?

Upper-grade and high school students have more access to and make greater use of technology than early childhood and elementary school children. Studies (Picciano & Seaman, 2009; Picciano & Seaman 2007; U.S. Department of Education, 2000; Quality Education Data, 1995; Becker 1994; Picciano, 1991) indicate that junior high and high school students typically make greater use of technology than do elementary school students. One major reason is that high schools and upper grades in the earlier years of instructional technology adopted computer science and computer literacy courses before the elementary schools did. Also, as students progress in their education there is a need to start developing career skills. Another important reason entails the debate within the elementary schools as to the appropriate age at which to introduce students to technology. Whereas some schools have adopted an "earlier the better" approach, others indicate that there is no need to rush and children can learn computer skills later on in their education.

One side of this issue is based on the concept that technology is good—therefore, the more (and earlier) students can learn it, the better off they will be. The other side of this issue concerns the readiness of children to use technology. Readiness in this regard can relate to a host of subissues including cognitive development, finger dexterity, eye–hand coordination in using keyboards, comprehension of computer instructions, and integration into content areas.

Papert (1980), who studied with Jean Piaget, believes that children are able to benefit from computer technology at a very early age. The fundamental Logo concept of manipulating a friendly-turtle icon was directed specifically at the young learner and is derived directly from Piaget's theories on cognitive development. Though children develop cognitively at different rates, Piaget (1952) proposed that logical thinking, at least as applied to physical reality, begins at approximately 7 to 11 years of age. The fact that, by the late 1990s, practically all elementary schools had acquired computer technology and were connected to the Internet for instructional purposes suggests that most educators believe children are ready to begin using computer equipment at an early age (U.S. Department of Education, 2000).

Logo and its derivatives, such as MicroWorlds, and many other software programs directed at the young learner have been used successfully in many elementary school programs. Although offered as a content area in which children learn about computer technology, Logo is also commonly integrated with other curriculum activities such as mathematics and problem solving. The success of Logo and other software packages designed for young children also suggests that many children of elementary school age are indeed cognitively ready to use and benefit from technology experiences. Furthermore, with the prevalence of the use of the Internet and the World Wide Web in American homes, the decision as to when to introduce technology to young people may be moot in that parents probably have already made a decision for their own children. But still there are concerns with which educators should be familiar.

Young children's finger dexterity is not the critical issue it once was because of recent hardware developments and advancements. Although the keyboard and mouse remain the major input devices for most computer systems, other devices now available—such as the joystick and trackball—are easier for children to use and manipulate. Home video games such as Nintendo's Wii continue to grow in popularity and expose children to these and other types of input devices. Special instructional input devices—such as the Muppet keyboard, which has oversized letters and keys—have also been designed for use in early childhood education and can be found in prekindergarten classes.

Computer instructions or message comprehension can be a problem in the early years if appropriate software has not been selected. Such errors in selection can result in young children staring at a video screen unable to respond to a command or becoming frustrated because they chose a logic path or continuous loop in a program from which they were unable to escape. Although these frustrating situations can and do continue to occur, even among older children and adults, careful software evaluation combined with proper supervision by teachers can minimize them.

In evaluating software for use by young children, planners should remember that children's reading comprehension level becomes most critical in determining whether they can follow the software's instructions. Educational software packages routinely include as part of the documentation the necessary reading levels required to use the programs effectively. Teachers evaluating software should match these suggested reading levels against those of their children.

In addition, teachers should not leave young children alone for extended periods of time when using technology. Young children need and appreciate regular assurance that they are doing what is expected of them.

Perhaps the most crucial decision regarding when to introduce technology into an elementary school program is its placement within the curriculum. When educational software was less abundant, the availability of software almost dictated the content areas in which computing would be used. In most cases, the targeted areas were basic skills, especially reading and mathematics. However, this has changed dramatically, with elementary schools using computers in a variety of content areas including art, social studies, and science. The abundance of quality software across content areas provides many options, and all of them should be explored. As a guiding principle, the computer should be viewed as a tool that can be integrated into various content areas of the elementary school curriculum, more so than as a subject of instruction in and of itself.

SPECIAL EDUCATION

In the past three decades, American schools have been trying to improve the education of children with special needs. Several pieces of legislation—including Section 504 of the Rehabilitation Act of 1973, the Education for All Handicapped Children Act of 1975 (Public Law 94–142), and the Individuals with Disabilities Act of 2004—prodded education policy makers to reexamine special education in the schools. An outcome of this legislation has been a movement toward inclusion of special education children into general education classrooms. This movement has presented opportunities for educators in preparing these children to participate more fully in American society. It has also presented challenges for educators to provide for the many special needs of these children.

The most fundamental tools used in education are books. Students use them in the classroom and at home to read and write. In addition to the spoken word, books are the primary means of communicating and conveying ideas. Yet, for many special education students, reading a book or writing—even simply turning a page—may be as formidable an obstacle as ascending a flight of stairs is to a person in a wheelchair. Technology is now being used by children who have difficulty learning through conventional means. Regardless of the challenge—whether hearing, vision, mobility, or learning disability—assistive technology is being used to help provide the links to learning that otherwise might not have been available to these children in years past.

For example, technology provides a variety of voice input and output devices that allow students with visual impairments to hear and respond to text that is stored on a DVD or a CD-ROM rather than printed on the pages of a book. Electronic or e-books are becoming more readily available that eliminate the need to physically turn a page. Video and text enlargers are available for students with limited vision, as are braille printers that produce embossed paper output. For students with severe motor control impairments who are unable to use their arms or hands, a number of innovative input devices have been developed that allow students to control or respond to a computer using other parts of the body. An electronic switch mechanism can be activated by wrinkling an eyebrow, moving one's jaw, puffing on a tube, or making contact with a metal plate. These switches enable students with disabilities to turn to the next page in an electronic book, respond to yes/no questions, and communicate using Morse code, which is instantly converted and displayed on a computer screen.

For a variety of other challenges including hearing, speech, and multiple disabilities, technology is also being used to provide the primary means of communication. Special education students are able to have computers in their homes, on their wheelchairs, and in minivans, in addition to the classroom. For many of them, especially those with severe physical disabilities but unimpaired brain functionality, the computer can become the primary means for communicating with the world around them.

The purpose here is not to review completely the various ways technology is being used in special education, but to emphasize the concept that technology can be used to provide tools that alleviate the hindrances that many special education children experience in their learning. When integrated with other support services and used by well-trained teachers, technology can be as beneficial to the special education child as to the general education child. Depending on the need or challenge, it may even be more beneficial because the special education child may have far fewer options for communicating and functioning in the general classroom environment.

Selecting appropriate technological aids for special education children can be complex. Given the limited market, these devices are also more expensive than other forms of educational technology. However, reimbursement for such technology may be available from governmental as well as private insurance agencies. Administrators and teachers involved with planning for technology should make sure that they have access to sources and individuals who can provide the appropriate expertise. Vocational rehabilitation agencies and national and local support groups can provide invaluable advice and assistance. A growing number of organizations that specialize in assisting and providing technology to persons with disabilities are available. The Web sites of the following organizations provide hundreds of resources for families and educators interested in assistive technology:

The National Center to Improve Practice in Special Education Through Technology, Media, and Materials

http://cecp.air.org/teams/stratpart/ncip.asp

The DRM Web-Watcher Assistive Technology Index

http://www.disabilityresources.org/AT.html

Selected Links to Assistive Technology and Augmentative Communication Resources for Children with Disabilities

http://www.lburkhart.com/links.htm

R.J. Cooper & Associates—Software and Hardware for Persons with Special Needs

http://rjcooper.com/

GENDER ISSUES

The issue of gender as it relates to the use of computers in education can be complicated, and to a degree it involves larger societal issues and sex stereotyping. Women demonstrate their abilities in using technology every day. However, much of the research and literature indicate that differences prevail in the way females and males approach the use of technology during their formative years. Much of this literature comprises two categories—one dealing with the performance of females and males in technology-infused courses, and the other dealing with the attitudes of females and males to technology. Very likely, a relationship exists between the two.

In earlier research, studies have shown differences in the outcomes of males over females in terms of performance and mastery of computer skills (Fetler, 1985; Hawkins, 1987; Martinez & Mead, 1988). Others show no differences (Linn, 1985; Robyler, Castine, & King, 1988; Webb, 1985). A possible explanation of the performance differences that showed boys performing at higher levels than girls is the assumption that technology is a skill that improves with use. If boys tended to use technology more than girls, then over time they would perform at higher levels or show greater competency, particularly in the upper grades (Sacks, Bellisimo, & Mergendoller, 1994). However, even in studies involving very young children who were first introduced to computer activities, the results were inconclusive. Using preschool samples, Schaefer and Sprigle (1988) found no gender differences in mastering Logo skills. On the other hand, Block, Simpson, and Reid (1987) reported gender differences favoring boys in learning Logo in a sample of kindergarten, first-grade, and second-grade students. Campbell, Fein, Scholnick, Schwartz, and Frank (1986) found gender differences in programming style but not in programming mastery in a sample of kindergarten children learning Logo.

Whereas technology performance research comparing gender differences has been inconsistent, research comparing gender attitudes is more consistent. Many studies involving the optional uses of technology indicate that males tend to favor these activities more so than females. These uses include taking elective courses, joining computer clubs, going to summer computer camps, and majoring in computer science in college (Pinchard 2005; Gibson & Nocente, 1999; Sanders & Stone, 1986). For example, Gehring (2001) reported that according to the College Board only 15% of those taking the Advanced Placement exam for computer science were girls. Cassell (2002) reported that boys play more computer games than girls. More recently, Heemskerk, Ten Dam, Volman, and Admiraal (2009) reported that girls prefer electronic games and software tools that emphasize creativity, collaboration, and cooperation, whereas boys prefer games that emphasize competition and are more action oriented.

The various reasons for attitudinal differences may relate to larger societal factors including parental influence, subject stereotyping, peer influence, and access to computers (including video games) in the home. Shashaani (1994), in a study involving 1,730 high school students in Pittsburgh, concluded that significant gender differences in computer interest, computer confidence, and gender-stereotyped views exist. Furthermore, she stated that parental attitudes and influences are directly associated with student attitudes about computing.

In more recent years, particularly with the proliferation of Internet tools, research indicates that some of the attitudinal issues have been changing. For instance, although females were slow to be active users of the Internet (fewer than 9% in the early 1990s), by the year 2000, women represented slightly more than half of all Internet users in the United States (Weise, 2000). However, how females use the Internet may be different. The latest results of a study by the Pew Internet and American Life Project indicate that teenage girls make greater use of social networking tools such as blogs than do teenage boys. More specifically, older girls ages 15–17 are more likely to have used social networking sites and online profiles; 70% of older girls have used an online social network compared with 54% of older boys, and 70% of older girls have created an online profile, whereas only 57% boys have done so (Lenhart, Madden, Macgill, & Smith, 2007).

However, Christie (1997) cautioned against reaching firm conclusions on gender studies regarding the use of technology, particularly for communication in education situations. In a study of female and male users of e-mail in an elementary school, Christie attempted to study the gender-stereotypical uses of the technology. She concluded that when using computers for communication, such as with e-mail, gender stereotypes cannot be understood as something apart from the social systems of particular classes (Christie, 1997). The technology is so woven into the social fabric of the class that to try to isolate it as a topic of study is difficult if not impossible.

In developing curricula, planners should keep in mind that these gender-based attitudes toward technology exist and that they most likely were established and reinforced outside the school. If technology is to be an important part of their curricula, schools should attempt to overcome these attitudinal problems. In one of the most extensive treatments of this subject, Sanders (1986a, 1986b) and Sanders and Stone (1986) suggested a variety of strategies for educational policy makers, including the following:

- Require students to take certain technology courses, because girls tend to enroll in much smaller numbers than boys if courses are optional.
- Expand technology curricula beyond mathematics and science courses.
- Integrate technology into the regular academic program.
- Educate parents at parent–teacher meetings to ensure that the home environment does not contribute to stereotyping.
- Educate the staff so that teachers are aware of the issue.
- Establish positive role models in the schools.
- Review and eliminate software and technology literature that might contain stereotypical characterizations or depictions.

For further information on gender equity and technology, readers may wish to visit the following Web sites:

Collaborative for Gender Equity

http://genderequitycollaborative.org/about.php

Anita Borg Institute for Women and Technology

http://www.anitaborg.org/

European Centre for Women and Technology

http://www.womenandtechnology.eu/digitalcity/w_homepage.jsp?men=AAABEAGE&
dom=AAABECDQ&prt=AAABDUAV&fmn=AAABEAGD

DIGITAL DIVIDE ISSUES

The concept of a digital divide was made popular during the presidency of Bill Clinton in the 1990s. It was a catchy phrase that resonated well with those making a case for the way different groups approached the use of technology. Of specific concern were minorities, lower socioeconomic populations, and non-English speakers who were not taking part in the same way as others in the technological advancements of the 1990s and especially the cyber world of the Internet.

In years past, there was definitely a large gap in terms of access to technology between schools with a large majority of white, higher socioeconomic students and schools with a large majority of minority, lower socioeconomic students. Quality Education Data (1991), after conducting three national surveys between 1988 and 1991, concluded that although all school districts had accelerated their acquisition of computers and other technologies, the typical leaders tended to be affluent suburban districts more so than inner-city and rural districts. The U.S. Department of Education (2000) reported that schools with a high percentage (in excess of 70%) of poor students have student-per-computer ratios of 16:1, whereas schools with a lower percentage (less than 11%) of poor students have ratios of 7:1. In a 129-page study of California schools conducted by the UCLA School of Education, Oakes (2003) concluded that problems of supply and adequacy of textbooks, curriculum materials, and instructional technology are most severe in schools that have a high enrollment of "the State's most vulnerable students" including low-income, minority, and English language learners. In a national study, one of the first of its kind of high school facilities, Singer, Hilton, and Schweingruber (2005) concluded that

> schools with higher concentrations of poor students are less likely to have adequate laboratory facilities than other schools. In addition to less adequate laboratory space, schools with higher concentrations of poor or minority students and rural schools often have lower budgets for laboratory equipment and supplies than other schools. (p. 8)

In sum, urban inner-city schools, schools in poor rural districts, and larger schools have less equipment including computer hardware per student than other schools; they also enroll much higher percentages of African American and Latino children. However, by the early 2000s, the issue of access to technology began to abate. In a national survey, Park and Staresina (2004) reported that the average student-per-microcomputer ratio was 4:1. In high-poverty and high-minority schools, the ratios are 4.2:1 and 4.3:1, respectively.

The question of technology access has to be viewed in the context of the larger societal issues. Minority students, poorer students, and children who are recent immigrants and whose home language is not English have a number of obstacles to overcome to succeed in American public schools. These obstacles go beyond technology education questions, and educational planners cannot be expected to resolve them simply by virtue of providing more computers in a school. Nonetheless, educators must be sensitive to these issues as they relate to their own schools. They should consider strategies that do not isolate one group from another but instead bring them together. Educators should be seeking to provide opportunities that allow children of all races, ethnicities, and socioeconomic backgrounds to not only have access to technology but also be able to use it well. The goal should not be simply to overcome the digital divide but to use technology to further the educational goals and aspirations of children.

Before concluding this section, it needs to be mentioned that this issue is not simply restricted to access in the school but also relates to ownership and access to technology in the home. For example, in a national study, the Kaiser Family Foundation (2004) reports that parents' education, occupation, race, and income, all influence ownership of technology. National surveys of computer use in the United States indicate that the percentage of households owning a computer is doubling every 5 years. However, this ownership is not even across all family characteristics. Figure 3.1 provides a comparison of home access to technology among a number of different subgroups (age, education, family income, race, ethnicity, locale), and basically it indicates that poorer, minority, lower income, less educated, and non-English-speaking Hispanic populations have less access to technology than do others. What this indicates is that even if the digital divide is reduced or eliminated within a school, it will likely continue to exist outside of school. If the assumption is that technology is good and can be beneficial in education, then students who have greater access may have an advantage over those who do not, regardless of where that access is. Technology offers access to a plethora of educational tools and information resources such as the World Wide Web that can significantly facilitate doing homework, writing papers, and doing research assignments. Simple access to word processing software can provide advantages to students doing compositions or essays. The final paper not only looks neater and cleaner than handwritten or typewritten work, but also has the advantage of the spell-checking, thesaurus, and grammar-checking features provided with modern word-processing software packages. In addition, students using word processors can correct and redo their work many times without the drudgery of rewriting or retyping it. Students who have access to technology in their homes can use the technology many hours each day if need be, whereas students without access may be limited to an hour here and an hour there in a school computer laboratory or library.

Administrators and teachers need to be aware of how many students in their schools have access to technology in their homes and consider doing something for those students who do not. Open access after school to equipment in laboratories, media centers, and libraries is becoming more and more common. However, these facilities are not as beneficial as having a computer in the home. The lending or purchasing of equipment for students will likely increase in the future as smaller portable and notebook computers become less expensive. States such as Maine, Michigan, and New Mexico have piloted programs to provide a laptop computer for every student. Some school districts have initiated similar programs specifically for homebound and other needy students. This equipment is used interactively to provide access to the Internet, e-mail, discussion groups, and other educational software.

With all the concerns that exist in education, access to technology in the home may not be a major consideration. However, with the growing acquisition of personal computer equipment combined with access to the Internet and national networks, opportunities exist for educators to use and provide experiences for their students that in the past were simply not possible. By the same token, educators increasingly will have to consider how they supply these experiences to those children who do not have access to such opportunities in their homes.

There may be some light in the "access to technology" tunnel. The Pew Charitable Trusts organization (http://www.pewtrusts.org/) has been conducting surveys on access to technology for a number of years. The data in Figure 3.1 was derived from one of its studies. Fortunately, its recent studies indicate that while the digital divide still exists, the gap is narrowing between the haves and have-nots. These studies also indicate that as minority families move into higher income brackets or attain more education, the gap narrows considerably.

	Use the Internet or E-mail Percent	Use High-Speed Internet Connection Percent
Total Population	73	55
Gender		
Female	73	52
Male	73	57
Age		
18–29 Year Olds	90	69
30–49 " "	85	68
50–64 " "	70	49
65+ " "	35	19
Race/Ethnicity		
Blacks	59	41
Spanish Dominant Hispanics	32	NA
English-Speaking Hispanics	80	55
Whites	75	56
Yearly Income		
Less than $30,000	53	31
Greater than $75,000	95	82
Education		
No High School Diploma	44	29
High School Graduates	63	39
College Graduates	91	78
Locale		
Rural	63	38
Suburban	77	59
Urban	74	56

FIGURE 3.1 Disaggregation of the U.S. Households Access to Technology. *Source:* Pew Internet & American Life Survey (2008).

CASE STUDY

Place: Sojourner Truth High School   Year: 2008

Sojourner Truth High School is the pride of Hewlitt County, a suburban community in the South. The community has grown in the past 10 years because the general metropolitan region around it has increased in population and has attracted businesses relocating from the Northeast and Midwest. The Hewlitt County School District is generally regarded as one of the best managed in the state.

Sojourner Truth High School has an excellent reputation. The principal, Mr. Wells, has spent his entire career in Hewlitt County, where he was first hired as a science teacher in 1976. The entire academic program is highly regarded; in fact, the science and technology programs are considered among the best in the state. Students from Sojourner Truth win both national and state awards each year in a variety of competitions, especially in science. In the past 10 years, several students have won prestigious national awards. In terms of computer education, the student-to-microcomputer ratio is 4:1. In addition to several central laboratories and open access areas, microcomputers with high-speed Internet connections are also located in each classroom.

It is Friday, June 7, and Dr. Lewis, the district superintendent, is finalizing the agenda for the monthly school board meeting that will take place Monday night. At the June meeting, Dr. Lewis usually has Mr. Wells give his annual high school report, during which he always introduces one or two students who have achieved some outstanding distinction. This was an especially good year in that four students (James H., Jason K., Roger S., and Miguel P.) won a national science award for developing a computer simulation program to predict drought conditions in the Southwest.

The telephone rings and it is Mrs. Elena Bodine, who wants to discuss a concern she has about her daughter, Caroline, a junior at Sojourner Truth. She says that her daughter would like to join the school's computer club but is reluctant to do so because she would be the only girl. Mrs. Bodine has had at least three conversations with Mr. Wells about this since last January. He promised to look into the matter but, according to Mrs. Bodine, "he has not done a thing about it." Although Dr. Lewis promises that he will address her concerns, she informs him that if she does not hear from him with an appropriate solution to her daughter's problem by Monday, she will attend the meeting and bring the issue up before the school board.

Discussion Questions

1. Assuming that you are Dr. Lewis, what actions do you take? Do you think it might be appropriate to change the agenda so as not to embarrass anybody? What additional information do you need?
2. What are some actions or policies that could be adopted to encourage more girls to join the computer club?

Summary

This chapter presents several issues regarding the use of technology in education. Although not as obvious as some of the basic hardware, software, and staff development issues, they are nonetheless important. Minimally, educators should be aware of them—but, more importantly, they should be sensitive to them early in the planning stages when considering the implementation or expansion of technology.

The primary learning issue to be considered is the extent to which technology is desirable in the school. Although enthusiasm about technology is desirable and even beneficial, too much enthusiasm can be disruptive and do more harm than good.

Technology in and of itself is limited. But as a tool and when placed in skillful hands, it can open new possibilities and enrich learning regardless of grade levels. Elementary, middle, and high school students are able to derive benefits from technologically based teaching techniques. Special education children, who because of various impairments are unable to use traditional educational tools, are using computer aids to provide the necessary links to learning.

In addition to educational issues, a number of equity issues are emerging. Administrators and teachers should be cognizant of gender and digital divide issues relating to minority, ethnic, and socioeconomic factors in their school districts that may affect the success of their academic computer programs. Some of these issues must ultimately be resolved in the larger society; however, educators should try not to add to the inequity that might already exist and instead employ technology to lessen it.

Key Concepts and Questions

1. Technology is being used in all aspects of our society. Use is growing in business, government, and homes. Many components of our society could not function without computer facilities and information systems. Has American education reached the point where teaching should depend more extensively on technology, which, in turn, may form the impetus for school improvement? Or is technology a simple tool that will have little impact on education? Explain.
2. Technology is generally available in high schools and upper grade levels, but major questions persist as to when it should be introduced in the elementary school. What are some of these questions? How would you respond to them if you were involved in planning or implementing technology in an elementary school?
3. Technology is proving to be especially effective for several special education populations. Do you agree with this statement? If so, provide examples. If not, which alternatives are more appropriate?
4. Equity issues and the use of technology relate to much larger societal issues involving gender, minority, and other socioeconomic factors that may be beyond the scope of most administrators' duties. What are some of these issues as they relate to technology in the schools? What strategies would you consider to lessen any inequities that might exist?
5. Americans are increasingly acquiring computer equipment for use in their homes. Does this pose any special consideration for educators? Is this a problem or an opportunity? Explain.

Suggested Activities

1. Review the educational policies that might exist in a (or your) school district regarding the use of technology in the elementary school program. At what grade level is technology introduced? Has technology been designated for specific applications? Do you have suggestions for improving these policies?
2. Observe several special education students in a school district. Do they make greater use of technology than other students? If not, do you have any suggestions for improving their learning environment by introducing technology?
3. Gather data on "digital divide" issues. Is the digital divide growing or narrowing? Why? Several excellent resources are available at the following Web location: http://www.digitaldividenetwork.org

References

Becker, H. J. (1987). The importance of a methodology that maximizes falsifiability: Its applicability to research about Logo. *Educational Researcher, 16*(5), 11–17.

Becker, H. J. (1994). *Analysis and trends of school use of new information technologies.* Irvine: Department of Education, University of California.

Block, E. B., Simpson, D. L., & Reid, D. K. (1987). Teaching young children programming and word processing: The effects of three preparatory conditions. *Journal of Educational Computing Research, 3,* 435–442.

Campbell, P. F., Fein, G. G., Scholnick, E. K., Schwartz, S. S., & Frank, R. E. (1986). Initial mastery of the syntax and semantics of Logo positioning commands. *Journal of Educational Computing Research, 2,* 357–378.

Cassell, J. (2002). Gendering HCI. In J. Jacko & A. Sears (Eds.), *The handbook of human-computer interaction* (pp. 402–411). Mahwah, NJ: Lawrence Erlbaum.

Christie, A. A. (1997). Using e-mail within a classroom based on feminist pedagogy. *Journal of Research on Computing in Education, 30*(2), 146–176.

Davy, J. (1984). Mindstorms in the lamplight. *Teachers College Record, 85*(4), 549–558.

Fetler, M. (1985). Sex differences on the California statewide assessment of computer literacy. *Sex Roles: A Journal of Research, 13*(3/4), 181–191.

Gehring, J. (2001, May 10). Not enough girls. *Education Week, 20*(35), 18–19.

Gibson, S., & Nocente, N. (1999). Microcomputers in social studies education. A report of teachers' perspectives and students' attitudes. *Computers in the Schools, 15*(2), 73–81.

Hawkins, J. (1987). Computers and girls: Rethinking the issues. In R. D. Pea & K. Sheingold (Eds.), *Mirrors of minds: Patterns of experience in educational computing* (pp. 242–257). Norwood, NJ: Ablex.

Heemskerk, I., Ten Dam, G., Volman, M., & Admiraal, W. (2009). Gender inclusiveness in educational technology and learning experiences of girls and boys. *Journal of Research on Technology in Education, 41*(3), 253–276.

Kaiser Family Foundation. (2004). *Children, the digital divide, and federal policy.* Issue brief of the Henry J. Kaiser Family Foundation, Menlo Park, CA. Retrieved February 15, 2004, from http://www.kff.org/entmedia/7090.cfm

Lenhart, A., Madden, M., Macgill, A. R., & Smith, A. (2007). *Teens and social media.* Washington, DC: Pew Internet and American Life Project.

Levy, F., & Murname, R. J. (2004). Education and the changing job market. *Educational Leadership, 62*(2), 80–83.

Linn, M. (1985). Fostering equitable consequences from computer learning environments. *Sex Roles: A Journal of Research, 13*(3/4), 229–240.

Maddux, C. (1989). Logo: Scientific dedication or religious fanaticism in the 1990s. *Educational Technology, 29*(2), 18–23.

Maddux, C. D., & Johnson, D. L. (1997). Logo: A retrospective. *Computers in the Schools, 14*(1/2), 1–7.

Martinez, M. E., & Mead, N. A. (1988). *Computer competence: The first national assessment* (Technical Report No. 17-CC-01). Princeton, NJ: Educational Testing Service.

Oakes, J. (2003). *Access to textbooks, instructional materials, equipment, and technology: Inadequacy and inequity in California public schools.* Los Angeles: Graduate School of Education and Information Studies. Retrieved February 28, 2004, from http://www.mofo.com/decentschools/expert_reports/oakes_report_2.pdf

Papert, S. (1980). *Mindstorms: Children, computers, and powerful ideas.* New York: Basic Books.

Papert, S. (1987). Computer criticism vs. technocentric thinking. *Educational Researcher, 16*(1), 22–30.

Park, J., & Staresina, L. (2004, May 6). Tracking U.S. trends. *Education Week, 23*(35), 64–67.

Pea, R. D. (1983). *Logo programming and problem-solving* (Technical Report No. 12). New York: Bank Street College of Education, Center for Children and Technology.

Pea, R. D. (1987). The aims of software criticism: Reply to Professor Papert. *Educational Researcher, 16*(5), 4–8.

Perelman, L. (1992). *School's out: Hyperlearning, the new technology, and the end of education.* New York: Morrow.

Piaget, J. (1952). *The origins of intelligence in children.* New York: Norton.

Picciano, A. G. (1991). Computers, city, and suburb: A study of New York City and Westchester County public schools. *Urban Review, 23*(3), 93–109.

Picciano, A. G., & Seaman, J. (2007). K–12 online learning: A survey of school district administrators. Needham, MA: The Sloan Consortium.

Picciano, A. G., & Seaman, J. (2009). K–12 online learning: A 2008 follow-up of the survey of U.S. school district administrators. Needham, MA: The Sloan Consortium.

Pinchard, N. (2005). How the perceived masculinity and/or femininity of software applications influences students' software preferences. *Journal of Educational Computing, 32*(1), 57–78.

Pew Internet and American Life Survey (2008). Degrees of access, May 2008. Retrieved February 4, 2010 from http://www.pewinternet.org/Presentations/2008/Degrees-of-Access-%28May-2008-data%29.aspx

Quality Education Data. (1991). *Microcomputer uses in schools: A 1990–91 Q.E.D. update.* Denver: Author.

Quality Education Data. (1995). *Education market guide and mailing list catalog, 1995–1996.* Denver: Author.

Robinson, H. E. (2008). *Emergent computer literacy.* New York: Routledge.

Robyler, M. D., Castine, W. H., & King, F. J. (1988). Assessing the impact of computer-based instruction. *Computers in the Schools, 5*(1), 1–149.

Sacks, C. H., Bellisimo, Y., & Mergendoller, J. (1994). Attitudes toward computers and computer use: The issue of gender. *Journal of Research on Computing in Education, 26*(2), 256–269.

Sanders, J. S. (1986a). Closing the computer gender gap. *Education Digest, 10,* 34–39.

Sanders, J. S. (1986b). Here's how you can help girls take greater advantage of school computers. In J. C. Arch (Ed.), *Technology in the schools: Equity and funding* (pp. 40–43). Washington, DC: National Education Association.

Sanders, J. S., & Stone, A. (1986). *The neuter computer.* New York: Schuman.

Schaefer, L., & Sprigle, J. E. (1988). Gender differences in the use of the Logo programming language. *Journal of Educational Computing Research, 4,* 49–55.

Shashaani, L. (1994). Socioeconomic status, parents' sex-role stereotypes, and the gender gap in computing. *Journal of Research on Computing in Education, 26*(4), 433–451.

Sherry, M. (1990). An EPIE Institute report: Integrated instructional systems. *Technological Horizons in Education, 18*(2), 86–89.

Singer, S. R., Hilton, M. L., & Schweingruber, H. A. (Eds.). (2005). *America's lab report: Investigations in high school science.* Washington, DC: National Academies Press. Available: http://www.nap.edu/catalog/11311.html

Trotter, A. (2003, November 5). Budget crises may undercut laptop efforts [Electronic version]. *Education Week, 23*(10), 1, 21.

U.S. Department of Education, National Center for Education Statistics. (2000). *Internet access in U.S. public schools and classrooms: 1994–99,* NCES 2000–086. Washington, DC: U.S. Department of Education, National Center for Education Statistics.

Walker, D. F. (1987). Logo needs research: A response to Papert's paper. *Educational Researcher, 16*(1), 9–11.

Warschauer, M. (2007). *Laptops and literacy: Learning in the wireless classroom.* New York: Teachers College Press.

Webb, N. M. (1985). The role of gender in computer programming learning processes. *Journal of Educational Computing Research, 1,* 441–458.

Weise, E. (2000, August 9). In a Web first, women are in the majority. *USA Today,* p. 1.

Section II

TECHNOLOGY IN ACTION

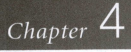
Technology for School Leadership

Since the introduction of microcomputer technology in the late 1970s, much of the literature on the uses of technology in schools has concentrated on instructional applications in the classroom. Thousands of books, professional journals, magazines, and newspaper articles have been written providing insights into the uses of technology for learning and teaching. However, for superintendents and principals, among the most successful technology applications have been those that support their administrative operations. The effectiveness of technology in instruction continues to be debated, but the effectiveness of technology to provide information, manage budgets, analyze test scores, and improve office operations is a foregone conclusion.

This chapter reviews major applications of technology in educational administration and provides an integrated framework for planning and implementing them. More importantly, it provides insights into how data and information can provide vehicles for administrators to evolve into leaders who use data and information to lead and maybe inspire teachers and parents to support educational goals and objectives. A principal with command of her/his school's data resources is in a much stronger position to inform and to persuade others to work for the betterment of children and their education.

KNOWLEDGE IS POWER

History abounds with examples of the concept that knowledge is power: the control of trade routes, the conquest of disease, and the development of the atomic weapons, to name a few. In organization theory, also, the power of knowledge has been well recognized. French and Raven (1959), in a series of studies on administrative management in organizations, were among the first theorists to identify "expert power" as a requisite to successful leadership among managers. They defined expert power simply as having access to critical information about one's organization and environment.

This concept that knowledge is power should not be viewed negatively. Because of public control and the number of constituents, schools generally require their administrative leaders to have expert or information power. Parents, teachers, staff, school board members, and the media seek out and rely on principals and superintendents to help them understand issues and events in their schools. An important characteristic of experienced and accomplished school leaders is to share freely their knowledge with others. Leaders who invest in and develop their information resources are better able to lead and manage their schools in all activities, be they program evaluations, budget presentations, or curricular improvements. Making good judgments in these areas requires accurate information about what is going on both inside and outside the schools.

Given the extensive reporting requirements of various governmental agencies, school leaders need to be able to demonstrate that they have access to and can provide critical data about their schools. Failure to do so can jeopardize budget requests, grant applications, and overall credibility with governmental officials.

Ready access to accurate information is indispensable to the functions of school leaders. Therefore, both time and monetary resources need to be devoted to planning administrative systems for a school district that carefully and efficiently provide for the integration of information needs with available computer technologies.

THE AGE OF KNOWLEDGE

In the 20th century, we witnessed major breakthroughs in humankind's activities and endeavors. Some of these have come to be characterized as periods of time, such as the age of the airplane, the atomic age, and the space age. The latter half of the 20th century, known as the information age, resulted from advances in the use of computer technology for collecting, sorting, manipulating, and reporting information. However, the information age is evolving into the age of knowledge. Educated people and their ideas, facilitated and augmented by information technology, have become key to our social well-being and a driving force for great change in all social institutions (Duderstadt, 1997). Success and progress will depend on the ability of institutional leaders to harness and convert information resources into knowledge about what is happening within an organization while monitoring the forces that influence it from the outside. Corporations, government agencies, and schools have made significant investments over the past five decades to take part in the information–knowledge age by developing, expanding, and improving their computer-based information systems.

These systems consist of three broad categories of administrative applications: (1) databases to manage data and information, (2) electronic spreadsheets to manage and manipulate numerical data, and (3) office automation to manage text and communications. Together, these three types of applications form the basis of any plan to develop and improve information systems in organizations.

Databases

Database applications are by far the most important of the three categories mentioned. They involve the management of information about the various activities of a school in the form of data elements, records, and files. Unlike spreadsheets and office automation applications that became popular relatively recently with the introduction of microcomputers, database management systems began evolving on large mainframe computers in the 1950s. IBM became a corporate giant in part because it was the first of the major manufacturers to realize the potential of the computer for managing data files rather than for manipulating and crunching numbers in scientific research and engineering applications.

In the past 40 years, database management systems have grown in complexity and sophistication, particularly for large organizations. The more data needed to be collected, verified, updated, and reported, the more complex and expensive the task of establishing and maintaining an accurate database becomes. However, the alternatives are unthinkable. Not having access to the data eventually becomes a serious problem and one that leaves an administration vulnerable. Collecting data manually can also be very expensive and prone to problems of inaccuracy and inconsistency. All school districts, regardless of their level of operation, should have as a priority in their plans the development, improvement, or upgrading of their database management systems.

The terminology used for describing databases has been inconsistent over the years, and certain terms mean different things to different people. Identifying and defining some of these terms here may be helpful. The general definition of a database is a collection of files in which data can be created, updated, and accessed. However, a more modern definition requires that data files be interrelated or integrated so that data can be accessed easily across all files and redundancy of the same data be kept to a minimum. The basic concept of databases involves the management of data in an increasingly more complex hierarchy. The members of this hierarchy, from least to most complex, are the *character*, the *data element*, the *data record*, the *data file*, and the *database*. These terms are defined as follows:

A **character** consists of a single letter of the alphabet (A through Z), a single digit (0 through 9), or a single special character ($, %, +).

A **data element**, also referred to as a *data field*, groups these characters to represent characteristics of a person, place, or thing. Examples of data elements include birth date, gender, mother's maiden name, family income, grade, course number, or room number.

A **data record** consists of a collection of related data elements for a single entity (person, place, or thing). Examples of data records include the personal record of an individual employee, the inventory record of a single piece of scientific equipment, or the transcript record of an individual student.

A **data file** is a collection of related data records. For example, the records of all employees would comprise a personnel file, or the records of all students would comprise a student file.

A **database** is a collection of data files and records. The database for a school district would encompass student, personnel, course (or curriculum), financial, and facilities files.

A **database management system** is a package of computer programs that allow the user to create, maintain, and access the data on a database. Examples of database management systems include Oracle for large computer systems and Microsoft's ACCESS for micro-computer systems.

Within a database management system, the data should be organized and documented in a **data element dictionary**, which is a table used to identify the content and coding schemes of the database. Table 4.1 is an example of part of a data element dictionary table that would be used to identify the content of a simple personnel record. This table would be stored in a computer file to be used by the database management system software and be included in a documentation manual for reference by the staff and teachers who need to maintain or access this file. Figure 4.1 is a page from a data element dictionary manual that describes the characteristics of one of the individual data elements in the personnel record represented in Table 4.1. Each data element should have a page in a paper or online manual similar to this.

As databases grow and become more complex, the task of documenting and maintaining a data element dictionary also becomes more complicated. School systems that operate a dedicated information service, data processing, or computer center frequently have full-time staff functioning as database administrators who have these responsibilities. All school districts, regardless of their size, should have someone performing these tasks. Failure to do so may render a database useless after a while because the staff will forget how to update or access the file.

TABLE 4.1 Sample Data Element Dictionary Table for a Personnel Record

Field Number	Field Name	Type	Width	Decimal	Comments
1	NAME	CHARACTER	25		Last, First, Initial
2	SOC-SEC-NO	CHARACTER	9		Social Security Number
3	SCHOOL-CODE	NUMERIC	2		School Assignment
4	DEPT-CODE	NUMERIC	2		Department Assignment
5	STARTDATE	NUMERIC	6		First Date of Employment
6	TENUREDATE	NUMERIC	6		Date Tenure Awarded
7	BIRTHDATE	NUMERIC	6		Date of Birth
8	GENDER	CHARACTER	1		Female/Male
9	STREET	CHARACTER	15		Street Address
10	CITY	CHARACTER	15		City Address
11	STATE	CHARACTER	2		State Abbreviation
12	ZIP	NUMERIC	5		ZIP Code
13	SALARY	NUMERIC	8	2	Current Salary
14	MARITAL-STAT	CHARACTER	1		Marital Status Code

```
                    DATA ELEMENT DICTIONARY
                NORTH CENTRAL SCHOOL DISTRICT NO. 1
                  PERSONNEL MASTER RECORD (PMR)

Field Number:                          14

Field Name:                            Marital-Stat

Definition:                            The legal status of the employed
                                       with respect to wedlock.

Coding Scheme/Comments:                S  = Single
                                       M = Married
                                       D  = Divorced
                                       W = Widowed
                                       L  = Legally separated
```

FIGURE 4.1   Sample Page of a Data Element Dictionary Manual.

One of the most important features of database software is the ability to generate reports. A query language is provided that enables users to access data in many different ways. These languages are very powerful for creating customized reports and temporary data files. Designed for nontechnical staff, they give users excellent access to data without having to wait for computer or data processing personnel to perform the task for them.

The number of software developers providing database management systems actually is shrinking as larger companies such as Microsoft and IBM acquire smaller companies. For microcomputer systems, Microsoft Access, Paradox (Borland), Approach (Lotus, now owned by IBM), and FileMaker Pro (FileMaker, Inc.) have proven to be very popular and are reasonably priced. For large computer systems, the selection of a database management system is a serious decision that should be made carefully with the advice of experienced and trained technical staff. These systems are expensive to acquire and more expensive to implement considering the planning, design, and computer programming required. Some of the major database management systems for large computers are Oracle, IBM DB2, and Microsoft SQL Server (developed originally with Sybase).

In reviewing and evaluating information about database management software, administrators will see references to the "data structure" or data organization used. Data structure is the method by which one data element relates to other data elements. Many books and articles explore and compare the benefits of the different data structures and approaches taken by software developers. Among the more popular structures is the relational database. Although a simple structure, a relational database views all data as being stored as tables or matrices, with each data element having access to the other data elements. Figure 4.2 is an illustration of how a student file and a course file might relate to one another in such a structure. In this illustration, the course codes serve to "relate" or link student records to course records.

Figure 4.3 illustrates some of the major administrative database applications. Each application area has a unique role in contributing to the overall data management resources of a school. The student applications tend to be the most complex because of the amount of data that needs to be collected. In addition, student data are volatile and subject to frequent change. Applications such as attendance reporting and scheduling require extensive data collection efforts and careful

Student Records

Name	ID	Year	Courses Codes
Smith, Jan	31122	10	A1,E2,S2,F2
Fox, Ann	21667	11	E1,S2,L3,M2
Feld, Lois	11233	9	E1,F1,L1,M1

Course Records

Courses Codes	Subject	Credits	Room
A1	ART 1	1.0	H100
E1	ENG 1	1.0	H101
E2	ENG 2	1.0	H110
E3	ENG 3	1.0	H102
F1	FRE 1	1.0	L100
F2	FRE 2	1.0	L110
L1	LAT 1	1.0	L103
M1	MATH 1	1.0	L101
S2	HIS 2	1.0	H120

Course codes (e.g., A1,E1,E2) are used to "relate" student records to course records.

FIGURE 4.2   Sample Relational Database Structure for Student and Course Files.

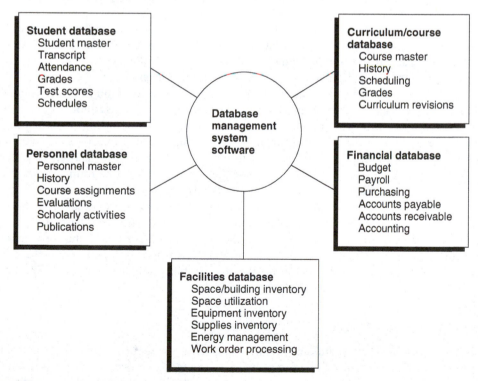

FIGURE 4.3   Common Database Applications.

coordination. Student applications are important because certain areas such as achievement and performance come under a good deal of scrutiny, especially from outside the school. Administrators need to have good access to data such as retention, attrition, graduation rates, and test scores. To give the reader a sense of the importance of such systems, the New York City Department of Education for instance recently awarded an $80 million contract to IBM to develop a comprehensive database system to monitor student performance. The new system, called ARIS (Achievement Reporting and Innovation System), will take approximately 5 years to develop. Student enrollment data are also usually critical for various state and local funding formulae, and accurate data on students in attendance become a necessity for various reporting purposes.

Curriculum and course applications are vital for a school's internal academic operations. Curriculum meetings and discussions are, in many schools, the centerpieces of academic planning. Administrators and teachers collect extensive amounts of data to develop new courses and modify existing ones. Data on student performance tied to curriculum and course enrollment become critical for such planning. A good curriculum and course database is also necessary for developing a student scheduling application, one of the most time-consuming activities when done manually.

Personnel and financial applications are frequently the first database systems to be implemented. In public schools, they may tie into other local governmental agencies for applications such as payroll, accounting, and purchasing controlled at the municipal or county levels. For any administrator, the management of a budget is a critical responsibility. Access to up-to-date and accurate information on budgets and finances is a necessity and affects all of a school's operations. Personnel files are important complements to the financial data files for purposes of managing a budget, because the major costs in school operations are for personnel items such as salaries and fringe benefits.

Facilities are generally the last of the database applications to be implemented. Facilities data are not as critical or volatile and do not need to be as tightly integrated. However, applications such as space utilization, equipment inventory, and supplies inventory should not be ignored because they contribute to overall effectiveness and efficiency.

The database management system software in Figure 4.3 is common to all of the applications and serves as an integration mechanism. By developing such a system, schools greatly enhance administrative cohesiveness because offices become more dependent on one another by virtue of sharing common data files. A single system also significantly improves the consistency of information and eliminates issues involving the accuracy of one office's data versus another's.

In developing an overall plan for database management systems, administrators should assess their ability to collect and maintain data in the five major application areas identified in Figure 4.3. More resources may have to be provided for those areas where data collection has been poor or nonexistent. In addition, all database applications, even the most established, need regular modifications and upgrades. In many cases, the ongoing costs for modifying and upgrading an existing database system, particularly when staff time is considered, may be as much as that of original implementation. Administrators believe that the ability to bring order and easy access to their information resources is well worth the price.

Electronic Spreadsheets

Electronic spreadsheets have significantly grown in popularity for applications that require frequent analysis and manipulation of numbers (e.g., budget, accounting, enrollment projections, and test scores). Electronic spreadsheets have become indispensable tools for planning and modeling.

Electronic spreadsheet software is an electronic grid or matrix of rows and columns. It replaces the accounting tablet as a tool for organizing numbers into appropriate boxes or cells, and it automatically performs all of the arithmetic operations that were formerly performed manually or with calculators on each individual cell. VisiCalc was the first popular spreadsheet package developed for use on microcomputers in the late 1970s. Presently, Microsoft Excel, Lotus, and Quattro Pro are among the most popular. Packages such as Microsoft Office and Lotus integrate spreadsheet software with database and office automation software. These packages also provide excellent graphics capabilities that enable users to present their worksheets in colorful and interesting ways.

Figure 4.4 is an example of an electronic spreadsheet for a school district's yearly budget summary and proposal. This figure shows a grid of numbered rows and lettered columns. Entries are made onto the spreadsheet by pointing or moving a cursor to the appropriate cell as identified by grid coordinates (A1, A2, B4, C6, etc.). Each cell can also have a *formula* or arithmetic operation that uses data existing in any of the other cells. The major benefit of spreadsheet software is that these arithmetic operations can be performed automatically so that a change in any one cell will almost instantaneously change all other cells that may be affected. This provides for a very rapid "what if?" facility, as popularized by media advertisements. For example, in doing a school's budget projections, if you wanted to know the effect of some percentage reduction on all the various cost centers or departments, this computation could be done almost instantaneously by just changing the entry in one cell. The calculation could also be performed over and over again with different percentages. Financial staff who regularly perform spreadsheet-type applications manually can learn to use an electronic spreadsheet in a matter of hours and become proficient after doing only a few applications. When proficiency has been achieved, electronic spreadsheets typically will replace all similar applications that had been performed manually.

Figure 4.5 provides a chart of some of the major administrative applications appropriate for electronic spreadsheet software. It is by no means a complete list of such applications (which easily number in the hundreds). They are grouped according to the major database file applications that are illustrated in Figure 4.3.

	A	B	C	D	E	F	G
1							
2			North Central School District No. 1				
3			Proposed Budget 2009/2010				
4							
5			2008-09	2008-09	2009-2010	Approved vs	
6			Estimated	Approved	Proposed	Proposed Budget	
7	Category		Expend ($)	Budget ($)	Budget ($)	Change ($)	
8							
9	General support		$ 3,888,500	$ 4,222,500	$ 4,100,000	$ (122,500)	
10	Instruction		38,250,500	39,000,000	42,000,000	3,000,000.00	
11	Transportation		3,555,000	3,550,000	3,600,000	50,000.00	
12	Plant operations		5,150,500	5,200,000	5,300,000	100,000.00	
13	Employee benefits		7,250,000	7,200,000	7,500,000	300,000.00	
14	Community service		3,050,000	3,150,000	3,100,000	(50,000.00)	
15	Intefund transfer		800,000	800,000	800,000	-	
16	Debt service		7,200,000	7,200,000	7,000,000	(200,000.00)	
17							
18		Total	$ 69,144,500	$ 70,322,500	$ 73,400,000	$ 3,077,500	

FIGURE 4.4   Sample Spreadsheet (School District Budget).

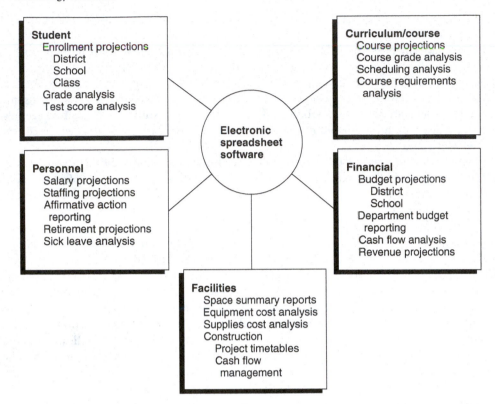

FIGURE 4.5 Common Electronic Spreadsheet Applications.

Because optimum management of information resources requires that all data files and applications be integrated where appropriate, the source data for electronic spreadsheet applications should come from the district's database files whenever possible and not gathered anew from other sources. This is generally referred to as downloading data from the database for use by other computer applications. It can be done electronically by creating aggregate data files that can be accessed by the electronic spreadsheet software. Of course, if a database does not exist or if the particular data needed are not available, then they must be gathered from other sources. This is necessary when attempting to do analyses involving phenomena that occur outside the schools. For example, an enrollment projection might require data on birthrates or the number of children under age 4 in a district.

Electronic spreadsheet software is effective in manipulating any aggregate data that are typically presented in tabular form. The number of reports using student data in this fashion is endless. Enrollment projections at various levels, test score analyses, and grade evaluations are common applications. For academic planning and scheduling, electronic spreadsheets can be very effective in doing course enrollment projections.

Personnel files are also important sources of data for spreadsheet applications. Staffing projections related to enrollment and course offerings can be routinely done. Personnel costs account for the major portion of the budget, and data such as salary projections are invaluable during budget planning and collective bargaining negotiations.

Designed initially for financial applications, spreadsheets have become commonplace in most accounting and budgeting offices. Entire budget-planning processes are conducted with

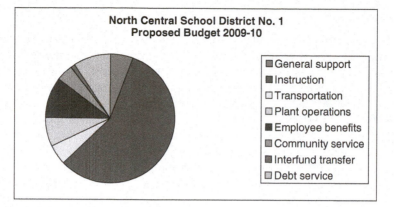

FIGURE 4.6 Sample Pie Chart Using Data from Figure 4.4.

school board members, superintendents, and others using the printed output from spreadsheets as the basis for discussion. These documents can easily be changed and recalculated many times over the course of the budget negotiation cycle. The graphics capabilities of spreadsheet programs can produce pie charts and bar graphs on budget information (see Figure 4.6 and Figure 4.7). Increasingly, these graphics are being used during public presentations of a budget and in mailings to residents on budget proposals.

Facilities applications such as space utilization reports and projections, as well as equipment and supplies inventory analyses, are also commonly done on spreadsheets. Project management timetables, cost projections, and cash flow analyses for capital construction can also be done effectively.

Spreadsheets are important tools in the presentation and manipulation of data and are most effective when integrated with database management systems. When planning these applications, keep in mind that the benefits of spreadsheet programs will best be realized if they have good data sources from which to draw aggregate data.

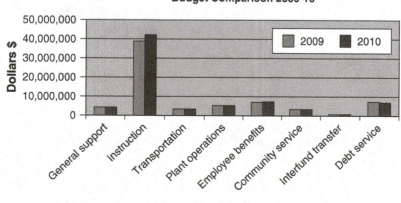

FIGURE 4.7 Sample Bar Chart Using Data from Figure 4.4.

Office Automation

Until the early 1990s, the concept of office automation essentially referred to word processing. It was a major step forward when secretaries and other administrators made the change from typewriters to microcomputers. Word processing continues to be by far one of the most frequently used microcomputer applications worldwide. Developing word processing software has become an industry in itself, with several fine products such as Microsoft Word, Corel WordPerfect, and the Web-based Google Docs. Most administrators and teachers have learned the basic features of word processing packages. Although one product might be a little easier to use and another might have a better spelling checker, they all do the job very well and certainly much better than typewriters can.

With the advent of the Internet, office automation applications have moved beyond word processing. Administrators should be thinking about how to use word processing with overall communications tools and integrating it into a "suite" of administrative software packages. In office automation, word processing is increasingly being used in conjunction with other software such as Webpage messaging, desktop publishing, electronic mail, voice mail, and databases. Word processing creates and edits text, and these other software tools print, report, and communicate the text to others. Unlike word processing, which essentially developed as a stand-alone application replacing the typewriter, these other office automation tools require either local and wide area data communications networks or the Internet to be effective. Lotus Notes and Microsoft Exchange are examples of software that links and integrates several office automation packages.

The first use of word processing with other software came with the need to merge data from database management systems with text. The best example is the merging of addresses from a database file with the text of a letter (i.e., mail merge). This not only saved the time that would have been needed to key the addresses but also made good use of the information resources available from the database management system. Today, there is much more merging of text with all sorts of data—attendance records, grades, test scores, and schedules—that are downloaded from databases. In most cases, this is an attempt to personalize the form letter and to relate the contents specifically to the recipients. Figure 4.8 provides a chart of some of the common uses of text with database information that are typically performed in school systems.

Electronic mail (e-mail) systems to distribute messages have grown in popularity. These systems concentrate on the distribution of communications throughout and beyond an organization by means of electronic mailboxes, which are data files containing text data such as messages. These systems also provide software for controlling who can send and who can receive messages and for alerting users when messages are in their electronic mailboxes.

To use these systems, a school district must develop a good data communications network that is used regularly by administrators and staff. Most school districts have established such systems. Variations of the electronic mail software include electronic bulletin boards and voice mail, which uses digitized voice messages rather than computer text files. The U.S. Department of Education reported that by 1999, 95% of all schools had acquired the necessary communications equipment to connect to the Internet (U.S. Department of Education, 2000). A good case study of the large deployment of a system-wide communications system for electronic mail is in the Jefferson County Public Schools, the largest school system in Kentucky. Jefferson County built a communications infrastructure that offers e-mail access to every 4th- through 12th-grade student, teacher, and staff member in the district. As the largest school system in Kentucky and the 26th largest U.S. district, this was no small task. Jefferson County has more than 92,000 students enrolled in its 88 elementary, 23 middle, and 20 high schools.

Desktop publishing software is also growing in popularity and is used increasingly by schools to produce their own printed materials such as newsletters, manuals, and other

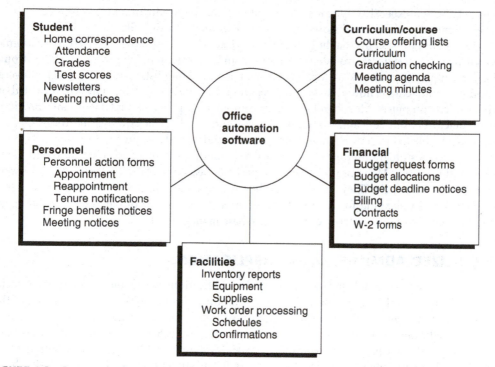

FIGURE 4.8 Commonly Merged Text and Data Applications.

documents. In addition to providing word processing capabilities, desktop publishing also provides easy-to-use graphics capabilities so that previously simple typewritten notices can include illustrations and become more colorful and interesting to the eye. Some of these publishing packages, such as Adobe PageMaker, Corel Ventura, Microsoft Publisher, and QuarkXPress, are highly rated and effective in supporting public relations activities. They can also save money by doing printed work in-house rather than sending it to a professional printer. These packages also provide World Wide Web interfaces so that material can be displayed on Web pages as well as printed pages.

The development of document storage and retrieval software that integrates computer and microform technologies is also advancing rapidly. Schools and many other people-oriented organizations are tremendous producers of paper documents that need to be stored and maintained for many years, in some cases "forever." Computer indexing systems help and in some cases replace the extensive paper file systems that are so common in a school's administrative office. These moderately priced systems provide rapid search capabilities for looking up key identifiers to microform (film or fiche) documents. They assume the existence of a microform system, which would be more efficient if a quick indexing or look-up capability was provided. They should also use existing databases for downloading index keys and other pertinent information.

With the rapid advancements in disc storage capacity, more and more documents that were being converted to microform are now being converted to digital form. These systems are being used mostly in larger school systems that maintain hundreds of thousands of past and current records. However, as this technology becomes less expensive and more readily available on microcomputer systems, with extensive read-and-write disc storage capacities, most school districts, regardless of size, will start to implement them and eliminate the need to keep paper documents.

Using relatively inexpensive optical scanners, almost any paper document can immediately be converted into digital form and stored on an optical or magnetic disk file.

Office support systems that help organize work activities are another type of office automation software. Such systems provide facilities for planning work activities and include electronic calendars, appointment books, address books, notepads, phone lists, and alarm clocks. Several computer manufacturers now include these as part of the standard software package provided on all their microcomputers. Most handheld microcomputers or personal digital assistants, provided by manufacturers such as Palm, Casio, Blackberry, and Hewlett-Packard, feature these applications and are able to integrate them with the Internet and other large proprietary networks.

The various programming packages that come under the rubric of office automation are diverse and extensive. Many of these packages perform tasks electronically that in the past were routinely done manually. They generally can be time savers and improve communications in a school district. In planning for such systems, administrators are encouraged to integrate them with other administrative systems, especially database management.

SPECIALIZED ADMINISTRATIVE APPLICATIONS

There are several additional specialized computer applications worth mentioning. First, technology is increasingly being used as an external communications tool. With the emergence of the Internet as the major technological communications tool, all organizations—including schools—are becoming a part of the global digital community. School technology leaders have begun to expand home pages and to develop "portals" or main points of entry to the Internet that provide a full range of Internet services to faculty, staff, and students. Typically a "portal site" has a catalog of Web sites, a search engine, e-mail, access to databases, and other Internet-based services. Most of the administrative applications mentioned earlier in this chapter can be integrated with Internet and World Wide Web software to communicate information and data beyond the school building (school to school, school to school district, school district to government agency, government agency to government agency, school to families, etc.). Using the Internet and other specialized networks, administrators can access a host of databases maintained by federal and state governments as well as other public or private agencies and corporations. Examples include the National Center for Educational Statistics (NCES), which maintains databases for the U.S. Department of Education on all aspects of education; Educational Testing Service Test Collection, which has thousands of descriptions of standardized tests and measures; and LexisNexis, which provides access to the full text of articles appearing in all the major newspapers and general-interest magazines. Access to these databases provides administrators with an important research tool allowing them to keep up-to-date on many aspects of the field of education.

Second, statistical software packages such as the Statistical Package for the Social Sciences (SPSS) and the Statistical Analysis System (SAS) can be valuable additions for institutional planning, evaluation, or research offices. They provide relatively easy-to-use programs for doing all types of statistical analyses involving treatments such as t tests, analysis of variance (ANOVA), correlation, and regression. They are not meant to replace electronic spreadsheet software for doing simple tables and summary totals but rather perform the advanced statistical analysis helpful in research and data-driven decision making.

Third, test-scoring equipment and software are common in many schools and provide quick marking of objective tests. Many of these systems are on the market and use some type of optical scanner to read the tests and provide the data to a microcomputer, which in turn provides the test results in the form of a printed report. The better packages also provide summary statistics such as group results, means, standard deviations, and item analysis. Teachers make good use of these systems in grading and analyzing student academic performance. Much of this specialized equipment is also being upgraded and provided by World Wide Web software packages.

Fourth, automatic telephone calling systems that combine telephones, computer equipment, and stored voice message equipment are used in some districts. Originally designed for use in telephone sales or telemarketing operations, these systems have found success in school districts for monitoring student attendance. Such systems generally require that a disk file of telephone numbers of the children absent from school be provided each day. These are automatically dialed, and a recorded message is played informing the parent that her or his child was not in school that day. These systems can also be used to notify parents of special meetings, school closings, and other news.

Fifth, energy management is an important means of generating substantial savings through the use of computer technology. Computer applications support energy management in two different ways. One is simply to use a database management system to keep detailed records on energy consumption by heating zones and time of day. Analyzing these data regularly allows facilities personnel to track down and eliminate wasteful uses of energy. A more sophisticated approach requires a computer system that is directly connected to all the physical plant's control mechanisms for electricity, heating, and cooling. These systems can be programmed to control (reduce, increase, or shut down) the amount of energy that is being used in all the various zones. Such systems are expensive to acquire and install but should be considered, especially when doing capital improvements.

INTEGRATING IT ALL TOGETHER: DATA-DRIVEN DECISION MAKING

Although all of the major administrative applications mentioned above are critical for the effective operation of a school or school district, they are incredibly powerful when integrated and used to inform decision making. In recent years, the term *data-driven decision making* has become popular in education. The simplest definition of data-driven decision making is the use of data analysis to inform when determining courses of action involving policy and procedures. It is important to note that data analysis is used *to inform* and does not replace the experience, expertise, intuition, judgment, and acumen of competent educators. Inherent in this definition is the development of reliable and timely information resources to collect, sort, and analyze the data used in the decision-making process. The next chapter is devoted entirely to the development of data-driven decision-making activities in schools and school districts.

CASE STUDY

Place: Lincoln Middle School, Rockwell City   Year: 2009

Lincoln Middle School is a 6th to 8th grade middle school located in Rockwell City. It has an enrollment of 600 students and its principal, Jan Marson, is generally recognized as one of the more effective school leaders in Rockwell City. Almost 90% of the students regularly pass the state-mandated competency tests. Ms. Marson credits the success of Lincoln mostly to a dedicated teacher corps and an involved community, especially the parents. About 4 years ago she and one of her assistant principals took a workshop—"Using Data to Guide Instruction"—offered by a local college. Both she and her assistant were impressed with the concepts and decided to try implementing some of them at Lincoln. The biggest obstacle was the absence of a user-friendly database system in their school and district. They were required to maintain basic student information on an old database system at the district office, but accessing the data was slow and very cumbersome. Nevertheless, working with data provided by the state education department and with several reports generated by the district, Ms. Marson and her assistant were able to establish a small but effective database that contained some basic student demographic information as well as performance data on mandated tests. Her assistant, Len Vasquez, was especially attentive in keeping the data accurate.

The following year, Ms. Marson and Mr. Vasquez introduced the concepts of data-driven decision making to the teaching staff. Teachers were generally willing to try it, and in 2006 a data-driven decision-making process was implemented with grade 6 teachers. The process is inclusive, with teachers meeting and discussing student performances class by class. Performance goals and strategies for each class are subsequently established for the following year with particular attention paid to individual students who did not pass the state competency tests. Teachers were responsive to the approach and the process was extended to the other grades in 2007.

Mr. Vasquez performs all of the responsibilities of a data analyst and coordinator for Lincoln, and he has had to invest many hours to collect and provide the data on a timely basis. He is having some difficulty meeting his other responsibilities and has expressed this to Ms. Marson. Ms. Marson recognizes that he is spending much more time on this than she originally anticipated and she is concerned.

In May, Ms. Marson received a telephone call from the district superintendent, Dr. Elizabeth Cope, asking her to serve on a district-wide committee to guide the development of a new student information system. Dr. Cope indicated that she chose Ms. Marson for this assignment because Lincoln Middle School is one of the few schools in the district that has managed to collect student information capable of supporting a data-driven decision-making process for instruction. In preparation for the first meeting of the committee, Dr. Cope has asked Ms. Marson to write a position paper on her experiences with data-driven decision making at Lincoln and more importantly to provide her views and recommendations on how the district should proceed.

Discussion Questions

1. Assume you are Ms. Marson. What are your recommendations for the district? Critical to your recommendations are whether or not what has been accomplished in one middle school can easily be adapted to the entire district.
2. Are the issues here simply technological, or are there important personnel considerations as well?

Summary

This chapter reviews the major administrative uses of computer systems. A framework is developed for planning that requires these systems to be integrated with one another as much as possible. Database management systems and the information they provide are critical for this integration; they are the resources on which all the other applications depend.

Database management systems, electronic spreadsheets, and office automation are the major software packages used to perform administrative applications. Extremely sophisticated but easy to use, they are evolving into indispensable administrative software tools. Various examples of the uses of these software packages in educational administration are also presented. In addition, several special-purpose applications of computer technology are described, including access to national information networks, statistical software, test scoring, automatic calling, and energy management systems.

Key Concepts and Questions

1. Developing the information resources of a school district is a critical goal of administrative computer systems. Why is this goal so important to school administrators? Who are some of the regular recipients of information from a school district? Is developing information resources a common goal in all organizations? Explain.

2. Database management systems, electronic spreadsheets, and office automation are the three major categories of administrative software applications. How do you define and compare them? Are they dependent on one another, or do they function independently? Explain. If starting administrative applications from the beginning, what would be your first priority? Why?

3. Database management systems are very complex applications. Identify some of the common database applications that exist in a school district. How do they relate to one another? What staff would be involved in designing a new database management system for student records? Personnel records?

4. Spreadsheet applications are used extensively in number manipulation exercises. Identify some common uses of spreadsheet applications in a school. How are the data generated for these applications? Who might be the major developers of spreadsheet applications in a school?

5. Office automation at one time essentially referred to word processing. How has it changed? What other applications does it include? Who are the major beneficiaries of office automation applications?

6. In addition to database, spreadsheet, and office automation applications, various other special-purpose applications can exist in a school district. Identify several special-purpose applications. For each one, consider (a) whether special hardware or software is required, (b) which individuals in a school would be involved in developing the application, and (c) how important you consider the application to the overall administrative operations.

Suggested Activities

1. Assume that you are responsible for initiating a 5-year administrative technology plan for a school district. For the first meeting of the new Administrative Systems Advisory Committee, you are to prepare a brief assessment of the school district's present level of administrative systems development. How would you outline such an assessment?

2. Familiarize yourself with some of the features of the database management, electronic spreadsheet, and office automation software that might exist in a school (or in your school). If available, also explore the facilities of an integrated administrative software package such as Microsoft Office. If you are not familiar with these software packages, try to develop simple applications for database, electronic spreadsheet, and office automation. Then try to integrate them. (For example, mail merge.)

3. Do a search (use Google, Bing, Yahoo, or some other popular search engine) on the World Wide Web for "school budget." Do a comparison of how school districts use Web pages to publicize their budgets. Also evaluate how newspaper articles, citizen groups, PTAs, and other community groups comment on school budget issues.

References

Duderstadt, J. J. (1997). The future of the university in an age of knowledge. *Journal of Asynchronous Learning Networks, 1*(1), 78–88. Retrieved March 15, 2004, from http://www.aln.org/publications/jaln/v1n2/v1n2_duderstadt.asp

French, R. P., & Raven, B. (1959). The bases of social power. In D. Cartwright (Ed.), *Studies in social power* (pp. 150–167). Ann Arbor, MI: Institute for Social Research.

U.S. Department of Education, National Center for Education Statistics. (2000). *Internet access in U.S. public schools and classrooms: 1994–99* (NCES 2000-086). Washington, DC: U.S. Department of Education, National Center for Education Statistics.

Chapter 5

Wisdom and Data-Driven Decision Making

Wisdom is usually associated with the great thinkers of philosophy and religion. Confucius, Abraham, Solomon, Socrates, Mohammed, and Gandhi are some of the "wise" men who have exhibited wisdom as well as commented on its nature. Through the ages, wisdom's definition has varied with peoples and cultures. However, its psychological and scientific study only goes back several decades. One of the first individuals to study wisdom, asking "what is it?", from a scientific point of view was a young graduate student from Brooklyn, New York, named Virginia Clayton (Hall, 2007). In the 1970s, Ms. Clayton was studying psychology at the University of Southern California with James Birren, one of the leading psychologists in the country. She chose the nature of wisdom as her dissertation topic. She wrote several papers, many of which are still referenced today. Her basic model for the essence of wisdom involved

1. knowledge as applied to human social situations;
2. involved judgment and reflection; and
3. compassion. (Hall, 2007, p. 59)

Data-driven decision making involving the education of children requires wisdom, and Clayton's model provides an appropriate starting point from which to discuss what it is and how to apply it.

Data-driven decision making is not simply the assembling, sorting, and analyzing of test scores and other quantitative data to determine a particular course of action. On the contrary, it requires the integration of the knowledge that educators have amassed during their careers (reflective decision-making process) to analyze information in a manner that considers carefully the educational conse-quences for the children who will be affected (compassion). Increasingly, data-driven decision making is being seen as a critical element for improving schools. Arne Duncan, upon his appointment as Secretary of Education in 2009, identified four key requirements needed to improve poorly performing schools:

1. Rigorous standards
2. Effective data systems to track student progress
3. Effective teachers
4. Good planning (Duncan, 2009)

This chapter examines data-driven decision making with an emphasis on those decisions that affect the way teachers teach and students learn. The development and nurturing of information resources is examined as the foundation for establishing effective data-driven decision making in a school or school district.

DEFINING DATA-DRIVEN DECISION MAKING

The simplest definition of data-driven decision making is the use of data analysis to inform courses of action involving policy and procedures. Note that data analysis is used *to inform* and does not replace the experience, expertise, intuition, judgment, acumen, and compassion of com-petent educators. Nevertheless, inherent in this definition is the availability of reliable and timely information resources to be accessed, sorted, and analyzed in the decision-making process. Although all schools have professionals with experience and expertise, not all have developed the information resources needed to support decision making.

Decision making may be simply defined as choosing between or among two or more alter-natives. In a modern school organization, however, decision making is an integral component of complex management processes such as academic planning, policy making, and budgeting. These processes evolve over time, require participation by stakeholders and, most importantly, seek to include information that will help all those involved in the decision process.

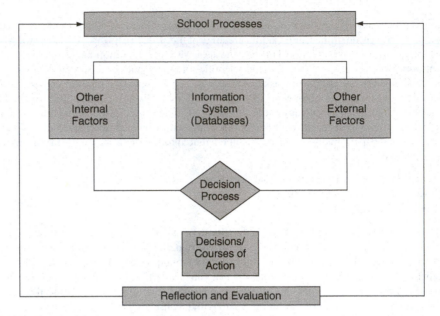

FIGURE 5.1 The Decision Process Model.

Figure 5.1 illustrates the basic data-driven decision-making process. It assumes that an information system is available to support the decision process, that internal and external factors not available through the information system are considered, and that a course(s) of action is determined. Preferably, the information system in Figure 5.1 is a computerized database software system, as discussed in Chapter 4, capable of storing, manipulating, and providing reports on a variety of data.

Some terms related to data-driven decision making that have become popular in recent years include *data warehousing, data mining,* and *data disaggregation.* Data warehousing is essentially a database information system that is capable of storing and maintaining data *longitudinally* (over a period of time). Data mining is a frequently used term in research and statistics that refers to searching or "digging into" a data file for information to better understand a particular phenomenon. Data disaggregation refers to the use of software tools to break data files down into various characteristics. An example might be using a software program to select student performance data on a standardized test by gender, by class, by ethnicity, or by other definable characteristics.

INFORMATION INFRASTRUCTURE

Webster's Third New International Dictionary (1986) defines infrastructure as the underlying foundation or basic framework of an organization or system. The term can be applied to a host of entities such as energy, water, or communications that undergird an organization—state, city, corporation, medical center, or school district—and its operations. An organization's infrastructure might include a central source such as an energy power station, water supply, communications center, or information system that distributes resources through a series of nodes. In many cases, the flow (see Figure 5.2) is top–down from the source (e.g., school district office) to the nodes (e.g., individual schools and administrative departments). Recently, however, in the case of

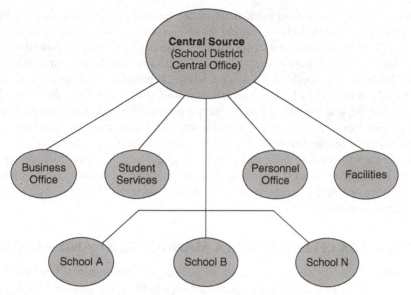

FIGURE 5.2   Central Source (Top-Down) Information Infrastructure.

information systems and the distribution of data throughout an organization, the emergence of digital communications and the Internet/World Wide Web has changed the conceptual framework of the infrastructure. Although central sources for communications and data processing activities still exist, a diagram (see Figure 5.3) of an organization's information infrastructure will more frequently show a hub-based network in which resources are shared across all nodes rather than moving back and forth or from the top–down between the central source and the nodes within the organization. Fundamental to this model is the ability of nodes to share resources with other nodes without necessarily going back to the source. This model is particularly important

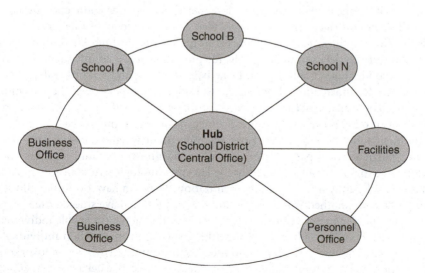

FIGURE 5.3   Hub-Based Information Infrastructure.

when developing the information infrastructure for data-driven decision making in a school district. All those involved in decision making are able to share activities, strategies, and data with one another. Although technical assistance, support, and databases may be provided centrally at the school district level, ultimately the success of the data-driven decision-making process will rest on the ability of individuals in the schools to effect changes in classrooms and offices. It is highly desirable, if not critical, for administrators and teachers in the schools to share their knowledge, expertise, and experiences with others across the district. This framework for sharing information resources across the school district is the foundation that will empower shareholders and enable them to realize the potential of data-driven decision-making activities in their schools. Note that when conceptualizing infrastructure, the tendency is to think about the physical elements of a system. With data-driven decision making, however, it is most beneficial to think of the infrastructure as composed of hardware, software, and especially people—their expertise, experience, knowledge, and compassion.

HARDWARE FOR EFFECTIVE DATA MANAGEMENT AND ACCESS

To support data-driven decision making, the school district's fundamental hardware configuration comprises computer workstations distributed on a high-speed digital network that is fully compatible with the Internet. Each node in the school district's network may be a school or office with its own mini-network capable of intercommunication with any other node in the district as well as with networks outside of the district. The details of establishing data communications networks will be further discussed in Chapter 8.

Once a network is in place, the next question is, "Where should the computer workstations be located?" The answer to this question is "everywhere." The Internet was established as a ubiquitous resource; users are able to connect to it from anyplace. Administrators have computer workstations in their offices, teachers in their classrooms, parents and students in their homes. As early as 1989, the National Education Association (NEA) recommended that a computer be installed on the desk of every teacher (National Education Association, 1989). The emergence of portable electronic devices, namely, laptop computers and personal data assistants (PDAs), allows connectivity to the network from anyplace there is a telephone connection or a clear satellite signal. All school districts have not yet provided computers to all of their teachers and staff, but this is the direction in which Internet-based technology is heading. The long-range plan for developing data-driven decision making calls for providing access to information resources to just about everybody in a school district. Principals, teachers, and administrative staff should have ready access to information about students, budgets, and personnel. Furthermore, these resources need to be available so as to allow access from anyplace (office, classroom, home) that a desktop, laptop, or other portable electronic device can connect to the Internet.

A comment about the power of networks is appropriate when discussing data-driven decision making, particularly as part of a process where administrators and teachers are sharing information. Networks are not just simply the latest technological advancement designed to move data more efficiently throughout an organization. They can have profound effects on how people work with one another. Watts (2003) and Birabasi (2002) have studied the effects of networks on various people-intensive processes. They found that networks enable individual behavior to aggregate into collective behavior. Something special happens when individual entities (nodes, components, and people) are able to interact to form larger wholes (networks, systems, and communities). Furthermore, the "interaction effect" or collective behavior may result in a far more productive environment than individuals acting by themselves: one individual working with another individual does not simply comprise two individuals but a third, more powerful collaborating entity that can extend the benefits beyond two. Modern data communications networks now make it possible for many individuals to share and work with one another, and their collective behavior can be most effective in supporting complex processes including data-driven decision making.

SOFTWARE FOR DATA MANAGEMENT AND ANALYSIS

The database management system, as discussed in Chapter 4, serves as the underlying software for developing and supporting a school district's information resources and also serves as an integration mechanism. It allows a school district to warehouse or maintain data longitudinally (over time). This becomes most critical in analyzing student progress from semester to semester and year to year. By developing such a system, schools greatly enhance administrative cohesiveness, because offices become more dependent on one another by virtue of sharing common data files. A single system also significantly improves the consistency of information and eliminates issues involving the accuracy of one office's data versus another's.

A database management system always provides a query language that enables users to access data. Query languages were the precursors to search engines popularized on the Internet and World Wide Web. The power of query languages, however, is that they can be customized to access data stored in a specific database system. For this reason, query languages are very efficient in providing specific information, creating reports, and establishing temporary data files for subsequent analysis. With some training, query languages can be used by nontechnical staff thereby eliminating dependence on others to perform data gathering tasks. They also allow teachers and administrators to customize output in addition to utilizing standardized reports that have a set format and cannot be manipulated and altered. Query languages can be used to create subsets of the database that can be analyzed and reanalyzed, delving deeply into a particular issue that pertains to a particular group of records. For instance, a committee of mathematics teachers could create a subset of the test scores of all the students in fourth grade in order to analyze and reanalyze performance as it relates to student demographics and characteristics. If they need additional information, they simply do another query on the data subset. This method of inquiry is far more sophisticated and effective than examining a preformatted (either on paper or on a display screen) report. This analysis and reanalysis is an example of data mining, as mentioned earlier in this chapter.

In addition to query languages, electronic spreadsheets and statistical software packages are important tools in supporting data-driven decision making. Electronic spreadsheets such as Microsoft Excel have already been discussed in Chapter 4 as important tools for the frequent analysis and manipulation of numbers such as budget, accounting, enrollment projections, and test scores. When integrated with query languages, spreadsheets become indispensable for all types of data-driven decision-making activities. A complementary and a more powerful tool for data-driven decision making is the statistical software package, such as the Statistical Package for the Social Sciences (SPSS) or the Statistical Analysis System (SAS). These packages can perform most of the data analysis routines that Excel and other spreadsheet programs do and in addition can more easily perform statistical routines such as contingency tables (crosstabulations), frequency distributions, and correlations. Although spreadsheet software is a good starting point for doing basic data analysis, statistical packages can take the analysis much further.

However, to use a package such a SPSS or SAS, a certain amount of training is required. These packages have extensive data analysis capabilities, and learning to use these capabilities requires practice. In larger schools and school districts, it might be difficult to train large numbers of administrators and teachers to use these types of packages, and so it may be preferable to appoint or designate one or more individuals as data analysts who will develop the technical expertise to provide and coordinate data analysis activities. The position of a data analyst will be discussed later on in this chapter.

PEOPLE, DECISION MAKING, AND THE SOCIAL NATURE OF INFORMATION

A good deal of literature exists on the importance of collaboration in decision making. Authors such as Senge (1990; learning organizations) and Wenger (1999; communities of practice) see collaboration as crucial to organizational growth and health. In a sense, organizations are transformed into organic entities that learn and advance, advance and learn. Sergiovanni and Starratt (1998) redefined educational administration as reliant on "organic management" that makes the promotion of the community the "centerpiece" of supervision. Each of these authors has promoted concepts that elevate school management above the bureaucratic, top–down, do-it-this-way style of administration to a higher level of collaborative, we-are-in-this-together activity. In more recent years, a link has been made between collaboration and information sharing, especially with regard to complex decision processes and the use of data as the fulcrum on which communities develop. Seeley Brown and Duguid (2002), in their work entitled *The Social Life of Information,* call for a better understanding of the contribution that communities and people make to complex decision processes and an enhanced realization that data, information systems, and technology only take the process so far. This concept is essentially an extension of the Nobel Prize–winning work of Herbert Simon (1957) on the "limits of rationality" or "bounded rationality" discussed in Chapter 2. Part of Simon's thesis posited that the emotions, cognition, and values underlying conditions make some decisions possible and some not.

Increasingly, dialogue and social interaction in decision making are being seen as critical to effective management and administration. Elmore and others have expressed concern that teachers, in particular, have not been encouraged to engage in dialogue, nor are they often given the time or support to allow such activity (Elmore, 2004; Wilhelm, 2007). Wilhelm begs the question: "Why are meaningful inquiry and exploratory dialogue so rare in American schools, despite the fact that leading researchers agree that it is essential to student learning?" (2007, p. 19). Although hardware and software are the vehicles for delivering accurate and timely information, there is still great concern that integrating these with the people element is lacking in many schools. Most of the people essential to the decision-making process are school-based and include administrators who know their schools and constituents, teachers who know their students and curricula, and staff who know their operations and services. All of them need to be trained and brought together to use the information resources that will help them make informed decisions.

Data-driven decision making requires enhanced leadership skills on the part of district supervisors, principals, and other administrative staff. School leaders must be capable of setting a climate that allows for a "we" process rather than a "me" process. Teachers and staff need to feel comfortable and to know that they are not the objects of data-driven exercises wherein their skills and abilities are constantly questioned. Given the current emphasis on accountability and standards, teachers have become a focus of attention in the success or failure of our children. Teachers and other staff are indeed critical to the educational enterprise; they should be treated, assigned, and developed with skill and competence. Price (2004), in an article entitled "New Age Principals" that appeared in *Education Week*, expressed the following concern:

> Both current principals, and those entering the principalship for the first time, find that they are ill-prepared to manage an infrastructure that supports instruction and has as its constant focus the technical core of teaching and learning. (p. 36)

He recommended that all principals, new and old, develop four key skills to create and manage the type of infrastructure needed to support instructional improvement:

1. Ability to manage information
2. Ability to analyze and use data to determine areas in need of improvement
3. Ability to align and monitor curriculum to meet needs
4. Ability to build a professional community of learners (stakeholders) committed to instructional improvement

Although all four of these skills are important, the last is the most critical and undergirds all the others.

THE DATA ANALYST

As school districts begin to invest in data-driven decision processes, the need for someone with technical expertise in data analysis becomes more apparent. The data analyst possesses a number of skills, especially familiarity with information systems and fundamental statistical analysis, and serves as an important resource person for others (administrators, teachers, parents) in using data effectively. The data analyst also performs a coordinating function by providing data in a timely manner to coincide with a district or school's planning activities. As data-driven decision-making activities evolve, districts will have minimally one person performing this function on a full-time basis. Large districts will have more than one person, depending on size. In addition, individual schools will have someone performing this function perhaps on a part-time basis, and large schools, especially middle and high schools, will likely have a full-time person.

The need for a data analyst has grown considerably as data are used more frequently in shaping instructional activities. In other areas where data are critical for decision making, such as budget and finance, it is more likely that the staff assigned to these areas will have had some formal training in information systems management and business statistics or quantitative analysis. In addition, generally a small cadre of business personnel work with data files on a daily basis and are comfortable "mining" these files to support decision-making activities. Instructional decision making, however, requires sharing data on students, testing, and other performance indicators with teachers and parents who are going to be less familiar with data analysis. The data analyst can be very helpful in designing standard reports that are produced on a cyclical basis and that serve as common resources in the discussion and planning of instructional activities. In addition, with some training and assistance, teachers will use the standard report to begin the process of mining the data as group and individual judgments about instruction evolve. The support of a data analyst with expertise in information processing and quantitative methods will facilitate their analysis and judgments.

Another way in which a data analyst can be helpful is in monitoring the external environment. Although much of data-driven decision making is internal to a district or school, scanning the external environment for resources or data-related mandates and compliance issues can be helpful if not critical. Front-line administrators have difficulty finding the time to do this effectively, whereas a data analyst may be able to do this quite easily.

Finally, data-driven decision making for instruction assumes that the community, especially parents, will also be invited to become involved in the process or at least to share in its results. To involve the community, reports will have to be easily understood by the broader population. Having a knowledgeable data analyst design, explain, and answer questions about these reports will contribute to the success of the activity and garner support from the community.

DATA-DRIVEN DECISION MAKING APPLICATIONS

Data-driven decision making can be applied to almost any school administrative activity including projecting school enrollments, budgeting, curriculum development, monitoring student progress, or surveying a community, although the sources of the data and the individuals involved in the decision making may change. It would be worthwhile to examine several typical data-driven decision-making applications. What follows are three case studies of data-driven decision making in action at the school district and school building level. The names of the schools and individuals have been changed.

School Enrollment Projections

School districts need to provide the leadership for developing and implementing data-driven decision-making processes especially with respect to large, "big picture" issues and questions. For example, how many students are in attendance or will be attending? Will they have any special needs? Will the staff and budget be adequate? Although these questions are important at any level of the education organization, they are critical to district-wide planning and decision making. In addition to the school superintendent, other district-level personnel (e.g., student services, facilities, business office) as well school-based personnel who may be impacted by changes in enrollment patterns should be included in the decision process. All of these individuals have expertise and experiences that can help planning for any significant changes in the student population.

Several reliable sources (e.g., census, county building department) collect data pertinent to enrollment from the community. However, even in the best of circumstances such data may be less than 100% accurate. A few percentage points can have serious ramifications with regard to a school district's operations. It is therefore incumbent upon the school district leadership to develop models that provide an accurate picture of enrollments for the coming 2 or 3 years. Every district office should have individuals who know the characteristics of the community, such as population growth and economic factors, and who can provide insights into trends and developments in the district that might effect enrollments. However, critical to every enrollment projection model is accurate data from the past.

The Haldane School District (name changed) is a medium-sized district with approximately 16,000 students spread over a significant geographic area in the southwest part of the United States and is divided into six attendance zones. It operates 16 primary schools (average enrollment = 490), 6 middle schools (average enrollment = 700), and 2 high schools (average enrollment = 2000).

Figure 5.4 is a spreadsheet for a simple enrollment projection for the Haldane School District. Enrollment data for the previous 5 years serve as the basis for projecting the enrollments for the subsequent 3 years. This is a common technique used by many school districts. In this

Haldane School District Enrollment Data and Projections

		Actual					Projected		
	Year 2000	Year 2001	Year 2002	Year 2003	Year 2004		Year 2005	Year 2006	Year 2007
Enrollment	15400	15550	15700	15750	16100		16275	16456	16645
Change		150	150	50	350		175	181	189
% Change		0.010	0.010	0.003	0.022		0.011	0.012	0.012

FIGURE 5.4 Basic Enrollment Projection Using Averages From Previous Years (Base Year, 2000).

example, in 2004, a Microsoft Excel spreadsheet was used to develop a model using data from the year 2000 as the base; the spreadsheet averages (calculates a mean) the actual enrollment increases of the subsequent 4 years (2001–2004) to project enrollments for the upcoming 3 years (2005–2007). The formula used is as follows:

Sum Each Actual Year's Enrollment Increase and Divide by N (4) Years OR

$$(150 + 150 + 50 + 350)/4 = 175$$

$$16100 + 175 = 16275 \text{ for Year 2005}$$

In this projection, the percentage change from year to year (shown in the bottom row of the spreadsheet and expressed as a decimal) is fairly stable except for a little move upward for Year 2004, when the enrollment in the district increased 350 students or 2.2%. The method used to make the projection (yearly average increase) is simple and direct, especially when enrollments are fairly stable and do not change significantly from one year to another.

Figure 5.5 depicts a second spreadsheet that also uses enrollment data for the previous 5 years as the basis for projecting the enrollments for the next 3 years. However, rather than computing simple averages of the enrollment increases of each of the previous years, weighted averages designed to give more "weight" to the immediate past year and less "weight" to the more distant past year are used. The formula used is as follows:

Each Year's Enrollment Increase is assigned a weight in increments of one as follows:

Year 2001 Increase $\times$ 1

Year 2002 Increase $\times$ 2

Year 2003 Increase $\times$ 3

Year 2004 Increase $\times$ 4

Haldane School District Enrollment Data and Projections

		Actual					Projected		
	Year 2000	Year 2001	Year 2002	Year 2003	Year 2004		Year 2005	Year 2006	Year 2007
Enrollment	15400	15550	15700	15750	16100		16300	16510	16729
Change		150	150	50	350		200	210	219
% Change		0.010	0.010	0.003	0.022		0.013	0.013	0.014

FIGURE 5.5 Basic Enrollment Projection Using Weighted Averages From Previous Years (Base Year, 2000).

Sum the weighted increases and divide by the sum of the weights as follows:

$$\text{Year 2001 Increase} (150 \times 1) = 150$$
$$\text{Year 2002 Increase} (150 \times 2) = 300$$
$$\text{Year 2003 Increase} (50 \times 3) = 150$$
$$\text{Year 2004 Increase} (350 \times 4) = 1400$$
$$\text{Sum} = 2000/10 = 200$$
$$16100 + 200 = 16300 \text{ for Year 2005}$$

The result of using weighted averages shows an increase of 200 students compared to 175 students using the nonweighted averages as shown in Figure 5.4. This result reflects the additional weight given to the larger increase (350 students) in the most recent year (2004) compared to the earlier years.

The superintendent chaired several meetings in early spring 2005 to discuss enrollment projections. Present at these meetings were 8 to 10 district-level administrators and 2 school principals. The two spreadsheets depicted in Figures 5.4 and 5.5 were used to support the planning process for the upcoming year. As it turned out, the projections in Figure 5.5 were closer to actual enrollments in the subsequent years. Furthermore, since most of the enrollment increase was the result of a single new housing development, most of the new students were concentrated in one student attendance zone effecting two primary schools and one middle school.

Improving Teaching and Learning

In this age of accountability and assessing student outcomes, one of the more important functions of school district personnel is to provide test results at the school building level so that principals, assistant principals, and teachers can understand the teaching and learning needs of their children and act accordingly. The data need to be timely, accurate, and readily available. Timeliness allows strategies to be developed before semesters and school years. Readily availability means that data are provided in electronic form and not on reams and reams of paper. Too often, data are made available to administrators on workstations where they are manipulated, sorted, aggregated, and disaggregated, whereas individual class data are printed in a "final" form for the teachers. The improvement of teaching and learning will succeed (or not) depending on what goes on in the classroom. Teachers need to understand and be able to "mine" the data with their particular students in mind to develop appropriate strategies and, more importantly, to implement the changes needed to give every child the chance to succeed.

Jefferson Middle School (name changed) operates a sixth- through ninth-grade program in a growing suburb of a metropolitan area in the southeast part of the United States. Figure 5.6 is a Microsoft Excel spreadsheet showing test results for students who took the eighth-grade statewide Language Arts Test in spring 2004 at Jefferson Middle School.

The example shows the first 10 records of the 106 students who took the test. In July 2004, the new principal established a committee to review the state test results and make plans for the next school year. In previous years when results were made available by the district, the former principal shared them individually with each teacher who then developed his or her own plans for the coming year. The new committee included an assistant principal, a former

	A	B	C	D	E	F	G	H	I	J	K
1					Jefferson Middle School						
2					Grade 8 Language Arts Test Results						
3					(Year 2004)						
4											
5			Special	Eligible	Assigned	Scale	Standard 1	Standard II	Standard III	Performance	
6	Student Id	Gender	Services	Free Lunch	Class	Score	Score	Score	Score	Level	
7	1	1	1	1	1	718	83	93	81	3	
8	2	2	1	1	3	689	72	85	63	2	
9	3	2	1	1	5	767	95	98	94	4	
10	4	2	2	1	2	697	75	88	69	2	
11	5	1	1	2	1	722	84	93	80	3	
12	6	1	1	1	2	728	87	95	83	3	
13	7	2	1	1	1	742	90	96	88	4	
14	8	2	1	1	5	770	96	98	94	4	
15	9	1	2	1	2	698	75	88	70	2	
16	10	2	1	2	3	755	93	97	91	4	

FIGURE 5.6 Jefferson Middle School Student Data File of the Results of the Eighth-Grade Language Arts Test (MS Excel Format).

teacher who was released from teaching to assist in data coordination for the school, and the three eighth-grade language arts teachers. To do the analysis, the assistant principal decided to use the Statistical Package for Social Sciences (SPSS) because certain statistical procedures comparing means and standard deviations will be done more easily in SPSS than in a spreadsheet program.

Figure 5.7 is an SPSS report providing basic information from the data file. The first part of the report is a simple frequency distribution showing the number and percentage of students in each performance level. The second part compares the means of the student scale scores by performance level. These reports provide a basic overview of the student performance on this test. Eight students (7.5%) did not meet the performance standard; 32 (30.2%) students partially achieved the standard; the remaining students met or exceeded the standard. The mean scale report is broken down by performance level. In addition to the means, the standard deviation is shown for each level. Note that the standard deviation is as important a measure as the mean in looking at summary test data. Just as the mean shows the central tendency of a group of numbers, the standard deviation shows the tendency of the group to disperse or spread from the mean. In essence, the standard deviation expands on the information provided by the mean by identifying the range within which most scores fell. In a normal distribution, the distance from one standard deviation (*SD*) above the mean to one *SD* below the mean includes approximately 68% of all the scores, +2 to −2 *SD* includes approximately 95% of all scores, and +3 to −3 *SD* includes over 99% of all scores. A low standard deviation indicates that the scores are closer together. A large standard deviation indicates that there is a wide spread in the group with more students scoring high and low. In Figure 5.7, the overall standard deviation is 34.96, which indicates that 68% of all of these test scores will range between 676.79 and 746.71 or plus and minus 34.96 from the mean (711.75). When developing a strategy for improving the test scores of this group of students, one goal would be to increase the mean of the scores while lowering the standard deviation. Increasing the mean translates into higher group performance, and decreasing the standard deviation indicates that the scores are closer to each other and that the group is moving forward as a coherent whole.

Performance Level

		Frequency	Percent	Valid Percent	Cumulative Percent
Valid	1 - Did Not Meet Performance Standard	8	7.5	7.5	7.5
	2 - Partial Achievement of Performance Standard	32	30.2	30.2	37.7
	3 - Met Performance Standard	43	40.6	40.6	78.3
	4 - Exceeded Performance Standard	23	21.7	21.7	100.0
	Total	106	100.0	100.0	

Language Arts Scale Score

Performance Level	Mean	N	Std. Deviation
1 - Did Not Meet Performance Standard	634.50	8	4.811
2 - Partial Achievement of Performance Standard	687.44	32	8.976
3 - Met Performance Standard	719.70	43	9.906
4 - Exceeded Performance Standard	757.61	23	13.197
Total	711.75	106	34.963

FIGURE 5.7 SPSS Report Showing a Frequency Distribution of Performance Levels and Mean Scale Scores.

The information provided in Figure 5.7 was a first step in understanding student perform-ance on the Language Arts Test. To provide more insight, a greater degree of data disaggregation and analysis was done and similar crosstabulations provided the results of disaggregating per-formance level by gender, by special education services code, and by eligibility for free lunch code. Essentially the data showed that

1. girls did better than boys;
2. general education students did better than special education, English language learners (ELL) and students designated as both special education and ELL; and
3. student not eligible for free lunch did better than students eligible for free lunch.

The results of the data analysis provided important information to the committee involved in developing strategies to improve teaching and learning. For instance, although the overall strategy was to improve learning for all students, the data indicate that a large percentage (30.2%) of the students is at level 2 (very close to meeting the performance standard). The data also showed that the eight students at level 1 (did not meet the performance standard) are special education/ELL students who will in all likelihood need a good deal of individual instruction to improve their performance. The committee continued to meet and asked for additional data that examined class assignments and the placements of special education students and ELLs.

During the committee's discussions, one of the teachers asked whether they should be considering any changes to the curriculum. Specifically, she was concerned with the articulation of Jefferson's language arts curriculum with the state standards. To assist in answering this question, the committee looked at the student performance subscore data (Standards 1, 2, and 3). Figure 5.8 is an example of one of the reports used. It provides a breakdown of the means for each of the subscores within each of the eighth-grade classes. For all groups, the lowest scores were in Standard 3–Critical Analysis and Evaluation. Furthermore, in all cases, Standard 3 was at least 10 points lower than Standard 2. The teachers on the committee agreed that more work in the language arts curriculum could be done to address this particular standard.

The committee at Jefferson Middle School continued to meet until the end of July. During its meetings, a good deal of discussion was dedicated to the special education and ELL programs. Committee members reviewed the individual records of a number of students in these programs and noted that many of them were close to meeting the standards. Although it would make recommendations that could benefit all students, the committee concluded that a

Class		S1–Information and Understanding	S2–Literary Response and Expression	S3–Critical Analysis and Evaluation
Grade 8A	Mean	85.64	93.88	82.52
	N	25	25	25
	Std. Deviation	5.722	2.833	6.734
Grade 8B	Mean	70.44	83.88	63.62
	N	16	16	16
	Std. Deviation	8.310	7.623	8.221
Grade 8C	Mean	82.37	91.58	77.67
	N	24	24	24
	Std. Deviation	9.098	5.356	11.378
Grade 8D	Mean	62.47	75.59	54.18
	N	17	17	17
	Std. Deviation	7.534	8.024	6.483
Grade 8E	Mean	87.92	95.00	84.37
	N	24	24	24
	Std. Deviation	5.389	2.554	6.781
Total	Mean	79.41	89.17	74.44
	N	106	106	106
	Std. Deviation	11.705	8.728	13.771

FIGURE 5.8   SPSS Report Showing a Breakdown of the Mean Subscores (Standards) by Class.

more extensive analysis was needed for special and ELL education. At the end of July, a plan was developed with immediate and long-term objectives. The overall goal of the plan was to improve the performance of all students in language arts. Elements of the plan included the following:

1. Develop a performance profile for each student to be shared with the teacher, the student, and the parents. This profile would also include performance data for other subject areas and be made available in electronic form on the Internet.
2. Establish a committee in the fall 2004 to consider revisions to the school report card to reflect performance and progress on standards.
3. Address the need for teachers to have greater access to electronic student databases to monitor progress and performance.
4. Do a more extensive review of the special education and ELL education programs. Consider specifically the establishment of more inclusive classes as well as more individual tutoring support.
5. Establish a committee in fall 2004 to review the eighth-grade language arts curriculum to include more activities related to Standard 3.
6. Increase resources to the Resource Room (Helping Place), which provides one-on-one support for students.

The school's principal endorsed the committee's recommendations and committed to doing whatever she could to provide the resources necessary for its implementation.

The Anatomy of a Survey

Richter Park (name changed) is an urban high school of approximately 2,300 students located in the northeast part of the United States. In 2007, Richter Park considered a plan to infuse technology into its programs and operations. A committee of teachers and administrative staff from the school district office had been considering this initiative for about 8 months. Two parents were also on this committee. Several of the academic programs at Richter Park made significant use of technology through computer workstations located in computer laboratories, the library, and the classrooms. The plan under consideration would make greater use of the Internet to connect the school to the students, parents, and community. Among other things, teachers and tutors would be available to students via e-mail, and parents would be notified of any concerns or questions regarding their children via e-mail as well. The sense among the staff was that many students had access to the Internet in their homes. However, there was also a suspicion that there was a "digital divide" within the school's population with many children from poor and recent immigrant families not having Internet access except at school.

During one committee meeting, the decision was made to survey the community. Both parents and students would participate in this survey in some way. Students would be given the survey at school to take home; responses would be completed for the household and signed off by a parent or guardian. A random sample of the students at Richter Park High was selected to participate in the family survey. Rather than ask for income information that some parents might consider sensitive, the superintendent indicated that these data could be provided from the district's student information system.

A major decision to be made in designing a survey is the size of the sample. An appropriate sample size is 10% to 20% of the population, as long as controls have been put into place to ensure that the sample is representative. The committee decided that 10% of the students would be sufficiently representative of the total Richter Park High School population. The fact that the survey was being given to students by name would maximize the probability of a good return. When the question of anonymity arose, the committee decided that since technology information was not particularly sensitive, parents or guardians would not have a problem being identified when answering it. Identification of the participants also made it easier to collect reliable data (e.g., income level, ethnicity) from the school district's student information system and to conduct a meaningful follow-up survey at a later date if needed.

The data to be collected centered on

- whether there is access to the Internet in the home;
- speed of access;
- type of equipment and location in home;
- typical uses of the Internet by children; and
- future plans to acquire or improve access to the Internet.

After several meetings that included members from the district office, the committee agreed on the format and content of the survey (see Figure 5.9). The superintendent also secured approval from the board of education to conduct this survey. A cover letter from the principal, Sandra Patterson, briefly describing the purpose of the survey would be included to allay any concerns from the students or parents.

To do a data analysis, a file layout and coding scheme was designed (see Figure 5.10). The data file layout contained data fields from two sources: the school district's student information system (SIS) and the survey. The school district coding schemes were used where appropriate. Data collected from the survey were coded using simple numerical codes. The data file was then constructed by downloading the data from the school district's information system and appending the survey results through individual data entry.

To perform the data analyses, the Statistical Package for the Social Sciences (SPSS) was used. It would have been possible to use a spreadsheet such as Microsoft Excel, but SPSS has greater facility in dealing with certain statistical procedures that are helpful for data disaggregation such as contingency tables or crosstabulations.

Two hundred and thirty surveys (10% of the total Richter Park High School population) were distributed. Two hundred and twelve surveys (92% of those distributed) were returned, an excellent response rate.

A major purpose for conducting this survey was to determine whether the students at Richter Park High School and their parents had access to the Internet in their homes. Figure 5.11 is a frequency distribution of the variable (Student Access) collected on Question 1:

Does the student named above have access to a computer outside of Richter Park High School?

Yes: _____   No: _____

Richter Park High School
Technology Survey

Dear Student:

You and your family have been selected to participate in a survey about technology use in your home. This survey will only be used to help our high school plan for the future technology needs of all of our students. Please have your parent or guardian complete the questions in this survey as best as he or she can. If you or your parent or guardian have any questions, feel free to contact either Ms. Laura Kelly or Ms. Yvonne Vasquez in the school office at 212-772-4666.

Thank you for your help in this important project.

Sandra Patterson
Principal

Student Name: Lisa Rogers

Name of the Person Completing This Survey: _____

Relationship to the Student of the Person Completing this Survey:

Father: _____   Mother: _____   Guardian: _____

1. Does the student named above have access to a computer outside of Richter Park High School?

   Yes: _____   No: _____

   If no, please go to Question 8. If yes, continue on to Question 2.

2. Where does the student have access to a computer?

   At Home: _____   At the Public Library: _____   At a Community Center: _____

   Other (Please Specify): _____

   If the student does not have access to a computer at home, please go to Question 8; otherwise go to Question 3.

3. What manufacturer/brand of computer do you have in your home? Check all that apply if you have more than one computer.

   DELL: _____   IBM: _____   Compaq: _____   Apple: _____   Gateway: _____

   Other(Please Specify): _____

FIGURE 5.9 Richter Park High School Access to Technology Survey.

4. How old is the computer (or main computer if you have more than one) that you have in your home?

   Less than 1 Year: _____   1–3 Years: _____   More than 3 Years: _____

5. Do you have Internet access for the computer (or main computer if you have more than one) in your home?

   Yes: _____   No: _____

   If yes, what type of Internet access do you have?

   Dial-Up: _____   DSL: _____   Cable Modem: _____   Wireless: _____   Other: _____

6. How often does the student named above use a computer in your home?

   Several Times a Day: _____   Once a Day: _____   Once a Week: _____

   Other (Please Specify): _____

7. Does the student use a computer mainly for:

   School Work: _____   Social Activities: _____   Games: _____   Other: _____

   Please go to Question 10.

8. If you do not have a computer in your home now, do you have any plans to purchase one in the immediate future?

   Yes: _____   No: _____

9. Would you like any assistance or help in selecting a computer?

   Yes: _____   No: _____

10. Do you have any suggestions for how Richter Park High School can use technology in its academic programs or to communicate with you? (Use the reverse side if you need more space.)

    _____

    _____

    _____

    _____

    _____

    _____

    _____

11. Would you like to be invited to a meeting to discuss further how Richter Park High School can use technology in its programs or to communicate with you?

    Yes: _____   No: _____

Thank you again for participating in this survey. Please mail the completed survey in the envelope enclosed. Again if you have any questions or wish to speak to anyone about this survey, please contact Ms. Kelly or Ms. Vasquez in the school office at 212-772-4666.

FIGURE 5.9   *(continued)*

Data Field	Source	Coding Scheme
Student ID	SIS	
Student Last Name	SIS	
Gender	SIS	1=Female, 2=Male
Grade Level	SIS	1=Freshman, 2=Sophomore 3=Junior, 4=Senior
Hispanic/Latino Ethnicity	SIS	1=Yes, 2=No
Race	SIS	U.S. Department of Education Code
Qualify for Free Lunch	SIS	1=Yes, 2=No
English Language Learner	SIS	1=Yes, 2=No
Special Education Indicator	SIS	1=Yes, 2=No
Name of Person Completing the Survey	Survey	
Relationship of Person Completing the Survey	Survey	1=Father, 2=Mother, 3=Guardian
Q1–Student Access	Survey	1=Yes, 2=No
Q2–Where Student Has Access	Survey	1=Home, 2=Public Library, 3=Community Center, 4=Other
Q3–Brand of Computer	Survey	1=Dell, 2=IBM, 3=Compaq, 4=Apple, 5=Gateway, 6=Other
Q4–Age of Computer	Survey	1=Less than 1 Year, 2=1–3 Years, 3=More than 3 Years
Q5A–Internet Access	Survey	1=Yes, 2=No
Q5B–Level of Access	Survey	1=Dial-Up, 2=DSL, 3=Cable Modem, 4=Wireless, 5=Other
Q6–Frequency of Use	Survey	1=Several Times per Day; 2=Once a Day; 3=Once a Week
Q7–Purpose of Student Use	Survey	1=School Work, 2=Social Activities, 3=Games, 4=Other
Q8–Future Purchase Plans	Survey	1=Yes, 2=No
Q9–Assistance	Survey	1=Yes, 2=No
Q10–Attend a Meeting	Survey	1=Yes, 2=No

FIGURE 5.10 Technology Use Survey Data File Layout/Coding Scheme.

Student Access

		Frequency	Percent	Valid Percent	Cumulative Percent
Valid	Yes	152	71.7	71.7	71.7
	No	60	28.3	28.3	100.0
	Total	212	100.0	100.0	

FIGURE 5.11   Frequency Distribution of Student Access to Technology.

The results indicate that 71.7% of the students have access outside of Richter Park and 28.3% do not have access. The percentage of students that do not have access was substantial enough to warrant further analysis to find out more about the two subpopulations.

Figure 5.12 is a crosstabulation of the variables Student Access and Qualifying for Free Lunch. Students who qualify for the U.S. federal government's Free Lunch program are considered to be members of low-income families. This is a standard measure maintained by all school districts. The data in Figure 5.12 indicate that 40.6% of the students who qualify for free lunch have access to computer technology outside of Richter Park High School as compared to 86.7% access for the students who do not qualify.

Figure 5.13 is a crosstabulation of the variables Student Access and English Language Learner. Students who are designated as ELL come from families where the home language is not English and the student receives additional services to learn English. Typically, students designated as ELL include large percentages of recent immigrants. The data in Figure 5.13 indicate that 51.7% of ELL students have access to computer technology outside of Richter Park High School as compared to 79.6% of the non-ELL students.

A good deal of additional data analysis was also conducted, much more than can be presented here. In sum, the data from the survey indicated that a substantial percentage of students who did not have access to technology were poor and designated as ELL. A large portion of these

Student Access * Free Lunch Crosstabulation

			Free Lunch		
			Yes	No	Total
Student Access	Yes	Count	28	124	152
		% within Student Access	18.4%	81.6%	100.0%
		% within Free Lunch	40.6%	86.7%	71.7%
		% of Total	13.2%	58.5%	71.7%
	No	Count	41	19	60
		% within Student Access	68.3%	31.7%	100.0%
		% within Free Lunch	59.4%	13.3%	28.3%
		% of Total	19.3%	9.0%	28.3%
Total		Count	69	143	212
		% within Student Access	32.5%	67.5%	100.0%
		% within Free Lunch	100.0%	100.0%	100.0%
		% of Total	32.5%	67.5%	100.0%

FIGURE 5.12   Crosstabulation of Student Access by Qualify for Free Lunch.

Student Access * ELL Crosstabulation

			ELL		
			Yes	No	Total
Student Access	Yes	Count	31	121	152
		% within Student Access	20.4%	79.6%	100.0%
		% within ELL	51.7%	79.6%	71.7%
		% of Total	14.6%	57.1%	71.7%
	No	Count	29	31	60
		% within Student Access	48.3%	51.7%	100.0%
		% within ELL	48.3%	20.4%	28.3%
		% of Total	13.7%	14.6%	28.3%
Total		Count	60	152	212
		% within Student Access	28.3%	71.7%	100.0%
		% within ELL	100.0%	100.0%	100.0%
		% of Total	28.3%	71.7%	100.0%

FIGURE 5.13　Crosstabulation of Student Access by ELL.

students also were children of recent immigrants from Latino countries. The conclusion was that a "digital divide" did in fact exist within the population at Richter Park High School.

The committee continued to analyze and review additional data from the survey to develop a recommendation for infusing technology into the programs at Richter Park High School. In continuing its deliberations, the committee also met with parents in the community and specifically invited the small group of parents who had indicated on the survey (Question 11) that they would be willing to attend such meetings. The committee finally issued a report in which they laid out a plan for infusing technology into Richter Park High School, including extended connections to the students' homes. Among its additional recommendations were the following:

1. The library, which housed a large computer center, should remain open until 7:00 P.M. each evening to allow students greater access to its computer equipment and other facilities. Weekend hours should also be considered.
2. Data with regard to student access to technology should be added to the district's student information system and be collected and updated on a regular basis along with other student demographic data.
3. Parents of students without access to technology would continue to be contacted by telephone or other means. Additional tutoring support would also be provided to ELLs and students who qualify for free lunch.
4. The district office should provide advice and assistance to parents wishing to purchase computers for their homes. A pamphlet describing appropriate equipment and desirable use of technology in the home should be developed and distributed to all students.
5. A group student discount policy with a major local computer retailer would also be explored in addition to group discounts that already existed with two computer manufacturers.

When the report was issued, the committee held an open meeting with the community to discuss its recommendations. More than 300 parents attended the meeting, more than any other open meeting held that year.

EVALUATION AND NURTURING THE PROCESS

The relationship between modern information systems and decision making has been evolving for many years. Although the term *data-driven decision* has gained popularity in K–12 education during the past 10 or 15 years and especially since No Child Left Behind was enacted in 2001, it has been used and studied conceptually in other organizations for decades. Mason (1969) and later Craven (1975) studied "information decision systems" to establish the importance of information to the decision process in private industry and public agencies. One important aspect of their approach was the evaluation of the decision-making process. Evaluation requires stakeholders (e.g., administrators, teachers, and staff) to review how well the process works and to reflect on the effectiveness of the decisions and courses of action taken. Unfortunately, the evaluation step is not always taken or is sometimes done very informally with little feedback into future decision-making activities. What Mason, Craven, and others recommended is that evaluation be formalized as part of the decision process and that the outcomes of the evaluation be used as input or "lessons learned" into future decision processes. In this approach, evaluation is never punitive but is used positively and formatively to help improve and nurture the process for the next decision-making cycle. Issues typically examined in an evaluation involve stakeholder access to accurate and timely data, knowledge of stakeholders and their readiness to engage in decision making, and a clear delineation of the outcomes of the decision. Regardless of the configuration of the evaluation, upon reflection, stakeholders do well to determine what worked well as a result of their decision making and to learn from those elements that did not work as well. It is in this manner that schools become less bureaucratic institutions and more organic communities that grow to be the best they can for their students.

This last point reflects back to the work of Senge, Wenger, and Sergiovanni and Starratt mentioned earlier in this chapter. Leaders and policy makers interested in promulgating effective decision-making processes in their schools need to develop communities in which all stakeholders see themselves as moving forward toward a common goal. Data-driven decision-making processes can help in this forward movement. In addition to solid operational conditions including current hardware technology, user-friendly software that provides accurate and timely data, and informed and knowledgeable people, data-driven decision making needs enlightened leadership integrating these into a dynamic process that fosters and utilizes a sense of community. The enlightened leader sets in motion group decision processes that trumpet "we are in this together" rather than "you better be careful if this does not work out." In sum, data-driven decision making is not simply a technology-based process but one that requires the human touch to reach its potential as an effective tool in moving the education of our children forward.

Summary

This chapter reviews data-driven decision making. Although hardware and software are important components of data-driven decision making, emphasis is placed on the importance of people in the decision process. Critical to the process is an information infrastructure that allows stakeholders throughout the school district to access data and reports and to share their expertise with one another. The role of a data analyst is described as someone who can facilitate the data-driven decision-making process.

Data-driven decision making can be applied to almost any school activity related to planning, instruction, curriculum, budgeting, and so on. Three examples of data-driven decision making applications are examined: enrollment projections, improving teaching and learning, and surveying a school's community. The chapter concludes with a discussion of the importance of evaluating and nurturing decision processes within the school or district.

Key Concepts and Questions

1. Developing data-driven decision-making processes requires integrating several key components. What are these components and why are they important?
2. Information infrastructure is discussed in this chapter. What is meant by this term? How does it relate to data-driven communications and networking?
3. Throughout this chapter, reference is made to stakeholders. Who are the stakeholders in a school or school district? How can they participate in data-driven decision-making processes? What tools do they need?
4. A data analyst is someone who develops expertise in accessing and presenting information from (a school district's) data resources. What other role(s) can a data analyst play in making data-driven decision-making processes effective?
5. Evaluation of data-driven decision-making processes is well-recognized as an important aspect of the decision process. Why is evaluation important? How would you characterize the nature of evaluation in a decision process?

Suggested Activities

1. Examine a data-driven decision-making activity at a school (or your school). Determine the main participants in the activity. Document the communications links (if any) between administrators and teachers.
2. Following up on Suggested Activity 1 above, how is data provided or delivered for the data-driven decision-making activity? Do you have any suggestions for improving the data delivery? Who do teachers or administrators go to if they have any questions (accuracy, currency, completeness) about the data?

References

Birabasi, A. L. (2002). *Linked: The new science of networks.* Cambridge, MA: Perseus Publishing.

Craven, E. C. (1975). Information decision systems in higher education: A conceptual approach. *The Journal of Higher Education, 46*(2), 125–139

Duncan, A. (2009, June 17). Start over: Turnarounds should be the first options for low-performing schools. *Education Week, 28*(35), 36.

Elmore, R. (2004). *School reform: From the inside out.* Cambridge, MA: Harvard Education Press.

Hall, S. S. (2007, May 6). The new middle ages. *New York Times*, Section 6 (Magazine), pp. 58–66.

Mason, R. O. (1969). *Basic concepts for designing management information systems.* (AIR Research Paper No. 8).

National Education Association. (1989, July). Report of the NEA special committee on educational technology. Paper presented at the 127th Annual Meeting of the National Education Association, Washington, DC.

Price, W. J. (2004, January 7). New age principals. *Education Week, 23* (16), 36–37.

Seeley Brown, J., & Duguid, P. (2002). *The social life of information.* Boston: Harvard Business School Press.

Senge, P. M. (1990). *The fifth discipline: The art and practice of the learning organization.* New York: Doubleday-Currency.

Sergiovanni, T. J., & Starratt, R. J. (1998). *Supervision: A redefinition* (6th ed.). Boston: McGraw-Hill.

Simon, H. A. (1957). *Administrative behavior* (2nd ed.). New York: Macmillan.

Watts, D. (2003). *Six degrees: The science of a connected age.* New York: Norton.

Wenger, E. (1999). *Communities of practice: Learning, meaning, and identity.* Cambridge, UK: Cambridge University Press.

Webster's Third New International Dictionary of the English Language (1986). Springfield: MA: Merriam-Webster Inc. Publishers.

Wilhelm, J. (2007). *Engaging readers and writers with inquiry.* New York: Scholastic Inc.

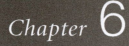
Technology in Instruction

During the 1980s and 1990s, the 15,000-plus school districts in the United States began making a substantial investment in computer technology to support instructional applications. In 1983, the student-per-microcomputer ratio in all public schools was approximately 125:1; by 2004, it was 4:1, where it has stayed for the past several years. In addition to hardware purchases, school districts also acquired software, developed technological infrastructure, trained teachers and staff, and built computer laboratories and centers. However, even though the investment in technology continues, the yield in terms of academic benefits is unclear. In some schools, technology applications have been heralded and showcased as models for delivering instruction. In others, these applications have not lived up to their promises. School administrators can sometimes find themselves caught in the middle, because some members of the school community request more resources for expanding instructional technology whereas others question its value. This chapter provides school leaders with a balanced assessment of instructional technology applications. This chapter is followed by three chapters, each dealing with a major instructional technology application, namely, multimedia, Internet/World Wide Web, and distance learning.

INSTRUCTIONAL COMPUTING: A NEW BEGINNING

In 1988, the U.S. Congress's Office of Technology Assessment (OTA) conducted a national study on the uses of computer technology for instruction in primary and secondary schools. Extensively researched and documented, the study provided one of the first glimpses of the investment that schools in all parts of the country were making in instructional technology. Millions of microcomputers costing billions of dollars had been purchased in the 1980s, and almost every school in the country had acquired some form of computer technology. This study was frequently cited in professional journals as evidence of the revolution under way in the schools. The study showed that a major new thrust in instructional computing was indeed occurring.

Based on data provided by Quality Educational Data (QED), the National Center for Education Statistics (NCES), and *Education Week*, Figure 6.1 provides the actual national student-per-microcomputer ratios in the public schools for 1983 to 2004. The most recent data show that the national average is presently 3.8:1 (Hightower, 2009).

The public schools spent approximately $2 billion per year on computer technology in the 1980s. Presently, schools are spending closer to $9 billion per year on technology. These figures are indeed significant considering that in 1975, computers for instructional purposes were nonexistent in many primary and secondary schools, and the expenditures for technology in general were negligible.

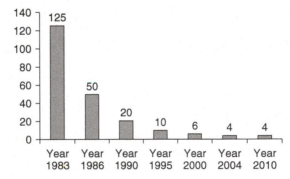

FIGURE 6.1 U.S. Public Schools Student-per-Microcomputer Ratios. *Source:* Based on data provided by Quality Education Data (1996), the National Center for Education Statistics (U.S. Department of Education, 2000), *Education Week* (Park & Staresina, 2004), and Hightower (2009).

Based on the number of machines purchased and the dollars invested, one might assume that computer technology has become an integral part of instruction in our nation's schools. This is debatable. Larry Cuban (2000, 2001), professor of education at Stanford University, observed that many teachers at all levels remained occasional users or nonusers and those who are regular users seldom integrate the machines with core curricular or instructional tasks. In a national survey conducted for *Education Week* in 2004, many teachers considered themselves beginners in the use of technology in their classes. Furthermore, in a survey of fourth-grade students, only 63% reported using a computer at least once a week in school (Park & Staresina, 2004). In two recent studies, while important, only about 35% of the responding school district superintendents considered teacher training as a barrier for the development of online learning in their schools, implying that teachers are able to engage in online coursework but are not necessarily doing so for other reasons (Picciano & Seaman, 2007, 2009).

The question is: Why then do the schools continue to make such a considerable investment in technology? The answer is not simple. If you see instructional technology as a mature activity with many well-known and well-understood applications, making this investment without substantial results becomes questionable. However, if you consider instructional technology as dynamically changing with a great deal of development still occurring, then this expenditure can be supported as a research or development activity. The presumption is made here that many schools find themselves in the latter situation, still in the developmental stages, responding to changes in the technology and perhaps seeing benefits that are not readily assessed.

Much of the hardware and software used in the 1970s and early 1980s have little application today. It is true that some of the early pioneers of instructional computing—such as Patrick Suppes, John Kemeny, Donald Bitzer, and Seymour Papert—have seen applications that they designed and experimented with in the 1960s evolve to take a major place in present-day instructional technology. But by and large, they are the exceptions. Computer hardware has changed radically, spurring new approaches to instructional software, most of which has been developed by companies founded after 1990. The advent of the Internet and World Wide Web in the mid-1990s spawned another new wave of instructional technology applications. Schools and most other organizations had to rethink how the resources of the new global network would be used. Schools are in a new beginning vis-à-vis instructional technology. They are still experimenting with and evaluating different applications, and slowly some of these applications are being accepted and added to the schools' instructional repertoire. Given demands for more technology by parents, the business community, and some teachers, administrators will continue to find themselves in positions of nurturing and helping technology applications to mature for the foreseeable future.

INSTRUCTIONAL COMPUTING: SOME HISTORY

Patrick Suppes is the individual most associated with computer-assisted instruction or CAI. Starting in 1959 at Stanford University, he conducted various experiments with CAI and eventually developed software especially designed for teaching basic skills such as reading, writing, and arithmetic. He was one of the founders of the Computer Curriculum Corporation in California, which is now part of Pearson Education Technologies. In 1990, he was awarded the prestigious National Medal of Science by President George H. W. Bush in part for his work with computer-assisted instruction.

In the late 1950s and 1960s, John Kemeny and Thomas Kurtz were among the first to envision personal computers. The product of their vision was Beginner's All-Purpose Symbolic Instruction Code (BASIC), a programming language that was really a variation of the FORTRAN programming language. BASIC was the first language designed to be used by anybody. Originally required of all freshmen entering Dartmouth College, with which Kemeny and Kurtz were affiliated, BASIC quickly gained wide acceptance throughout the country. When microcomputers were introduced in the late 1970s, most of the manufacturers decided to provide BASIC as part of their operating systems. As a result, it became the most popular programming language ever developed. Microsoft's Visual BASIC evolved from the original BASIC language developed by Kemeny and Kurtz.

Donald Bitzer developed Programmed Logic for Automatic Teaching Operations (PLATO) at the University of Illinois in the 1960s. PLATO was the first popular authoring system for developing instructional applications. Designed to run on a large computer network, it sought to bring quality and innovative instructional material to students over wide geographic areas. PLATO's unique feature was the use of a plasma display tube for producing exceptionally interesting graphics. Bitzer is generally credited with foreseeing the importance of graphics and sound in developing instructional computer applications. The National Academy of Television Arts and Sciences awarded Bitzer an Emmy in 2002 for his work on plasma display tube technology.

Probably the best-known developer of instructional computing software for primary and secondary schools is Seymour Papert. He was a founding member of the Massachusetts Institute of Technology (MIT) Media Lab. Logo, which many consider the first language developed for children, embodies his philosophy of experiential and discovery learning. The name derives from the Greek word *logos*, meaning "word, thought, or discourse." Although developed and well received in the late 1960s, like BASIC, Logo really became popular when it was made available on microcomputers in the late 1970s and 1980s. Logo Computer Systems, Inc., a company that Papert founded in 1981, has continually improved it, and versions that incorporate multimedia (MicroWorlds), word processing (LogoWriter), and mechanical interfaces (MicroWorlds Robotics, LEGO Logo) are used in schools today. Papert's (1980) major book, *Mindstorms: Children, Computers, and Powerful Ideas*, is recommended reading for any educator interested in instructional computing. It is one of the first books to relate the development of an instructional software package to a particular educational philosophy: namely, experiential or discovery learning.

These software developments are well respected among technology educators, but their impact on academic achievement remains questionable. Although thousands of studies have been conducted, the acceptance of instructional technology as having a definitely positive effect on academic achievement is still being debated.

A BRIEF REVIEW OF THE RESEARCH

James Kulik and his associates at the University of Michigan conducted some of the most extensive reviews of the research on computer education. In the 1970s and 1980s, they conducted a series of meta-analyses of hundreds of studies dealing with the effects of computer education at different grade levels (elementary, secondary, college, and adult). Their general conclusion was that computer-based education had a beneficial effect on academic achievement, although it was not uniformly true at all grade levels (Kulik, 1984; Kulik, Bangert, & Williams, 1983; Kulik, Kulik, & Bangert-Downs, 1984; Kulik, Kulik, & Cohen, 1980; Kulik, Kulik, & Schwab, 1986). However, Richard Clark (1983, 1985. 1989) refuted the findings by questioning the research controls of most of the studies that were included in the Kulik meta-analyses. Clark further concluded that the computer was basically a vehicle carrying an instructional substance and that real improvement in achievement only comes with improving the substance, not the vehicle. Clark's position has been challenged over the years by a number of researchers including Kozma (1991, 1994a,

1994b) and Koumi (1994) who see the medium as integral to the delivery of instruction. However, the two differing opinions on this issue remain, and the "great debate" continues to this day. As an indication of the importance of this debate, a search of "Clark Kozma" on Google or Yahoo provides hundreds of hits, many of which refer to Web sites and blogs created in the past couple of years.

In the late 1980s and early 1990s, educators saw value in providing instructional computer experiences for reasons other than improving student performance. Benefits such as ensuring computer literacy, providing variety in instructional delivery, or releasing teacher time from record-keeping tasks were considered important enough to continue investing in technology. However, even with objectives that might not directly affect academic performance, schools were having problems implementing effective instructional applications.

Sheingold, Kane, and Endreweit (1983) identified six issues critical to planning and implementing instructional computer applications:

1. Access to hardware
2. New roles for teachers and administrators
3. Integration of technology into the curriculum, especially at the elementary school level
4. Quantity and quality of software
5. Teacher preparation and training
6. Effects and outcomes of the instructional use of technology (p. 426)

These six issues are still appropriate in helping us briefly assess the conditions that exist when planning and implementing instructional applications in schools today.

Access to hardware, as documented by the QED, NCES, and *Education Week* data cited at the beginning of this chapter, has improved dramatically. Despite the considerable progress, however, improving student access to hardware continues to be a priority in schools. Even in school districts with very favorable student-per-microcomputer ratios, the priority among computer coordinators continues to be the acquisition of more hardware—either to upgrade existing equipment or make more machines available to students. As discussed in Chapter 3, a number of school districts have initiated "one to one" computing or "laptop per child" programs. Also, the popularity of the Internet and the World Wide Web has forced all technology planners to upgrade their information infrastructure to provide faster and more dependable data communications services.

New roles for teachers and administrators have become evident as more and more school districts employ full-time technology coordinators. In districts with many schools geographically dispersed, it is common to have building-level coordinators in addition to district-level coordinators. Graduate schools at many universities across the country have also developed new specialized programs that provide concentrations in technology-related teacher education. In addition, in technology-infused classrooms, teachers are seeing themselves more as guides for learning as more instruction becomes differentiated and centered to meet individual student needs. A popular description of the teacher in such a classroom is the "guide on the side" rather than the "sage on the stage."

Integration of technology into the curriculum, especially at the elementary school level, has improved but still requires a good deal of attention on the part of administrators. Studies (Becker, 1994; Fatemi, 1999; Park & Staresina, 2004; Picciano, 1991; Sheingold & Hadley, 1990; U.S. Congress, 1995) have continually indicated that this is a most serious issue. Resources, especially time, are needed for teachers and curriculum coordinators to do the detailed curriculum design work necessary for successful integration.

Even though the quantity and quality of software improved considerably over the past decade, the overall investment and interest in educational software has undergone a significant shift. Many school districts, as well as parents buying software for their children for home computers, have reduced their purchases of educational software. One review of the industry had overall spending on software by K–12 schools at $2.3 billion in 2004, up 2% from a year earlier but down from $3.4 billion in 2001 (Richtel, 2005). The instructional software industry, which only started in the late 1970s, had grown considerably through the 1990s but now seems to be contracting. Much of this is due to the fact that educators prefer generic Internet tool software, much of which is available as free downloads on the World Wide Web. In sum, although the quantity and quality of software have improved, the need for more and better software will continue especially as the technology in general advances and forces software providers to keep up and remain current with their competition or risk loss of interest in their products.

Most teacher education colleges have begun to make technology a basic requirement. In a 1998 survey of 416 colleges of education, the International Society for Technology in Education concluded that teacher preparation programs were not giving future teachers the kinds of experiences they needed to use technology in the classroom (Trotter, 1999). Park and Staresina (2004) report that only 15 states required technology course work as part of their colleges' teacher education programs. Regardless, new teachers now entering the education field are more technology literate than their predecessors. Much of this started to change when the National Council on Accreditation of Teacher Education (NCATE), the major accrediting agency for teacher education programs, revised its standards to include instructional technology. NCATE's (2009) Standard 1 requires teacher candidates to demonstrate that they are able to facilitate student learning of the subject matter through the integration of technology. However, even if teachers receive sufficient training to use technology as part of their initial teacher education programs, they will need sustained, ongoing, and systematic training and development, as the technology changes and advances, to maintain their skills.

Studies and reviews of the literature on the effects and outcomes of instructional technology (Campuzano, Dynarski, Agodini, & Rall, 2009; Dynarski et al., 2007; Christensen & Knezek, 2001; Archer, 1998; U.S. Congress, 1995; Becker, 1994; Robyler, Castine, & King, 1988) continue the debate of its effectiveness. Two recent large-scale randomized studies (see Dynarski et al., 2007, and Campuzano et al., 2009) conducted by the U.S. Department of Education National Center for Education Statistics that examined student outcomes of a number of reading and mathematics educational software programs concluded that there were few significant learning differences between students who used the technology and those taught using other methods. These well-funded studies were part of the No Child Left Behind federal appropriations. Proponents of the benefits of instructional technology have questioned the methods used and pointed to several flaws in these studies. However, the fact remains that research has a long way to go to establish the effectiveness of technology on student achievement. It may be that Richard Clark's position mentioned earlier is correct or minimally that the Clark–Kozma debate will continue.

One last comment on the effectiveness issue is in order. An earlier meta-analysis by Robyler and colleagues (1988), which concentrated on more than 80 studies conducted in the 1980s, concluded that "Computer applications have an undeniable value and an important instructional role to play in classrooms of the future. Defining that role is the task [for the future]" (p. 131). Trotter (1998) defined "that" role as being beyond student achievement and should include teaching high-tech skills, providing access to information, making learning more fun, promoting problem-solving skills, and providing individual student attention. Today's school leaders are in the pivotal positions in their schools to define further and perhaps to expand technology's role, and perhaps its role is beyond student achievement.

DEFINING TECHNOLOGY'S ROLE: A TOUCH OF PHILOSOPHY

In defining technology's role in instruction, discussing and identifying an overall philosophy of learning is appropriate. As any undergraduate in an education foundations course will attest, the literature on learning theory is immense. It is not the intent here to cover this extensive literature. School district leaders, school building administrators, and teachers within schools pride themselves on their own philosophical approaches to teaching and learning that frequently have been developed from their studies and experiences. Attention should be given to developing a philosophical framework when using instructional technology.

Dewey, Piaget, Bloom, Gagné, and Vygotsky are well-recognized theorists in the area of learning theory. Dewey (1915) and later Piaget (1952) provide the foundations for experiential learning. *Experiential learning* is defined here simply as learning by doing. Bloom (1956) and Gagné (1977) each established taxonomies of learning that related to the development of intellectual skills and stressed the importance of problem solving as a higher order skill critical to the learning process. Vygotsky (1978) also posited that problem solving and the construction of knowledge were the essence of the learning process. Vygotsky described the learning process as the establishment of a "zone of proximal development" in which exists the teacher, the learner, and a problem to be solved. The teacher provides an environment in which the learner can assemble or construct the knowledge necessary to solve the problem.

Evolving from Dewey, Piaget, Bloom, Gagné, and Vygotsky is a constructivist theory of learning that stresses the importance of experiences, experimentation, problem solving, and the construction of knowledge. Constructivism draws on the vast experiences of the learner. Applying this to instructional technology translates into presenting problems and learning situations to which the learner can relate as well as providing the materials, media, and informational resources needed to solve the problems. Seymour Papert (1980), in describing the popular Logo programming language, talks about creating a highly interactive, technology-based microworld in which children solve problems by drawing on the resources of a computer. The learner, with guidance from a teacher, can actively access databases, test mathematical equations, or manipulate a geometric figure by using a computer. This concept can be broadened and applied to the design of any instructional technology application. The designer considers the technology-supported learning environment as a microworld in which problems (mathematical and scientific problems, social issues, case studies, etc.) are presented. A teacher or tutor who acts as a guide is available to the learner, as well as numerous informational tools and resources (World Wide Web, databases, media, analytical tools, and written materials) that enable learners to engage in and solve the problems. The learner learns by interacting with the available resources (teacher, tutor, information, media, etc.) and drawing on his or her own experiences to construct the knowledge to solve the problem. In this scenario, the ability to interact with teachers or tutors as well as to access other materials becomes most important—and designers must ensure that the ability to do both is available in the environment. The technology tools become integrated with, and facilitate, the problem-solving activity. Given the vast information and other resources that technology can provide, how this is done is left to the creativity of school leaders, teachers, and instructional designers.

CLASSIFICATION SYSTEMS AND DEFINITIONS OF TERMS

Widely accepted classification systems are elusive in education. This is also true in instructional technology. Although various attempts have been made to establish classification systems for instructional software, very little agreement exists. The Educational Software Preview Guide identified

19 different software classifications or modes as part of its reviews. One of the simpler and better-known classification systems, and the one referenced in many standard technology education textbooks over the years (e.g., Bullough & Beatty, 1991; Lockard, 1992; Merrill et al., 1992; Simonson & Thompson, 1997), is Robert Taylor's (1980) trichotomy of "tutor, tutee, tool." In tutor mode, the technology or computer possesses the information and controls the learning environment. In tutee mode, the student possesses the information and controls the learning environment. In tool mode, the technology is used to assist or act as a tool in the learning activity. However, as straightforward and flexible as this trichotomy is, it has possibly outlived its usefulness because of the dynamic and ever-changing nature of software. Some of the newer software programs such as course management systems do not fit neatly into any of the three categories. Also many instructional software products are incorporating features that overlap these classifications. For instance, many tutor-type applications such as tutorials or simulations incorporate word processing and database "tool" features. Increasingly, instructional software is being viewed as a "tool" for teaching and learning, and maybe we have reached a point in education where this is a sufficient description. The presentation in the remainder of this chapter will concentrate on instructional software programs as technology "tools."

The classification issue is also complicated because there are no commonly accepted definitions associated with instructional technology applications. Many terms—particularly when used by their acronyms such as CAI, CMI, or CBE—have been a source of more confusion than clarification among educators. In some cases, they are used interchangeably; for example, computer-based education (CBE), computer-based instruction (CBI), and computer-assisted instruction (CAI) are all frequently used to refer to any type of learning environment in which a computer is used. Sometimes, the definition of a term has changed over time—such as that of computer-assisted instruction, which originally was a generic term applied to all instructional uses of computers but now is used more frequently to refer only to programmed instructional software. Figure 6.2 provides a list of common instructional technology terms that serve to illustrate the nature of the problem more so than to clarify the nature of instructional software definitions. Readers may wish to familiarize themselves with these terms but also to assume that it is probably best to establish a basic vocabulary in their own environments for use in discussions, printed materials, and technology activities.

INSTRUCTIONAL SOFTWARE TOOLS

Basic Technology Tools

Chapter 4 included an extensive discussion of various software programs appropriate for administrative applications, namely, word processing, spreadsheets, and databases. This type of "tool" software is also an appropriate starting point for a discussion of instructional applications.

WORD PROCESSING AND DESKTOP PUBLISHING   Word processing is frequently used to assist in teaching writing. Word-processing software makes revisions easy and avoids the drudgery of handwriting or retyping extensive amounts of text. Students at various grade levels commonly use commercial word-processing packages to do writing assignments. In addition, some word-processing packages have been developed specifically for use by young children in classrooms.

When word processing is implemented as part of a writing program, questions frequently arise regarding the use of spell-checking and grammar-checking features. In most cases, these features are optional and can be deleted if a decision is made that these aids are not appropriate for

---

Computer-assisted instruction (CAI). The use of the computer to assist in the instructional process. One of the earliest used terms to refer generically to computer applications in education, it is used now to refer to tutor-type applications such as drill and practice and tutorials.

Computer-assisted learning. See Computer-assisted instruction.

Computer-augmented learning. See Computer-assisted instruction.

Computer-based education (CBE). A generic term used to refer to the broad array of instructional computer applications.

Computer-based teaching (CBT). The use of a computer by teachers as part of an instructional presentation such as an interactive video.

Computer-managed instruction (CMI). The use of the computer in an instructional process in which student progress is monitored and recorded for subsequent instructions and review. Most CMI applications are also able to adjust material to each individual student's level of understanding.

Computer-mediated communications (CMC). The use of computer systems that incorporate communications software such as e-mail and electronic discussion boards and blogs to enhance distance learning and computer-managed instruction applications.

Integrated instructional system (IIS). See Integrated learning system.

Integrated learning system (ILS). A single computer package for delivering instruction that combines hardware, software, curriculum, and management components. It is usually supplied by a single vendor.

Intelligent computer-assisted instruction (ICAI). Similar to CAI but also uses a substantial database of information for presenting material and selecting instructional paths.

FIGURE 6.2 Instructional Computing Terminology.

teaching writing. Students exposed to word processing early in school generally continue to use it and become more proficient as they grow older.

A variation of word processing software that has grown significantly in popularity is desktop publishing software, which combines standard word processing features with graphics capabilities to produce visually stimulating print material. Desktop publishing can be used to create professional-quality newsletters, school newspapers, and flyers. It can also be easily integrated into course work and extracurricular activities. Typical applications might be clubs doing flyers on recent activities, social studies classes preparing a newspaper article on some important historical period such as the French Revolution or the first landing of men on the moon, or students designing banners for sports and dances. Students usually collaborate on desktop publishing projects that can translate into motivation for completing the final products. In recent years, desktop publishing software programs have advanced to the point where in addition to printed material, they are also able to generate World Wide Web pages and media files. Yancey (2004) reports that desktop publishing programs may be fundamentally changing the way students approach writing. Because of the ease with which photographs, audio files, and video files can be integrated into presentation activities, students are able to express themselves in ways that were not easily possible before the development of word processing/desktop publishing technology. Using both text and visual material makes it easier for many students "to focus on, analyze, and improve their writing" (Yancey, 2004, p. 39). Besides basic word-processing programs such as Microsoft Word, several products such as The Print Shop and The Amazing Writing Machine (both from Broderbund) have been very popular in K–12 education.

SPREADSHEETS Standard electronic spreadsheet programs are being used for a variety of subjects. Mathematics, the sciences, and business education make extensive use of spreadsheet software for all sorts of instructional applications involving the manipulation of numbers. Almost any subject where mathematical formulas or statistical analyses are used can integrate spreadsheets into the curriculum. Just as word processing takes the drudgery out of typing text, spreadsheets take the drudgery out of doing hand calculations. They should not be used in courses where it is desirable or necessary for students to do hand calculations as practice in refining their mathematics skills. However, there are many instructional situations where the nature or understanding of a formula is more important than the mathematical practice of adding, subtracting, multiplying, or dividing numbers. In these situations, spreadsheets can be most effective.

Commercial spreadsheet packages also provide easy-to-use graphing features that allow students not only to do a mathematical formula but also to visualize it. Microsoft Excel and Lotus 1-2-3 are examples of the commercial packages commonly used in many schools. Integrated packages such as Microsoft Office also provide excellent spreadsheet programs along with word processing and database software. These integrated packages can be particularly effective in instructional applications where data collection using a database is combined with data analysis using a spreadsheet. Examples include research activities on voting behavior, economic forecasting, and analyses of local census data.

DATABASES Database software is also finding its way into a variety of instructional applications. Data collecting and data searching skills are being taught by having students use the World Wide Web to access databases maintained by government agencies, universities, and research institutions. During research projects, students build their own databases with information that they have collected on animals, weather, states, famous people, minerals, places, and so forth. A popular long-term assignment is to have all the students in a class contribute to building a database over the course of a semester or year and then to do some type of statistical analysis as a culminating experience.

Standard database packages such as Microsoft Access and FileMaker Pro can be readily learned by older students. For younger children, it may be more desirable to acquire database software packages such as Friendly Filer, which have been designed specifically for instructional applications. Some of these packages provide databases on a variety of subjects in addition to the software for collecting and manipulating data.

In planning the instructional applications of databases, educators interested in building employment skills should recognize the increasing importance of reference and researching skills, as many professions rely more on the ability to access information from a variety of sources. Online databases are not simply the domain of research organizations and graduate schools but are used routinely in all types of everyday businesses. Students should be prepared to use them along with other standard tool software programs as part of their basic education.

ELECTRONIC ENCYCLOPEDIAS AND REFERENCE WORKS One of the most popular instructional software packages that have a good deal of ready application for K–12 instruction are electronic encyclopedias and other types of reference works. Some of these electronic encyclopedias are distributed on DVDs or CD-ROMs, and others are accessible via Web sites. Wikipedia, the most popular of online references, maintains a list of approximately 200 online encyclopedias at http://en.wikipedia.org/wiki/List_of_online_encyclopedias, many of which are available free of charge. For younger students, especially those doing their first research assignments on a subject, an electronic encyclopedia provides an easy-to-use resource that gets started in the right direction by providing materials that have been reviewed by experts. This is an increasingly important issue because a certain amount of material on the World Wide Web is based on dubious authority. In addition to text descriptions, the electronic encyclopedias provide excellent graphics, sound, and video clips, all of which add to the initial understanding of a subject. In addition to encyclopedias, other reference works available on CD-ROM or DVD include atlases, dictionaries, literary works, classical music, and works of art. Examples include *Compton's Electronic Encyclopedia*, *The Digital Universe*, *National Geographic Maps*, and *Grolier's Multimedia Encyclopedia*.

SPECIALIZED TOOLS AND PROBEWARE   Tool software packages are also being developed for special-purpose instructional applications. In many cases, the software is combined with computer hardware to perform specific functions. The popular graphing calculator is an early example of software combined with hardware to perform a specific function. In recent years, digital scientific probes or sensors that collect data on temperature, motion, gas pressure, light, and other characteristics have been gaining in popularity. Other devices called "data loggers"—either handheld computers or interface boxes attached to computers—compile the data from probes, display them in real time, and transfer them to software that can analyze and present the information in various ways. Collectively, these devices and the computer software with which they are integrated are called "probeware." Vernier's LabQuest handheld device, PASCO's SPARK Science Learning System, and Data Harvest's EasySense Q5 data logger are examples of popular educational probeware. As this technology improves, specialized software will grow in popularity especially in science, mathematics, music, and special education applications.

ELECTRONIC TEXTBOOKS (eBOOKS)   By far the most commonly used technology in instruction is print. Textbooks, journals, newspapers, syllabi, tutorials, assignments, tests, and papers commonly consist of printed materials. Although the demise of the printed word has been predicted as a result of the growth of mass media and the evolution of the electronic age (Birkerts, 1994), in education the printed word continues to be alive and well. It will be a number of years before the standard textbook is replaced completely by another form. By the same token, educational planners should also be aware that electronic textbooks on CD-ROM or DVD and Web-based curricula are also becoming more common. A number of states (e.g., Maine, Texas, Virginia) have piloted programs that replaced printed textbooks with electronic ones on laptop computers. Major benefits include the ability to keep up with rapidly changing information and to alleviate the problem of replacing aging textbooks, which costs school districts hundred of millions of dollars every year. As an example, in 2008, the Westport (Connecticut) School District replaced its 1,000 plus-page high school Algebra I textbook with a completely online curriculum developed by its mathematics teachers in cooperation with HeyMath!, an online program developed in India (Hu, 2009). Despite some start-up problems, both teachers and students appear to be happy with the new online curriculum. Regardless, although print material enhanced, replaced, and integrated with electronic technology will continue to evolve and will play a significant role in instruction in the years to come, the combination of cost and ease of revision will likely lead more and more school districts to consider electronic alternatives. At the time of this writing (June 2009), Governor Arnold Schwarzenegger had just announced the Digital Textbook Initiative, a program designed to begin the process of replacing printed K–12 textbooks with digital books in California schools.

Learning Tools

Learning tools are software programs that have been designed to provide instruction on a specific topic or subject area. Generally, the computer presents some information or subject matter, the student responds, the computer evaluates the response and presents additional or new information, and the cycle repeats itself. The more sophisticated versions of these programs can also maintain student assessments and can report the same to a teacher. Among the most popular of these types of programs are drill and practice, tutorials, simulations, and instructional gaming.

DRILL AND PRACTICE   Drill-and-practice applications are usually used to reinforce a lesson or material that has already been presented to the student. They have been much maligned as too boring and mechanistic. This view is not entirely unjustified in that many of the drill-and-practice applications developed in the 1960s and 1970s could have been more interestingly designed. However, technological limitations existed in the early years of computing that made some pedagogically important features, such as graphics and sound, difficult to program. Many of these applications have since been improved by making greater use of graphics, motion, color, and sound to keep students interested in the activity.

Teachers regularly use drill and practice manually (e.g., flash cards, worksheets) as part of their normal instructional repertoire. The benefits of a computer drill-and-practice program can include immediate feedback, automatic adjustment of the level of difficulty depending on student responses, and record keeping on student performance that can be reviewed as needed by teachers. In reviewing and planning instructional applications, administrators should assume that some drill and practice is common in most schools' software libraries; however, it should not dominate the collection.

Drill-and-practice computer applications are used in many learning situations at different grade levels. Much of the earliest drill-and-practice software packages concentrated on basic skills and have continued to evolve as the technology has improved. They are most commonly used in mathematics, basic language skills, grammar, and spelling. They are also popular in special education classrooms where they have been combined with specialized speech and visual equipment. Among the popular drill-and-practice software programs available is the Edmark House Series (Houghton Mifflin Harcourt) and the Math Blaster Series originally developed by Davidson Software and taken over by Knowledge Adventure Incorporated. A version of Math Blaster has also been developed to be used on the Nintendo game products.

TUTORIALS   Tutorial applications are similar to drill-and-practice applications in design and appearance. An important distinction between the two is that tutorial programs attempt to teach something new and are not used specifically to reinforce material already presented—although they can do that, too. Tutorial programs have been criticized for the same reasons as have drill-and-practice programs, but they too have improved in recent years. They are used regularly in advanced technologies such as interactive video and integrated learning systems.

In many schools, the emphasis on using computers has been to try to integrate them into a regular curriculum. When used for stand-alone instruction, tutorial programs tend to keep the computer as something separate; they have not been as popular as other software programs for this reason. Tutorial programs can, however, be very effective in certain situations, such as for students who have missed a good deal of class time because of illness, who are homebound, or who live in rural areas where teachers may not be available to teach certain specialized subjects. The A.D.A.M. Essentials High School Suite (Science) and Rosetta Stone (Foreign Languages) are among many successful tutorial programs.

SIMULATIONS   Simulations attempt to represent on a computer certain real-life situations that would be impossible to duplicate in most classrooms. For instance, scientific experiments, ecological systems, and historical or current events can be duplicated by using computer models to represent the real-life situations. Students interact with the simulation and influence decisions and outcomes. Simulation software keeps growing in popularity, and many educators consider it a more effective use of computers than drill-and-practice programs or tutorial software.

Simulation software is also considered to be appropriate for beginning the teaching of higher-order thinking skills. It can easily be used to supplement a lesson to allow students to apply what they have learned to different situations. Increasingly, simulations are combined with instructional games and problem-solving applications.

The Learning Company (now part of Houghton Mifflin Riverdeep Group) has been successful in developing a wide variety of stimulating and pedagogically appropriate simulations in social studies (Oregon Trail), ecology (Amazon Trail), science (Discovery Lab), and other subject areas. Tom Snyder Productions (now part of Scholastic) has also developed a series of excellent simulations—called Decisions, Decisions—that cover subjects such as colonization, immigration, city management, and teenage drug use. Simulation software is also being integrated into interactive video games where the use of motion and sound adds significantly to the pseudoreality of the computer models.

INSTRUCTIONAL GAMING, PROBLEM SOLVING, AND MUVES   Instructional gaming software attempts to make learning fun by combining learning, entertainment, and gamesmanship. Although some instructional games continue to be poorly designed, many are well done and have instructional value. Of the various types of instructional software packages, games are frequently successful in using current technology, especially graphics and sound, to heighten student motivation and interest. Instructional games should be used to supplement other lessons; they are excellent when used to add some variety to a student's day. This is more important in elementary school programs and especially with younger children.

Problem-solving software is frequently subcategorized with instructional games, although it can also be considered a separate category. Problem-solving software is significantly gaining in popularity because of its primary focus on thinking skills. Students typically are presented with situations in which they use and develop cognitive, analytical, and other thinking process skills. In many cases, the material is presented in game format in which students compete with one another or with the computer. The literature on teaching and learning thinking skills is very extensive and open to much debate.

Discussion of the future of instructional gaming and its prodigies such as multi-user virtual environments (MUVEs) are provocative. Some of the best minds in instructional technology such as Chris Dede have invested significant energies in developing first-rate programs or virtual environments such as The River City and Alien Contact. However, implementing and integrating these programs into a school's curriculum takes a significant amount of resources, especially time, so that while the promise of these programs are generally acknowledged, the realities of curriculum requirements frequently make it difficult for schools to adopt them.

More recently, generic MUVEs have evolved as part of the social networking phenomenon that is incredibly popular among young people on the World Wide Web. A generic MUVE such as Second Life provides tools for developing and manipulating avatars and virtual environments. They leave the nature of the interaction and activities to the imaginations of the participants. Teachers, for example, could develop a lesson or augment a lesson with a Second Life experience. At the time of this writing, the educational value of a Second Life–type environment for young people was much debated. Proponents argue that the freedom to develop and manipulate avatars in a virtual environment unleashes a plethora of creativity on the part of the users that can be beneficial to a wide range of educational activities. Detractors question Second Life–type environments that have steep learning curves and make excessive demands on a user's time. The loss of control of the software development, that is, the investment in using a product like Second Life is not transferable to other software environments thereby locking users into this particular environment, is also a serious concern. Regardless, instructional technology support personnel would do well to keep up their knowledge of this type of software because sooner or later it will likely become a significant part of the instructional software application landscape.

Programming and Authoring Tools

In the discussion of Second Life above, a comment was made that a user has to spend a good deal of timing learning how to develop an application that might have educational value. Second Life is a generic MUVE that requires users to learn a substantial set of tools with which to develop an activity and crosses over into the realm of programming and authoring tools. The basis of such tools is that the teacher and student learn to direct or control some aspect of technology (e.g., a computer) to perform some task. In years past, many high schools introduced computer programming as an activity to learn how a computer works. It was a worthwhile instructional activity especially for students who were interested in the computer itself as an object of learning.

Developing computer programming skills provided several worthwhile instructional experiences. Programming languages such as BASIC and Pascal required students to learn rules, syntax, and logic constructs. The nature of computer programming was also one of problem solving and developing plans (programs) for solutions. It is a higher-order thinking exercise formalized via programming instructions that can be visualized to a certain degree on a computer.

Debate persisted, however, regarding the value of a computer programming exercise in actually teaching thinking skills. Some educators, such as Papert (1980) and Luehrmann (1980), supported the use of computers for this purpose. Others, such as Linn (1985) and Pea (1987), accepted programming as a thinking exercise but cautioned that there is no proof that it actually improves the teaching of thinking. Perhaps Vockell and van Deusen (1989) summarized the issue best by making the "chicken and egg" comparison: Do clear and logical thinkers become successful computer programmers, or do people become clear and logical thinkers by writing computer programs? These theorists concluded that computer programming undoubtedly requires and exercises higher-order thinking skills, but it is illogical, though tempting, to assume that teaching programming will also *teach* higher-order thinking skills. In offering computer programming courses, administrators and teachers should feel confident that they are providing a higher-order thinking and problem-solving experience for their students. They are also offering one of the better experiences for learning about computers.

In recent years, however, educators have questioned whether programming languages should be taught in primary and secondary schools at all. One practical reason is that to teach programming well requires a significant amount of class time as well as significant investment in teacher training and development. Furthermore, the technology industry is prone to rapid changes, so that computer programming languages such as BASIC and Pascal that once were very popular are now being used less and less. Increasingly, presentation software and Internet and Web-based software tools (e.g., Java) are replacing the traditional computer programming activities. A discussion of several popular programming and authoring tools follows.

LOGO   The most popular programming language taught in primary schools is Logo and its derivatives, which were designed and developed by Seymour Papert of MIT specifically for young children. Logo can be used to experiment and explore or to develop sophisticated computer programming procedures. Logo was designed so that a "friendly turtle" in the center of the screen became the vehicle whereby children learned to master and control the computer by drawing different shapes, developing geometric patterns, or designing a computer game. However, Logo was sophisticated enough that it could also be used at many grade levels.

For educators wishing to provide programming experiences in the early grades, Logo and its derivatives (LogoWriter, MicroWorlds, and LEGO Logo) are among the best software packages available. MicroWorlds, available from Logo Computer Systems, Inc. (LCSI), is a powerful Logo-based multimedia authoring tool that allows students in grades 2 and up to create impressive projects incorporating movies, photos, sound, graphics, text, and animation. In planning to implement Logo into a curriculum, educators need to provide a good deal of computer access on a regular basis.

HIGH-LEVEL PROGRAMMING LANGUAGES   High-level programming languages such as Beginner's All-Purpose Symbolic Instruction Code (BASIC) or Pascal were once very popular in advanced high school classes. A BASIC programming experience combined with a general understanding of computer hardware served to define computer literacy in the schools throughout the 1980s. Microsoft's Visual BASIC is a derivation of the original BASIC and is one of the more popular programming languages for doing multimedia programs. However, in response to the way technology has changed in general, schools have begun to replace BASIC and other programming experiences with authoring tool software packages, especially those such as Java, designed to develop World Wide Web materials. However, high schools that offer a computer science or technology track for students continue to favor a high-level language such as Visual BASIC.

AUTHORING LANGUAGES   Computer programming over the past four decades has gradually become easier. The computer software industry has been moving in the direction of providing simpler tools and techniques to communicate with a computer. High-level languages such as BASIC and Pascal were easier to use than their predecessor languages, but they could not in any way be considered simple languages to learn. They have their own special syntax, verbs, constructs, and rules for developing logical plans for directing a computer to perform a task. In recent years, simpler software development tools have evolved that are generically referred to as "authoring languages."

Authoring languages are much easier to use than other programming languages and were originally designed to be used for specific applications by people without special computer training. For instruction, several authoring languages are available to aid teachers in developing lessons, in doing multimedia presentations, and in creating pages for the World Wide Web. They are designed specifically to make it easier to present material, ask questions, and interpret student responses. They can also be used to control other equipment such as CD-ROMs and DVDs to provide a multimedia presentation.

The first authoring languages—such as TUTOR, MicroTUTOR, Coursewriter, and PILOT—were designed strictly for instruction, and although some teachers were willing to make the effort to use these languages, the time needed to learn to use them proved burdensome. Authoring languages developed in the 1980s and early 1990s—such as Apple's HyperCard, IBM's Linkway, and Asymetrix's ToolBook—were appropriate for lesson development as well as other applications such as building databases, maintaining inventories, or keeping a telephone directory. Though relatively easy to use, these newer authoring languages were not adopted by very many teachers because they too required a good deal of time and effort to master.

Newer authoring languages—such as HyperStudio and Microsoft's PowerPoint—are designed for doing multimedia presentations. They are more widely used by teachers, especially those who have had some technical training. Using a series of programming objects such as buttons, fields, and graphics, these languages can provide a very stimulating learning environment. They are especially effective in combining graphics and animation with instructional text and other written material. These languages are fast becoming the basic tools for developing multimedia materials using video and audio. They are also easy enough to use so that technology instructors are teaching students how to "author" or use an authoring language. Authoring languages will continue to evolve and will play a large role in the future in computer education curricula.

During the late 1990s, there was an evolution of authoring software packages for the development of hypertext markup language (HTML) documents for distribution as World Wide Web pages. Dozens of Web authoring programs have since been developed that make creating and editing Web pages no more difficult than using a word-processing program. The newest version of Microsoft Word has a built-in Web-authoring facility. These authoring packages are becoming popular in schools, where teachers and students are using them for a host of Web-related activities.

INTEGRATED LEARNING SYSTEMS

Integrated learning systems (ILSs) are integrated systems of hardware, software, curriculum, and management components that are generally marketed by a single supplier. Also referred to as integrated instructional systems (IISs), they are probably the most sophisticated examples of computer-managed instructional products on the market. The hardware usually consists of a microcomputer that can function as a file server in a local area network (LAN). The software is generally tutorial and drill and practice. The curriculum provided can range from kindergarten through 12th-grade subjects, although many of the most popular ILSs are used for basic skills instruction in language arts and mathematics. In recent years, a number of ILS vendors have converted their materials to be accessed by the World Wide Web. Especially popular are a number of adult education software products designed to improve job and career skills.

Critical to all ILSs is a student management system (computer-managed instruction) that tests students, keeps records of their performance, and adjusts lesson material depending on their progress. The management system usually produces automated individual student and group progress reports that can be used by teachers and administrators for instructional planning.

Many educators consider an ILS as the total solution for implementing instructional computing in their schools. All the major components provided are already integrated. The problems of integrating computer technology into the curriculum are solved because the computer provides the curriculum as well as a major portion of the instruction. Pearson Digital Learning's SuccessMaker and the Waterford Institute's Waterford Early Learning are examples of popular integrated learning systems.

Why, then, have most school districts not acquired these systems? The major reason is their cost. Depending on the number of computer workstations, such systems can easily cost hundreds of thousands and, in some cases, millions of dollars. After the initial investment, there are yearly costs for maintenance and upgrades, which can range from 7% to 12% of the original purchase price. Many school districts simply cannot afford an ILS. To be used effectively, these systems require extensive training of the teaching staff and may require teachers to become managers of instruction rather than simply instructors. On the other hand, an ILS with extensive reporting capabilities can be a powerful tool for monitoring student progress and customizing lessons to individual needs.

In planning to acquire an ILS, administrators need to do a careful analysis to ensure that the benefits of such a system will be realized in their districts. Because of the costs, administrators cannot afford to experiment; they must be sure that the curriculum provided is appropriate and consistent with their own curriculum goals and objectives. Most importantly, teachers need to be well trained to take full advantage of the many technological and pedagogical tools that an ILS provides.

MULTIMEDIA: A BRIEF WORD

Most of the instructional software packages mentioned above have been available for several years. In some cases, they are in their seventh or eighth versions. Perhaps the most significant changes or improvements from version to version have been the addition of multimedia (sound, pictures, and video) to the basic software program.

The power of images and sounds expands every year. Television and digital versatile discs (DVDs) are common in homes and in schools. Children, especially teenagers, frequently are more knowledgeable about these media than adults. School administrators and teachers need to understand and, where appropriate, tap into the power of multimedia if they have not already done so. In acquiring instructional software, multimedia features are important complements—especially when the program has a good pedagogical foundation to begin with. This will be discussed further in Chapter 7, which is devoted entirely to the topic of multimedia.

DATA COMMUNICATIONS

Data communications provide facilities for a wide range of instructional applications. Local area networks (LANs) are used to support central computer laboratories, integrated learning systems, and other instructional applications. Using a file server, the LAN can provide software programs to all the users on the network, which thereby precludes the need to purchase multiple copies of the same software packages for use on stand-alone machines.

Wide area networks (WANs), in addition to offering all of the services of a LAN, allow access to a variety of instructional applications. The Internet, as will be discussed in greater detail in Chapter 8, emerged in the 1990s as the epitome of the wide area network, providing access to a wealth of resources throughout the world. The Internet has had such an impact on technology that software vendors are preparing to offer World Wide Web versions of many of their products and services. Even before the advent of the Internet, several networks were established to supply specific services directed to teaching and learning that involve the sharing of information not ordinarily available at the local school. Either by way of the Internet or as separate entities, many of these networks are still providing specialized instructional resources and applications that are important to educators.

Probably the most common service provided by national networks is access to databases. Students and teachers can access encyclopedias, research databases, information exchanges, and technical documentation. The most important benefit of databases via national online services is that they provide the most current and up-to-date information. Educational networks such as GTE Education Services provide several services: ED-LINE for general education news; SpecialNet for databases and information exchanges directed to the special education profession; Youth News Service Newsline for news and journalism activities appropriate for primary and secondary school children; and CNN Newsroom for curriculum and other instructional materials based on daily news reports.

Some of these services combine information access with e-mail and bulletin boards so that students can exchange information with other students across the country and across the globe. National Geographic's Kids Network, for instance, provides services for students to share information about the environment, weather, geography, current events, and so forth. National Geographic even provides curriculum material so that teachers can develop research projects and share reports with other schools doing similar projects.

Possibly the greatest potential for WAN services involves integrating them with television and distance learning technologies. Learning Link and IntroLink, for instance, are designed to be used in conjunction with Public Broadcasting Service (PBS) television. Curriculum information and classroom activities based on current PBS offerings can expand the uses of educational television for instruction. Distance learning, which has been emerging as an important educational technology for several years, is greatly enhanced when a two-way communication link is established that allows for interactivity between students and teachers. State education departments in Minnesota, Wisconsin, Alaska, Kentucky, and Iowa, for example, have taken the lead in developing distance learning facilities for a number of school districts. Most state education departments, if they have not already done so, are planning to provide distance learning facilities for use by local school districts in the near future. This topic will be discussed in greater detail in Chapter 9.

CURRICULUM INTEGRATION AND PLANNING

Curriculum integration is a simple concept but is proving difficult to realize with instructional technology applications. Integrating computer tools into the classroom is conceptually similar to integrating other tools such as chalkboards, overhead projectors, or paints and crayons. Teachers and students have few problems, however, using these other, more familiar, tools in teaching and learning. Furthermore, these tools have limited application, so mastering them is an easy task.

Modern technology—especially the computer—on the other hand, provides more sophisticated, expensive tools, and mastering them is a more complex and ongoing undertaking. Integrating computers into the curriculum starts with making sure that teachers and students have developed a basic understanding and knowledge of technology. Once this basic understanding has been achieved, mastery involves developing a knowledge base of the many different ways computers can be used. Teachers need to feel comfortable using technology and developing a repertoire of instructional applications. Integrating technology into the curriculum is therefore closely tied to professional development, which is therefore one of the critical components of any technology-based plan, along with hardware, software, facilities, and finances.

Integrating instructional applications is not something that can be accomplished overnight. Quick fixes in implementing technology usually have very little, lasting impact and frequently only delay serious planning activities. Administrators should not be thinking about quick fixes but instead should be evaluating whatever instructional technology is already occurring in their schools and building on that which works.

Planning requires the involvement of those who possess expertise and who ultimately may be responsible for implementing new applications. The fulcrum for curriculum integration and planning instructional applications is the teaching staff. The teachers are critical for identifying applications and evaluating software, hardware, and professional development needs. Administrators must work with teachers to provide leadership in these activities, ensuring that resources are available for training, facilities, and staffing, as well as for hardware and software.

Finally, because of the many applications and alternatives available, teachers and administrators need to develop a process in which priorities can be established and plans developed for the long term. No school district in the country—even with the best tax base, the most competent teachers, and most enlightened administrators—can afford to do everything it might wish to do; however, every school district can and does do something well. This should be kept in mind when planning for instructional technology.

CASE STUDY

Place: Silicon City   **Year: 2009**

Silicon City, an urban school district on the West Coast, has an enrollment of 20,000 students in 31 schools. The population has been increasing significantly during the past 10 years, particularly with students needing bilingual education. The voters approved a bond issue in 2004 to build a new high school. As part of the bond issue, $4 million was budgeted for purchasing new instructional equipment, of which $1.5 million would be used district-wide for educational technology.

A district-wide planning committee was established in 1994 with a standing technology subcommittee. This subcommittee has been very effective in securing funds and helping the district implement technology in the schools. Each school has one or more centralized computer laboratories and a building coordinator. Computer equipment is also available in many classrooms, especially in the middle schools and high schools. A major goal of the district has been to integrate technology into the regular classrooms rather than providing it only in centralized computer laboratories. The district has a student-per-microcomputer ratio of 4:1.

In addition to acquiring basic computer hardware and software for the new high school comparable to what exists in the two other high schools in the district, the technology subcommittee would like to use a portion of the instructional equipment budget to make a major thrust into newer technologies that might benefit the entire district. As part of the planning process in 2008, the technology subcommittee asked a task force of administrators, teachers, building computer coordinators, and parents to develop proposals to help in this regard.

The subcommittee was provided with three proposals, each of which would cost approximately $1 million to implement initially. They were as follows:

Proposal 1: Upgrade data communications in the classrooms.

This proposal would allow each school to be wired for higher speed data communications access in each classroom. Presently, some schools have high-speed (T1) access and some have modest (ISDN) speed. In some schools, high-speed access is available in the central computer laboratories but not in individual classrooms. Each microcomputer in each classroom would be wired for higher speeds and equipped with the necessary software for tying into the Internet and other national networks. A variety of instructional applications were identified as benefiting from this upgrade, including accessing databases, monitoring seismographic data, using CNN curriculum materials for teaching current events, and establishing electronic pen pals in Latin America.

Proposal 2: Set up a One-to-One Laptop program.

This proposal would provide funds so that all middle and high school students could be given a laptop computer. Funds would also be used to expand district-wide software licensing agreements to ensure that each student laptop was equipped with a basic suite of software tools. It was also suggested that this proposal be implemented in phases over 3 years:

Academic Year	Grades
2010–2011	11–12
2011–2012	9–10
2012–2013	7–8

Parents on the task force that was involved with developing proposals were most supportive of this initiative.

Proposal 3: Develop an integrated learning system to teach basic skills.

This proposal would use the funds to establish a district-wide ILS. Each school could tie into the system via the computer laboratories at all of the schools. Although the ILS could be used for several instructional applications, it would be used initially for basic skills and bilingual education. One ILS vendor based on the West Coast indicated great interest in working with the school district to establish a model for using its products and offered very attractive pricing.

The subcommittee, before it proceeds with making a recommendation to the planning committee, has asked the assistant superintendent for curriculum for her recommendation. It is unlikely that the district could afford to fund more than one of these proposals over the next 3 years.

Discussion Questions

1. Assuming that you are the assistant superintendent, analyze the three proposals. What observations can you make regarding the appropriateness of the three proposals from technological, pedagogical, and programmatic perspectives?

2. Although you have been provided with only a summary of each proposal, what additional information on each proposal would you consider critical to making a recommendation?
3. Finally, given the information provided and assuming you felt compelled to support one proposal, which would you recommend? Why?

Summary

This chapter reviews the development and issues surrounding instructional technology. All school districts have made some investment in instructional technology, with varying degrees of success. Although some question the benefits of this investment, every indication is that this investment will only increase in the future.

This chapter also attempts to provide administrators with a balanced picture of instructional applications: their problems, benefits, and potential. With the proliferation of the microcomputer in the 1980s followed by the emergence of the Internet in the 1990s in all aspects of businesses, the professions, and everyday living, schools throughout the country are attempting to ensure that their students are prepared to use this technology.

The research on instructional technology is conflicting. Some researchers conclude that it is beneficial and improves academic achievement, whereas others dispute these claims. Much of the recent literature also identifies implementation problems such as difficulty in integrating technology into the curriculum, the need for more teacher training, and limited resources as the root of many problems. Some of these issues are gradually being resolved.

Looking at the evolution of instructional computing applications, much of the work done in earlier years is not relevant because of the radical changes that have occurred in the technology. Several exceptions, though—including the pioneering efforts of Suppes, Kemeny, and Papert—have continued to evolve, and the fruits of their labor can be seen in many schools today.

Instructional computer applications have grown, with tens of thousands of software and media products on the market. Classifying and developing a framework for understanding the various applications is prone to a good deal of overlap. Although Robert Taylor's "tutor, tool, tutee" approach is referenced, it has probably outlived its usefulness as more and more educators refer to all types of software as "tools." A review of popular instructional software tools is presented.

Computer technology is also merging with other technologies—namely, multimedia and communications—to create a variety of new instructional applications. The Internet of the 1990s is evolving into the major medium of the 21st century. New applications using these technologies are far more exciting and pedagogically more stimulating than anything that the individual technologies alone provided in the past. The potential of these merged technologies is great and will be more evident as they improve and as educators learn how to use them.

Key Concepts and Questions

1. Schools are investing significant resources in instructional technology. How have the schools benefited from this investment to date?
2. Instructional technology has been evolving since the 1950s and 1960s. Some computer educators consider that much of the early work has very little application in today's schools. Do you agree? If so, why? If you do not agree, provide examples of early work in instructional technology that are commonly used in today's schools.
3. In implementing instructional technology, administrators may have several objectives. What are some of these

objectives? What do you consider the most important objective for using technology in the classroom?

4. Developing a classification system for instructional technology has proved to be an elusive endeavor. Why?

5. Integrated learning systems are probably the most complete instructional computer applications available. If this is so, why have most schools not acquired them? Do you see any change in their acquisition in the near future? Explain.

6. Computer technology is gradually merging with video and communications technologies to provide instructional applications. Give examples and discuss the potential of the following: (a) computer and video; (b) computer and communications; and (c) computer, video, and communications.

7. Integrating technology into the curriculum is proving to be a major problem in many school districts. Why? How do you see this problem being resolved?

Suggested Activities

1. Examine the types of instructional technology applications that exist in a school (or in your school). Evaluate whether any patterns develop according to grade level, subject, or year of acquisition.

2. If you are not familiar with instructional software, consider examining several instructional software packages that might exist in a school (or in your school). Try to select a variety of programs (drill and practice, simulations, and instructional games). Take notes on your impressions of the educational value of these programs.

3. As a follow-up to the preceding activity, search and review a Web site(s)that provides information on instructional software. The following Internet sites can be used to start your search:

International Society for Technology in Education

http://www.iste.org/

Technology and Learning

http://www.techlearning.com/

California Learning Resource Network

http://www.clrn.org/home/

World Village Schoolhouse Software Review

http://www.worldvillage.com/wv/school/html/scholrev.htm

References

Archer, J. (1998). The link to higher scores. *Education Week, 18*(5), 10–21.

Becker, H. J. (1994). *Analysis and trends of school use of new information technologies.* Irvine: Department of Education, University of California.

Birkets, S. (1994). The Gutenberg elegies: The fate of reading in an electronic age. Boston: Faber & Faber.

Bloom, B. S. (1956). *Taxonomy of educational objectives handbook: Cognitive domains.* New York: David McKay.

Bullough, R. V., & Beatty, L. F. (1991). *Classroom applications of microcomputers.* Upper Saddle River, NJ: Merrill/Prentice Hall.

Campuzano, L., Dynarski, M., Agodini, R., & Rall, K. (2009). *Effectiveness of reading and mathematics software products: Findings from two student cohorts* (NCEE 2009–4041).

Washington, DC: National Center for Education Evaluation and Regional Assistance, Institute of Education Sciences, U.S. Department of Education.

Christensen, R., & Knezek, G. (2001). Instruments for assessing the impact of technology in education. *Computers in the Schools, 18*(2/3), 5–25.

Clark, R. (1983). Reconsidering research on learning from media. *Review of Educational Research, 53*(4), 445–459.

Clark, R. (1985). Evidence for confounding in computer-based instruction studies. *Educational Communications and Technology Journal, 33*(4), 249–262.

Clark, R. (1989). Current progress and future directions for research in instructional technology. *Educational Technology Research and Development, 37*(1), 57–66.

Cuban, L. (2000, February 23). Is spending money on technology worth it? [Electronic version]. *Education Week, 19*(24), 42.

Cuban, L. (2001). *Oversold and underused.* Cambridge, MA: Harvard University Press.

Dewey, J. (1915). *Democracy in education.* New York: Reprinted by Dover Publications (2004).

Dynarski, M., Agodini, R., Heaviside, S., Novak, T., Carey, T., Campuzano, L., Means, B., Murphy, R., Penuel, W., Javitz, H., Emery, D., & Sussex, W. (2007). Effectiveness of reading and mathematics software products: Findings from the first student cohort. Washington, DC: U.S. Department of Education, Institute of Education Sciences.

Fatemi, E. (1999). Building the digital curriculum. *Education Week, 19*(4), 5–8.

Gagné, R. M. (1977). *The conditions of learning.* New York: Holt, Rinehart & Winston.

Hightower, A. (2009). Tracking U.S. trends. *Education Week, 28*(26), 30–31.

Hu, W. (2009, June 8). Throwing out the textbook in favor of homegrown, online Algebra lessons. *New York Times.* Retrieved June 9, 2009, from http://www.nytimes.com/2009/06/08/education/08math.html?scp=8&sq=winnie%20hu&st=cse

Koumi, J. (1994). Media comparison and deployment: A practitioner's view. *British Journal of Educational Technology, 25*(1), 41–57.

Kozma, R. (1991). Learning with media. *Review of Educational Research, 61*(2), 179–211.

Kozma, R. (1994a). Will media influence learning? Reframing the debate. *Educational Technology Research and Development, 42*(2), 7–19.

Kozma, R. (1994b). A reply: Media and methods. *Educational Technology Research and Development, 42*(3), 11–14.

Kulik, J. A. (1984). Evaluating the effects of teaching with computers. In G. Campbell & G. Fein (Eds.), *Microcomputers in early education.* Reston, VA: Reston.

Kulik, J. A., Bangert, R., & Williams, G. (1983). Effects of computer-based teaching on secondary students. *Journal of Educational Psychology, 75*(1), 19–26.

Kulik, J. A., Kulik, C., & Bangert-Downs, R. (1984). Effectiveness of computer-based education in elementary schools. *Computers in Human Behavior, 1*(1), 59–74.

Kulik, J. A., Kulik, C., & Cohen, P. (1980). Effectiveness of computer-based college teaching: A meta-analysis of findings. *Review of Educational Research, 2*(2), 525–544.

Kulik, J. A., Kulik, C., & Schwab, B. (1986). The effectiveness of computer-based adult education: A meta-analysis. *Journal of Educational Computing Research, 2*(2), 235–252.

Linn, M. C. (1985). The cognitive consequences of programming instruction in classrooms. *Educational Researcher, 14*(5), 14–29.

Lockard, J. (1992). *Instructional software: Practical design and development.* Dubuque, IA: Wm. C. Brown.

Retrieved March 29, 2004, from http://www.lcsi.ca/company/profile.html

Luehrmann, A. (1980). Should the computer teach the student, or vice-versa? In R. Taylor (Ed.), *The computer in the school: Tutor, tool, tutee* (pp. 127–158). New York: Teachers College Press.

Merrill, P., Tolman, M., Christensen, L., Hammons, K., Vincent, B., & Reynolds, P. (1992). *Computers in education.* Upper Saddle River, NJ: Prentice Hall.

National Council of Accreditation of Teacher Education. (2009). Facts and questions about NCATE Standards. Retrieved April 11, 2009, from http://www.ncate.org/boe/faqStandards.asp#faq11

Papert, S. (1980). *Mindstorms: Children, computers, and powerful ideas.* New York: Basic Books.

Park, J., & Staresina, L. (2004, May 6). Tracking U.S. trends. *Education Week, 23*(35), 64–67.

Pea, R. D. (1987). The aims of software criticism: Reply to Professor Papert. *Educational Researcher, 16*(5), 4–8.

Piaget, J. (1952). *The origins of intelligence in children.* New York: Norton.

Picciano, A. G. (1991). Computers, city and suburb: A study of New York City and Westchester County public schools. *Urban Review, 23*(3), 93–109.

Picciano, A. G., & Seaman, J. (2007). *K–12 online learning: A survey of school district administrators.* Needham, MA: The Sloan Consortium.

Picciano, A. G., & Seaman, J. (2009). *K–12 online learning: A 2008 follow up of the survey of U.S. school district administrators.* Needham, MA: The Sloan Consortium.

Quality Education Data. (1996). *Education market guide and mailing list catalog.* Denver: Author.

Richtel, M. (2005, August 22). Once a booming market, educational software for the PC takes a nose dive. *New York Times.* Retrieved April 11, 2009, from http://www.nytimes.com/2005/08/22/technology/22soft.html

Robyler, M. D., Castine, W. H., & King, F. J. (1988). Assessing the impact of computer-based instruction. *Computers in the Schools, 5*(1), 1–149.

Sheingold, K., & Hadley, M. (1990). *Accomplished teachers integrating computers into classroom practice.* New York: Bank Street College of Education, Center for Technology in Education.

Sheingold, K., Kane, J. H., & Endreweit, M. E. (1983). Microcomputer use in the schools: Developing a research agenda. *Harvard Educational Review, 53*(4), 412–432.

Simonson, M. R., & Thompson, A. D. (1997). *Educational computing foundations* (3rd ed.). Upper Saddle River, NJ: Merrill/Prentice Hall.

Taylor, R. P. (Ed.). (1980). *The computer in the school: Tutor, tool, tutee.* New York: Teachers College Press.

Trotter, A. (1998). A question of effectiveness. *Education Week, 18*(5), 7–9.

Trotter, A. (1999). Preparing teachers for the digital age. *Education Week, 19*(4), 37–46.

U.S. Congress, Office of Technology Assessment. (1988). *Power on: New tools for teaching and learning* (Report No. OTA-ETA-379). Washington, DC: U.S. Government Printing Office.

U.S. Congress, Office of Technology Assessment. (1995). *Teachers and technology: Making the connection* (Report No. OTA-EHR-616). Washington, DC: U.S. Government Printing Office.

U.S. Department of Education, National Center for Education Statistics. (2000). *Internet access in U.S. public schools and classrooms: 1994–99,* NCES 2000-086. Washington, DC: U.S. Department of Education, National Center for Education Statistics.

Vockell, E., & van Deusen, R. M. (1989). *The computer and higher-order thinking skills.* Watsonville, CA: Mitchell.

Vygotsky, L. (1978). *Mind in society: The development of higher psychological processes.* Cambridge, MA: Harvard University Press.

Yancey, K. B. (2004). Using multiple technologies to teach writing. *Educational Leadership, 62*(2), 38–40.

Chapter 7

Multimedia in Education

Responding in an interview to a question about a leading soprano's singing and acting talents, James Levine (1995), the artistic director of the Metropolitan Opera in New York City, commented that good music does not need words. His point was that music alone was enough to communicate emotion and beauty between those with talent and those with the ability to appreciate it. However, when a Verdi melody is combined with words, the result is an aria that touches and appeals to many more people who can better appreciate the melody within the context of a story or event. Add actors in colorful dress, a set depicting a quaint mountain village, some graceful dancers, and the result is opera that appeals and communicates to the world.

The expansion of a libretto into an aria and an aria into an opera is an appropriate metaphor for introducing the subject of multimedia as applied to teaching and learning. Indeed, words conveyed by writing and reading alone may not be sufficient to reach all students. Combining words with images, sounds, and movement can extend the teaching/learning process and help communicate a lesson to many more students.

MULTIMEDIA DEFINED

The term *multimedia* refers to many types of communication processes, delivery systems, and events. It is a buzzword that is used in connection with entertainment, advertisement, museum exhibitions, theme parks, video games, and dozens of other areas of human endeavor. Multimedia adds a certain technological chic that conjures up images of color, movement, dazzling special effects, and provocative sounds. Because of the variety of ways in which the word has been used, multimedia has come to mean different things to different people.

Generically, multimedia can be defined as any combination of two or more media such as sound, images, text, animation, and video. When used with computer technology, multimedia refers to a variety of applications that combine media and that utilize audio, video, DVD, CD-ROM, and other media equipment.

In addition to this basic definition, multimedia, when used with computer equipment, also implies interactive navigational or hypermedia capabilities that can be invoked and controlled by the user. *Hypermedia* is the integration of sights, sounds, graphics, video, and other media into an associative or linked system of information storage and retrieval. It is an extension of the concept of hypertext, which links text information in an associative system. Ted Nelson, an engineer, coined the term *hypertext* in 1965 to describe computer-based document retrieval systems that could be used in a nonlinear fashion as opposed to the traditional linear format of other document retrieval systems such as books and microfilm.

Hypermedia allows users to navigate in a nonlinear manner from one topic to another by the use of information linkages built into the associative system. The navigational system for the entire World Wide Web is based on this concept. Linkages are usually presented in the form of icons, active screen areas or buttons that, when clicked on by a mouse, transfer or link the user to some other material. Examples of these linkage techniques are commonly found in electronic reference and resources such as Wikipedia, Microsoft's Encarta, and Grolier's Multimedia Encyclopedia. For educational technology purposes, multimedia refers to computer-based systems that use associative linkages to allow users to navigate and retrieve information stored in a combination of text, sounds, graphics, video, and other forms of media.

MULTIMEDIA FOR MULTIPLE INTELLIGENCES

For educators, multimedia may seem like nothing more than a higher technological use of sounds and sights to stimulate instruction. Educators have been using slide projection, film, videotape, and videodisc for decades to enhance student interest. However, in addition to being a point on the media continuum, multimedia also relates to theories of brain functioning and learning theory, especially those that relate learning to sensory stimulation and multiple intelligences (Armstrong, 2000).

Since the early 1980s, Howard Gardner, a psychologist at Harvard, has been popularizing a theory of *multiple intelligences* (see Table 7.1). He posits that intelligence has been too narrowly defined; it is not a singular entity that can be measured by standard intelligence tests but rather is composed of multiple entities. Gardner (1983) identifies nine basic or multiple intelligences (MI) that all humans possess to some degree or another:

- *Linguistic intelligence*—the capacity to use words effectively, either orally or in writing (e.g., writers, poets, orators)
- *Logical–mathematical intelligence*—the capacity to use numbers effectively and to reason well (e.g., mathematicians, accountants, computer programmers)
- *Spatial intelligence*—the capacity to perceive the visual-spatial world accurately, including the capacity to visualize and graphically represent visual and spatial ideas (e.g., architects, designers, artists)

TABLE 7.1 Theory of Multiple Intelligences

Intelligence	Definition	Learning Needs
Linguistic	Capacity to use words effectively	Books, writing, discussion, debate
Logical-mathematical	Capacity to use numbers effectively	Manipulatives, science puzzles
Spatial	Capacity to perceive the visual-spatial world accurately	Art, video, slides, building blocks
Bodily-kinesthetic	Capacity to use one's body to express ideas	Movement, dance, drama, sports, hands-on learning
Musical	Capacity to perceive and express musical forms	Song, instrumental music, background music
Interpersonal	Capacity to perceive moods and feelings of others	Group activities, social gatherings
Intrapersonal	Capacity to know oneself	Self-paced learning, quiet time
Naturalistic	Capacity to perceive and understand things in the world of nature	Field trips, garden projects, animal and pet care
Existential	The capacity to locate oneself with respect to the furthest reaches of the cosmos and to locate oneself with respect to the meaning of life, the human condition, the meaning of death, and fate of the physical and natural worlds	Activities centered on human issues such as suffering and mercy, total immersion, and looking for meaning in a work of art

Source: Based on Gardner (1983, 1993, 2000).

- **Bodily-kinesthetic intelligence**—the capacity to use one's body to express ideas and feelings and the facility to use one's hands (e.g., athletes, dancers, craftspeople)
- **Musical intelligence**—the capacity to perceive, discriminate, and express musical forms (e.g., musicians, composers, singers)
- **Interpersonal intelligence**—the capacity to perceive and make distinctions in the moods and feelings of other people (e.g., counselors, social workers)
- **Intrapersonal intelligence**—the capacity to know one's strengths and limitations and to act according to this knowledge (e.g., psychotherapists, religious leaders)
- **Naturalistic intelligence**—the capacity to perceive and understand things of the natural world (e.g., farmers, gardeners, veterinarians)
- **Existential intelligence**—the capacity to ask about life's questions (e.g., philosophers, cosmologists)

Gardner's theory has been questioned and debated, particularly whether he has really expanded the concept of intelligence or simply extended it to long-recognized talents or aptitudes. Regardless, his theory makes a good case for using multimedia and other multisensory techniques in teaching and learning. Applied to instruction, his theory supports a concern that U.S. education at all levels (primary, secondary, and higher) is too linguistically oriented. Teacher talks, students listen; teacher writes, students read; students write, teacher reads; and so forth. If we accept Gardner's theory—or even if we simply accept that people have different talents, aptitudes, or modalities for learning similar to the multiple intelligences—then should we not be teaching in a way that can tap into these multiple intelligences instead of relying on one of them while neglecting the others?

This concept has generated an extensive debate that cannot be treated fairly here. Readers interested in pursuing this topic are encouraged to read Gardner's books, especially *Frames of Mind: The Theory of Multiple Intelligences* (1983), *Multiple Intelligences: The Theory in Practice* (1993) and *Intelligence Reframed: Multiple Intelligences for the 21st Century* (2000). An excellent review of Gardner's theory can also be found in Thomas Armstrong's (2009) *Multiple Intelligences in the Classroom, Third Edition*. The Association for Supervision and Curriculum Development (ASCD) has also provided coverage of Gardner's ideas in its main publication, *Educational Leadership,* and maintains a Teaching for Multiple Intelligences network.

The application of the MI theory to multimedia and other computer technologies is apparent. If materials can be developed and used that extend instruction beyond the linguistic intelligence and make greater use of visual stimulation, sounds and music, logic and mathematics, and so forth, then perhaps a more-effective teaching and learning process could evolve. The literature includes many examples of multimedia technology as an outgrowth of Gardner's theory. David Thornburg (1989), who has been involved in designing provocative educational technology such as the Muppet Learning Keys and the Koala Pad, bases much of his application designs on MI theory. Thomas Armstrong (2009) also advocates using multimedia for implementing MI theory in the classroom. Researchers at the Center for Media and Learning at the City University of New York likewise have developed interactive video models for teaching history based on MI and modalities of learning (Picciano, 1993).

MULTIMEDIA LITERACY

Fred Hofstetter (1994), a professor at the University of Delaware, raised this question for educators: "Is multimedia the next literacy?" It was a serious question not only for the future, as Hofstetter implied, but for the present as well.

The question concerns the manner in which society receives its information. Essentially, since the advent of television (a multimedia technology in its own right) in the 1940s, Americans have been receiving ever-increasing amounts of their information from the moving images and sounds emanating from their TV sets. In 1991, most Americans did not read about the Gulf War in the Middle East in the morning paper; they saw it on TV in real time. Scud missiles firing, tanks rolling, soldiers running with guns, and reporters ducking for cover were flashed on television sets all over the world by the Cable News Network (CNN). In 1995, they did not read about the O. J. Simpson "trial of the century" either; it was fully covered on a daily basis by several of the major networks. People watched in real time or set their VCRs to tape portions of the trial and watched it at night. For those without VCRs, several stations devoted as much as an hour each night recapping the trial's daily events. Other major events—such as the death of Princess Diana in 1997, the impeachment proceedings of President Bill Clinton in 1998 and 1999, the recounting of election ballots in Florida during the 2000 presidential election, and the terrorist attacks on the World Trade Center and the Pentagon in 2001—have likewise been followed by hundreds of millions of people on television.

Without question, for the average American, television has evolved into the most powerful information delivery mechanism ever—supplanting newspapers, magazines, and other material. On the other hand, television can generate so much interest in a subject that viewers actually seek out additional reading. Shelby Foote, playwright and author of a trilogy on the Civil War, was an adviser for, and appeared in, the award-winning PBS documentary *The Civil War,* which was viewed by more than 40 million people. In an interview, he commented that in the 15 years before the PBS broadcast, his trilogy sold about 30,000 copies. In the first 6 months after the broadcast, his trilogy sold more than 100,000 copies (Toplin, 1996).

For young people, not only television but also other multimedia technologies have become a fact of their daily lives. A generation or two ago, music was essentially heard on the radio, the phonograph, or the cassette player, but now it is heard and seen on MTV, the Internet, iPods, and Zunes. Pop singers and rap music artists are not simply heard but also seen in colorful costumes and designer clothes, dancing and acting while provocative still and moving images are displayed in the background. Highly sophisticated morphing technology is routinely used in these music videos and motion pictures, too, to dazzle and capture the viewers' imaginations. These displays are dominating how young people receive information and are creating a new generation that increasingly expects and responds to multisensory delivery systems. Competing with such stimulating visual and audio presentations is becoming a challenge for educators.

This challenge has three important components. First, if the American people, especially the younger generations, are becoming a multimedia-dependent society, should schools take advantage of the technology and use it in delivering instruction? Could it be that today's students, who do not read as well and are not as literate in the traditional sense as past generations, are developing a "multimedia literacy"? If this is the case, educators should begin to capitalize on this state of affairs by channeling their students' multimedia literacy into educational activities. More teachers, for instance, are integrating and assigning documentaries and educational programs aired by PBS, the Discovery Channel, or the History Channel into their lessons. Some are requiring students to research and download media-rich materials from Web sites such as The Digital Universe, National Geographic Maps, or NASA Education.

The second component of the educator's challenge is more complicated and involves the ability of young people to discern what is real and what is fake. American society has begun to ask: What is fact and what is fiction? For instance, are the events depicted in docudramas true or false? Some of them are true and some are false. How do viewers, especially young people, discern the truth? Oliver Stone's 1991 movie *JFK* is a case in point. Parts were footage or images of the actual assassination of John F. Kennedy and related events. Other images were enactments of a script written by Hollywood fiction writers. However, given the technical superiority of the movie and its extensive treatment of the topic, many viewers, especially those born after the events in 1963, came to accept this movie's version as fact. Errol Morris, director of the 2003 Oscar-winning documentary, *The Fog of War*, about former defense secretary Robert McNamara, responded to a question about the truth of documentary filmmaking with this observation:

> Does it make sense to talk about a movie being true or false? I'm not sure it does. In fact, I am pretty sure it doesn't. Movies are movies. (Waxman, 2004, p. E5)

American educators must consider teaching how media, particularly multimedia, can be manipulated to display events so that fiction appears to be fact.

In addition to television and film, which are nondigital and essentially passive technologies that do not require computer interfaces, young people today are the biggest consumers of video games such as Nintendo Wii, Sega, and others provided on CD-ROMs and DVDs. These games are highly sophisticated, interactive multimedia computer systems that take advantage of the latest digital technologies to deliver stimulating activities. Go into a retail computer store and look at the software product displays; there will be sections for business software, educational software, and games. Invariably, the sections for games are generally three to four times larger than the others. Young people, especially males, are not only seeing and hearing multimedia presentations but also actually manipulating and interacting with them to create and control outcomes. Thus, the third challenge for educators is to develop and provide beneficial content that moves multimedia beyond the action game genre.

Hofstetter, quoted at the beginning of this section, raised the issue of multimedia literacy as a requirement for basic functioning in the evolving American society. He provided examples of how everyday existence will depend on multimedia delivery systems in the form of home shopping, electronic publishing, banking, worldwide communications systems, telecommuting or working from home, and so forth. The future society that Hofstetter (2000) envisioned as needing to be multimedia literate is already here for many of the young people in our primary and secondary schools. Multimedia will dominate the world in which they will function as adults. For further information and resources on media literacy, readers may wish to contact the National Association for Media Literacy Education at http://www.amlainfo.org/.

MULTIMEDIA TECHNOLOGY

In years passed, planning for multimedia applications required consideration of specialized hardware and software components. This is no longer the case and except for higher-end video and audio production, most microcomputers (including laptops) now provide basic video and audio capture components. Several manufacturers such as Apple, Dell, and Sony market microcomputers with special "multimedia packages," which essentially means more sophisticated sound and video boards, a good deal more disk space, and audio and video editing software. These machines are ideal for audio and video production but are not an absolute necessity.

Through the end of the 1990s, any discussion of media would have entailed differentiating analog versus digital formats. Examples of each would have been presented and likely compared. Analog formats typically referenced were audiotape and videotape. Digital formats in electronic (stored in binary computer-coded formats) were evolving but had not reach maturity yet, and users were typically conflicted between which format to use. Even with the movement to digital, users still spent significant time working with both formats. During the first decade of the 21st century, the issue of media formats has pretty much been resolved, and most media companies and suppliers are moving to all-digital format. Most media-based educational applications likewise are now using digital format.

Five Levels of Digital Media

There are essentially five levels of digital media: text, still images, animation, audio, and full-motion video. A brief review of these will be helpful as part of this discussion on the use of multimedia in instruction.

Text (letters of the alphabet, numbers, and special characters) is handled very efficiently in any digital media whether on stand-alone or networked computers or the Internet. By far, the most popular applications worldwide are text-based and include word processing, e-mail, text messaging, and database/data file manipulation.

Still images and photographs likewise are also handled well in digital format. Increasingly, still images and photographs are becoming standard accompaniments to text on digital applications and are important enhancements to learning. Standard word processors such as Microsoft Word have made adding an image or photograph to a text document a routine, click-the-menu item. Most Internet and e-mail service providers encourage subscribers to attach a photograph to their e-mail messages. Digital cameras, which were a rarity and quite expensive a decade ago, can now be purchased for less than $100. These cameras attach to a computer or produce images on a disk, flash drive, or other data storage device for immediate use in any digital-based application. Digital camera technology is also being added for very little cost to other devices such as cell phones. Today, Kodak, Fuji, and other film developing companies will develop a roll of the analog 35-mm film into digital format on a CD-ROM or DVD for the same price as standard 4-by-6 snapshots. Increasingly, it is less expensive to provide the developed photographs in digital format than as snapshots.

Animations are still images to which motion has been added. As a field, digital animation grew considerably in the 1990s. Major film producers such as Disney and Lucasfilm depend on digital animations for special effects. In 1997, the highly acclaimed movie *Titanic* relied almost exclusively on digital animation for the sequences in which the doomed luxury liner was seen cruising the Atlantic. In the summer of 2004, the immensely popular animation movie *Shrek* led all movies in total revenues. For the average individual, developing high-quality animation is not easy and requires many hours of editing and refining the images and sequencing flow. On the other hand, with some technical assistance and expertise, developing a good animation can significantly enhance a presentation, including a class lesson. Animations have been used very successfully to add meaning to complex processes in many subject areas, especially in the sciences. For students, viewing an animation on a stand-alone or locally networked computer is relatively simple. Many educational Web sites such as NASA Education make available educational animations that can be freely downloaded for use in lessons, research, or homework assignments.

Digital audio and sound files without images are also becoming easier to develop. An inexpensive microphone (less than $20) can be attached to an input jack on the back of most computers, and a lecture or presentation can be converted into digital form. If done in an acoustically controlled environment with more sophisticated recording equipment, the quality of a digitally produced sound file can be superb. Playing the sound file of a lecture on a stand-alone or locally networked computer is easy and can be more effective than reading a comparable amount of text.

To enhance understanding, instructional applications can combine the two (text and audio). On the Web, technologies such as podcasting can be easily and efficiently used to upload and download sound files.

Thirty frames of still images per second accompanied by a sound track is the recognized standard for full-motion video digital or analog productions. Fewer than 30 frames per second provides a "jerky" and poor-quality video, with the accompanying audio frequently out of synchronization with the images. Producing high-quality, full-motion video in digital format, likewise, is becoming easier but will likely require assistance for the average teacher or student to get started. Good-quality video may require the assistance of technical support staffs that can easily spend days editing 1 or 2 hours of digital video to produce an acceptable product. Playing digital video on a stand-alone or a locally networked computer works well, and Web-based streaming technologies have begun to mature. Full-motion video requires extensive digital storage, running into hundreds of millions if not billions of bytes or more. Students and other users attempting to download or play large video files need substantial computer capability (disk space, processor speed, and input–output transfer rate) as well as high-speed modem and communications capabilities. Digital video cameras that typically cost several thousand dollars at the beginning of the 21st century have come down considerably in price. Flip Video Inc. makes an easy-to-use camera for under $200, which can record up to 2 hours of digital video. Once the video has been recorded, the camera attaches directly to a computer for subsequent playback and editing. The popular YouTube Web site (www.youtube.com) provides a simple-to-use format for uploading and sharing video on the Web.

The Evolution of Video Technology

The emergence of DVD technology has added a significant new option to multimedia development. A review of the evolution of video technology as used in instruction is appropriate.

VIDEOCASSETTE   Videocassette technology, which gained considerable popularity in the 1980s, is still used in many schools for instruction. Videocassette libraries in some schools are quite extensive mainly because the technology is so simple to use. Teachers and students alike have no problem dropping a videocassette into a VCR and hitting the "Play" button to provide video clips on subject matter. Teachers and students also increasingly have become familiar with using camcorders for creating videocassettes for classroom projects. The major limitation of videocassette technology is its noninteractive or passive nature. Viewing a videocassette in a class requires the teacher to stimulate discussions and activities. Videocassette is also a sequential medium with little or a generally clumsy Rewind/Playback facility for randomly selecting segments or clips from the larger videotape. Although a good deal of pedagogically valuable material is available on videocassette from organizations such as Public Broadcasting Service (PBS) and the Discovery Channel, the days of the videocassette are numbered. Most schools have already begun to or are planning on replacing their videocassette collections with DVD.

ANALOG VIDEODISC TECHNOLOGY   In the 1990s, one of the promising breakthroughs in analog video technology was the emergence of videodisc (or laserdisc) as a direct-access video medium. A videodisc is organized as frames stored on a series of concentric tracks on 12-inch or 8-inch metallic disks. Laser (light) technology is used to read the frames. Any individual frame or segment of frames can be accessed directly and played independently of any other frame. This technology was popular for delivering instruction mainly because of its direct access capabilities.

It was a much more advanced technology than videocassettes or other sequential media and could be easily integrated with computer technology to provide interactive capabilities.

There were several levels of interactivity. Level I provided no actual computer interactivity, but assumed that the person using the videodisc had a handheld controller for directly accessing desired frames or chapters. The simplest controllers were similar to those used to change channels on television sets.

A Level II interactive system was a videodisc player with a built-in internal microprocessor. The microprocessor received its instructions from programs that must be added onto the discs. These systems were never very popular for several reasons, mainly because they were programmed specifically for a particular manufacturer's disc player.

Level III interactivity combined a videodisc player with a standard microcomputer. The microcomputer controls the player through programs usually supplied by the videodisc vendor. Using authoring languages such as Authorware Professional or Asymetrix's ToolBook, a teacher could also develop programs to control a videodisc presentation.

In the 1990s, a number of excellent videodisc titles were produced specifically for education in the sciences, social studies, literature, art, and music. Optical Data Corporation produced a highly acclaimed Windows on Science series. In one of the first such actions taken by a state board of education, this series was approved in Texas in 1990 for adoption in the science curriculum for grades 1 through 6. Unfortunately, analog videodisc technology has been pretty much subsumed by the movement to DVD formats.

DIGITAL VERSATILE DISC TECHNOLOGY   Digital versatile (or video) disc (DVD) is a small plastic disc used for the storage of digital data and is the successor to the compact disc (CD). A DVD may have as much as 26 times the storage capacity of a CD and has better graphics and greater resolution. A DVD stores digital data as a series of microscopic pits on an otherwise polished surface. The disc is covered with a protective, transparent coating so that it can be read by a laser beam. The playback or record heads never touch the encoded portion, and the DVD is not worn out by the playing process. Because DVD players are backward compatible to existing optical technologies, they can play CD and CD-ROM discs; however, CD and CD-ROM players cannot play DVD discs.

At the time of this writing, a standard DVD format had not been established. DVDs can hold data in a number of evolving formats depending on the application. DVD formats include DVD-Video (often simply called DVD), DVD-ROM, and DVD-Audio. DVD-Video discs hold digitized movies or video programs and are played using a DVD player connected to a standard television monitor. DVD-ROM (read-only memory) discs hold computer data and are read by a DVD-ROM drive hooked up to a computer. These discs are impressed with data at the point of creation and once written cannot be erased and rewritten with new data. DVDs also include recordable variations. DVD-R (Recordable) discs can be written to sequentially but only once. DVD-RAM (random-access memory), DVD-RW, and DVD1RW (ReWritable) discs can be written to thousands of times.

The amount of content available in DVD format is growing, especially for entertainment purposes. Educational content likewise has grown significantly and a number of instructional media suppliers such as PBS, National Geographic, and the Discovery Channel pretty much provide all of their new material in DVD format. Most microcomputer manufacturers now provide DVD drives or combined DVD/CD-ROM drives as standard equipment. Because of the backward compatibility mentioned earlier, most buyers are naturally opting for the newer DVD technology. All of this bodes well for the future of DVD.

MULTIMEDIA SOFTWARE

Authoring

Authoring languages are especially popular for doing multimedia applications. Easier to use than traditional programming languages, authoring has become the software of choice for teachers and students developing multimedia. The many authoring languages now available allow users to integrate text, images, digital and analog video, sound, and so forth, merely by selecting screen objects such as buttons, fields, and hotwords with the click of a mouse. Authoring languages such as Microsoft PowerPoint, HyperCard, HyperStudio, ToolBook, and Authorware Professional are increasingly being used by educators for instructional applications.

In acquiring authoring languages, ease of use should be of paramount importance, as will be discussed further in Chapter 10. Ease of use is relative to the skills and talents of the users, and although designed for the nontechnical individual, a certain amount of training and practice is necessary for the average teacher to use this software effectively. However, these packages are easy enough to use so that even students can become proficient in developing multimedia applications. One of the more popular student assignments is to take the traditional composition or essay and make it into a multimedia project that incorporates sights and sounds with the text material. Word processing and desktop publishing software such as The Print Shop and The Newsroom incorporate pictures and graphics into their programs so that even primary school children are capable of expanding the traditional writing assignment into something beyond simple text.

Image, Video, and Sound Editing

In addition to preparing multimedia presentations using authoring languages, image, video, and sound editing software is being used to assist in acquiring and editing visual and audio materials for inclusion into multimedia projects.

Simple image editing such as sizing and cropping a digital photograph can be easily accomplished with a wide range of software products including Adobe's Photoshop, Aldus's PhotoStyler, and Kodak's Photo-CD. Simple image editing is being directly incorporated into authoring and other multimedia software packages. More sophisticated image-editing software packages, such as North Coast Software's PhotoMorph, allow users to convert one image into other images using a variety of transitions such as pinpoint size reduction or expansion, color, and special effects. PhotoMorph can also be used to create effects on digital video files.

For simple video editing projects, Microsoft and Apple provide media editing products that can be freely downloaded. For more sophisticated video projects, video-capturing and video-editing software packages such as Adobe Premiere are more desirable. *Video capturing* is the term used for converting analog video as it exists on a videotape or videodisc into a digital video file. A video board is necessary to accomplish video capturing. Once captured into a digital file, the video material can be edited for subsequent multimedia projects. Likewise, sound-capturing software packages such as Creative Labs' Sound Blaster Pro allow users to capture sound either through a microphone or a MIDI device and save it as a digital file. The digital file is usually stored in a wave format that can be subsequently edited to reduce or expand portions of waves and add echo, bass, and other sound effects.

Digital Animation

Digital animation as a field grew considerably in the 1990s. No longer are simple "jerky" movements of a single figure the norm. Digital animation packages have become sophisticated enough to provide animations to multiple objects on a screen, special effects such as three-dimensional images, and high-color resolution approaching photograph quality. Because the animation is all digital, computer processing is simplified and faster. Digital animation is also an important area for future development as major international industries in film, music video, television advertising, and video games continue to invest significant capital and human resources in advancing and perfecting digital animation technology. Reasonably priced, high-level digital animation software products that are appropriate for use in schools today are available from companies such as Adobe and Macromedia.

MULTIMEDIA FOR TEACHING AND LEARNING

When planning and implementing multimedia applications in schools, one should make a distinction between using this technology for teaching and using it for learning. For teaching, the emphasis is placed on the presentation of lessons, with the teacher as the center of the lesson delivery and the use of equipment. For learning, the emphasis is on the use of multimedia by students either for discovery learning, accessing information, or developing projects. For the latter, a good deal more hardware and software need to be acquired, and an investment must be made in class time to train students to use the technology. The possibilities are endless and limited only by the teacher's imagination and creativity. Several common educational uses of multimedia are described here.

For teaching applications, software packages such as PowerPoint (Microsoft), HyperStudio (Knowledge Adventure), and Harvard Graphics (Software Publishing) provide templates or ready-to-use models for doing simple multimedia presentations. Teachers with a basic understanding of computers can learn presentation software relatively quickly, given some support by a technology coordinator or other expert. Once the software is mastered, a 50-minute multimedia lesson incorporating images, sound, animation, or video into a text outline can be completed in 1 or 2 hours. Usually, the greatest effort in developing a multimedia presentation is spent in locating appropriate images, sounds, or video. In planning presentations, a large monitor or overhead projection system is necessary so that a class can easily see the presentation. Increasingly, intelligent whiteboards are being used. These "boards" generally integrate a range of digital software tools for presenting digitally formatted information, be it text, images, sound, or video. Furthermore, they come with interactive features so that teachers and students can manipulate the displayed information. SMART Technologies is one of the leading manufacturers of whiteboards.

Teachers may also wish to develop their own custom multimedia programs for use by students in a discovery learning or other pedagogical mode. Custom multimedia programs make extensive use of interaction and the ability of students to select options and direct the flow of the program. More advanced authoring languages such as Authorware Professional (Macromedia) and ToolBook (Asymetrix) are ideal for these applications. Teachers will have to devote considerable time to learning these software packages, and although easier to use than other instructional programming languages, they will test the technical abilities and skills of the average teacher. Most likely, custom-designed and developed multimedia programs will require a team effort on the part of teachers and technical support staff. The time required to develop a custom multimedia program will depend on a number of factors, including the scope of the project, whether it will be incorporating digital video, and the availability of video. Such projects usually require several months, if not more, for design and development.

Doing a customized multimedia project should be carefully considered, with serious planning devoted to training, design of the project, and the availability of media. This is especially true if part of the work involves doing video production. Even with the latest editing hardware and software, 30 minutes of quality video can require weeks of scripting, shooting, and editing.

Readers interested in designing such a project are encouraged to refer to Simkins, Cole, Tavalin, and Means's (2002) *Increasing Student Learning Through Multimedia Projects,* Semrau and Boyer's (1994) *Using Interactive Video in Education,* or Kemp and Smellie's (1989) *Planning, Producing, and Using Instructional Media.* In addition to technical factors, teachers designing a custom project will also have to consider the abilities and learning styles of their students. Multimedia programs should not be designed for only the higher ability students but should be easy enough for all students to use. This means that careful consideration is given to "help" features, navigational techniques, and program prompts.

For student learning, the use of commercially developed multimedia is appropriate for many learner-centered activities for studying a topic. Figure 7.1 provides a list of commercial multimedia packages that are appropriate for use in classroom activities. The World Wide Web has a plethora of Web sites that contain freely downloadable media. Electronic multimedia encyclopedias such as Grolier's Multimedia Encyclopedia are prevalent in school libraries and media centers and are excellent sources of media. They incorporate sophisticated but easy-to-use search tools for finding not only text but images, sounds, and video. Custom software products dealing with a specific topic—such as A.D.A.M. The Inside Story (of the human body) from A.D.A.M., Inc.—are available for all the major subject areas. The Florida Virtual School markets a fully online multimedia gaming course, Conspiracy Code, to teach American history. In addition to the appeal of pictures, sounds, and moving images, the benefit of using multimedia Internet resources and encyclopedias is that students begin to learn how to use this technology easily.

A more advanced level of learning applications would be for students to develop their own multimedia project. Examples include the following:

- Compiling a photo essay
- Doing a news report on an event using video
- Collecting oral histories from family members
- Doing a weather report using maps and animations
- Creating an artistic or musical piece using multimedia

Program	Developer	Subject
A.D.A.M. The Inside Story	A.D.A.M., Inc.	Science–Biology
Amazon Trail	The Learning Co.	Social Studies–Ecology
American Sign Language Dictionary	Multimedia 2000	Special Education
Children's World Atlas	Rand McNally	Geography
Conspiracy Code	Florida Virtual School	Social Studies
Eyewitness Series	DK Interactive	Children's Encyclopedia
Great Ocean Rescue	Tom Snyder	Environment
Magic School Bus Series	Scholastic	Science
Music Loops for Multimedia	FTC Publishing	Music
National Geographic Series	National Geographic	Geography, Culture
Operation Frog	Scholastic	Science
Oregon Trail	The Learning Co.	Social Studies
Point of View Series	Scholastic	Social Studies
Science Explorer Series	Riverdeep Interactive	Science
Who Built America?	American Social History Project	Social Studies

FIGURE 7.1 Samples of Instructional Multimedia Software.

Planning and implementing these applications require training students to use the necessary hardware and software. Sufficient equipment must also be available for the students to use for extended periods. Because of the amount of preparation and work involved, student multimedia projects are generally group or collaborative activities involving two or more students. One of the benefits of multimedia projects for learning is that students need to use a variety of skills, including reading and writing, in developing the project. Additionally, student-developed projects are excellent for helping children develop multimedia literacy; with guidance from teachers, students can begin to learn how media, in general, can be manipulated and edited to fit the message that they wish to deliver. In recent years, most of the popular multimedia authoring languages have also provided options to save files in hypertext markup language (HTML) format so that they can easily be made available and shared as pages on the World Wide Web.

MULTIMEDIA RESOURCES AND COPYRIGHTS

All of the major educational software developers and suppliers have begun to market multimedia programs that would be appropriate for school use. If a multimedia program that meets a school's instructional needs is available, then certainly it should be acquired. No need exists for teachers to reinvent materials that already exist. Annual catalogs, guides, and compendia are readily available from a variety of sources. These are frequently provided free of charge to educators by journal and other publishers. Highly recommended are Public Broadcasting System Web sites such as WUFT (http://www.wuft.tv/teachers/) that provide multimedia guides for teachers. *The Multimedia Home Companion Guide for Parents and Kids* published by Warner Books is also an excellent resource. Keep in mind that commercial multimedia packages are subject to the same copyright stipulations that apply to other software products. Generally, programs and files including image, sound, and video files cannot be copied or used in a manner inconsistent with their original intent.

For those educators who plan to develop their own materials either for presentation or for student use, locating images, sounds, and video in digital format can be time consuming. The first source of multimedia materials in digital format would be the files available as part of the authoring or presentation software being used to develop the application. All of the major multimedia authoring or presentation software tools provide clip media libraries or files containing materials that can be readily incorporated into multimedia projects. In some cases, both a standard version of the package without the clip media and a deluxe or all-inclusive version of the package with the clip media files are available. The deluxe versions are generally worth the additional cost and can save hours of searching for images and sounds. Clip media libraries generally can be used freely by educators without the need to secure permissions for their use.

A second source of digital media would be electronic encyclopedias and multimedia databases. In many cases, the developers allow users to copy a photograph or image for limited use, as would be appropriate in a class presentation. Microsoft and Grolier are two of the major marketers of electronic encyclopedias that allow for a limited amount of copying of their materials, generally through a copy-and-paste mechanism.

A third source for digital multimedia materials would be commercially available clip media CD-ROMs and DVDs. Companies such as Aris Entertainment (Marina Del Ray, California) and Corel Corporation (Ottawa, Canada) provide clip media libraries of multimedia materials that can be freely used for educational purposes.

The Internet is a fourth source that will be discussed in more detail in the next chapter. Sites around the world make available images, sound, and video, which can be accessed and copied by educators for classroom use. The Internet, in fact, has emerged as the major source for all types of digitally formatted data.

Local video stores maintain up-to-date lists and provide search services to locate titles of commercially available materials on DVDs. Copyright restrictions generally prohibit copying this material or converting it into other formats.

Recording television programs is also another source of video; however, using this material is also subject to copyright laws.

In using any copyrighted materials (text, images, sound, and video), educators should be aware of the restrictions on their use. Generally, but not always, educators have a fair or limited use of copyright materials as long as they are used for instructional purposes. However, even here prohibitions exist against the unauthorized use or proliferation of copies. It would be safe to say that any attempt to profit by selling or showing copyrighted materials, even for educational purposes, is generally prohibited. For educators unfamiliar with copyright issues, especially as applied to instructional multimedia, an excellent source of information is the Fair Use Center at Stanford University, which maintains an Internet site (http://fairuse.stanford.edu/) dedicated to copyright issues. Another excellent guide written specifically for school administrators can be found at Hall Davidson at http://www.halldavidson.net/CopyrightGuideadmin.pdf.

MEDIA DISTRIBUTION SYSTEMS—WHITEBOARDS

Media distribution systems integrate several media sources (computer, DVD, Internet, document camera, etc.) and are able to distribute to an intelligent display device(s). Whiteboards, such as SMART Board, have become popular in the last several years as intelligent display devices for use in classrooms. A report by SMART Technologies (2009) concluded that more than 2 million whiteboard units have been purchased by schools worldwide. Figure 7.2 shows a flow diagram of

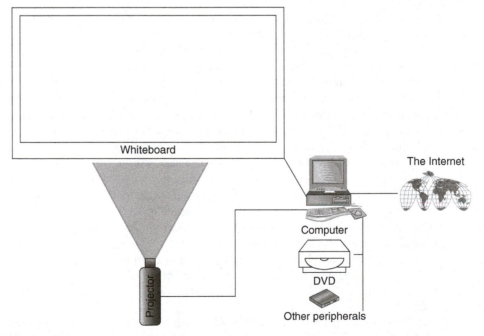

FIGURE 7.2 Whiteboard Configuration.

such a whiteboard system that shows a computer with various peripheral media devices connected to a large whiteboard display unit. In these systems, a computer can connect directly to the whiteboard and through an overhead projector. An overhead projector is usually needed if there are analog media devices (e.g., document camera, videotape player) as part of the system.

A whiteboard can be used for a variety of instructional activities, including

- displaying any software program that is loaded onto the connected microcomputer such as Internet browsers, presentation software (e.g. PowerPoint), and any other proprietary software;
- showing images, animations, and video clips;
- capturing notes and illustrations that are part of a lesson; and
- videoconferencing.

A whiteboard can also come with its own software allowing a teacher or student to interact with whatever is being displayed on its surface. Increasingly, teachers are involving students in projects by requiring them to use the whiteboard for displaying their work.

Depending on size, level of interactivity, and screen resolution, a whiteboard can cost from a little over a thousand dollars to several thousand dollars. In purchasing a whiteboard, it is also a good idea to budget for installation charges and maintenance contracts. The EdVenture Group maintains an excellent resource Web site for using whiteboards in instruction at http://www.theedventuregroup.org/21stcentury/whiteboards.html.

Another excellent resource for lessons using whiteboard is Lesson Planet–A Search Engine for Teachers (subscription service). It has hundreds of lesson plans using whiteboards.

CASE STUDY

Place: Redwood Middle School   Year: 2009

Redwood Middle School is located in an urban center in the northwestern part of the United States. Redwood provides a 6th to 8th grade program for approximately 500 students. The school enjoys an excellent reputation in its community, and the administrators and teachers are generally regarded as doing a good job of educating the children. Technology is apparent throughout the school, with computer equipment located in classrooms as well as in three central laboratories. The library media center maintains an excellent videotape selection and arranges for loans of portable (VCR/large monitor) workstations to teachers. The coordinator of the library media center would like to upgrade the video collection by adding DVD titles and players and has been in discussions with the Redwood site-based management (RSBM) team. An active Parent-Teacher Association has been helpful in securing additional resources for Redwood and has been particularly supportive of instructional technology.

Redwood is one of five pilot schools in the district that plans and administers much of its program under the auspices of a site-based management team. The members of the RSBM team are as follows:

The cochairs of the PTA (one parent and one teacher)

Two teachers elected by the staff

Two parents appointed by the PTA

A representative from the school district's central office

A guidance counselor

A librarian

The assistant principal

The principal

Decisions are made as much as possible through consensus, with most issues being decided by unanimous vote. When opinions are divided, issues are generally tabled for further discussion.

A special (one-time infusion) city appropriation for the advancement of instructional technology has been made available to all the schools in the district for the 2009–2010 fiscal year. Redwood's share of these funds is $75,000. Each school is required to come up with a plan on how it would use these funds. It is October 2009, and all plans for using this appropriation must be submitted by February 2010 to secure funding in the current fiscal year.

The RSBM team has been discussing upgrading its instructional technology equipment for more than 2 years, especially with regard to multimedia applications. Several approaches have been discussed, with members of the team leaning toward installing intelligent whiteboards into classrooms. It is estimated that 15 classrooms can be upgraded for approximately $4,000 per classroom. The remaining $15,000 would be used to start a DVD collection in the library media center. However, at the first meeting in September, the school district representative suggested using the entire $75,000 appropriation for a wireless data communications system and 25 laptop computers that can be stored in a mobile cabinet for transportation throughout the school. The district representative reported that this was the way many schools were now accessing the Internet and its rich array of data resources.

At a second meeting in October 2004, the RSBM team seemed evenly split, with most of the administrative members supporting the school district representative's suggestion of the wireless/mobile laptop system, and the teachers and parents supporting the plan to upgrade the classrooms with intelligent whiteboards. It appears that the team will have difficulty reaching a consensus by February 2010.

Discussion Questions

1. Assume that you are the principal and have not yet committed yourself to a position on this issue. Given that you are concerned with developing a plan by February 2010 so as not to risk losing the funds, explain what your plan would be for ensuring that the team will reach a consensus by the deadline. In developing your strategy, you should have a clear understanding of your own position on the technological merits of the two proposals.
2. Assuming the team makes the decision by February 2010, how do you present it to the school community? Do you have any fallback strategy for those who might not agree with the team's decision?

Summary

This chapter reviews the development and use of multimedia technologies in education. Particular emphasis is put on the instructional uses of multimedia. Interest and investment in this technology are increasing, and indications are that it has appeal to both teachers and students.

Multimedia can be defined generically as any combination of two or more media such as sound, images, text, animation, and video. For educational technology purposes, multimedia refers to computer-based systems that use associative linkages to allow users to navigate and retrieve information stored in a combination of text, sounds, graphics, video, and other media.

Howard Gardner's theory of multiple intelligences establishes a theoretical framework for using multimedia in instruction. This theory relates to other widely recognized theories on learning styles and modalities of learning.

Multimedia literacy is a growing concern among educators as American society continues to depend on image technologies such as television, video, and film. Educators need to prepare children to live and function in a society that relies more on multimedia for information storage and dissemination.

Components of multimedia systems have been reviewed. Hardware components include a variety of both basic and specialized equipment. Software components include authoring languages, image handling software, and digital animation packages.

Multimedia can be used in instruction in a variety of creative and stimulating ways. Applications include teacher presentations, student projects, and discovery learning. Although teachers are encouraged to develop their own materials, many excellent educational multimedia products are available and should be considered rather than "reinvented."

In developing multimedia applications, many resources are available to educators. Educators should be aware of copyright issues and infringements when acquiring and using materials, especially video, images, and sound. The chapter concludes with a discussion of intelligent whiteboard systems.

Key Concepts and Questions

1. Multimedia technology has been evolving slowly but steadily during the past decade. How has this technology affected your daily activities? How do you see multimedia developing in the 21st century?
2. Multimedia means different things to different people. How do you define *multimedia*?
3. Multimedia is frequently used in conjunction with the application of technology for a variety of applications. Is multimedia strictly a technological phenomenon? Or does it have some theoretical basis for teaching and learning? Explain.
4. *Literacy* is a frequently used term in education and generally refers to language (reading and writing). Explain literacy in conjunction with multimedia. Does a need exist for developing multimedia literacy? Explain.
5. Multimedia can include a variety of hardware components. How are multimedia hardware components changing? Which do you consider the most beneficial for education? Why?
6. Multimedia can be used in a variety of applications. How would you differentiate multimedia applications as used by teachers for presenting lessons as opposed to use by students in learning?
7. Locating multimedia resources such as video, images, and sounds can be a time-consuming activity. If you were to design a multimedia project, how would you locate appropriate material? Do you need to be concerned about copyright in using this material? Explain.

Suggested Activities

1. Take an inventory of media (video, film, television) facilities presently being used in a school or school district. Where are they located? When were they acquired or established? How do you see them evolving in the future?
2. Look at your inventory and consider how, if at all, these facilities are integrated with computer facilities. Do you see any trend in this integration? How are the Internet and World Wide Web used, if at all?
3. Multiple intelligences (MI) has become popular as a learning theory, especially in connection with instructional technology. Write a brief paper (3 to 5 pages) evaluating MI theory. Use and cite at least five World Wide Web resources to support your views.

References

Armstrong, T. (2000). *Multiple intelligences in the classroom.* Alexandria, VA: Association for Curriculum Development and Supervision.

Armstrong, T. (2009). *Multiple intelligences in the classroom* (3rd ed.). Alexandria, VA: Association for Curriculum Development and Supervision.

Gardner, H. (1983). *Frames of mind: The theory of multiple intelligences.* New York: Basic Books.

Gardner, H. (1993). *Multiple intelligences: The theory in practice.* New York: Basic Books.

Gardner, H. (2000). *Intelligence reframed: Multiple intelligences for the 21st century.* New York: Basic Books.

Hofstetter, F. (1994, Winter). Is multimedia the next literacy? *Educator's Tech Exchange, 2*(3), 6–14.

Hofstetter, F. (2000). *Multimedia literacy* (3rd ed.). New York: McGraw-Hill.

Kemp, J. E., & Smellie, D. C. (1989). *Planning, producing, and using instructional media.* New York: Harper & Row.

Levine, J. (1995, September 26). Interview with Charlie Rose, on *Charlie Rose* [Television broadcast]. New York: Public Broadcasting Service.

Picciano, A. G. (1993). The Five Points: The design of multimedia model on teaching social history. *Journal of Educational Multimedia and Hypermedia, 2*(2), 129–147.

Semrau, P., & Boyer, B. A. (1994). *Using interactive video in education.* Boston: Allyn & Bacon.

Simkins, M., Cole, K., Tavalin, F., & Means, B. (2002). *Increasing student learning through multimedia projects.* Alexandria, VA: Association for Supervision and Curriculum Development.

SMART Technologies. (2009, February 13). SMART's 2008 sales more than double its nearest competition. Retrieved April 17, 2009, from http://www2.smarttech.com/st/en-US/About+Us/News+Room/Media+Releases/2009+Media+Releases.htm?guid={BB764E4A-7B94-4D01-B006-B34CD310913D}

Thornburg, D. (1989). *The role of technology in teaching to the whole child: Multiple intelligences in the classroom.* Los Altos, CA: Starsong.

Toplin, R. B. (1996, August 4). Plugged into the past. *New York Times,* section 2, pp. 1, 26.

Waxman, S. (2004, July 5). Nonfiction films turn a corner; "Fahrenheit" shows approval of audiences and of distributors. *New York Times,* pp. E1, E5.

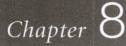

Chapter 8

Data Communications, the Internet, and Educational Applications

Vladimir Zworykin, the "father of television," invented the iconoscope and kinescope, which became the basic technologies used for broadcasting and receiving television signals in this country. Born in Russia, he immigrated to the United States in 1919 and was hired by the Radio Corporation of America (RCA) in 1929 to do research and development in communications technology.

In the early years of the development of television, Zworykin envisioned a technology that could be useful in a free and democratic society. He struggled to receive funding for his work and had to convince others of its benefits. In later years, even while rising to the position of vice president at RCA, he became concerned, even dismayed, at the commercialization of broadcast television. In 1962, he met President John F. Kennedy, who praised him for his contributions to this country, especially for his invention of the television. Zworykin replied wryly, "Have you seen television recently?" (Negroponte, 1995, p. 82).

In his later life, Zworykin commented frequently on the commercialization of television as a necessary evil. In an interview he gave in 1975, 8 years before his death, he expressed deep emotion over the "violence and murder" that we teach our children through television. But commercial television was driven by ratings, and the ratings ironically provided the funding for much of his and others' research and development.

Zworykin's surprise at the direction taken by his own invention serves as an apt vignette to introduce this chapter on data communications and the Internet. The Internet is a relatively new medium with a greater potential for societal influence than television. Observations and concerns have emerged regarding the content on the Internet. Those involved with its original development had no idea what the Internet would become.

Without a doubt, the Internet is evolving into a major technology within which a host of information, communications, entertainment, and educational services are being provided. In December 1995, an education advisory council to President Bill Clinton recommended that every school in the United States be connected to the Internet. The basis for this recommendation was a carefully done, 2-year study conducted by McKinsey & Company, an international management consulting firm. The study estimated that every school in the country could establish a new 25-station computer laboratory with connections to the Internet via ordinary telephone lines for a cost of approximately $11 billion. Educators and newspaper editorials ("Connecting Every Pupil," 1995) praised this recommendation and commented that such an undertaking could "democratize education by bringing the world's best materials into the classrooms of the nation's . . . schools" (p. A20).

This recommendation is worth citing for several reasons. First, its specificity was unusual; recommendations regarding national policies for all schools in the country tend to be very general. Here, the recommendation specifies the number of workstations per school, as well as details on the nature of the application and costs. Second, the recommendation also highlighted the importance of the Internet, not simply in terms of teaching and learning but by characterizing its information resources as the "world's best materials." Lastly, by the early part of the 21st century, practically all schools in the United States were connected to the Internet, of which the vast majority had high-speed (T1, T3, or cable modem) connections (Park & Staresina, 2004).

These developments are indicative of how far communications technologies, especially as integrated with computer and video technologies, have come. The American public is aware of the extensive use that television has made of advanced communications systems to reduce the distance between audiences and live events. Major happenings—whether NASA space exploration projects, international crises, or the Olympic Games—are brought into living rooms in real time as they occur. The same advances that have been made in the television or video communications industry are now beginning to be made in the digital or computer communications industry. In the 1990s, terms such as *the Internet, the World Wide Web, cyberspace,* and *the information superhighway* became household words, whether used by government officials espousing national policy or children asking parents to subscribe to America Online so they could e-mail their friends. Data communications (i.e., the methods and media used to transfer data from one computer device to another) provide opportunities for a wide range of educational applications. Whether browsing the Internet, accessing a government database, or participating in a social network, teachers and students are discovering that data communications systems are becoming a major technology to support teaching and learning.

In this chapter, we examine data communications systems in schools, especially those provided by the Internet. Before continuing, readers are encouraged to review the material in Appendix A that covers the basic components of most data communications systems.

DATA COMMUNICATIONS IN THE SCHOOLS

During the past several decades, educators have seen data communications systems and networks expand in size, sophistication, and the ability to communicate over distances. In the late 1970s and 1980s, schools began to install their first *local area networks (LANs)* (see Figure 8.1). The use of these LANs in computer laboratories, libraries, and administrative offices has become commonplace. In larger school districts, *wide area networks (WANs)* are in evidence, connecting computers and LANs, which are dispersed miles apart throughout the district (see Figure 8.2).

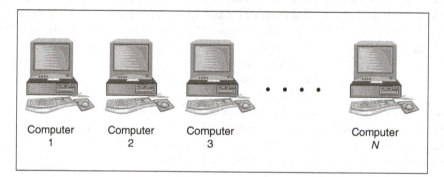

FIGURE 8.1 Simple Local Area Network.

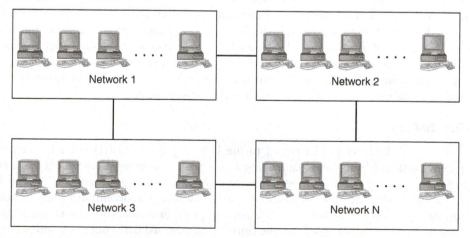

FIGURE 8.2 Multiple Networks.

The essential concept here involves a large computer network integrating the activities of smaller computer networks. Using district-wide networks, a student in one school can determine whether a library in another school has a particular book, an assistant principal can examine the transcript of a student who has just transferred from another school, or a district business manager can monitor the daily expenditures of several schools.

The data communications technology that enables a computer in one school to communicate with a computer in another school is essentially the same, whether the schools are one mile apart or many miles apart. Once a WAN has been established in a locality, the distance between sites does not make that much difference in the ability of individual sites to communicate with one another. In the late 1980s, this concept was taken a step further as computers in school districts began to communicate with computers on networks outside the school district. A student looking for a particular book was able to use a computer in the school's library to locate the book at a local public library or perhaps even a local college library. A superintendent using a computer in the school district office was able to transfer data on student demographics to a computer located in the state education office.

In the 1990s, data communications technologies advanced to the point where a computer on one network could easily communicate with a computer on another network hundreds or even thousands of miles away. The grants officer in a local school district office in Juneau, Alaska, could examine a database of funded programs that existed on a computer network maintained by the U.S. Department of Education in Washington, DC. A state education department administrator in Albany, New York, could e-mail a new curriculum proposal to all 800 school district superintendents on a statewide education network. A social studies teacher in Tulsa, Oklahoma, developing a module in cultural studies could access a database of curricular materials maintained by the National Geographic Society.

With the expansion of data communications capabilities over the past several decades, networks likewise have expanded to cover greater distances and to link with many other networks. At some point, all of this data traffic occurring on thousands of networks throughout the country, and the world could pass over a common universal network.

THE INTERNET

The Internet (see Figure 8.3) is an international computer network consisting of hundreds of thousands of smaller networks that link schools, colleges, government agencies, research organizations, and private businesses through satellites and other high-speed data communications facilities. The essential function provided by the Internet is to allow users to transfer and receive data. The data can be a simple, one-line e-mail message, a complex weather map, or a huge subset of the United States 2010 census. The Internet also provides the conceptual framework for a universal computer network and has evolved into the network of networks.

A Brief History

The roots of the Internet can be traced to the U.S. Department of Defense in the 1960s. Concerned about establishing and maintaining a worldwide communications system in the event of a major disaster such as nuclear war, engineers and scientists from Rand, UCLA, and MIT designed a "doomsday" data communications system that would be decentralized and capable of functioning regardless of whether any single node or point in the network was no longer available. This design was a departure from the common centralized data communications systems that required a hub or center point to control the entire network.

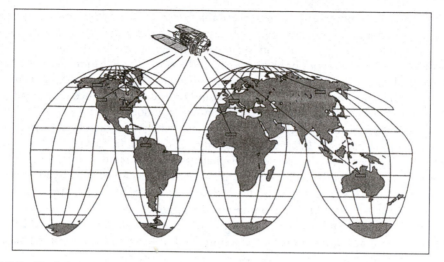

FIGURE 8.3 The Internet.

In 1969, the Pentagon's Advanced Research and Projects Agency established the first node of this new network—called Advanced Research and Projects Agency Network (ARPANET)—at UCLA. Throughout the 1970s, the ARPANET grew but was used essentially by government officials, engineers, and scientists connected with research for the U.S. Department of Defense. In 1983, the military segment of ARPANET developed a separate network called MILNET, and access to ARPANET was expanded to include other computer networks worldwide that used its standard *protocol* or method of transferring data.

Also in the early 1980s, the higher education, government, and research communities established other international networks. The City University of New York, Yale University, and IBM established Because It's Time Network (BITNET) to link university mainframe computers. The U.S. National Science Foundation (NSF) funded Computer Science Network (CSNET) to provide data communications facilities for industry, government, and university groups engaged in computer science research. Later, several U.S. agencies—namely, the NSF, the National Aeronautics and Space Agency (NASA), and the U.S. Department of Energy—funded and established networking facilities that eventually would be used to enhance the aging ARPANET system. By the late 1980s, all of these major networks were communicating with one another, either using or converting to the standard protocol established on ARPANET; hence the birth of the Internet.

The Internet Today

Since the early 1990s, the Internet community has grown exponentially. The number of users was estimated to be increasing at the rate of 20% per month, or doubling every 5 to 6 months. These numbers were strictly estimates because no one really knew at the time how many people were using the Internet. The art of estimating how many people are online throughout the world is an inexact one at best. Surveys abound, using all sorts of measurement parameters. However, from examining many of the published surveys, one educated guess has the number at 1.6 billion people, with 255 million in the United States and Canada (Internet World Stats, 2009).

This growth and popularity is understandable because joining the Internet is relatively inexpensive, voluntary, and service is equitable. The cost of using the Internet is not based on usage. For example, sending an e-mail message costs the same whether the message is going a mile down the road to a neighbor or halfway around the world. Furthermore, a user incurs very few obligations by joining the Internet and can use its resources as needed. Although connecting to the Internet depends on acquiring equipment and online services, once on the Internet all users are equal. A major corporation or government agency does not receive quicker or better service than a group of fourth graders using the Internet to help with their homework.

The types of users on the Internet are changing significantly. In the late 1980s, the Internet was dominated by the nonprofit, research, university, and government sectors. Since the 1990s, many private enterprises, both small and large, joined the Internet for marketing, sales, and other commercial purposes. Likewise, private individuals are using the Internet daily for such routine activities as reading the news, checking on the weather, purchasing goods and services, or communicating with friends and relatives around the globe. Although still dominated by users in more technologically advanced countries, the number of Internet users in developing nations has also increased significantly in the past few years.

This expansion has significant implications. A major issue facing the Internet is in administration; presently, no single organization is really responsible for the Internet. Various government-sponsored arrangements and consortia exist in different countries to administer the Internet on a voluntary basis. In the United States, for instance, the NSF sponsors and funds the Internet Network Information Center (InterNIC) that maintains information, database directories, and registration services for the Internet. However, the funding for this center is not guaranteed, and the providers of the services do not accept responsibility for the accuracy of their information and services.

Interestingly, whereas data communications technology usually requires a good deal of precision in developing procedures, protocols, and access, the Internet has evolved with little planning or administrative precision. When it first came on the scene in the 1990s, some observers (Shirky, 1995; Stoll, 1995) referred to the Internet as not much more than *information anarchy* and predicted that it would outlive its usefulness. On the other hand, others (Ellsworth, 1994; Williams, 1995) considered the voluntary, loosely administered digital community as the very essence of freedom and equality in accessing and sharing information. In the 21st century, it is clear that the latter is the case.

The Future of the Internet

Speculation on the future of the Internet is difficult given its dynamic nature. However, the Internet has attracted a good deal of attention, and because planning requires consideration of the future, a few comments and concerns about the Internet in the coming years are appropriate.

The Internet has been, perhaps, the most dynamic digital technology ever introduced. Computer industry analysts and software developers believe that it set "a new computing standard or platform much as the personal computer did in the 1980s," (Fisher, 1996, p. C15). In a period of a few years, hundreds of millions of people, most of whom did not even know of its existence as late as 1990, have used its services. Its growth rate in the mid-1990s, doubling the number of users approximately every 6 months, was nothing short of phenomenal.

This dynamism is stimulating for those who believe in the benefits of technology for the general populace, but it is a cause for concern as well. The Internet is a voluntary community with few rules and little formal administration. In the future, attempts will be made to impose rules and regulations, some of which will require administration and oversight. As an example, the U.S. Congress has considered censorship legislation for the Internet, particularly as it applies to child pornography and other sex-oriented material. Given the absence of mechanisms in place capable of controlling such activity, combined with the international character of the Internet, such legislation, whether warranted or not, would have limited impact. In the years to come, if the Internet continues to evolve into the network of networks, some international effort will likely be made to administer, and to some degree, control it. Whether this will be good or bad for the Internet is difficult to predict. If its growth continues, some technological administration, planning, and funding will have to be implemented. On the other hand, the same forces that provide administration and planning may also bring control, which has the potential of changing the free and voluntary access and sharing of information that has made the Internet so popular.

An issue related to administration and control is the commercialization of the Internet. The Internet evolved from the nonprofit (government, research, and university) sectors. Commercial use of the Internet came afterwards; however, much of the growth in the Internet during the past several years has been fueled by commercial activities—everything from private entrepreneurs selling crafts to international corporations marketing goods and services. The Internet was designed primarily for information access and sharing, not necessarily for high-volume commercial transaction processing.

Furthermore, security on the Internet is limited. Security breaches happen regularly on many commercial networks, but the Internet is far more vulnerable to such breaches because it lacks any security oversight. Whether using a credit card or banking at home, the possibility exists that the Internet will always be vulnerable for high-volume commercial transaction processing typically found in banking, retail, and financial services. For a number of years, engineers at the Stanford University Clean Slate Project have been involved with building a new Internet with improved security and the capabilities to support a new generation of not-yet-invented Internet applications, as well as to do some things the current Internet does poorly, such as supporting mobile users. A rationale for the new Internet is the concern that a major security breach wreaking havoc on millions of users, government agencies, and businesses is only a matter of time. Furthermore, the estimated $80 billion a year Internet security industry will be powerless to stop this "digital Pearl Harbor" (Markoff, 2009).

The nature of commercial enterprise and high-volume transaction processing significantly adds to the traffic on the Internet. Most nonprofit uses of the Internet, such as information access, do not compare in volume with commercial activity in financial services, retail sales, and marketing. The Internet is already suffering from growing pains, as access and searches have slowed considerably, particularly during the prime business usage hours of 9:00 A.M. to 10:00 P.M. (Some critics have begun to refer to the World Wide Web as the "World Wide Wait.") Spamming, or mass e-mailing from marketing enterprises, has begun to jam e-mail inboxes. If commercialization of the Internet continues with its concomitant high-volume transaction processing, then access and search speed will continue to slow considerably, possibly changing its character and usefulness.

The basic hardware and software technology that is the foundation of the Internet was conceived in the 1970s and 1980s; the designers, however, were not envisioning a network that would meet the needs of hundreds of millions of people throughout the world. Data communications, as most technologies, evolved and improved in a steady, predictable fashion. Recently, however, the rapid growth of the Internet has fueled a significant increase in research, development, and new products meant to improve the hardware and software that all data communications systems require. The speed of modem equipment rises every year while its cost comes down. The introduction of handheld information appliances is adding a whole new dimension to accessing the Internet. Using wireless communications (satellite transmissions) and palm-size microcomputers, anybody is able to access e-mail and surf the Web literally in any place and at any time.

As we entered the early years of the new millennium, almost 158 million people in the United States used cell phones and other wireless devices (CTIA, 2003). It is only a matter of time and a bit more refinement of the technology before these people use wireless information appliances for most of their Internet activities. The future evolution of Web browser software is impossible to predict because new companies and products seem to appear almost overnight. The speed with which this technology is changing is unprecedented and generating new products with technological life cycles of no more than 1 or 2 years. The very nature of the providers of Internet access—whether public or private telephone companies, cable TV companies, satellite services, or strictly commercial Internet service providers—is not at all settled and can change significantly in the future. Such rapid change requires the most flexible of planning strategies as organizations, including schools, attempt to keep up with and adjust to newer data communications hardware and software technologies.

While considering the future of the Internet, it is most important for schools to provide experiences and opportunities for children to learn to use this rapidly evolving technology. Schools have traditionally prepared children to contribute, work, and play in the larger society—and using the Internet exemplifies the facility that will be required of individuals to technologically function in the future. Golden and Katz (2008) report that the share of U.S. workers directly using computers on the job increased from 25% in 1984 to 57% in 2003. Nicholas Negroponte (1995) relates a discussion that he had with the late Jerome Wiesner, then president of MIT, on considering the advances of technology and the evolution of a "digital" society. Although optimistic, Wiesner was concerned that such a society "takes jobs and may have fewer to give back" (p. 233). The Internet and/or its successors will require users in all sectors of society to continually hone their skills as they adjust to rapid advances and changes in using data communications and other technologies. Educators would be wise to include, as part of their technology planning, the establishment of goals and objectives that require students to be prepared for a digital society that will be largely dependent on a worldwide data communications system similar to, but more advanced than, the Internet of today.

An excellent reference for technology standards for students has been developed by the International Society for Technology in Education (ISTE) and is available online at http://www.iste.org and listed under NETS (National Educational Technology Standards).

THE WORLD WIDE WEB

Terms for the Internet, such as *cyberspace* or the *information superhighway,* are designed to provide a descriptive character to this network of networks. Another term that is used in conjunction or interchangeably with the Internet is the *World Wide Web,* or simply the Web. The Web is actually a software system that introduced hypertext and multimedia capabilities to the Internet. Originally developed in the early 1990s at CERN (the European Particle Physics Laboratory in Switzerland), the Web was designed to provide hypertext and full multimedia support in a relatively easy-to-use language for physicists and other scientists using the Internet. This concept of a hypertext-based software system for the Web is generally credited to Tim Berners-Lee, currently director of the World Wide Web Consortium, who envisioned an Internet that would be much easier to use.

Hypertext, as used on the Web, is a nonsequential retrieval system for accessing data on the Internet. Rather than sequential searching, hypertext relies on linkages of data files to one another in a complex "web" of associations. Hypertext is not a new software search concept, having been routinely used in large databases for years. Electronic encyclopedias, for instance, employ hypertext searching when a particular topic or passage has links or "hotwords" that users can click on to jump to a related topic, which in turn has links to other related topics. The same approach is used on the Web to locate data files on the Internet.

Protocols and Client Servers

To understand the nature of the Web in relation to the Internet, a brief discussion of protocols, as used in data communications, is necessary. *Protocol* is a general term for a set of rules, procedures, or standards that are used in exchanging data in a data communications system. Examples of these rules would be a code or signal indicating the beginning of a message, a code or signal indicating the end of a message, or a code or signal indicating that a device is busy. Computer and communications equipment manufacturers established different protocols for exchanging data, which complicated the ability of one manufacturer's computer to communicate with another manufacturer's computer. This protocol incompatibility problem was resolved to some degree by the development of protocol conversion software that enabled computers to translate and convert data messages of other computer protocols. The Internet established a standard protocol for all its activity, called *transmission control protocol/Internet protocol* (TCP/IP). All computers using the Internet had to exchange data using TCP/IP. The Web's data transfer method or protocol, called *hypertext transfer protocol* (http), was designed to run "over" or to be in conjunction with the TCP/IP, the standard Internet protocol. Many other protocols have also been designed to run in conjunction with TCP/IP on the Internet; however, because of its hypertext and multimedia capabilities, the Web has become the most popular.

Because of its hypertext facilities, the Web is also an excellent software system to run on a client–server data communications system, which is how the Internet functions. In the early days of data communications, the standard network model was for a central computer to control all the activity on a network and also function as the central depository for data files and programs. The client–server data communications model does not require a central depository or controlling computer. The basis for the Internet and its predecessor, ARPANET, was to distribute or share control broadly among the networked computers.

In a client-server model, computers essentially perform two major functions. The client or end-user function makes a request or query for data to a server. The server function, performed by one of many computers sharing network control, processes the request and returns the results to the client. Many computers, not just one, can function as servers and can locate data on a network. Furthermore, servers can forward requests to other servers and create a chain reaction to process the original client's data request.

Uniform Resource Locator

Within the client–server environment of the Web, the uniform resource locator is the standard method of accessing the location of information resources on the Web. *Uniform resource locators* (URLs) are electronic addresses that identify a unique location of a data file. URLs serve the exact same function as an address in the U.S. Postal Service. If a letter is to be delivered in a timely fashion, an envelope is generally addressed with the recipient's name on the first line, the house number and street on the second line, and the city, state, and Zip code on the third. The standard for addressing envelopes is well known and works well. The standard format for entering a URL address is as follows:

protocol://host/path/file

where

> **protocol** is the method of transferring data from one computer to another (i.e., http)
>
> **host** is the name of the host computer
>
> **path** is the name of the directory on the host computer
>
> **file** is the name of a file in the directory

For example, the following URL uses the hypertext transfer protocol (http) to access a file that contains an index of education resources at the College of Chemistry at the University of California, Berkeley:

http://www.cchem.berkeley.edu/Education/index.html

where

> **http** is the protocol
>
> **www.cchem.berkeley.edu** is the host computer name
>
> **Education** is the path or directory
>
> **index.html** is the file name

For new users of the Web, the format of URLs may seem complicated. However, after frequent use they become second nature. Software browsers that provide the software facilities for locating information on the Web also provide URL address lists that can simply be clicked on to access the data file at the desired host computer or site.

The most commonly used protocol on the Web is *http*. Other less frequently used protocols are

FTP	file transfer protocol
Gopher	database and communications software system for searching for data in files
WAIS	wide area information server

The host name on many URLs will contain a suffix designating a type of organization. In the previous example, *edu* represents an educational institution. Other commonly used suffixes include

com	commercial enterprise
gov	government agency
mil	military agency
net	network service
org	nonprofit organization

These suffixes are not required but are considered good form conventions when establishing a host name.

Web Browsers and Search Engines

Searching for data and information on the Web using URLs requires software browsers. The most popular browsers—Mozilla Firefox and Internet Explorer—are available in versions for both Windows and Macintosh computers. It is quite possible that by the time this book is in print, new software browsers will be in use. However, the basic concept and nature of Web browsing is expected to remain the same.

Browsing software is used to access data files that are generally displayed as "pages" on the Web. Figure 8.4 is a sample page from the Mozilla Firefox Web browsing software. Web browsers generally provide a series of pull-down menus or navigation buttons that allow users to navigate or "surf" the Web. The location where a user starts a Web browsing session is referred to as the user's home page. Besides standard features such as save, copy, paste, and help, common basic navigational functions of browsers include the following:

Back	Returns to the previous page
Forward	Goes to the next page
Reload	Reloads the current page
Home	Returns to the user's home page

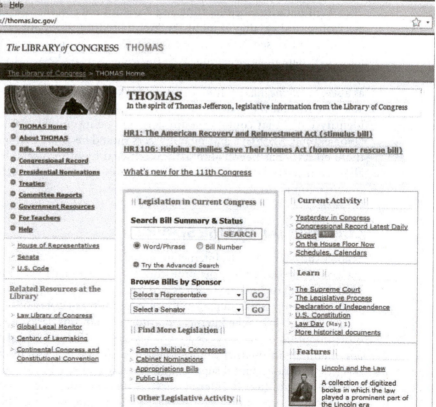

FIGURE 8.4 Sample Web Page.

Search	Transfers the user to a search engine
Print	Prints the current page
Security	Provides security information
Stop	Stops the current operation
Bookmark	Stores/lists frequently used URLs

Web browsers allow users to enter URLs in some designated areas to access the page of the requested data file. Depending on the overall traffic on the Internet, the number of users requesting data from the same host computer, and the speed of the data communications line being used to make the request, requests are usually processed in a matter of seconds. If too much traffic exists or if the host does not respond to a request, a message is displayed within a reasonable period of time, giving the user the option of continuing or canceling the request.

Web browsers rely on software called *hypertext markup language* (HTML) to establish and convert data files. "Filter" or conversion programs are available that will convert documents produced by word processing or some other software into an HTML or Web page document. However, other software languages—such as Java and JavaScript, developed by Sun Microsystems—have been introduced that are enhancing the way data are established and displayed on the Internet. Java adds a great deal more programmability and multimedia capabilities to data files on the Web.

Without assistance, locating and accessing data on the Web can be a formidable task. An electronic card catalog of all of the Web's holdings does not exist and never will, given its dynamic and loosely administered nature. Users can easily spend hours trying to locate some particular data or information. Web browsers provide keyword search capabilities that work similarly to database query languages. In addition, another type of software, referred to as a *search engine*, has evolved that provides keyword search facilities. Search engines are available at URLs on the Web and can save users a significant amount of time in attempting to identify URLs that contain the information being sought. Popular search engines include Google, Bing, AltaVista, and Yahoo!. Users should be aware that much of the data searched by these engines has been voluntarily submitted by other users or is gathered using various algorithms. By no means do search engines conduct complete searches of all the data resources on the Web.

COMMERCIAL ONLINE SERVICES

Schools can connect to the Internet in several ways. They establish their own Internet connection via a SLIP (serial line Internet protocol); they can connect via an online service provided by a local nonprofit organization such as a college, university, or government agency; or they can subscribe to a commercial online service such as an Internet service provider (ISP). When contemplating connecting to the Internet, educators should consider commercial providers, especially if other nonprofit online services are not available or if the technical expertise needed to establish and maintain an Internet connection is limited in the school district. The commercial online services provide technical support and are very effective in getting new users connected to the Internet. In addition to Internet service, they also provide access to content such as online newspapers, home shopping, financial reports, and so forth. Although users of commercial Internet providers can sign up for various usage plans, most schools will do well to negotiate a flat-rate fee plan that allows for unlimited usage. The competition among commercial online service providers such as Optimum Online or Verizon is keen and prices have generally been holding steady.

If commercial providers are not required for a school's connection to the Internet, educators may still want to become familiar with them for their own professional development and to understand what their students are likely using in their homes. The major commercial providers have not ignored education as part of their menu of services. On the contrary, educational services such as professional homework assistance, educational databases, and standard reference materials are available. Educational blogs and discussion groups sponsored by the National Education Association, the United Federation of Teachers, the National Principals Center, and the Association for Supervision and Curriculum Development are also available via these services and are excellent forums for communicating with other professionals on national issues.

The Internet has been described in this chapter as a dynamic, free, and voluntary community. Commercial activity has grown significantly, which means that commercial providers are having and will continue to have a more significant role in defining the Internet in the years to come. Based on such speculation, major corporate entities in the telephone, computer, and cable television industries have been developing strategies to provide Internet services and are willing to make significant financial investments to corner a substantial part of this market.

APPLICATIONS ON THE INTERNET

The Internet is a dynamic communications and information resource. Information of all sorts is constantly being added, deleted and, most importantly, shared among millions of people. For educators, the Internet can provide a pedagogically valuable array of skill activities such as writing, reading, and research, as well as a content-rich resource for culture, science, current events, and so forth. The list of possibilities and specific applications is endless, but most of these activities fall into several broad categories.

Global electronic mail (e-mail) is the most popular activity on the Internet. Although e-mail has existed for almost four decades, the Internet has made it available to the masses worldwide, making it easy to send or receive messages over thousands of miles or across the street. Teachers and students are establishing pen pal correspondences with others all over the globe. Furthermore, any delay in sending and receiving messages is limited only to the time it takes to collect, organize, and write one's thoughts; there is no waiting period of days or weeks while paper letters are hand delivered.

The Internet does not actually provide the e-mail software itself but works through URLs to route messages that have been composed and stored on local e-mail software systems. A school or school district that has established a local e-mail system would continue to use that same system and integrate it for use on the Internet.

Group e-mail including discussion groups, newsgroups, or electronic mailing lists such as LISTSERV extend the e-mail concept beyond the individual. E-mails can be sent to preestablished groups of individuals or posted to an electronic bulletin board for members of a group to read and respond as they wish. The messages stay on the electronic bulletin board for a given period of time. Generally, these groups identify a topic of common interest to all their members.

Electronic bulletin boards exist at all levels of education and in all subject areas. Activity-related bulletin boards on a host of topics, sponsored by state education departments, professional societies, museums, and libraries, are regularly being established. In addition to supporting discussion groups on the Internet, electronic bulletin boards are also being used by educators on local and commercial computer networks to discuss locally important issues.

Live conferencing organizes the discussion group concept into a real-time activity. The Internet provides a software system known as Internet Relay Chat (IRC), commonly known as *chat*. On the Internet, text-based "chat areas" or "chat rooms" are available on a host of topics. Live conferencing differs from discussion groups in that the discussion is live and text messages are posted as they are written and answered.

Organizing a real-time discussion group requires familiarity with the IRC software, which can be complicated for the average person using the Internet. However, commercial online services such as America Online and Elluminate provide software facilities for setting up chat and live conferencing areas that are easy to use. Administrators and teachers might use this feature to carry out informal conferences, thus eliminating the necessity of traveling many miles. The nature of live conferencing has also taken on another dimension, as live audio and video facilities are advanced for use on the Internet. This topic will be discussed more fully, later in this chapter, in the section titled "The Internet and Distance Learning."

File transfer protocol (or FTP) refers to the transfer and receiving of data files on the Internet. These files can include text, pictures, sound, and video. File transfer can occur in several ways, depending on how a user is connected to the Internet. In some cases, FTP is automatically included as a feature of the e-mail software system wherein users can send and receive files as attachments to a specific message. In other cases, files are made available to all members of the Internet community by invoking specific FTP software. The acts of sending and receiving data files are generally referred to as *uploading* and *downloading,* respectively. The Internet community is generous in what it allows users to access, especially for educational purposes. The National Aeronautics and Space Administration (NASA), for example, makes data resources available on many of its active space exploration projects, and the U.S. Weather Service updates data files on weather conditions throughout the world on a timely basis. When downloading and uploading files, users should be sure to have virus protection software installed to scan files that are made available to the public. Also, when accessing data files, especially images, sound, and video, users should be aware of any copyright restrictions associated with the further use of the data. The copyright guidelines discussed earlier in Chapter 7 also apply to materials downloaded from the Internet.

Through a software feature known as Telnet, a user on one computer can literally connect to and use the resources of another computer. Rather than downloading a single file from NASA's central computer system, for example, a user might actually be able to connect to and use all the resources available on NASA's computer. Though theoretically possible, most computer facilities on the Internet do not allow outside users to access their computers directly for practical and security reasons. Permission is required along with establishing proper sign-on procedures with user IDs and passwords.

Information navigation, also known as "Net surfing," "cruising," and "Web browsing," continues to grow in popularity. Using Web browser software such as Internet Explorer or Firefox Mozilla, students, teachers, and administrators can access volumes of information that have been made available by schools, museums, businesses, and other organizations. Furthermore, navigating the Web no longer simply means accessing information that others have published but increasingly involves publishing and posting one's own information using blogs, wikis, podcasts, and YouTube videos. Although not all of this information is educationally valuable, a certain amount of it is. Students and teachers can spend hours looking up pages of pertinent information on a topic and not even touch the surface of all that is available on the Internet. Reference materials, maps, art collections, frog dissection simulation software, the Periodic Table of Elements, the White House, and the U.S. Congress are all available with a click of a mouse. Never in the history of humankind has such an extensive collection of informational resources been so readily available. However, given the availability of all of this information, much of which is uncensored and not reviewed for accuracy, users and especially young people need to be educated on how to sift the Web for the valuable material. Once proficiency is developed in browsing the Web, the informational rewards can be abundant. Andrew Keen (2007) in his provocatively titled book, *The Cult of the Amateur*, rails against the "self-broadcasting" culture that has evolved on the Internet, particularly on social network Web sites, blogs, and wikis. He expresses concern that the sources of the material published and posted on the World Wide Web cannot be determined: a trained expert or a poorly informed amateur. He posits that these Web sites are places where mob rule has replaced expertise. Jeff Howe (2008), in his book *Crowdsourcing*, agrees with Keen to a degree but also sees a fine distinction between mob rule and democracy and that some tolerance of the former is needed to allow the latter to survive. Even though a good deal of the material on the Web is questionable, it still provides a medium where everybody can state a position and contribute their opinion.

Social networking is emerging as one of the most popular activities on the Internet, especially among young people. The fundamental Internet application for most of them is a social networking site where they digitally establish who they are and have access to friends and digital acquaintances. Social network sites (SNS) such as MySpace, Facebook, YouTube, and Twitter attract millions of individuals. For many, these SNSs have become part of their daily routine, comparable to eating, bathing, and sleeping. Rather than reading a newspaper or watching television, many young people spend hours upon hours sharing information about themselves and reading about others on SNSs, blogs, and instant messages. Furthermore, they are no longer constrained by access to a desktop computer but increasingly utilize portable digital appliances (PDAs) to maintain contact with their Web world.

According to a national survey by the Pew Internet & American Life Project:

- 55% of online teens have created a personal profile online, and 55% have used social networking sites like MySpace or Facebook.
- 48% of teens visit social networking websites daily or more often; 26% visit once a day, 22% visit several times a day.
- Older girls ages 15-17 are more likely to have used social networking sites and online profiles; 70% of older girls have used an online social network compared with 54% of older boys, and 70% of older girls have created an online profile, while only 57% boys have done so. (Lenhart & Madden, 2007)

The Pew study defined a social network site as a Web site where users can create a profile and connect that profile to other profiles for the purposes of making an explicit personal network. Boyd and Elison (2007) expanded the definition as follows:

> We define social network sites as web-based services that allow individuals to (1) construct a public or semi-public profile within a bounded system, (2) articulate a list of other users with whom they share a connection, and (3) view and traverse their list of connections and those made by others within the system. (Boyd & Elison, 2007)

SNSs have been expanding and integrating their services by providing access to blogs, instant messaging or texting services, and a host of other informational facilities so that a social networker's day is filled with engaging in one-to-one messages with friends, reading and contributing to their favorite blogs, and accessing a plethora of information on a variety of subjects, interests, and hobbies. Users of these services are not simply passive receivers of information but providers as well. All of this Internet activity has important implications for educators, especially in providing the guidance needed for young people to use these facilities safely and effectively. Young people have to be educated about how much information they make available about themselves in the digital world. The Internet lacks oversight and supervision, and unfortunately, predators—be they sexual, commercial, deviant, or hate mongering—actively seek out impressionable young people. Stories are reported almost on a daily basis about someone who was able to take advantage of a young person because of access to personal information found on a social networking site. There is also a concern that overuse of the Internet is leading to an addiction that precludes young people from participating in other activities. Byun and colleagues (2009) identified 120 studies over a 10-year period that examined this issue. Although the data is still emerging, Byun and colleagues speculate that adolescents are at a point in their life cycle where they are very vulnerable to harmful addictive agents and that the Internet may be one of these agents. In sum, the Internet provides the most significant communications and information tool ever developed; however, young people need guidance on how to use its resources. Along with parents, educators are in pivotal positions to provide this guidance.

MULTIMEDIA AND THE WEB

Many educational applications on the World Wide Web rely extensively on text (e-mail, discussion groups, bulletin boards, instant messages, etc.) for instruction and communication. In the early 1990s, the usefulness of extending this discussion to other media such as audio or video would have been questionable because the Internet—mainly because of limited bandwidth—did not handle media beyond text very well. Now multimedia applications on the Web are becoming commonplace. In teaching and learning, a picture can indeed be worth a thousand words. Full-motion video, capable of transmitting thousands of pictures accompanied by an audio track in minutes, can perhaps be worth much more. However, even though pedagogically important, producing high-quality multimedia material for the Web is still evolving and can require substantial resources, particularly in the time it takes to script, develop, and edit quality instructional multimedia. Nonetheless, the potential of multimedia for Web-based learning activities cannot be ignored and needs to be considered. Readers may wish to review the material in Chapter 7 on the "Five Levels of Digital Media," namely, text, stilled images, animations, audio, and video.

Designing Multimedia for Web-Based Learning

In developing multimedia for Web-based learning applications, teachers and technical assistants should start by considering student access to the Internet. The effective transmission of sound, animation, and full-motion video on the Internet depends on computer hardware and communications capabilities. If the goal of the application is to provide learning opportunities to students in their homes, then teachers should carefully consider the extent to which multimedia can be effectively used, because not all students have access to the Internet in their homes and some of those who do are using slow-speed modem connections. Providing a good deal of multimedia content requiring students to download large media files may be frustrating if hardware capability or transmission speeds are not available in the home environment or unaffordable to the targeted population. On the other hand, where teachers control students' computer environments, such as in a school's media center or computer laboratory with high-speed modem access, then Web-based multimedia applications can be very successful.

In developing multimedia materials for the Web, teachers must strive for decent quality. A video that has the look or feel of amateurism will not be effective in many learning environments. Given the superb media quality that students are accustomed to viewing on television, in films, and in video games, educators have found it difficult to compete. In traditional classrooms, instructors rely on materials such as videocassettes, videodiscs, or DVDs that they have purchased or rented from commercial or other professional producers. Delivering these same materials over the Web, even locally to a school's media center, may be impossible because they may not be available in digital form. To copy them for use on a computer network may be a serious infringement of copyright laws.

Given the issues of student access to technology, technical support requirements, and difficulties involved in producing or obtaining high-quality multimedia materials, teachers should consider providing substantive Web-based animation, audio, or video material only if it in fact adds to the instructional value of an activity—not merely to add pizzazz or technological glitz to the course content. Certain subject matter is significantly enhanced when multimedia illustrations, animation, or video are added to the presentation. The sciences make extensive use of computer simulations to conduct experiments and should seek to continue to do so in Web-based applications. High-quality documentaries such as those produced by educational television, National Geographic, or the Annenberg Media Project can add significant pedagogical value to a class presentation. Although teachers have to consider the costs and benefits carefully, costs alone should not preclude schools from engaging in multimedia production. The technology for producing video is becoming easier and more common. With Webcams, Flip Video portable recording devices, and relatively inexpensive microphones, anybody can develop a decent quality multimedia presentation. Furthermore, with facilities such as YouTube, podcasting, and SlideShare (for sharing PowerPoint presentations), it has become relatively easy to upload this material on the Web at minimal cost.

Desktop Videoconferencing

Point-to-point videoconferencing using analog television transmitters and receivers has been available for many years. This analog format, however, does not work on the World Wide Web. Most point-to-point analog videoconferencing systems operate in dedicated spaces or distance learning classrooms in which students attend at specific times. Desktop videoconferencing systems using digital transmission via the Internet, on the other hand, have the potential of operating at any place and any time.

On the Web, desktop videoconferencing is being used to replace synchronous chat areas in which students and/or instructors establish some specific time to be available to each other to answer questions or to collaborate on a project. Rather than being limited to text messages, digital videoconferencing allows participants to see and speak to each other in a more efficient and personal manner.

Desktop videoconferencing technology has continued to evolve over the past 15 years. The popular CUSeeMe technology, developed at Cornell University in the 1990s, has advanced beyond the postage-stamp-sized jerky image. Streaming audio techniques have evolved to include streaming video capable of providing relatively high-quality images in synchronization with the audio track. Live Meeting (Microsoft) and iChat (Apple Macintosh) are examples of commonly used software products that allow desktop audio and video conferencing.

Access to sufficiently high-speed computer and communications resources remains a must. As mentioned earlier in this section, educators need to be aware of what access their students have to the Internet. Slow-speed access or no access at all are still evident in students' homes in many school districts, particularly among poorer and immigrant populations. As communications technology advances and the movement to high-speed Internet access continues in the United States, desktop videoconferencing and video streaming, whether used in real-time (synchronous) or anytime (asynchronous), activities will play a more significant role in Web-based instruction.

THE INTERNET AND EDUCATION

In developing Internet applications for education, administrators should consider how to integrate the Internet with other data communications facilities in a school district. Although many school districts rely on the Internet exclusively for their data communications systems, it does not necessarily have to replace existing facilities such as LANs and WANs but can be used to enhance them. *Intranets,* which are LANs or WANs that use Internet software tools such as Web browsers, are mini-Internets that are useful for controlling access to sensitive data, reducing data traffic, and speeding access to frequently used data files. An intranet depends on local software systems (e-mail, file servers, databases, etc.) to accomplish much of its activity.

Global E-Mail

Global e-mail applications have educational value mainly because they require and aid in the development of basic skills such as reading, writing, and researching. In addition, they can literally be conducted around the world so that electronic cultural exchanges take place with minimal cost or effort. Once a school has access to e-mail, implementing provocative e-mail applications is relatively easy. Examples of e-mail applications abound in the professional literature, including these:

- *Local news reporters:* Have students assume the role of local news reporters and have them swap news stories with students in other locales.
- *Local weather forecasters:* This activity is the same as the previous one but asks students to report on weather conditions. Expand on this same theme and trace weather patterns (rainfall, snowfall, days hotter than 90°) over the course of a semester or academic year.
- *Conduct surveys:* Conduct surveys with a number of schools around the country or world on a variety of topics (important people, favorite singer, most important event in the 21st century, most important event of the current year).
- *Problem solvers:* Develop a problem (mathematical, scientific, riddle) and solicit opinions for its solution.
- *Story starters:* A very popular activity is to start a story and have others add to it to see how long the story can become.

Organizations such as NASA, with its K–12 Project, and the National Geographic Society, with its Kids Network, provide ideas and limited assistance in helping teachers develop e-mail activities. Several sites on the Internet, such as Kidlink, are set up specifically to facilitate worldwide communications among students through e-mail and discussion groups.

Information Navigation

Navigating the Web for information and communication is becoming one of the more popular applications. Students as well as teachers and the general public do it just for fun. Internet cafes have opened up around the country, providing a social environment in which people hang out and surf the Web. For a modest fee, one sits at a computer workstation or hooks up a laptop and communicates with colleagues on a social network, participates on a blog, collects information on a term paper that is due, checks up on a local sports team, reviews the stock market, or starts looking up airline flights on Travelocity. They may take a break, sip espresso, and then go back to the workstation for more Net surfing.

Schools are already providing this type of environment—minus the espresso—in school media centers, computer labs, and libraries. Navigating the Web can be a significant "time sink" and is especially enjoyable when valuable informational experiences result. Educators should develop activities such as WebQuests that encourage both fun and more serious uses of the Internet. Ideas for navigating the Web for educational activities should be predicated upon the age of the navigators, subject area, and skill level. Visiting the numerous Web sites that contain resources and activities related to education demonstrates the value of the Web. Administrators might find interesting information on school policy at the Council of the Great City Schools Web site or become acquainted with new grant programs in the NSF database. Teachers can get lesson plans and other teaching ideas from the Galaxy directory or the Texas Education Network. For students, Ask Jeeves is both fun and educational, the Kidlink site is excellent for participating in international discussion groups, and the University of Arizona site provides many useful resources for high school students engaged in space research projects.

Several education-oriented Web sites relate to specific subject areas and disciplines. If a particular subject area is not listed, readers are encouraged to use a search engine such as Google or Yahoo! where, in addition to keyword searching, a list of subject categories is provided. Generally, when looking for information on broad subject areas such as history, biology, or mathematics, so much information will be provided that it will take hours to read and consider. Searching for resources on the Internet is like using an electronic card catalog or database: Users need to practice to hone and narrow a request for information. One benefit of using a Web browser for this activity is that users can easily collect useful URLs and store them electronically on address lists, bookmarks, and other Web site organizing programs. For new users, allow time for practice and provide instruction on using address lists and bookmarks to save URLs. As with other applications of instructional technology, particularly for new or intermediate learners, collaborative activities should be encouraged.

In developing Internet navigating applications for students, educators must take on some responsibility for screening the materials that students might accidentally or purposefully come across. The Internet is a free and voluntary community with little oversight. Some of the material is unsuitable for children, including child pornography and hate-group activity. Children need to be educated about the world around them; however, schools have some obligation to protect children from material that might be harmful. Presently, adults (teachers, parents, and paraprofessionals) may simply have to provide guidance and be alert to damaging uses of the Internet. Software—such as CYBERsitter and Net Nanny—has been developed that will assist schools and other organizations in screening some of the material that is delivered from the Internet on to their networks.

Creating Web Sites

The development of Web sites is growing in popularity as an educational activity. Developing a Web site is not as complicated as one might assume but requires becoming familiar with a programming language such as HTML or an HTML authoring or filtering program. Dozens of Web authoring programs have been developed that make creating and editing Web pages no more difficult than using a word processing program. Most schools have created their own Web sites. To develop a Web site, a school either has to have its own server with a direct connection to the Internet, generally referred to as a *serial line Internet protocol* (SLIP), or, if connected via commercial or public online service, it must obtain permission from the provider to develop a Web site. Many commercial providers make this service available for free, but some will charge a modest fee.

Developing a school Web site is a stimulating and educationally valuable activity; however, schools must think seriously about how they want themselves portrayed to the Internet community. The major purposes of the Internet are communication and information sharing. When establishing a Web site, schools become information providers and should provide useful information about their students, academic programs, and related activities. Suggestions for developing a Web site abound. For instance:

- Avoid too much clutter per page, which can make it difficult for readers to access important information.
- Avoid "electronic vanity plate" syndrome via extensive photographs of one or two individuals.
- Highlight the school, not the technology itself.
- Keep current events current.
- Assume that many computers in students' homes have limited-speed modems, so use graphics in moderation or allow for text-only access options.

For more information, Exworthy Educational Resources maintains an excellent Web site that provides ideas, templates, and examples of Web sites of schools from around the world as well as a plethora of resources for educators.

Increasingly, individuals, small groups, a class, an individual teacher, a student, or group of students doing a class project are now developing their own Web sites. As the Internet continues to evolve, providing information on a Web site is becoming a routine activity for all educators and students.

Blogging on the Web

As mentioned earlier in this chapter, social networking sites (SNSs) are increasing in popularity among young people. Perhaps the most popular technological tool used in most SNSs is a blog. A blog, abbreviation for Weblog, is a Web site that can easily be updated and edited with entries or postings that appear in reverse chronological order. Most blogs provide facilities for posting text, images, and increasingly sound and video clips. The following are examples of the variety of ways they can be used in classrooms:

- *Sharing News*   teachers and students can share news about events and happenings in the class or school.
- *Homework Assignments*   students share ideas and comments on a reading assignment or a homework problem.
- *Showcase Student Work*   teachers use the blogs to post student artwork and writings assignments.
- *Individual or Group Reflection*   individual students or groups of students reflect on what they have learned.

Most course management systems (CMSs) provide blogs as part of their repertoire of tools; however, if a school does not have a CMS, there are a number of companies that provide blogging services free of charge for education purposes:

- 21Classes Cooperative Learning—www.21classes.com
- ePals SchoolBlog—
- www.epals.com
- Edublogs—edublogs.org

A number of articles have been written giving credence to using blogs in classroom activities for student writing, higher-order thinking exercises, new information literacy, and reflective practice (Zawilinski, 2009; Leu et al., 2007; Coiro & Dobler, 2007). It is likely that blogging will advance as an instructionally valuable aspect of the Internet and World Wide Web.

Course Management Software

Up until a few years ago, teachers wishing to develop a Web site for their classes would have had to use hypertext markup language (HTML) as their software base for creating all Web pages. Figure 8.5 is an example of the HTML language for a sample course Web page (see Figure 8.6). HTML is not a difficult language to use, but because of its cryptic style that makes use of various special characters, tags, and two-character instruction codes, it may prove difficult to the average teacher. In the past, teachers who wanted to teach on the Web either learned this language to produce the Web content or would be provided with the technical assistance to do so.

Web developers now have the option of using an HTML filter, authoring, or conversion software program to develop HTML documents. These filters generally provide a menu-driven, relatively easy-to-use interface for developing Web pages in HTML. They are continually evolving so that even sophisticated routines such as those generally provided by more advanced software languages such as Java and JavaScript are now becoming available by pointing and clicking on a menu. Learning to develop relatively straightforward Web pages is now no more difficult than learning an advanced feature on standard word-processing software packages. In fact, the latest version of Microsoft Word allows the user to automatically save any word processing document in HTML format. Even electronic presentation software packages, such as Microsoft's PowerPoint, which are designed to integrate images, text, sound, and animation into digital slide shows, have "Save as HTML" features for automatically converting these shows into Web pages. The point here is that developing HTML documents is becoming relatively easy and, with a little bit of guidance, requires about the same technical skill as using a standard word-processing program.

More recently, course management software (CMS) (also referred to as learning management software or LMS) packages designed specifically for teaching on the Web have become available. CMS packages provide a complete set of software tools for creating Web-based course materials, including Web sites, electronic bulletin boards, e-mail systems, test generators, chat areas, and multimedia facilities. Almost all of these packages provide a course template that makes developing Web-based course materials no more difficult than filling in the blanks and selecting menu options. CMS packages are frequently used to enhance lessons and materials presented in traditional classrooms. Students at home can continue to discuss a lesson via e-mail or chat rooms, participate in a collaborative project, review reading and other materials, or ask a

```
<TR ALIGN = "LEFT" VALIGN ="TOP"
<TD NOWRAP = "NoWrap"><IMG SRC = "bullet.gif"><A HREF=
"a722week.html"></A><B>Communications Center</B></TD>
<TD><IMG SRC = "bullet.gif">
<AHREF = "http://listserv.cuny.edu/archives/ADSUP-
722.HTML"></A><B>Archives</B></TD>
<TD NOWRAP = "SNoWrap"><IMG SRC = "bullet.gif"><A HREF =
"a722pics.html"></A><B>Getting Started/Help Desk</B></TD>
</TR></TABLE><$><B>Figure 7.6- Sample Course Home Page </B></P></BODY></HTML>
```

FIGURE 8.5 A Portion of the HTML Code for the Course Home Page in Figure 8.6.

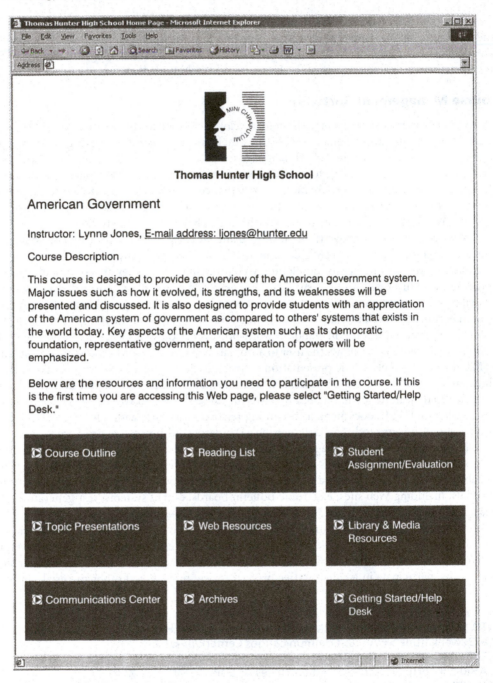

FIGURE 8.6 Sample Course Home Page.

teacher a question about an assignment. CMS packages are also being used to develop entire Web-based, distance learning instructional modules and courses, which will be discussed further in Chapter 9.

In years passed, there were a number of excellent CMS products available. For better or worse, Blackboard, Inc., has been most aggressive in acquiring CMS companies and products such as WebCT and ANGEL and has eliminated much of the competition for this software. Currently it has about 80% share of the commercial CMS market. Furthermore, Blackboard, Inc., filed for and has been involved for several years in a major patent infringement lawsuit against one of its remaining major competitors, Desire2Learn. As a result, the CMS acquisition decision has basically been reduced to selecting Blackboard or an open source product such as Moodle or Sakai, neither of which provide the full range of features that Blackboard supports. Figure 8.7 provides a list of some of the features that a CMS typically provides.

In deciding to acquire a CMS, good practice suggests establishment of a school-district-wide committee or task force that includes teachers, technical support staff, and students. A district-wide approach is suggested so that a common Web interface can be provided to facilitate teacher training, technical support, and student access to course materials. Evaluation criteria should be established on which all faculty users and support staff can agree. Ease of use, training and staff development requirements, and software stability and reliability may be more important in certain environments than more-advanced technical features or capabilities.

In adopting a CMS for a district, evaluators should also keep in mind that they are dealing with a rapidly evolving technology. CMS and other software systems that support applications on the Internet are being pioneered by small companies where competition is fierce and unpredictable. To remain competitive, software products are being upgraded and enhanced with new features every few months. Although desirable with respect to improving product capability, this rapid change can be unsettling for long-range course planning where design, development, and

---

Chat (synchronous discussions)
Conversion tools (e.g., from word processing files)
Desktop videoconferencing
Whiteboard
Discussion groups
Student groups
Electronic mail
Grading
Indexing of course material by instructor, major, field, course name
Individualized student assignments
Multimedia support
Related resources
Sharing materials across courses
Standard design with flexible customization
Student progress reporting
Blogging
Wiki
Template development tools
Test generator

FIGURE 8.7 Features/Capabilities Provided on Course Management Systems.

evaluation can take several years. Web-based course designers and planners have to be prepared to be flexible and open to new products and/or changes in existing products. Small school districts and school districts with modest resources, which want to experiment with a CMS, can contract with established vendors such as Blackboard, Inc., to provide hosting services. Rather than actually acquiring the software, school districts pay Blackboard to host the CMS software for them on Blackboard's own servers. School districts can continue with this arrangement or can decide at a later date to purchase the full CMS. One of the significant benefits of contracting for hosting services is that school districts do not have to invest in the technological hardware, software, and people infrastructure to maintain the integrity and stability of the CMS.

Open source CMSs such as Moodle or Sakai are pretty much free to acquire, but the school district takes on a good deal of responsibility for installing and maintaining the software. If a good technology infrastructure and experienced technical staff are in place, school districts might find open source CMSs cost-effective investments.

The Internet and Distance Learning

With the expansion of the Internet into people's homes and places of business, distance learning is becoming more popular in the United States. Early distance learning projects employed passive analog communications such as one-way television and radio. In the 1980s, two-way analog communications using videoconferencing technologies began to dominate distance learning applications. Today, data communications facilities as provided by the Internet and other large networks are beginning to redefine distance learning. Initiatives such as the Florida Virtual School, the Georgia Statewide Academic and Medical System (GSAMS), and the Iowa Communications Network (ICN) are making excellent use of data communications networks in providing highly interactive distance learning activities.

The Internet is a fully interactive, digital technology that will eventually redefine distance learning in several ways. First, students will no longer have to group themselves together into a common classroom or space to participate. Internet technology is such that students can actively participate in a lesson from any place (schools, day care centers, business establishments, or homes) with a connected computer. Second, students will no longer necessarily have to participate at the same time. In digital format, lessons can be delivered and stored and then called up by students as needed. Interactivity is achieved asynchronously through electronic bulletin boards, discussion groups, and e-mail. Third, instruction delivery will be an integration of several resources from which students can customize their lesson. Multiple resources may already exist, but students need to budget their time and schedule their learning in a sequential mode, such as (1) attend a lecture, (2) go to the library, (3) collect thoughts, (4) write a paper, (5) receive teacher comments, and so on. On the Internet, students may have at their immediate disposal a resource that includes the teacher as well as other instructional materials such as videos, computer simulations, and reference works. A student could possibly integrate the sequence by listening to the teacher for a while, consulting a reference work, looking at a simulation, sending an e-mail message, and then once again listening to the teacher. In the not-too-distant future, new digital facilities such as video on demand and split-screen monitors will allow students to do several of these tasks simultaneously.

Advances are being made in communications technology such as wireless digital communications, digital subscriber lines (DSL), cable modems, integrated service digital network (ISDN), and other high-speed transmission rates. In the future, much of what can be done with text on the Internet will be done routinely with live or real-time digital videoconferencing.

Educators, especially those already investing in distance learning applications, should keep abreast of these and other developments that will have a significant impact on the potential of the Internet as a distance learning medium. This will be discussed further in Chapter 9.

Summary

This chapter reviews the state of data communications as applied to education—specifically, the evolution of the Internet in terms of its applicability for instructional activities. Important concepts associated with global communications, information access, and new learning technologies are considered.

Data communications have been evolving and expanding for almost five decades. In the 1990s, this evolution resulted in the Internet or network of networks. It is a truly global network that expanded rapidly in the 1990s and now reaches hundreds of millions of people worldwide. Every indication is that the Internet will continue to evolve and become a major component of computer and communications applications in all areas of endeavor, including education.

A critical catalyst for the Internet's evolution was the development of the World Wide Web, a hypertext- and multimedia-based software system for establishing and sharing information resources. Through user-friendly Web browser software, individuals and groups throughout the world can access and share information on a system with standard protocols.

The major applications of the Internet are global e-mail, discussion groups, live conferencing, file transfer, direct access to other computer systems, information navigation, and social networking—all of which can be adapted for instructional activities. More detailed examples of Internet-based instructional activities for e-mail, information navigation, and information sharing are also presented.

Increasingly, course management software (CMS) packages are being used to develop Web-based course materials. As school districts do more online instruction, they will likely have to consider whether or not to use—purchase or contract for hosting services—CMS packages.

The chapter concludes with a brief examination of and speculation on the role that the Internet will play in defining and expanding the possibilities for distance learning applications. Future advances in digital video communications will significantly expand present concepts of distance learning.

Key Concepts and Questions

1. Data communications have evolved steadily for almost five decades. How has this evolution affected your daily activities? How do you see this evolution continuing over the next 10 years?

2. The Internet is a relatively new phenomenon. How do you explain its popularity and growth from the 1990s to the present? Will this popularity and growth continue? Explain.

3. Many terms such as *cyberspace, information superhighway,* and *the Web* are used interchangeably to refer to the Internet. How do you explain the World Wide Web in relation to the Internet? Why has the Web become such an important aspect of the popularity of the Internet?

4. Applications on the Internet are almost endless and depend on users' imagination and creativity. How do you categorize the major Internet applications? Are they adaptable for instructional and other educational uses? Explain. In developing a plan for using the Internet in an instructional program, what applications would you consider first? Why?

5. Distance learning has had limited applications in education. How do you see distance learning evolving or changing? What role, if any, will the Internet play in changing or redefining distance learning? Explain.

Suggested Activity

Hands-on activity: Using a search engine such as Google, Bing, or Yahoo! identify, visit, and develop lists of useful URLs for the following individuals:

- A school building administrator (to help in his or her day-to-day activities)
- A district-level curriculum specialist

- A teacher in designing new lessons (select whatever subject area or level with which you are familiar)
- A technology coordinator, in keeping abreast with the latest developments in integrating technology into the curriculum

References

Boyd, D. M., & Elison, N. B. (2007). Social network sites: Definition, history, and scholarship. *Journal of Computer-Mediated Communication, 13*(1). Retrieved May 11, 2009, from http://jcmc.indiana.edu/vol13/issue1/boyd.ellison.html#history

Byun, S., Ruffini, C., Mills, J., Douglas, A., Niang, M., Stepchenkova, S., Lee, S., Loutfi, J., Lee, J., Atallah, M., & Blanton, M. (2009). Internet Addiction: Metasynthesis of 1996–2006 quantitative research. *CyberPsychology & Behavior 12*(2). Retrieved May 12, 2009, from http://www.liebertonline.com/doi/abs/10.1089/cpb.2008.0102

Coiro, J., & Dobler, E. (2007). Exploring the online reading Comprehension strategies used by sixth-grade skilled readers to search for and locate information on the Internet. *Reading Research Quarterly, 42*(2), 214–257.

Connecting every pupil to the world. (1995, December 28). *New York Times,* p. A20.

CTIA. (2003). CTIA's annualized wireless industry survey results. Retrieved April 2, 2004, from http://files.ctia.org/img/survey/2003_endyear/752x571/Annual_Table_Dec_2003.jpg

Ellsworth, J. H. (1994). *Education on the Internet.* Indianapolis: Macmillan Computer.

Fisher, L. M. (1996, January 2). Surfing the Internet sets the agenda for software. *New York Times,* p. C15.

Golden, C., & Katz, L. F. (2008). *The race between education and technology.* Cambridge, MA: Harvard University Press.

Howe, J. (2008). Crowdsourcing: *Why the power of the crowd is driving the future of business.* New York: Crown Business.

Internet World Stats. (2009). *World Internet and population statistics.* Retrieved May 5, 2009, from http://www.internetworldstats.com/stats.htm

Keen, A. (2007). *The cult of the amateur.* New York: Doubleday.

Lenhart, A., & Madden, M. (2007, January 3). Social networking websites and teens: An overview. Internet Project Data Memo. Pew Internet & American Life Project. Retrieved May 11, 2009, from http://www.pewinternet.org/~/media//Files/Reports/2007/PIP_SNS_Data_Memo_Jan_2007.pdf.pdf

Leu, D. J., Zawilinski, L., Castek, J., Banerjee, M., Housand, B., & Liu, Y. (2007). What is new about the new literacies of online reading comprehension? In A. Berger, L. Rush, & J. Eakle (Eds.), *Secondary school reading and writing: What research reveals for classroom practices* (pp. 37–68). Chicago: NCTE/NCRL.

Markoff, J. (2009, February 15). Do we need a new Internet? *New York Times,* p. AR27. Retrieved February 15, 2009, from http://www.nytimes.com/2009/02/15/weekinreview/15markoff.html?th&emc=th

Negroponte, N. (1995). *Being digital.* New York: Knopf.

Nichols, P. M. (1999, January 17). The newest wave: Made-for-the-Internet movies. *New York Times,* p. AR27.

Park, J., & Staresina, L. (2004, May 6). Tracking U.S. trends. *Education Week, 23*(35), 64–67.

Shirky, C. (1995). *Voices from the Net.* Emeryville, CA: Ziff-Davis.

Stoll, C. (1995). *Silicon snake oil: Second thoughts about the information superhighway.* New York: Doubleday.

Williams, B. (1995). *The Internet for teachers.* Foster City, CA: IDG Books Worldwide.

Zawilinski, L. (2009). HOT blogging: A framework for blogging to promote higher order thinking. *The Reading Teacher, 62*(8), 650–661.

Zworykin, V. (1975, July 4). Interview conducted by M. Heyer and A. Pinsky [Broadcast by the Radio Corporation of America, Inc.]. IEEE History Center, Rutgers University, New Brunswick, NJ. Retrieved April 5, 2004, from http://www.ieee.org/organizations/history_center/oral_histories/transcripts/zworykin21.html

Chapter 9

Distance Learning

In April 1997, educators from 22 countries met in Salzburg, Austria, to attend a 9-day seminar, the focus of which was planning and implementing distance learning projects for teaching English as a foreign language in their countries. Participants shared the experiences of their homelands. In Iceland, radio transmission and the Internet were being used to provide instruction to fishermen who spend weeks at sea. In Indonesia, television was being used to provide basic language literacy to inhabitants of the hundreds of islands that make up this country. In Pakistan, a combination of mail and satellite television was being considered to improve English language skills in villages in the remote northern mountain provinces. These images of great distances, geographic obstacles, and scattered populations are frequently invoked as the basic rationale for distance learning programs or courses. At this same seminar, participants from Great Britain and the United States also described programs for students in large metropolitan areas, such as London or New York City, who take asynchronous Internet courses "at a distance" within a mile or two of their schools for the convenience of studying in their homes or places of business.

Educators throughout the world, whether in rural or urban areas, are increasingly considering developing distance learning as part of their academic programs. For rural and isolated communities, distance learning can be the vehicle to conquer geography and space between teachers and students. In populous metropolitan areas, distance learning is sometimes seen as a mechanism for fitting education into the busy lives of older students who struggle to find the time to balance careers, family responsibilities, and schooling.

Distance learning through the mail, radio, and television has an extensive history, but newer technologies such as digital communications and networking now make it much easier for educators to provide some form of distance learning for their students. Conquering space and time—a daunting venture in the not too distant past—is becoming more commonplace as computers, communications, and video technologies are being used to bring learning to virtually any place on earth at anytime. The implications of the newer digital and communications technologies for education are extensive and are being recounted in journals, newspapers, and books every day. Neil Rudenstine (1997), former president of Harvard University, observed that the Internet and other electronic networks allow communications to take place at all hours and across distances and permit a significant extension of the scope, continuity, and even the quality of certain forms of instructional interaction. Indeed, these technologies are having an enormous influence on traditional education while redefining our concept of distance learning.

In this chapter, we examine distance learning from several perspectives, including the postsecondary level. The rationale is that many school districts have collaborated with colleges and universities or as participants in regional and state consortia for developing and delivering distance learning to adult as well as K–12 students.

DISTANCE LEARNING DEFINED

Distance education, distance teaching, distance learning, open learning, distributed learning, asynchronous learning, telelearning, and blended learning are some of the terms used to describe an educational process in which the teacher and students are physically separated.

Distance education is the term that has most commonly been used for several decades. As an all-inclusive term, *distance education* has served well to define the physical separation of teaching and learning. However, in recent years, the term *distance learning* has become popular, particularly in the United States, to define this separation. Although used interchangeably with *distance education*, *distance learning* puts an emphasis on the "learner." Indeed, the concept of student-centered learning has become popular for all forms of education, distance or otherwise, but is especially appropriate when students need to take on greater responsibility for their learning, as is the case when doing so from a distance.

Within this definition, distance learning can take on many different forms. Figures 9.1, 9.2, and 9.3 illustrate three common forms of distance learning. Although they all fall within the definition of distance learning, they have very different components and characteristics.

DISTANCE LEARNING TECHNOLOGIES: A QUICK OVERVIEW

Figure 9.1 is an illustration of distance learning using broadcast television. In this model, a teacher delivers a live lecture over a television network into student homes via video technology synchronously (at the same time). The benefit of this format is that the lesson can be sent

FIGURE 9.1 Broadcast Television. *Source: Distance Learning: Making Connections Across Virtual Space and Time,* by Anthony G. Picciano, © 2001.

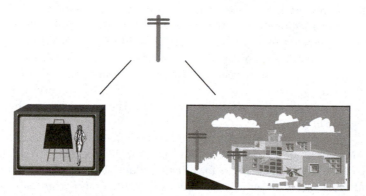

FIGURE 9.2 Two-Way Videoconferencing. *Source: Distance Learning: Making Connections Across Virtual Space and Time,* by Anthony G. Picciano, © 2001.

FIGURE 9.3 Asynchronous Learning Network.   *Source: Distance Learning: Making Connections Across Virtual Space and Time,* by Anthony G. Picciano, © 2001.

into many student homes over a broad geographic area and can include media-rich illustrations, simulations, and video clips. In recent years, instructional material used originally for broadcasting purposes have also been converted into videotape or DVD formats so that they can be rebroadcast over and over again as preprogrammed televised courses. Television, whether live broadcast or preprogrammed, is most effective in distance learning when accompanied by well-designed study guides. As a passive medium, television requires support systems that enable students to ask questions using telephone, the Internet, or some other communications systems.

Although most distance learning television is broadcast—that is, sent over the airwaves for anyone with an antenna to receive—some schools also use "narrowcast" transmission for limited distribution to a region or locality of approximately 20 to 25 miles. Narrowcast for distance learning, also referred to as Instructional Television Fixed Service (ITFS), requires a microwave transmitter and a transmission studio. Special receiver antennae are required by the students to access the microwave transmission. ITFS is especially effective in rural and less-crowded airwave spaces where interference is at a minimum. ITFS can also relay transmissions or "feed" from other sources such as satellite or cable television systems, thereby expanding the programming available.

Television will continue to be used for distance learning in the future; however, the technologies used for transmission are evolving rapidly. In the 20th century, broadcasting over the airwaves using transmitters and antennae for reception dominated television in most countries. But satellite and cable television services that can significantly improve and integrate television transmissions with digital technologies have evolved. Direct satellite services are now available for the modest cost of a small (18-inch diameter) satellite dish. Cable television and telephone companies have invested billions of dollars in providing fiber-optic, satellite, and broadband services to people's homes. One of these will likely emerge as the dominant technology of the 21st century. Regardless, it is safe to say that distance learning will benefit significantly from an integrated digital system capable of delivering video, telephone, and digital (computer, Internet) services via one transmitting and receiving technology.

Figure 9.2 is an illustration of distance learning using videoconferencing technology. In this model, a college professor is teaching a "live" course that is also being videoconferenced to a class at a local high school. In this format, both the instructor and students can interact with one another synchronously in a point-to-point, two-way delivery mode.

Videoconferencing (or teleconferencing) technology provides all the benefits of television and, in addition, allows the audience or students to interact in real time with the instructor and other students. Videoconferencing approximates the traditional classroom more than any other distance learning technology. Instructors conduct classes, students can see the instructor, instructors can see students, and students can ask questions of the instructor or each other by pushing a button on a microphone situated on a desk. When accompanied by electronic whiteboards and other imaging systems, instructors can use illustrations, write notes, and use images or video to enhance their class presentations. Videoconferencing is most frequently being used in a two-way interactive mode, but technology has also evolved so that students at multiple sites can participate. Using digital technology, videoconferencing is also now available on desktop computers so that a session may include individuals in many different locations. The delivery technologies being used for videoconferencing include high-speed telephone systems, satellite (wireless), cable, and dedicated fiber-optic networks. Several statewide systems (e.g., Oklahoma, Iowa, Wisconsin, Maryland) support videoconferencing links for a variety of educational, medical, and other nonprofit agencies. The Georgia Statewide Academic and Medical System (GSAMS) is a videoconferencing system that connects most of the state's colleges, school districts, and hospitals. GSAMS is especially effective in bringing distance learning programs to health care and medical professionals who regularly need to update their skills and knowledge of current medical practices and techniques.

Figure 9.3 illustrates distance learning using the Internet and World Wide Web. Using technology tools such as course management software systems (discussed in Chapter 8), a teacher can deliver Internet-based "online learning" to many students who are connected to the World Wide Web in their homes, schools, or places of business. Online learning activities can be *synchronous* (that is, instruction happening at a specific time), or they can be *asynchronous* (instruction happening at any time).

Synchronous distance learning via the Internet or other computer networks can use text-based, audio, or video technologies to enable teacher and students to interact with one another. The benefits of this approach are that there can be immediate interactions between teacher and student and student and student. The major difference between synchronous online learning and videoconferencing, as discussed in the paragraphs above, is that students normally participate while sitting at a computer workstation rather than as part of a class viewing a large monitor of an instructor presenting material at a distant site. Rather than pushing a button on a microphone to ask a question, a student might key in the question in text mode and receive a prompt text reply. Videoconferencing using standard video technologies almost always assumes that an instructor is leading the presentation, whereas with online technology the presentation may also be "led" by a packaged software program with the instructor acting more as a facilitator available to answer a question or help a student having some other difficulty.

Synchronous online learning without packaged software—which depends on an instructor to present, control, and interact with the students—is similar to other videoconferencing techniques. However, if there are large and widely dispersed student audiences, the instructor will likely need the assistance of facilitators to help answer questions or assist with technical difficulties. This can become costly. As a result, schools and other organizations using computer networks for distance learning tend to favor less costly asynchronous approaches.

Perhaps the most significant development in distance learning is the use of asynchronous learning networks. An asynchronous learning network (ALN) is generally defined as using computer networking technology to provide instruction at any place and any time. An instructor provides a file of instructional materials that students can access remotely from any computer workstation that has a modem or other communications capability. Interaction, discussion, and questions are handled through group software systems and course management software (e.g., Blackboard or WebCT) that provide e-mail, electronic bulletin board, threaded discussions, blogs, and other communications facilities.

In an example of an asynchronous learning session, an instructor introduces a topic or provides a file of materials that students can read or otherwise use for some activity at a Web site, say on a Sunday evening. The instructor might supplement the materials by posing key questions on a discussion board, group e-mail system, or blog that all students in the class are able to access. Students access this material at any time during the week, can post comments to the discussion board or blog for the entire class to see, and may ask questions directly of the instructor or of other students. An assessment or review of the material and the week's instructional activity (discussions, questions, etc.) is conducted on Saturday. The cycle begins again on the following Sunday evening with a new topic. In this example of asynchronous learning, the instructor and students did not communicate synchronously—that is, at the same time—but instead accessed all materials or asked questions anytime as needed from computer workstations in their homes, at a school, or in their places of business. Asynchronous online instruction can also easily be blended with other asynchronous technologies, synchronous technologies, or face-to-face instruction making it by far the most popular of all distance learning approaches being used.

The intent here is not to cover all the various possibilities, but to emphasize that distance learning can take on many different forms to meet different needs. The possibilities are extensive and will likely increase in the future, especially as digital technology continues to expand and integrate with other technologies.

BLENDED LEARNING

A wide variety of technologies are available for distance learning. Each of these technologies has certain benefits and certain limitations, and a "best" technology does not yet exist for distance learning. Educators should attempt to use the technology that will best meet their goals, that is most readily available, and that will be educationally sound as well as cost effective. Internet-based computer technology will be used more extensively in the future for distance learning but even within this technology, various options are available.

In selecting a technology for distance learning, educators should assume that they may blend technologies or options within technologies to provide the optimal approach. Although one technology may be the primary means chosen to deliver instruction for a particular distance learning course, other technologies or even face-to-face instruction may be more appropriate for some other aspect of the course. In recent years, distance learning approaches have been integrated with face-to-face instruction to deliver "blended" or "hybrid" courses. Figure 9.4 depicts a

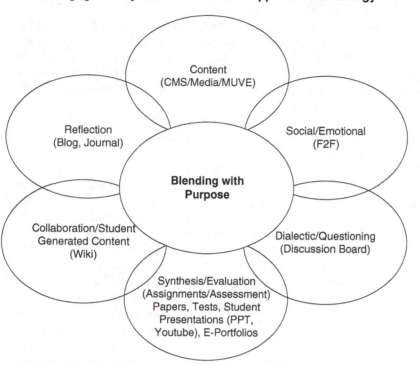

Blending with Purpose – The Multimodal Model
Pedagogical Objectives/Activities -> Approach/Technology

Content
(CMS/Media/MUVE)

Reflection
(Blog, Journal)

Social/Emotional
(F2F)

Blending with Purpose

Collaboration/Student
Generated Content
(Wiki)

Dialectic/Questioning
(Discussion Board)

Synthesis/Evaluation
(Assignments/Assessment)
Papers, Tests, Student
Presentations (PPT,
Youtube), E-Portfolios

FIGURE 9.4 Blending with Purpose: The Multimodal Model.

Blending with Purpose model that is appropriate for designing blended courses. It recommends that pedagogical objectives and activities should drive the approaches that teachers use in instruction. It also suggests that blending these objectives, activities, and approaches within multiple modalities might be most effective for and appeal to a wide range of students. The model presents six basic pedagogical objectives/activities and approaches for achieving them. It should be a given that other objectives can be added where appropriate. The most important feature of this model is that teachers need to carefully consider their objectives and understand how to apply the technologies and approaches that will work best for their students. A quick review of the objectives used in the model and their concomitant technological approach will be helpful in understanding the overall model.

Content is one of the primary drivers of instruction, and there are many ways in which content can be delivered and presented. Even though much of what is taught is delivered linguistically (teacher speaks—students listen; or teacher writes—students write), this does not have to be the case either in face-to-face or online environments. Certain subject areas such as science are highly dependent on using visual simulations to demonstrate processes and systems. The humanities, especially art, history, and literature, can be greatly enhanced by rich digital images. Increasingly, course management systems such as Blackboard or WebCT can provide basic content delivery mechanisms for blended learning. CMS software easily handles the delivery of a variety of media including text, video, and audio. Multi-user virtual environments (MUVEs) and gaming are also evolving and playing more of a role in providing instructional content. In providing and presenting content, the Blending with Purpose model suggests that multiple technologies and media be utilized.

The Blending with Purpose model posits that instruction is not always just about learning content or a skill but is also about supporting students *socially and emotionally*. Perhaps more readily recognized for younger K–12 students, social and emotional development is an important part of anyone's education. Faculty who have taught advanced graduate courses know that the students, even at this advanced level, frequently need someone with whom to speak, whether for understanding a complex concept or providing advice on career and professional opportunities. Although fully online courses and programs have evolved to the point where teachers can provide some social and emotional support where possible and appropriate, in blended courses and programs this might best be provided in a face-to-face mode.

Dialectics or questioning is an important activity that allows teachers to probe what students know and to help refine their knowledge. The Socratic Method remains one of the major techniques used in instruction, and many successful teachers are proud of their ability to stimulate discussion by asking the "right" questions that help students think critically about a topic or issue. In many cases, these questions serve to refine and narrow down a discussion to specific "points" or aspects of the topic at hand and are not meant to be open-ended "anybody can say anything at anytime" activities. For dialectic and questioning activities, a simple-to-use, threaded electronic discussion board is as or more effective than most other approaches. A well-organized discussion board activity generally seeks to present a topic or issue and has students respond to questions and provide their own perspectives while evaluating and responding to the opinions of others. The simple, direct visual of the "thread" also allows students to see how the entire discussion or lesson has evolved. In sum, for teachers wanting to focus attention and dialogue on a specific topic, the main activity for many online courses has been and continues to be the electronic discussion board.

Incorporating *reflection* can be a powerful pedagogical strategy under the right circumstances. There is an extensive body of scholarship on the "reflective teacher" and the "reflective learner" going back to John Dewey and more recently to the work of Donald Schon. Although reflection can be a deeply personal activity, the ability to share one's reflections with others can be most beneficial. Pedagogical activities that require students to reflect on what they are learning and to share their reflections with their teachers and fellow students extend and enrich reflection. Blogs and blogging, whether as group exercises or for individual journaling activities, are evolving as appropriate tools for students reflecting on their learning and other aspects of course activities.

Collaborative learning has been evolving for decades. In face-to-face classes, group work has grown in popularity and has become commonplace in many course activities. Many teachers rely heavily on collaborative learning as a technique for group problem solving. In the past, the logistics and time needed for effective collaboration in face-to-face classes were sometimes problematic. However, with e-mail and other electronic communications, some of these logistical problems are alleviated because the group can continue to communicate beyond the normal class period. More recently, wikis have grown significantly in popularity and are becoming a staple in group projects and writing assignments. Furthermore, unlike group work that typically ends up on the teacher's desk when delivered in paper form, wikis allow students to generate content that can be shared with others during and beyond the end of a semester. Papers and projects developed with wikis can pass seamlessly from one group to another and from one class to another.

Perhaps the most important component of the model is *synthesizing, evaluating, and assessing* learning. CMSs and other online tools provide a number of mechanisms for assisting in this area. Papers, tests, assignments, and portfolios are among the major methods used for assessing student learning and are increasingly being done electronically. Essays and term projects pass back and forth between teacher and student without ever being printed on paper. Oral classroom presentations are giving way to YouTube videos and podcasts. The portfolio is evolving into an electronic multimedia presentation of images, video, and audio, which goes far beyond the 3-inch, paper-filled binder. Weekly class discussions that take place on discussion boards or blogs provide the instructor with an electronic record that can be reviewed over and over again to examine how students have participated and progressed over time. They are also most helpful to instructors in assessing their own teaching and in reviewing what worked and what did not work in a class. In sum, online technology allows for a more seamless sharing of evaluation and assessment activities and provides an ongoing record that can be referred to over and over again by both students and teachers.

The six components of the model, as described above, should blend together in an integrated manner that appears as seamless as possible for students. Furthermore, not every course must incorporate all of the activities and approaches of the model. The pedagogical objectives of a course should drive the activities and hence the approaches. For example, not every course needs to require students to do group work or rely on reflective activities.

Many of the technologies discussed above are evolving. In planning distance learning programs, educators must remain flexible in their selection of a technology. Using several technologies may seem complex but, in the long run, may protect against major shifts or advances in technological approaches. Change, and in some cases rapid change, is becoming a dominating characteristic of many of the newer video and digital technologies. The Internet is being used by hundreds of millions of people from every walk of life on every continent. Internets II and III are already evolving. Flexibility as provided by blending different technologies with cognizance of major trends will best serve planning activities for distance learning.

THE EXTENT OF DISTANCE LEARNING IN K–12 EDUCATION

The U.S. Department of Education (Zandberg& Lewis (2008) reported that 37% of all school districts offered some type of distance learning courses in the 2004–05 academic year. Table 9.1 provides data on the distance learning technologies being used by these school districts comparing

TABLE 9.1 Primary Technology Used in K–12 School Districts to Deliver Distance Learning Courses

Percent of K-12 school districts currently offering distance education courses, showing the primary technology used in 2002–03 and 2004–05 school years.

Hardware Technology	2002–03	2004–05
Two-way interactive video with two-way audio	55	47
One-way prerecorded video	16	11
Internet using synchronous communications	21	24
Internet using asynchronous communications	47	58
Other	4	2

Source: U.S. Department of Education, National Center for Education Statistics, Fast Response Survey System (FRSS), "Distance Education Courses for Public School Elementary and Secondary Students: 2002–03," FRSS 84, 2003; and "Distance Education Courses for Public Elementary and Secondary School Students: 2004–05," FRSS 89, 2005.

the 2002–03 and 2004–05 school years. Essentially these data show that the Internet using asynchronous communications has evolved as the most popular technology for delivering distance learning courses. Two-way interactive video, the Internet using synchronous communications, and one-way prerecorded video also are commonly being used.

Note that school districts are not necessarily using only one technology but are mixing and matching technologies depending on individual circumstances. Although the trend to digital, Internet technologies predominates, it is not all-inclusive—and many institutions are planning to continue to use other technologies as well. It is likely that in many of these institutions, the infrastructure for Internet access has been established for reasons other than distance learning. Why not also use it for distance learning applications?

The data in Table 9.1 were collected for the 2004–05 school year and represent the best comparison of the different technologies being used for distance learning in these years. However, other more recent studies provide further insight into K–12 distance learning, particularly Internet-based applications. In addition, the blended or hybrid learning format discussed above has also been gaining in popularity. Picciano and Seaman (2007, 2009) conducted two national studies on the extent and nature of online learning in K–12 school districts. The 2007 study was based on a national survey of school district administrators during the 2005–2006 academic year. It was one of the first studies to collect data on and compare fully online and blended learning (part online and part traditional face-to-face instruction) in K–12 schools. The purpose of the 2009 study was to replicate the earlier study in order to substantiate its findings and to examine what, if any, changes occurred in online learning in K–12 school districts. The 2009 study was based on a national survey of school district administrators during the 2007–2008 academic year. A summary of the findings of the later study are as follows:

1. Three-quarters of the responding public school districts were offering online or blended courses:
   - 75% had one or more students enrolled in a fully online or blended course.
   - 70% had one or more students enrolled in a fully online course.
   - 41% had one or more students enrolled in a blended course.
   - These percentages represent an increase of approximately 10% since 2005–2006.
2. Two-thirds of the school districts with students enrolled in online or blended courses anticipated that their online enrollments will grow.
3. The overall number of K–12 students engaged in online courses in 2007–2008 was estimated at 1,030,000. This represented a 47% increase since 2005–2006.
4. Respondents reported that online learning was meeting the specific needs of a range of students, from those who need extra help and credit recovery to those who want to take Advanced Placement and college-level courses.
5. School districts typically depend on multiple online learning providers, including postsecondary institutions, state virtual schools, and independent providers as well as developing and providing their own online courses (Picciano & Seaman, 2009, p. 1).

The voices heard most clearly in this study were those of respondents representing small rural school districts. For them, the availability of online learning was a lifeline and enabled them to provide students with course choices and, in some cases, the basic courses that should be part of every curriculum. However, it is likely that all school districts will consider using some form of fully online or blended distance learning courses in the future.

DESIGNING INSTRUCTIONAL MATERIALS: A COMPARISON OF DISTANCE LEARNING MODELS

Figure 9.5 is an outline of a lesson plan or study guide for a multi-week course module on the U.S. Supreme Court's landmark 1954 decision, *Brown v. Board of Education of Topeka, Kansas*, its aftermath, and its relevance to modern American society. This content is commonly used in American history, sociology, political science, cultural studies, education, and constitutional law courses at the secondary and postsecondary education levels. Figures 9.6, 9.7, and 9.8 are examples of distance learning materials appropriate for three different delivery systems: the interactive videoconference, asynchronous learning using the Internet and World Wide Web, and a blended learning course. All three use the same general content. Each example concludes with a similar written assignment. Although the content is the same, the materials and presentations have been customized to suit the benefits and limitations of the distance learning technology used.

Module Objectives:

1. To study the checks and balances system in the American governmental system.
2. To analyze how a democracy responds to crisis.
3. To explain events before and after the Brown v. Board of Education Decision.

Key Questions:

1. Why is the Brown v. Board of Education decision regarded as one of the most significant decisions of the U.S. Supreme Court in the 20th century?
2. What was the reaction to the Brown decision on the part of various segments of American society?
3. What has been the effect of the Brown decision on American society in general?

Synopsis of the Case:

In the early 1950s, de jure (by law) segregation in public schools was well-established in seventeen states and Washington, D.C. In Topeka, Kansas, a black third-grader named Linda Brown had to walk one mile through a rail-road switch yard to get to her black elementary school, even though a white elementary school was only seven blocks away. Linda's father, Oliver Brown, tried to enroll her in the white elementary school, but the principal of the school refused. Brown went to McKinley Burnett, the head of Topeka's branch of the National Association for the Advancement of Colored People (NAACP), and asked for help. Other black parents joined Brown, and, in 1951, the NAACP requested an injunction that would forbid the segregation of Topeka's public schools.

The U.S. District Court for the District of Kansas heard Brown's case from June 25–26, 1951. At the trial, the NAACP argued that segregated schools sent the message to black children that they were inferior to whites; therefore, the schools were inherently unequal. . . .

(continued)

FIGURE 9.5 Excerpt of a Lesson Module (Study Guide). This excerpt is part of a larger instructional unit on the civil rights movement in the United States.

The Board of Education's defense was that, because segregation in Topeka and elsewhere pervaded many other aspects of life, segregated schools simply prepared black children for the segregation they would face during adulthood. The board also argued that segregated schools were not necessarily harmful to black children; great African Americans such as Frederick Douglass, Booker T. Washington, and George Washington Carver had overcome segregated schools to achieve what they achieved. The request for an injunction put the court in a difficult position. On the one hand, the judges agreed with the expert witnesses; in their decision, they wrote: "Segregation of white and colored children in public schools has a detrimental effect upon the colored children. . . . A sense of inferiority affects the motivation of a child to learn."

On the other hand, the precedent of Plessy v. Ferguson (1896) allowed for "separate but equal" public facilities including school systems for blacks and whites, and no Supreme Court ruling had overturned Plessy yet. Because of the precedent of Plessy, the court felt "compelled" to rule in favor of the Board of Education.

Brown and the NAACP appealed to the Supreme Court on October 1, 1951, and their case was combined with other cases that challenged school segregation in South Carolina, Virginia, Delaware, and the District of Columbia. The Supreme Court first heard the case on December 9, 1952, but failed to reach a decision. In the reargument, heard from December 7–8, 1953, the Court requested that both sides discuss "the circumstances surrounding the adoption of the Fourteenth Amendment in 1868.

"On May 17, 1954, Chief Justice Earl Warren read the decision of the unanimous Court: (Brown I) "We come then to the question presented: Does segregation of children in public schools solely on the basis of race, even though the physical facilities and other "tangible" factors may be equal, deprive the children of the minority group of equal educational opportunities? We believe that it does. . . . We conclude that in the field of public education the doctrine of 'separate but equal' has no place. Separate educational facilities are inherently unequal. Therefore, we hold that the plaintiffs and others similarly situated for whom the actions have been brought are, by reason of the segregation complained of, deprived of the equal protection of the laws guaranteed by the Fourteenth Amendment."

With this decision, the Supreme Court struck down the "separate but equal" doctrine of Plessy and ruled in favor of the plaintiffs. One year later, the Supreme Court issued its implementation decree ordering all segregated school systems to desegregate (Brown II).

Major Personalities:

Oliver Brown – father of Linda Brown . . .
Thurgood Marshall – lead attorney for the case for the NAACP Legal Defense Fund . . .
John W. Davis – lead attorney for the defense . . .
Kenneth Clark – social scientist and expert witness in the case . . .
Charles Houston – dean of Howard University's Law School . . .
Earl Warren – Chief Justice of the U.S. Supreme Court . . .

Aftermath of the Brown Decision:

Integration of Central High School in Little Rock, Arkansas (1950s) . . .
School decentralization and community power in New York City (1960s) . . .
Busing as a remedy for segregated schools in Boston (1970s) . . .

FIGURE 9.5 *(Continued)*

Legacy of the Brown Decision:

Provided the legal foundation for the American civil rights movement . . .
Catalyst for federal legislative initiatives and entitlement programs . . .
Established the legal precedent for other groups on constitutional issues of equality . . .

Reading Assignments:

Kluger, Richard (1976). Simple justice: The history of Brown v. Board of Education and black America's struggle for equality. New York: Alfred A. Knopf. (Selected Chapters)

Carter, R. L. (1995). The unending struggle for equal educational opportunity. Teachers College Record, 96(4),619–626. Miller, L. P. (1995). Tracking the progress of Brown. Teachers College Record, 96(4), 609–613.

Writing Assignment:

On the occasion of the anniversary of Brown v. Board of Education, The Nation conducted interviews with a number of activists and scholars on the relevance of the decision to present-day America. Ben Chavis, civil rights activist and former head of the NAACP, and Jack Greenberg, an attorney who assisted Thurgood Marshall in preparing the case in 1954, and professor emeritus at Columbia University's School of Law, gave the following responses to the question, "Does Brown Still Matter?":"

"In many cases access to schools has been achieved while access to knowledge has not. African-Americans and Latinos are disproportionately isolated in underfunded school systems and substandard schools. Wealthier school systems provide their mostly white students with experienced teachers, modern technology, better facilities and lower student/teacher ratios"—Ben Chavis

"There is now a large black middle class and substantial black political power (forty members of Congress, many mayors) as a result of a civil rights revolution, of which Brown was one of the main progenitors. This political and economic power is a direct consequence of Brown's perceptions and requirements."—Jack Greenberg

After studying the Brown v. Board of Education decision, do you tend to agree more with Chavis or Greenberg? Prepare a brief (1,200 words) paper explaining your position and cite examples either from your personal experiences or publicized current events to support it.

If you have any questions, do not hesitate to contact your instructor.

FIGURE 9.5 (*Continued*)

In reviewing the three examples, readers should compare the benefits and limitations of each of the distance learning methods. All three methods provide for routine communication and interaction among the instructor, the student, and the curriculum material. The issue of interaction (teacher to student, student to student, student to material) has long been recognized as an important element of well-designed instruction (Moore & Kearsley, 1996). The use of high-quality media such as a video documentary is highly desirable in all learning, distance or otherwise, but may not be possible or cost-effective depending on the technology used. Of the three examples, video is provided in the interactive videoconference and the blended learning environment. In terms of student convenience in taking classes, the asynchronous learning is best suited for students to learn at their own pace or according to their daily schedules.

The Interactive Videoconference

Figure 9.6 provides an excerpt from a script for a 3-hour interactive videoconference in which an instructor will teach to both a local and a distant student audience. Scripting is highly recommended in developing any type of conference (audio, video, one-way, two-way, or multipoint). The conference should be carefully organized according to a time schedule so that the parties at

1:00 P.M.	Prepare audio-visual setup for today's session. Test interactive video connection for audio and video quality. Test instructor and student microphones. Discuss with teaching assistants at the remote and local sites that they have received back-up material and understand lesson and procedures for today's session.
1:30 P.M.	Interactive video session starts. Welcome the students at both sites and verify that they can see and hear you. Take attendance.
1:40 P.M.	Begin the lesson. Orally present the synopsis of the U.S. Supreme Court's Brown v. Board of Education decision from prepared notes.*
2:00 P.M.	Ask for questions from each of the sites.
2:10 P.M.	Orally present background of major personalities involved with the decision from prepared notes.*
2:30 P.M.	Ask for questions from each of the sites.
2:40 P.M.	Break
2:50 P.M.	Welcome the students back. Provide a brief summary of the material/discussion during the first half of this session.
3:00 P.M.	Show a series of video clips from the award-winning documentary Eyes on the Prize from DVD player. These clips will include the following: Additional background on the Brown Decision; Footage of the integration of Central High School in Little Rock, Arkansas, in the 1950s; Footage of the school decentralization movement in New York City in the 1960s; Footage of the school busing issue in Boston in the 1970s.
3:40 P.M.	Highlight pertinent comments/scenes made in the video clips.
4:00 P.M.	Ask for questions from both of the sites.
4:15 P.M.	Distribute/announce/refer students to the reading and writing assignments.*
4:20 P.M.	Ask if there are any questions with the assignment.
4:30 P.M.	Interactive video session ends.

FIGURE 9.6   Excerpt of a Script for a Two-Way Interactive Videoconference.   This excerpt is part of the module on the Brown v. Board of Education decision in 1954.
  NOTE: Prepared notes, reading and writing assignment are the same as those described in Figure 9.5

all sites have a clear understanding of the sequence of a lesson's activities. In addition to helping an instructor organize his or her lesson, the script is used extensively by site facilitators to prepare for and assist in the delivery of the conference.

For the oral delivery in an interactive videoconference, an instructor can adapt much of his or her own traditional teaching style to the lesson. However, encouraging the students to ask questions, particularly at the remote site(s), is critical. A major advantage of interactive videoconferencing is its inherent interactivity, and instructors should plan their lessons accordingly. Study and observation of videoconferences indicate that the students at the local sites are frequently able to read the body language and energy of the instructor better than those at the remote sites, especially at the beginning of a course. It is not unusual to see students at a local site asking more questions than do students at the remote sites. A good script will identify specific periods for questions from all sites. Instructors should also be comfortable with camera angles and positioning and, to the extent possible, look into the camera. Another advantage of interactive videoconferencing facilities is the ability to incorporate media such as videotapes, videodiscs, slides, and document cameras. Where appropriate, instructors are encouraged to use media to enhance their basic oral delivery.

The script excerpted in Figure 9.6 starts with a testing of all technology, especially audio and video connections. Site facilitators or teaching assistants should be familiar with the session's activities. A backup plan is highly recommended in case a connection is lost or some other technical difficulty occurs. The session starts promptly at 1:30 P.M. with a welcome, another brief test of audio and video quality, and the taking of attendance. The instructor proceeds to introduce the topic orally, pretty much as he or she would in a traditional class. The script allocates frequent and specific times for questions to ensure that the students at the remote site(s) are encouraged and have the opportunity to interact. In a videoconference of 2 or more hours, at least one break is recommended. The example script also makes use of videodisc material to illustrate and support the oral presentation. PBS markets the highly acclaimed Eyes on the Prize documentary series of the civil rights movement in the United States in both videotape and DVD formats. In this particular situation where several video clips are being used, DVD with its rapid direct accessing capability is the recommended choice.

Distributing prepared notes on the topic is generally the prerogative of the instructor. Some instructors in traditional classes make their notes available; others do not. The same is true in distance learning lessons. Minimally, it is assumed that teaching assistants and site facilitators have received a copy of the instructor's notes. For this particular script, assume that the notes are similar to those in the lesson plan or study guide that are presented in abridged form in Figure 9.5.

The lesson concludes with the same reading and writing assignments that were required in the lesson plan. The reading assignments are generally provided as part of the entire schedule of assignments in the course syllabus. It may be helpful to students to have writing assignments scheduled in advance, but some instructors prefer to distribute writing assignments as needed.

Asynchronous Learning Using the Internet and World Wide Web

Figure 9.7 provides the outline for an asynchronous learning class using the Internet and the World Wide Web. Instructional activities described in this outline rely on Internet-based facilities typically found in a course management software (CMS) system. Students participate from their homes, places of business, or wherever they have access to the Internet, within given parameters, convenient for them. A good CMS package, as discussed in Chapter 8, will facilitate developing many of these materials for the Web.

Friday	Remind students to please do the readings for the Brown v. Board of Education Decision and are familiar with key questions.*
Monday	Review the topic concluding with the following open-ended question: "Why is the Brown v. Board of Education decision regarded as one of the most significant decisions of the U.S. Supreme Court in the 20th century?" Refer students to a synopsis and major personalities of the case that is available at the class Web site. Remind students that if they have any questions, feel free to e-mail the instructor at any time.
Monday	Monitor student comments and questions on the discussion board and individual e-mail.
Tuesday	Compliment students who made exceptionally good postings to the discussion board over the past 48 hours. Review the wording of the Brown decision (Brown I) and the implementation decree (Brown II). Conclude with an open-ended question: "What did the Brown decision mean to those states that had established de jure segregated school systems? How did these states attempt to implement the Brown decision?" Remind students that if they have any questions, feel free to e-mail the instructor at any time.
Wednesday	Monitor student comments and questions on the discussion board.
Thursday	Compliment and refer to students who made exceptionally good postings to the discussion board over the past 48 hours. Briefly review the discussion for the week. Emphasize that the Brown decision did not just affect the states that had established de jure segregated Provide examples in New York City in the 1960s and Boston in the 1970s. Conclude with an open-ended question: "What has been the effect of the Brown decision on American society in general?" Remind students that if they have any questions, feel free to e-mail the instructor at any time.
Friday	Monitor student comments and questions on the discussion board.
Saturday	Compliment and refer to students who made exceptionally good postings to the discussion board during the past week. Indicate that a summary of this week's discussion and further information from the instructor's notes** will be available at the class's Web site by 4:00 P.M. this (Saturday) evening. Refer students to the class Web site to a written assignment.** Thank student facilitators for their contribution to this week's discussion. Wish everybody a Happy Weekend!

FIGURE 9.7 Excerpt of a Script for an Asynchronous Learning Class. This excerpt is part of the module on the Brown v. Board of Education decision in 1954. This class is conducted entirely online in asynchronous mode over the Internet. Students access all material in their homes or places of business remotely via the Internet and World Wide Web. Each class session lasts one week beginning on Sunday evening and ending Saturday morning.

NOTE: Reading assignment includes material available at a Web site maintained by the Woodstock Center at Georgetown University commemorating the 50 Anniversary of the Brown Decision.

NOTE: Instructor notes and written assignment are the same as in Figure 9.5

In this example, the course is organized according to weekly discussion topics. The discussion commences on Sunday evening on a discussion board and formally concludes on Saturday morning. Additional material is also provided at a class Web site. Several students are selected each week to serve as facilitators of instruction and are reminded on Friday of this assignment via e-mail. Student facilitators are expected to be especially active in making comments, in responding to questions, and in moving the discussion along for the week. In asynchronous learning, open-ended questions are very effective in allowing students to express themselves and are highly recommended. In the example outline, each scheduled posting by the instructor concludes with an open-ended question. In addition to the discussion board, students are encouraged to contact the instructor directly via individual e-mail if need be throughout the session. In the absence of face-to-face contact, positive feedback and reinforcement techniques such as frequent compliments or references to students are desirable.

In this particular outline, the discussion continues for a week and ends with the instructor providing a summary of the week's discussion and posting his or her notes on the class Web site. At the Web site, students can also find the reading and writing assignments. In this example, the reading assignment includes material provided on the Web at another site from a symposium that was held on the *Brown v. Board of Education* decision. Where possible, using the information resources of the Web is highly recommended for asynchronous, Internet-based learning. Students in these classes are familiar with the Web and generally can access Web-based materials. Unfortunately, depending on the topic and content, quality reading and other instructional materials are not always available online. Although the book and journal publishers are moving toward providing access to some of their materials on the Web, too frequently user fees are required that may be prohibitive for students. An instructor might be tempted to scan in an excerpt from a particularly useful article and post it at a Web site; however, if the material is copyrighted, permission will have to be secured. The writing assignment in this example is the same as in the previous examples and can be submitted electronically via the course management system's "digital drop box."

Blended Learning Course

Figure 9.8 provides the outline for a blended learning course that meets face-to-face and online. The course normally would be meet 3 days per week (e.g., Monday, Tuesday, and Friday); however, the instructor with approval from his department chairperson has developed a blended learning version of this course that meets face-to-face 2 days (Monday and Friday) per week and meets online during the week instead of attending a Tuesday class session. Several students are selected each week to serve as facilitators of instruction, especially, for the online portion of the course and are reminded on Friday of this assignment. Student facilitators are expected to be especially active in making comments, in responding to questions, and in moving the discussion along for the week.

In this particular outline, the class covers a week's worth of instruction and ends with the instructor providing a summary of the week's discussion. At the Web site, students can also find the reading and writing assignments. In this example, the reading assignment includes material provided on the Web at another site from a symposium that was held on the *Brown v. Board of Education* decision. The instructor also makes use of video clips for the face-to-face sessions on Monday and Friday. The writing assignment in this example is similar to the examples in Figures 9.6 and 9.7 but also has been modified to be a more-reflective learning activity. The blog is used so that the student entries can be shared with others and possibly serve as discussion point for a future class.

Friday	Remind student facilitators via e-mail for the coming week's discussion that they should have read all the material and are familiar with key questions.[*]
Monday	In Class Session: Initiate week's discussion in class by introducing the topic and concluding with the following open-ended question: "Why is the Brown v. Board of Education decision regarded as one of the most significant decisions of the U.S. Supreme Court in the 20th century?" Show two video clips from the award-winning documentary Eyes on the Prize from DVD player. These clips will include the following: Additional background on the Brown Decision; Footage of the integration of Central High School in Little Rock, Arkansas, in the 1950s; Ask students to discuss this topic on the discussion board. Each student is to make at least two postings between now and Friday. Refer students to a synopsis and major personalities of the case that are available at the class Web site. Remind students that if they have any questions, feel free to post to the discussion board or to e-mail the instructor at any time.
Tuesday	Monitor student comments and questions on the discussion board.
Wednesday	Compliment students who made exceptionally good postings to the discussion board over the past 48 hours. Review the wording of the Brown decision (Brown I) and the implementation decree (Brown II). Conclude with an open-ended question: "What did the Brown decision mean to those states that had established de jure segregated school systems? How did these states attempt to implement the Brown decision?" Remind students that if they have any questions, feel free to e-mail the instructor at any time. Ask students to continue their discussion on the discussion board.
Thursday	Monitor student comments and questions on the discussion board.
Friday	In-Class Session Compliment students who made exceptionally good postings to the discussion board over the past three days. Briefly review the online discussion. Emphasize that the Brown decision did not just affect the states that had established de jure segregated. Show two video clips from the award-winning documentary Eyes on the Prize from the DVD player. These clips will include the following: Footage of the school decentralization movement in New York City in the 1960s; Footage of the school busing issue in Boston in the 1970s. Conclude with an open-ended question: "What has been the effect of the Brown decision on American society in general?" Ask students to post a brief reflective essay by Sunday summarizing this question on their blogs.
Sunday	Read, grade and comment on student reflective essays.
Monday	Compliment the students who wrote exceptionally good essays. Start next lesson on the Brown v. Board of Education module.

FIGURE 9.8 Excerpt of a Script for a Blended Learning Class.   This excerpt is part of the module on the Brown v. Board of Education decision in 1954. This class would normally meet face-to-face on Monday, Tuesday, and Friday. However, the instructor has decided to replace the Tuesday class activities with online activities so that class now meets face-to-face only two days per week (Monday and Friday).

NOTE: Prepared notes, reading and writing assignment are the same as those described in Figure 9.5

DISTANCE LEARNING PROVIDERS

Academic programs are designed with a consideration of the basic characteristics of students, including their age, interests, skill levels, academic preparedness, and career goals. With respect to distance learning, these same characteristics must be considered.

Much of the literature suggests that older students and adults are the primary targets and enrollees in distance learning programs. For example, distance learning institutions around the world patterned on the British Open University model were established essentially for adult populations. American higher education currently enrolls about 4 million students annually in online distance learning programs, the vast majority of which have been designed by faculty and support staff within the colleges and universities themselves. Most of these colleges have invested in their own technology infrastructure, acquired course management software, and trained their own faculty to design and develop their own online courses or modules that are blended into their face-to-face courses.

In recent years, a growing number of distance learning programs have been directed to primary and secondary school students. Large-scale literacy programs in developing countries with geographically remote or dispersed populations have been established for younger students as well as for adults. In the United States, rural school districts unable to offer courses to fulfill graduation requirements to small student populations have relied for many years on distance learning programs offered by other districts, colleges, or statewide consortia. Distance learning is also increasingly being viewed as an important instructional component for students who, by necessity or by choice, are being educated in their homes. However, the vast majority of these programs are not designed by the school districts themselves but by distance learning providers.

Picciano and Seaman (2009) reported that the major providers of online distance learning programs to K–12 schools were

1. postsecondary institutions,
2. state virtual schools within the district's home state,
3. independent vendors, and
4. education service agencies.

Also important is the fact that most school districts were using multiple providers and did not rely exclusively on one provider. Parsad and Lewis (2008), in a study for the U.S. Department of Education, estimated that more than 500 colleges and universities were providing distance learning services to K–12 school districts.

During the past 10 years, most states have also established "virtual" primary or secondary schools using the Internet for course delivery. The purposes of virtual schools vary, but essentially they are designed to provide online alternatives to traditional primary and high schools. The Kentucky Virtual High School, for example, is aimed in large part at students in small, rural school districts that suffer from a shortage of teachers qualified to teach upper-level math, science, and foreign language courses. Originally the Florida Virtual School offered only a few core high school courses such as algebra and English; however, now it offers all the courses necessary for a student to earn a high school diploma. Most of the students enrolled are public high school students, but a substantial minority are home-schooled students. The Florida Virtual School projects it will enroll more than 100,000 by the year 2011. The Virtual High School Global Consortium, or VHS, financed in part through a U.S. Department of Education grant and operated by the nonprofit Concord Consortium in Concord, Massachusetts, is operated as a cooperative, with schools in 30 states and a number of countries agreeing to design and teach Internet-based courses in exchange for their students being able to participate. The VHS has won international recognition for the quality of its programs, including the 2001 Stockholm Challenge Award for Global Excellence in Information Technology.

In addition to programs funded by state governments and individual school districts, for-profit ventures are also targeting distance learning students. Companies such as Kaplan Education, K–12, Inc., and Apex Learning are aggressively pursuing primary and high school students for specialized courses and educational needs. Apex Learning is a Seattle-based company originally established as a demonstration project by Paul Allen, the cofounder of Microsoft. The company provides courses that rely on the interactivity and accessibility of the Internet as well as the experience of master teachers and content specialists. Apex Learning originally concentrated on providing Advanced Placement online courses in several subject areas and the AP Exam review. The subject areas include calculus, statistics, U.S government and politics, microeconomics, macroeconomics, U.S. history, and English language and composition. It has broadened its course catalog in recent years to provide credit recovery, dropout recovery, remediation, intervention, and alternative school programs. Apex Learning was honored with a *Technology & Learning* Software Award of Excellence for its calculus and U.S. government and politics courses and for its CramCentral Web site.

In sum, most school districts are viewing themselves as customers who purchase seats in distance learning courses depending on the needs of their individual students. Furthermore, the vast majority of the school districts are selecting multiple online learning providers depending on their needs rather than contracting exclusively with one provider. Some may develop their own online courses, but more likely they might partner with another provider to offer a course, contract with a virtual school for a course that they are not able to offer, or rely on a postsecondary institution for students to enroll in college-level work. The use of multiple vendors makes sense and allows the school districts to be most flexible in meeting the specific needs of their students. Figure 9.9 provides a sample of popular K–12 distance learning providers.

DISTANCE LEARNING: SOME ISSUES

Distance learning is increasingly being viewed as an important alternative to traditional in-class instruction. Michigan, in 2007, passed a new requirement that all high school students must take and complete one online course or its equivalent in order to receive a diploma. Other states are considering a similar requirement. Yet there are issues that have not been fully resolved regarding distance learning in K–12 schools. Several major issues—including instructional quality, for-profit enterprises, student access to technology, scalability, and social interaction and development—need to be considered.

First, the issue of instructional quality in distance learning has and will continue to be closely monitored. Most of the research literature finds well-delivered distance learning in various forms on a par with traditional face-to-face instruction. Regardless, some forms of distance learning especially the online model continue to receive scrutiny, with many educators expressing concerns (Viadero, 2009). Picciano and Seaman (2009) in a national study reported that the quality of online courses was the number-one concern for most school district administrators. They expressed concern that students needed more discipline and maturity to do well in an online

- Apex Learning Inc. offers a range of online courses from credit recovery to advanced placement.
  http://www.apexlearning.com/
- Babbage Net School is a virtual high school that offers online courses in English, math, science, social studies, and other subjects.
  http://www.babbagenetschool.com/
- Christa McAuliffe Academy is a popular online private school, serving grades K–12.
  http://www.cmacademy.org/
- Florida Virtual Schools is perhaps the most popular K–12 state virtual school in terms of enrollments.
  http://www.flvs.net/
- Fraser Valley Distance Education School is one of the largest K–12 distance learning schools in Canada.
  http://www.fvdes.com/
- Kaplan Virtual Education offers a wide range of online classes and tutoring services.
  http://www.kaplanonlinehighschool.com/
- K^{12} Inc. offers online learning for kindergarten through high school students.
  http://www.k12.com/
- Michigan Virtual School offers online high school and middle school classes.
  http://www.mivhs.org/
- North Carolina School of Science and Mathematics Online offers a 2-year blended learning high school program in science and mathematics.
  http://online.ncssm.edu/
- North Dakota Center for Distance Education offers online high school and middle school classes.
  https://www.ndcde.org/
- Virtual High School Global Consortium offers a wide range of online high school and professional development (for teachers) classes.
  http://www.govhs.org/

FIGURE 9.9   Sample of Distance Learning Providers.

course. However, the extent of this concern has not prevented these same administrators from making online distance learning available to their students. For many years, when the popular thinking was that only advanced students or students looking to accelerate their time to graduate were being considered for online learning, it was assumed that these students possessed the discipline needed to do well in the online environment. However, this has begun to change as online learning is increasingly being used for a wide spectrum of students needing to make up courses in order to graduate (e.g., credit recovery) as well as Advanced Placement students (Picciano & Seaman, 2009). Other school district issues (e.g., small student populations, funding, scarcity of qualified teachers) have forced school districts to utilize online learning to fill basic instructional needs.

Second, the issue of instructional quality also relates to the number of for-profit digital schools that have emerged in recent years. Apex Learning, mentioned earlier, is an award-winning for-profit distance learning provider, but not all distance learning providers have been so honored.

Apex Learning is a legitimate, conscientious company trying to provide a valuable service and has been candid in reporting its results, both successes and problems. However, some for-profit distance learning providers are little more than "digital diploma mills." College learners, especially those who make individual decisions about their higher education, are vulnerable to such institutions. George Connick, in a *Distance Learner's Guide*, clearly alerts prospective students "to beware of diploma mills" and a small minority of low-quality or no-quality distance learning providers that have cast a shadow on others. (Connick, 1999). Distance learning providers and regional accrediting agencies need to be scrupulous in ensuring the quality of courses and programs offered and publicizing the same to prospective students. This might be more of an issue for higher education than K–12 students where decisions for enrolling in an online course are made in consultation with school administrators and advisors.

Third, the issue of student access to technology was discussed in Chapter 3 but deserves consideration with respect to distance learning. In the United States, concern has existed regarding the "digital divide" and the evolution of a nation of information haves and have-nots. Although the digital and communications technology industries offer excellent products for reasonable cost, distance learning providers, particularly those supported by public resources, need to be mindful that these products do not always exist in poorer, minority, lower income, less educated, and non-English-speaking homes. Developing academic programs that are not accessible to a large—and often the most needy—segment of a student population will rightfully be questioned. K–12 school districts that rely on online learning for a part of their academic programs need to make sure that their students have proper access to technology including facilities such as high-speed modem connections.

Fourth, the issue of scalability is becoming more important as schools attempt to broaden the scope or scale of programs. Many teachers in schools with little experience in distance learning have begun to experiment by offering one or two courses in selected programs. This is desirable and worthwhile experimentation. However, some concerns exist. For example, Park and Staresina (2004) reported that 10 states have found it necessary to require that teachers of online courses receive formal training in online instruction. In expanding programs, distance learning providers have learned that other issues, particularly related to student and academic support services (staff development, counseling, tutoring, library, etc.), will need to be addressed and provided for (Watson & Ryan, 2008). Failure to do so will leave schools, teachers, and students vulnerable to a number of logistical and policy problems that will be more difficult to resolve after the program has commenced. These problems, in turn, will lead to negative perceptions of the quality of the programs and will hinder their future development.

Lastly, given the complexity of the educational enterprise, educational policy makers and planners should ensure that distance learning programs take into consideration all of their learners' needs. Magellan University, for example, originally operated out of 600 square feet of office space in Tucson, Arizona. William R. Noyes, with 26 years at the University of Arizona as a professor and administrator, started Magellan University in 1996 with $1 million provided for the most part by Research Corporation Technologies. Magellan has directed most of its courses to adults over the age of 25, specifically for the professional development of K–12 teachers. In an interview in 1998, Noyes indicated that he carefully considered the academic quality and rigor of the program at Magellan. By design, class size was small, tutors were always available, and writing was an important component of all courses. However, in comparing

Magellan to a traditional university, Noyes indicated that he favored the conventional university setting for an 18-year-old because of the social interaction and "the breadth of the educational experience" (Christman, 1998). His point was that care must be taken that distance learning is not seen as the quick, easy, or inexpensive way to provide all the education needs for all students.

Decisions involving new distance learning courses and programs should involve administrators, faculty, and students to ensure that such offerings are appropriate and well prepared. Administrators, elected officials, and corporate sponsors cannot simply embrace the new technology as a way of servicing many or all students at reduced costs. The classroom has been evolving for centuries and will continue to do so. Where distance learning technology is appropriate and can be effective, it should be used. If it is not effective, it should be adjusted or abandoned. Finding the proper fit of academic program, student need, and instructional tools is the essence of good educational planning. Noyes's insight is essential to the successful planning and development of quality distance learning programs. Schools are not only places where teachers teach and students learn. The bottom line cannot simply be how well students performed on a test or how many were accepted by good colleges and universities. The place called *school* is a microcosm of society where values are transferred and people, especially the young, are developed. Learning is not simply knowing how to do one or two things well but involves understanding where one's knowledge fits in the broader context of life.

THE FUTURE OF K–12 DISTANCE LEARNING

In 2008, Clayton Christensen, Michael Horn, and Curtis Johnson published a book entitled *Disrupting Class: How Innovation Will Change the Way the World Learns.* Christensen is a professor at the Harvard Business School and the best-selling author of *The Innovator's Dilemma.* In *Disrupting Class,* Christensen, Horn, and Johnson present a compelling rationale for changing education in a way that makes far greater use of online technology to provide more student-centered and individualized instruction. The book's call for change is being cited by a host of respected educators as something policy makers need to consider in looking at the future of American education. The most provocative aspect of this book is the prediction that by the year 2019 about one-half of all high school courses will be online.

In the 1990s, the Internet and digital networks almost doubled the number of students taking distance learning courses. Data collected more recently (U.S. Department of Education, 2003; Zandberg & Lewis, 2008; Picciano & Seaman, 2009) suggests that growth in distance learning will continue for the foreseeable future. Online learning especially will continue to grow. How much is difficult to say. In the two academic years between 2005–2006 and 2007–2008, estimates of enrollments in K–12 online learning increased 47% to just over 1 million students (Picciano & Seaman, 2009). If this trend continues, it is likely in the next several years that there will be several million students enrolled in online distance learning courses. However, if more states follow the recent policy initiatives that Michigan (Merit Curriculum) and Alabama (Alabama Connecting Classrooms, Educators, and Students Statewide) have enacted, it is likely that enrollments in online distance learning will increase quite substantially. If we add to this the potential for blended learning courses to change the nature of K–12 learning in general and especially at the high school level, Christensen, Horn, and Johnson's prediction does not seem so daring.

CASE STUDY

Place: Clifton High School   **Year: 2009**

Clifton High School is a small rural high school located in the farm belt of the United States. The enrollment at Clifton is approximately 550 students. Clifton's academic programs are excellent, and it has a good deal of support from the community. One ongoing issue has been attracting and hiring teachers—particularly in the sciences, mathematics, and foreign languages. Fortunately, in the 1990s a statewide distance learning consortium was established and housed at the state's University Center. The consortium is subsidized by the state, and for a nominal fee Clifton may enroll any of its students in the program, which is based on interactive video technology delivered over the state's fiber-optic network. Clifton enrolls approximately 50 to 75 students per year in consortium courses, especially in Advanced Placement subjects, mathematics, and foreign languages.

Sandra Parks, the principal at Clifton, has been concerned about the science program. She has had trouble recruiting qualified science teachers, especially in physics and chemistry. Even if she could hire two science teachers, she is not sure she has a full teaching program for them. In recent years, a number of her students have been taking science courses via distance learning (interactive video) provided by the state's University Center. Although the lecture and discussion portions of these courses are appropriate, the laboratory experiences have been problematic. Students can view the laboratory exercises that are demonstrated at the University Center's site, but they cannot participate in a hands-on fashion. Ms. Parks sees the distance learning program in the sciences as "better than no science courses" and as very cost-effective given the fact the state subsidizes them—however, she is convinced that students learn science by doing, not simply by watching. She has approached the University Center's distance learning coordinator regarding whether the science offerings could be improved with some type of hands-on activity at Clifton High School. The coordinator has indicated that he would be more than happy to have several of his science faculty meet and discuss this with Clifton faculty, but that he could not possibly afford to send his faculty to Clifton. Ms. Parks has also recently seen advertisements in *Education Week* for a new Internet-based distance learning program offered by a for-profit company on the West Coast. The program includes several science courses provided on DVD-based instructional software packages that are designed to simulate laboratory experiments. Students not only are able to view graphically rich experiments but also can actually manipulate variables and hence change outcomes and results. These DVD software packages are to be used in conjunction with asynchronous Internet-based courses taught by highly qualified high school science teachers.

Discussion Questions

1. Assume you are Ms. Parks. Review your two alternatives for improving Clifton's science program and develop a plan for improvement. Consider carefully all options, costs, and academic issues as well as who should be involved with developing your plan.
2. Are there other alternatives besides the two described in the case study that are appropriate for Clifton High School?

Summary

This chapter introduces the topic of distance learning. Distance learning has an extensive history, including mail, radio, and television, but newer technologies such as digital communications and networking have begun to emerge that make it much easier for educators to provide some form of distance learning to their students. However, distance learning means different things to different people and can take many forms. This discussion includes an analysis and comparison of the various technologies. In selecting a technology for distance learning, educators should assume that they may pick and choose or blend technologies to provide the best approach.

The chapter also includes a presentation on design considerations for developing distance learning materials for three different delivery systems: the interactive video conference, Internet-based asynchronous learning, and a blended learning course. This is followed by a section on identifying who the major providers of distance learning are.

The chapter concludes with a discussion of emerging issues including instructional quality, for-profit enterprises, student access to technology, scalability, and social interaction and development.

Key Concepts and Questions

1. Distance learning means different things to different people. How do you define distance learning?
2. Distance learning can use several different delivery technologies. Identify and compare several different distance learning delivery technologies. What do you see as the future of these technologies?
3. Distance learning seems to be growing in popularity, especially in adult learning programs. What do you see as the growth of distance learning in primary schools? And high schools?
4. The terms *synchronous* and *asynchronous* distance learning are referred to several times in this chapter. Define and compare the two approaches. Especially identify the pedagogical benefits of each.
5. Many educators do not see distance learning as ever replacing the teacher in the classroom. Do you believe that distance learning technologies will ever substantially replace teachers in K–12 classrooms? If so, under what circumstances would this occur or be appropriate?
6. Many issues have arisen as a result of the expansion of distance learning in the United States. Identify and compare some of these issues. Are they significant issues in your school or district?

Suggested Activities

1. Visit the Florida Virtual School Web site (http://www.flvs.net/) or the Kentucky Virtual High School (http://www.kvhs.org/). Do you believe that a distance learning high school designed along the lines of these schools would be appropriate in your school district? Why or why not?
2. Assume you are designing a Web-based distance learning course in earth science for a high school class. How would you go about collecting material for this course? What are some of the important design criteria you need to consider for developing such a course?
3. Do a search on Google, Yahoo!, or some other search engine on the Internet and collect information on at least 10 distance learning providers that target their programs on K–12 students. Can you determine whether there are any similarities or differences (target student population, locale, or subject area) among these distance learning providers?

References

Christensen, C. M., Horn, M. B., & Johnson, C. W. (2008). *Disrupting class: How innovation will change the way the world learns.* New York: McGraw-Hill.

Christman, B. (1998). *Information revolution fills space between the ears: Magellan abandons bricks and mortar.* Originally retrieved from the Web site of Magellan University, no longer available online.

Connick, G. P. (Ed.). (1999). *The distance learner's guide.* Upper Saddle River, NJ: Prentice Hall.

Moore, M., & Kearsley, G. (1996). *Distance education: A systems view.* Belmont, CA: Wadsworth Publishing.

Park, J., & Staresina, L. (2004, May 6). Tracking U.S. trends. *Education Week, 23*(35), 64–67.

Parsad, B., & Lewis, L. (2008). *Distance education at degree-granting postsecondary institutions: 2006–2007* (NCES 2009–044). Washington, DC: National Center for Education Statistics, Institute of Education Sciences, U.S. Department of Education.

Picciano, A. G., & Seaman, J. (2007). *K–12 online learning: A survey of school district administrators.* Needham, MA: The Sloan Consortium.

Picciano, A. G., & Seaman, J. (2009). *K–12 online learning: A 2008 follow-up of the survey of U.S. school district administrators.* Needham, MA: The Sloan Consortium.

Rudenstine, N. (1997, February 21). The Internet and education: a close fit. *Chronicle of Higher Education,* 37–38.

U.S. Department of Education, National Center for Education Statistics. (2003). *Distance education at degree-granting postsecondary education institutions, 2000–2001* (NCES 2003-017). Washington, DC: Author.

Viadero, D. (2009, March 26). Research shows evolving picture of e-learning. *Education Week, 28*(26), 9–11.

Watson, J., & Ryan, J. (2008). *Keeping pace with K–12 online learning: A review of state-level practice.* Evergreen, CO: Evergreen Consulting Company.

Zandberg, I., & Lewis, L. (2008). *Technology-based distance education courses for public elementary and secondary school students: 2002–03 and 2004–05* (NCES 2008–008). Washington, DC: National Center for Education Statistics, Institute of Education Sciences, U.S. Department of Education.

Section III

PLANNING
AND IMPLEMENTATION

Chapter 10

Hardware and Software Evaluation

Hardware, with its flickering lights, modern designs, and colorful screens, may seem like the exciting component of digital technology, but among many computer professionals, software is where the action is. A computer cannot perform a single function unless a software program has been developed to provide instructions for the hardware. Some programs can be easily written with several basic commands, whereas more complex programs may require millions of instructions. Programmers who are involved in such large-scale software development are among the most talented and creative in the computer industry. Their completed work can engender feelings of accomplishment similar to those of an artist who has just completed a painting or a writer who has completed a new novel.

On the other hand, when something goes wrong, when a computer bug occurs, feelings of accomplishment can quickly fade. If a program is critical to an operation, a great deal of stress and frustration develop that evoke mental images of other, more appealing lines of work. These feelings last until the bug is found and corrected, and a sense of accomplishment returns, beginning the cycle again, waiting for the next bug to emerge.

With the proliferation of computing technology over the past several decades, this scenario occurs at many levels—perhaps involving a team of software engineers correcting the transmission of data from a NASA satellite, a staff of computer programmers in an education department implementing a new statewide school report card system, a secretary experimenting with new features of the latest version of a word-processing package, a high school class creating an interactive Web site, or a group of fourth graders completing their first newsletter with a desktop publishing program. Software surely is where the action is, where things happen, and where feelings of joy and frustration come and go in relation to successes and problems.

The fact is, however, that every technology application has a hardware and a software component, each of which is crucial to its eventual outcome and effectiveness. Planning the application, therefore, must involve an integrated approach to planning, evaluating, and acquiring both components. In many school districts as well as in many other organizations, there frequently has been too much emphasis on the acquisition of hardware alone. A common assumption was that once the hardware was acquired, the other components would follow. This unfortunately did not always happen, and as a result, some schools invested in hardware but did not always realize the benefits they expected.

This chapter presents the major criteria for evaluating hardware and software, concluding with an examination of several issues associated with hardware and software evaluation and acquisition.

DECISIONS, DECISIONS, DECISIONS

Tom Snyder Productions, one of the more successful instructional software development companies, markets a series of excellent simulation programs titled Decisions, Decisions. These simulation programs require students to make frequent decisions regarding real-life phenomena. Depending on the decision selected, new situations are created, each requiring the students to make additional decisions. The series title provides an *almost* adequate description of the real-life activity of evaluating and selecting hardware and software: "Decisions, Decisions, and More Decisions" may be more appropriate. With thousands of products available, the possibilities are mind boggling. Even after hardware or software has been selected, new models or new versions quickly appear—requiring yet another decision. Hardware add-ons, software updates, modifications, and new releases are commonplace in computing life. As a result, the number and types of decisions have grown considerably in the past 20 years.

A Look at Hardware

Planning for computer hardware requires planning for the long range. The life cycle of most computing equipment is 4 to 7 years, but it is not unusual to see equipment used longer. In fact, many schools continue to use computer hardware until the equipment literally no longer works.

As a result, when acquiring hardware, decision makers should be aware that this equipment may be used for a long time and evaluate it accordingly.

The durability of hardware also tempts administrators and others to look at their available hardware, which may have been acquired for one purpose, and to consider using it for other purposes. This is desirable as long as the hardware is appropriate, not too old, and can meet the needs of the application. However, the normal modus operandi should not be one of searching for applications for underutilized hardware, which reflects poor planning and an overemphasis on hardware. Rather, planning for hardware should be integrated with the other components of an application. If available hardware is appropriate, then it should be used. Otherwise, new hardware should be considered.

In buying hardware, most schools find themselves making decisions from two different perspectives: acquiring new hardware for new applications and replacing hardware for existing applications. In acquiring new hardware for new applications, the purchasing pattern is more varied, with buyers attempting to select the best equipment to meet the needs of the application. When replacing hardware for existing applications, the pattern reveals a tendency to continue with the same manufacturer and platform, simply upgrading to a newer model with greater capacity or speed. The various reasons for this include familiarity with the equipment and concern about retraining and conversion costs, particularly if larger computer systems are involved.

This approach is similar to the way people purchase most personal equipment, such as home appliances or automobiles. If they have had a good experience with a particular manufacturer, they go back to that manufacturer and buy a newer model when the old one needs replacing. There is one significant difference when it comes to computers, though. Once someone knows how to drive a car, for example, he or she is able to drive a new car of almost any manufacturer with relative ease. With computers, the "driving" is performed via software, and changing the hardware manufacturer may require changing the software, which in many cases means learning to "drive" all over again. The reason for this is that software standards generally do not exist, and software that drives one manufacturer's machine will not necessarily drive another. This is especially true for large mainframe computer systems and servers and less so for microcomputers.

Large urban school districts and other organizations with mainframe computer systems have shown a reluctance to change hardware manufacturers even if a better performing and less-expensive piece of hardware is available, because they do not want to change or convert the software. With microcomputers, the situation is somewhat different. Although several companies dominate the market, hundreds of microcomputer manufacturers exist, which makes for very keen competition. Most of these manufacturers have designed their products to be compatible with the dominant manufacturers and to use the same software. Another interesting phenomenon unique to microcomputers is the fact that much of the software being used, including the operating systems, is not being provided by the hardware manufacturers; the exception is Apple, which does provide the operating system for its Macintosh computers. The term *software platform* is used for foundation software (operating system and other fundamental programs of a computer system). Software companies such as Microsoft Corporation (DOS/Windows) are providing software that runs on a wide variety of manufacturers' microcomputers and is not entirely machine-dependent. These factors have combined to create a more-dynamic hardware acquisition pattern than exists with mainframe computer systems. However, these factors have also combined much of the hardware and software decisions together since the hardware manufacturers have financial arrangements with software providers to bundle their microcomputers with some basic suite of software products. As a result, when a school district purchases a Dell microcomputer, for instance, it is also acquiring Microsoft software.

A Look at Software

Although the fundamental nature of software has not changed over the past several decades, its acquisition, people-interface formats, and implementation have changed radically. Throughout the 1970s, all computer installations required a well-trained software staff to develop application programs using high-level languages such as COBOL, FORTRAN, or PL/1, provided by the hardware manufacturer. Today, in large computer installations, a good deal of application program development still exists, but programmers are also making much greater use of software development tools such as database management systems, communications control software, and HTML filters, which significantly reduce the number of high-level language instructions. In some cases, these software tools are provided by the hardware manufacturers, but more likely they are supplied by software development firms.

Once major software applications such as a database management system or a course management system are established in a school district, users such as administrators and teachers become dependent on the programming staff for support, documentation, maintenance, and modification of the software. A major application such as a student record-keeping system or a financial management system can have a useful life cycle of 15 years or more. As a result, users and programmers must have good working relationships and procedures for regularly maintaining and upgrading these systems. Clear lines of responsibility may be drawn, with the users identifying needs and improvements and the programming staff modifying the software. In the most successful situations, the overall software decisions are shared between the users and the technical staff.

The movement to microcomputer technology has also changed the technician–user relationship. The vast majority of microcomputer users do not program in a high-level language but instead use software packages for word processing, spreadsheets, desktop publishing, and a host of other applications. Most of these packages require only a basic understanding of how to load a CD-ROM or download a program from a vendor Web site and to respond to a series of menus, prompts, and alternatives. With good documentation and minimal technical support, users are expected to be able to master enough of the features of these packages to do most of what they wish to accomplish. Not unexpectedly, the degree of user success in these environments varies. User aptitude and experience are factors, but the choice of appropriate software is also a critical and determining factor.

The Internet and World Wide Web have also significantly changed the way software is developed and acquired. With so many companies, schools, and individuals using the Internet, many companies have had to reconsider how their software products can be used in a networked environment. As a result, many of them are now providing Web versions and interfaces to be used on the Internet or on local intranets. In many cases, stand-alone software products are being completely redeveloped as Web products.

For most administrative users, the major applications and appropriate software programs center on database, spreadsheet, word processing, Web browsing, and office automation, including e-mail applications. Although many packages exist for these applications, Microsoft has come to dominate the market. It is estimated that Microsoft has more than 90% of the market share for some of its products. For instructional microcomputer users, the number of applications and appropriate software packages are almost unlimited. Depending on subject, grade level, and student interests and abilities, thousands of software packages exist, and the number keeps increasing every day. However, with some instructional software programs such as course management systems, Blackboard, Inc., has been aggressive in acquiring its competition and holds about a 70% share of this market.

School districts have begun to establish instructional software evaluation teams to sort through and evaluate all that is available. Large school systems such as those in Chicago and

New York City employ full-time staffs whose major responsibilities involve evaluating and selecting software for use in their schools. Some states have established effective statewide software evaluation services that publish or provide online databases of their software reviews along with suggestions for developing lesson plans. Despite this centralization, a good deal of instructional software evaluation is being done at the school level. Frequently, it is an opinion-driven activity, with people liking or disliking certain products based on their knowledge, experiences, or teaching philosophies. Technology coordinators may have the greatest influence in evaluating and selecting software for use in the schools, but committees or teams of teachers and other professionals are increasingly involved in evaluating software as they would any other curricular or academic materials. Involving end users in software selection may seem obvious, but stories abound of teachers and others questioning the value of software products acquired by somebody else.

Regardless of the process by which software is selected in a district or school, administrators have a responsibility to ensure that the software is appropriate for its intended use. Although administrators need not be involved in every software evaluation activity, they should establish procedures to ensure that the appropriate technical and application (administrative or instructional) criteria are considered.

HARDWARE EVALUATION CRITERIA

Evaluating hardware can be a complicated process. For school districts with large mainframe computer systems, acquiring hardware means the investment of millions of dollars for many years with a particular vendor. As an example, in 2007, the New York City Department of Education awarded IBM an $80 million contract to install a mainframe computer-based Achievement Reporting and Innovation System (ARIS). The purpose of ARIS is to keep detailed records of students, which can aid in improving student achievement. Making such large investments requires the careful development of specifications and evaluation of equipment. In the public sector, administrators will likely use competitive bidding procedures that may require identifying a formalized evaluation procedure to prospective bidders.

Figure 10.1 identifies seven important factors for evaluating and selecting computer hardware:

1. *Performance:* How well does the hardware work?
2. *Compatibility:* Does the hardware work with other equipment?
3. *Modularity/expandability:* Can the hardware grow as applications grow?
4. *Ergonomics:* Is the hardware designed with people in mind?
5. *Software availability:* Is the software you wish to use currently available?
6. *Vendor:* What is the reputation of the manufacturer in terms of technical support, maintenance, and industry position?
7. *Cost:* What are the costs?

A serious hardware evaluation will take each of these factors into account when comparing different products. As much as possible, quantitative assessments should be developed. Certain factors such as capacity, speed, and costs are easily quantified. However, other factors such as ergonomics or software availability lend themselves better to qualitative assessments.

Site visits or field tests should be part of every major acquisition, particularly when purchasing new models. Perhaps the most revealing activities in evaluating hardware are visits to comparable schools or districts that are using the hardware and running similar applications. In addition, popular vendors of both large and small hardware systems are generally most cooperative in demonstrating their products. For larger mainframe computer systems and servers, vendors

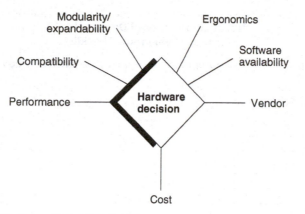

FIGURE 10.1   Major Hardware Evaluation Factors.

will also assist in conducting benchmark tests of typical applications. A *benchmark test* consists of running the same computer program on several different machines and comparing speed, response time, hardware resource requirements, and other factors. For microcomputer systems, local retail businesses are most accommodating in providing demonstrations. Trade journals and consultants should also be employed. Commercial research services such as the Gartner Group of Stamford, Connecticut (http://www.gartner.com), do periodic hardware evaluation reports and ratings based on national surveys. Although expensive, they can be valuable starting points in assessing the performance and customer satisfaction with various products.

In conducting an evaluation, one approach is to provide a hardware checklist or evaluation form to assist evaluators. However, the factors that go into a hardware evaluation can be very complex, especially for larger and more-expensive systems. Hardware evaluations are not easily reduced to a simple checklist and should have substantial qualitative as well as quantitative backup material. Figure 10.2 provides a checklist that one district used to summarize and compare hardware evaluation ratings. The most appropriate use of a checklist like this would be as part of an evaluation summary and a discussion among administrators and teachers.

All of the evaluation criteria identified here are important for an effective evaluation, but in some circumstances one or more factors may carry more weight than others. A brief review of each of these factors will help clarify their general importance in the evaluation process.

Performance

Most hardware performance indicators attempt to assess capacity, speed, or quality of output. Table 10.1 provides some of the common performance criteria in evaluating major computer hardware components.

Large mainframe manufacturers generally customize their central processing units (CPUs), and an in-depth evaluation requires a good deal of technical expertise. For microcomputers, the most commonly used CPU components are provided by Motorola, Inc. (for Apple computers) and Intel Corporation (for DOS/Windows computers). Several major attributes of all CPUs can be understood by many nontechnical people. For example, CPUs are frequently compared based on the capacity of the primary storage units as measured in bytes. Generally, the more primary storage a CPU has, the more processing that can be accomplished, assuming other factors such as software and other hardware components are equal.

North Central School District No. 1
Hardware Evaluation Checklist

Hardware Description (Type of equipment; also include/identify three manufacturers or models evaluated)

Manufacturer/Model 1 _____

_____

_____

_____

Manufacturer/Model 2 _____

_____

_____

_____

Manufacturer/Model 3 _____

_____

_____

_____

	Ratings		
Evaluation Criteria	Mfg. No. 1	Mfg. No. 2	Mfg. No. 3
Performance (capacity, speed)	_____	_____	_____
Compatibility	_____	_____	_____
Modularity/expandability	_____	_____	_____
Ergonomics	_____	_____	_____
Software availability	_____	_____	_____
Vendor	_____	_____	_____
Costs	_____	_____	_____
Final Ratings	_____	_____	_____

FIGURE 10.2   Hardware Checklist.

In terms of processing capacity, one of the most important factors in evaluating a CPU is the size of the data path within the CPU itself. These are usually established in 8-bit increments (8, 16, 32, 64, 128, etc.), each designed to carry instructions or data from one CPU subunit to another. A 32-bit data path can carry twice as many instructions or data in the same time as a 16-bit data path; a 64-bit data path can carry twice as many as a 32-bit data path and four times as many as a 16-bit data path. Theoretically, the size of the data path should directly relate to processing speed. In practice, however, although larger data paths are without a doubt faster, a direct proportion of speed to size is not realized because of software and waiting for other hardware components such as input and output devices.

Evaluating the speed of a CPU can be confusing because different terminology and measures are used. The term *megaflop* (MFLOP) is used to compare the processing speeds of different types of computers. A megaflop is defined as a million mathematical calculations per second. This is similar to the commonly used acronym MIPS, which designates a million instructions per second. However, in comparing CPUs, probably the most common speed measure is megahertz (MHz), which is a million machine cycles per second. A machine cycle is defined as the number of electronic pulses that a CPU can generate as controlled or timed by its own internal clock.

TABLE 10.1 Performance Criteria of Major Hardware Components

Component	Criteria
CPU	Capacity of the primary storage unit as measured in millions (megabytes) or billions (gigabytes) of bytes
	Size of data paths within the CPU as measured in bits (8, 16, 32, 64, 128, etc.)
	Machine cycle time as measured in millions (megahertz, MHz) or billions (gigahertz, GHz) of cycles per second
	Number of input and output devices that can be connected to the CPU
Disk storage (magnetic or optical)	Capacity as measured in megabytes, gigabytes, or terabytes
Video display	Quality of visual image as measured by resolution and color capability
Printer	Print technology (laser, ink-jet, etc.)
	Quality of print image (text and graphics)
	Speed as measured by characters per minute, pages per minute, or lines per minute
Modem	Speed as measured by kilobits or megabits per second

A machine cycle can be compared to a traffic light that goes through a timed sequence of red, yellow, and green signals. When the timing sequence changes (speeds up or slows down), the lights change accordingly. In the case of a CPU, the time pulses control the execution of instructions so that the more pulses that can be generated, the faster the CPU operates.

Performance of various input and output devices is also frequently measured in terms of capacity or speed. Storage capacity of magnetic disk equipment is measured in megabytes (millions of bytes), gigabytes (billions of bytes), and terabytes (trillions of bytes). The most important speed measure for disks and most input/output devices is transfer rate, which is simply the speed of moving data from the device to the CPU as measured in millions of bits per second.

These various measures may seem a bit confusing, or perhaps even alarming, because they involve speeds and numbers that are impossible for most people to conceptualize. However, in evaluations, the relative speeds and capacities are more important than the absolute. A 240-MHz machine is twice as fast as a 120-MHz machine, which is twice as fast as a 60-MHz machine.

For devices such as video displays and printers, the quality of the output is as important as speed. As an example, many users prefer the quality of a laser printer even though it might be slower than other types of printers. Readers may wish to review Appendix A, which compares the characteristics of various output devices.

Reliability and durability are important factors but are sometimes overlooked because they cannot be measured with the same precision as other performance criteria. Evaluation of these factors is best handled by contacting other users or research services. Computer operations managers frequently keep logs of hardware downtime and are willing to share this information with colleagues. In evaluating durability, keep in mind that usage variables may exist that might not apply in all situations. For example, keyboards in a primary school computer lab used frequently by many young children might not last as long as keyboards used occasionally by adults. In evaluating reliability and durability, the best approach is to seek information from similar environments.

Compatibility

Compatibility is a common term in technology but is used two different ways—referring to either the capability of one device to work well with another device or the capability of one device to work the same way as another device. An important element of compatibility is whether the hardware manufacturer supports *open system architecture,* which essentially means that all hardware specifications are made public so that third-party manufacturers can develop components that are in fact compatible. Many smaller hardware manufacturers market their products based on their compatibility (to work well) with other equipment. Manufacturers of peripheral equipment such as disk drives or printers will always identify their products' compatibility with various central processing units. For example, Hewlett-Packard makes laser printers that are fully compatible with Dell PC and Apple Macintosh microcomputers. As more school districts have become involved in designing WANs or LANs, it has become critical for them to know whether the various hardware components (CPUs, printers, disk devices, etc.) of these networks are compatible and can connect to one another.

The ability to meet compatibility criteria is easy to judge because no relative measures are involved. The equipment is either compatible or not. Qualified compatibility, percentage compatibility, or other "gray area" compatibility should not be accepted. The vendor should be able to demonstrate to a customer's satisfaction the complete compatibility of the equipment.

For a computing device to work the same way as another means that it will execute a program in the exact same fashion. This is critical for any applications that are expected to share the same programs, such as a common database system or an instructional local area network. Generally, the hardware products from a common vendor will execute programs in the same way. Historically this was not always the case. As an example, Apple Computer marketed two popular microcomputers in the 1980s—Apple IIs and Macintoshes—that were not compatible or were incapable of running the same programs.

In plans for technology at the district level, compatibility is frequently considered as an overall policy issue and one that is not left to individual schools. Many districts establish compatibility guidelines that restrict the types of equipment that can be purchased. It is an excellent discussion item for any planning committee because it leads naturally into long-range thinking about hardware.

Modularity/Expandability

Modularity and expandability are also very important factors for long-range planning. Some hardware analysts consider these to be two different factors that should be evaluated separately. However, the importance of modularity frequently manifests itself when considering expansion, and therefore these two features can be evaluated together. *Modularity* refers to the interchangeability of components or parts of a hardware system. For example, can RAMs or ROMs easily be replaced in a CPU, or can several different types of devices be used or interchanged on an input/output port? *Expandability* is the ability of computer hardware to grow or expand as new applications are developed or as old applications become larger.

The evaluation of modularity and expandability is critical, especially in the acquisition of mainframe computer systems and servers. Because of the costs involved, computer operations managers tend to develop equipment plans that stagger the replacement of certain components of a large hardware system at set intervals. A simplified example of the replacement cycle for a mainframe computer might be as follows:

Component	Replacement Cycle
CPUs	Years 1 & 2
Data communications controllers	Year 3
Secondary storage devices	Years 3 & 4
Input/output devices	Years 5, 6, & 7

At the end of 7 years, the cycle repeats itself depending on application growth, financial condition, and available technology. As a result, mainframe systems are acquired as a series of upgrades rather than as onetime, total system replacement. It would be impossible to function in this mode unless the equipment was both modular and expandable. For microcomputers, the expected life cycle can vary from 4 to 7 years depending on their usage.

Modularity and expandability should also be considered in acquiring microcomputer systems. For example, as with large systems, users should know how many and which type of input and output units can be attached or whether the primary storage can be expanded. Information on these issues is readily available from manufacturers and retailers. However, these factors are not quite as critical because at some point the entire microcomputer system will be replaced.

Modularity and expandability depend to a certain extent on the currency of the equipment's technology. Technology is constantly evolving. To expand, newly purchased equipment should not reflect old technology being phased out or considered "dead-ended." By the same token, some new technology is experimental and may not catch on or may quickly be replaced by newer technology. This is not a common problem, but even the major manufacturers have had to discontinue products (e.g., IBM PC) because of changes in technology, competition, design problems, or customer apathy. Information is readily available from user groups and trade journals on the nature of the technology being used on most major manufacturers' equipment. If serious doubts exist about the technology of equipment under consideration or if information is difficult to come by, this might indicate a problem and should be evaluated accordingly.

Ergonomics

Ergonomics describes hardware features directly related to whether the equipment is user friendly. Is it pleasant to use? Is it easy to use? Most manufacturers of hardware—particularly items such as keyboards, video displays, and other widely used devices—do consider the people who have to use their equipment. For example, the basic color patterns for most computer equipment are soft, pleasing to the eye, and blend into office and classroom environments.

For administrative applications, the feel of a keyboard is very important to staff who may be using the equipment for many hours at a time. Some of the early microcomputers used what was known as a "chiclet" keyboard, so named because the keys were small plastic pegs that looked and felt like Chiclets chewing gum. Although fine for occasional use, they were a problem for many typists. Their feel was different from a standard typewriter keyboard, and their spacing was more compact, which caused coordination problems. Although they are still available on some portable computers, they have been replaced on desktop microcomputers by the standard keyboard. Several manufacturers also offer keyboards that are designed to reduce stress to ligaments and muscle tissue in the wrists and lower arms. These may be more appropriate, especially for secretaries and other staff who use a computer for long periods of time.

For instructional applications, various ergonomic features such as video display resolution, color, and sound capability can add significantly to lessons and presentations. However, the potential of these features is generally realized only through appropriate graphics and audio software. Other ergonomic features and options important for instruction include the availability of special hardware features for younger children, such as the enlarged Muppet keyboard and voice synthesizers, Braille keyboards, and large video screens for special education students.

Software Availability

In evaluating hardware, it is most desirable to identify the software that will meet the needs of an application. A determination can then be made as to whether the identified software can run on the hardware being evaluated. This principle may seem obvious, but situations abound in which schools have acquired equipment without consideration of software. Administrators or teachers then search for applications that in some cases cannot be found or do not exist.

Such situations are typically more of a problem with small manufacturers but can also arise with the major manufacturers. A good example of this occurred when the Apple Macintosh microcomputer was first introduced in 1985. In terms of most hardware evaluation criteria such as performance, ergonomics, and vendor, the Macintosh rated very highly. However, very little software was available for it. Although the Macintosh provided a very advanced authoring language in HyperCard, none of the popular software products developed by independent software companies could run on it. As a result, many schools that had invested significant resources into Apple II microcomputers were slow to acquire the newer Macintoshes. Although many instructional software developers caught up with Macintosh hardware technology in the early 1990s, software availability is still an issue, especially when one considers the number of software products available for DOS/Windows machines. Apple has basically solved this problem now by allowing Microsoft's Windows Operating System to run on Macintosh computers.

Vendor

Hardware is usually a long-term investment. Through the purchase of hardware, schools are also buying into a long-term relationship with a vendor. This is particularly true for mainframe systems and servers but exists to a certain degree for all hardware acquisitions. The vendor should be evaluated in terms of reputation, technical support, training, hardware maintenance, and industry position.

Most schools find themselves in situations in which they have already had experience with one or two manufacturers. These experiences are valuable and provide the best information regarding a vendor's performance. Additional information is easily obtained from services such as CNET, journals such as *Technological Horizons in Education,* and buyers' guides such as ZDNet. However, the computing industry is dynamic; many new companies have entered it, and many have left. School administrators should be open to, and aware of, some of these dynamics.

For example, IBM was a dominant manufacturer of mainframe, minicomputer, and microcomputer equipment for decades. Its reputation for technical support, maintenance, and software availability, among other things, was excellent. For certain segments, especially in private businesses and corporations, IBM cornered in excess of 70% of the world market. However, IBM struggled in the 1980s and 1990s to keep up with the competition in the microcomputer market and failed to maintain its base as customers switched from larger to smaller computer systems. As a result, relatively new companies such as Dell, Compaq (now a division of Hewlett-Packard), and Gateway became the dominant manufacturers of microcomputer systems. In December 2004, IBM announced the sale of its entire PC division to a Chinese manufacturer (Lenovo) of microcomputers.

In the primary and secondary school instructional microcomputer market, the market share picture is different. Apple Computer had dominated this market for many years. The foundation of Apple's success was based on the wide acceptance of the Apple II microcomputers, which were first introduced in the late 1970s, followed by the introduction of the Macintosh in the 1980s. Apple is a classic example of the dynamics of the computer industry and how a new company that began in 1976 can become a major player in a short time. In the 1980s, Apple was clearly a leader in microcomputer design and manufacturing. In the 1990s, because of increasing competition from new companies, Apple struggled to maintain its leading position and began to lose its market share, even in the primary and secondary schools. However, in the first decade of the 21st century, Apple has rebounded, and its share of the total microcomputer market is approximately 10% with about a 25% share of the education market.

Cost

School administrators understand the importance of costs as a factor in all equipment acquisitions, including computer hardware. Defining costs for hardware can be complex and involves initial acquisition, yearly maintenance, lease purchases, and a host of other possible arrangements. School administrators, particularly in public bidding situations, find the competition very keen. Many of the smaller companies provide attractive proposals that can result in substantial savings. Needless to say, all proposals, regardless of the source, need to be carefully reviewed and evaluated. In considering hardware costs, administrators need to approach hardware acquisition as the total cost of ownership (TCO), which takes into account not just the purchase price but also ongoing maintenance, upgrade, and support costs. TCO will be discussed more fully in Chapter 13.

SOFTWARE EVALUATION CRITERIA

The most important factor in evaluating and selecting software is determining how well it meets the application's needs. For example, a multimedia authoring program might need to have extensive facilities for developing and controlling sound, images, and video, whereas a database package might be evaluated for its file-handling capabilities such as data merging, query language, and sort features. These evaluation factors can be extensive. For example, depending on the nature of the application, the Baltimore County Public School District (2009) recommends from 30 to more than 50 software evaluation criteria be used in acquiring instructional software. All of the criteria for every school application will not be reviewed here; however, several major evaluation criteria (see Figure 10.3) are common to all computer software packages, as follows:

1. *Efficiency:* How well are the programs written?
2. *Ease of use:* How easy is the software to use?
3. *Documentation:* What is the quality and quantity of the documentation?
4. *Hardware requirements:* What hardware is needed to run the software?
5. *Vendor:* What is the reputation of the developer in terms of support, maintenance, and industry position?
6. *Cost:* How much does it cost?

These factors should be considered in the evaluation and selection of every software product. As is the case in judging hardware, one or more of these factors may be more important than the others, depending on individual circumstances and applications. Together with a determination of how well the software meets the needs of a particular application, they form the basis for evaluating all types of software.

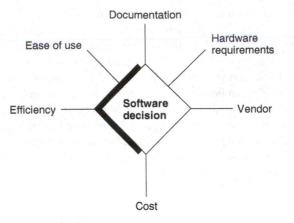

FIGURE 10.3   Major Software Evaluation Factors.

Efficiency

Most software efficiency measures relate to the speed with which a program executes. Overall response times, data access or search time, and sort time all relate to the operational speed of a program and are easily quantified. For software packages that are to run on mainframe systems, technical staff are needed to evaluate efficiency. For microcomputer software, users with some assistance from technical staff can evaluate basic speed measures such as response time and access time. Response time measures how quickly a program responds with the desired computer activity once a request has been made. It can refer to fetching a record from a database, answering a Help inquiry, or performing a calculation. Data access or search time refers specifically to locating data on a disk file. It directly relates to the number of records on the database and, more importantly, to the manner in which they are stored.

In evaluating data access times, the same disk equipment must be used when comparing software, because the speed of the disk hardware can greatly influence access times. In fact, the term *access time* is also used to measure the speed of disk equipment itself in fetching records, and this factor must be neutralized. For large record-keeping applications involving thousands or tens of thousands of records, *sort time* or the time required to sequence or merge data is also frequently used to test the efficiency of file-handling software.

Professional software research firms such as the InfoWorld Test Center (http://www .infoworld.com/) generally use a method of measuring software efficiency called the benchmark test. Benchmark tests can be developed by technical staff in any organization, including schools. As described earlier in this chapter, these tests consist of identifying tasks that the software being evaluated would be expected to perform, which are then executed on different software packages and measured in terms of speed. For example, in evaluating a sort feature of a database program, an appropriate benchmark test might be to sort the typical number of student records that might exist in a school's student files.

Benchmark tests are easy to perform but, again, it is essential to make sure that the hardware, data files, and any other factors that can influence speed are identical. Hardware characteristics, even within a family of computers, are very different, and software will perform differently depending on these characteristics. For example, a software benchmark test that compares two programs by running one on an Apple iMac 2.66 GHz computer and the other on a iMac 3.6 GHz computer is not valid because the inherent CPU speed of the iMac 3.6 GHz is much greater than that of the iMac 2.66 GHz.

Efficiency also relates to how well a program is written in terms of structure, logic flow, programming language, and so forth. When the source code (high-level language instructions) is open and available, it is desirable to have the technical staff evaluate the quality of the programs. This is generally a subjective evaluation dependent on the staff's knowledge and expertise. In cases in which only the object code (machine language instructions) is provided, this type of evaluation is not possible.

Ease of Use

The software evaluation factor of ascending importance in the past few years is ease of use. With machines being placed in offices, libraries, classrooms, and teacher prep rooms, their utilization depends significantly on how easy the software is to use. This factor relates directly or perhaps inversely to the level of knowledge of the intended users. Software that is to be used by a professional technical staff may be more difficult to use and may require a certain amount of training. Software that is to be used by occasional or beginning users such as students should be as user friendly as possible. Menu-driven screens, online Help features, and good supporting documentation are characteristics of user-friendly software and should be evaluated accordingly. These are generally subjectively evaluated, although they can be reduced to a quantified individual or group rating.

In evaluating ease of use, seeking input from the target users is very desirable. Secretaries may be the best choice for evaluating a desktop publishing package, accountants for a financial accounting program, teachers for a course management system, and students for instructional software. This approach is an obvious example of involving users at various levels in a school in technology planning and implementation activities. Not only is their opinion important to the decision maker, but their involvement enhances the environment required for moving ahead with technology.

Documentation

The importance of documentation in software evaluation is consistently recognized regardless of the type of computer being used, the nature of the applications, or the level of expertise of the target users. The critical questions that should be clearly answered in the documentation are: What does the software do? How does it do it? and How do you use it?

Documentation standards have grown considerably since the proliferation of microcomputers; therefore, good documentation is to be expected and should be evaluated most rigorously. In recent years, the documentation manual has been supplemented or replaced by user-friendly Help files. Product updates, frequently asked questions (FAQs), and troubleshooting services also are provided on the software vendor's Web site. Software designed to execute on mainframe computer systems and most administrative software tend to be well documented, mainly because of the competition but also because this kind of software has matured. Word processing, spreadsheet, and database packages from the major vendors come with a good deal of high-quality documentation. These vendors have learned that to be competitive in these markets, they must have comprehensive, easy-to-understand manuals and intuitive, online Help features.

For instructional software, however, the quality and quantity of documentation varies. Some instructional software comes with little more than a CD-ROM and one or two pages of installation instructions. On the other hand, the more established companies will provide a complete set of installation and operating instructions. The best instructional software documentation will also include curricular materials and suggestions for integrating the package into classroom activities. Tom Snyder Productions, Broderbund, and Pearson Digital Learning are some of the major instructional software developers that have been attentive to providing good documentation with their products.

One of the exceptions to good documentation standards is software that may be available at little or no cost from software exchanges and individuals. It frequently may not have high-quality documentation, but this is to be expected given that the software is usually provided for free or just a nominal fee.

Hardware Requirements

This evaluation factor is the corollary to the software availability criterion used in evaluating hardware. Just as any hardware purchased must have available software, software being evaluated, likewise, may have specific hardware requirements. Generally, the following are hardware requirements for software:

Specific computer manufacturer/model/platform or CPU

Minimum primary storage capacity

Minimum magnetic disk space

Specialized input/output devices

This information, along with any other specialized hardware requirement, is readily available from the software supplier.

Most major software developers provide products for all major software platforms, but some smaller companies only market for a specific machine. Because it has the largest share of the market, DOS/Windows is usually the preferred platform for these companies.

All software programs have some minimum primary storage requirements. For popular software products reissued periodically as newer versions, purchasers should try to determine future primary storage requirements. Microsoft's Office 2003 requires a minimum 128 megabytes (MB) of RAM, whereas Microsoft Office 2007 requires 256 MB. Users might question the need for additional storage. However, the software developers are attempting to provide additional options and capabilities to make their products more attractive and competitive. It is highly recommended that extra primary storage space exist on all computing equipment so that this particular requirement can be easily met when evaluating software.

Any software packages that perform some type of file handling will require disk space. As with primary storage, the basic rule is that whatever is needed presently will surely increase in the future. A standard computing adage is "You can never have enough disk space." You should remember this when evaluating the hardware requirements of software, especially for applications using large databases and multimedia files. For example, going back to the Microsoft Office products, Office 2003 requires 400 MB of disk storage whereas Office 2007 requires 1.6 gigabytes (GB).

Many software products also identify certain specialized input/output or other peripheral equipment to use all of their features and options. For example, many software packages for microcomputers provide deluxe versions that require certain levels of sound and video capabilities. Many packages providing color images and graphs may require certain levels of screen resolution on video display equipment. Some instructional software packages used in science, music, or art may require certain quality soundboards, custom probe, synthesizer, or other specialized input equipment. When these packages are evaluated, this information is generally available and must be considered when selecting software. Failure to do so may result in acquiring software that will not run as planned on the school's hardware or, in the worst cases, not run at all.

In some situations, such as in selecting an integrated learning system, both hardware and software are evaluated together. This is a desirable situation and streamlines evaluation activities considerably. In general, when the hardware and software can be planned and acquired together, one can expect a smoother implementation of the application.

Vendor

All of the vendor characteristics that apply to hardware evaluation—such as support, maintenance, industry position, and reputation—also apply to software. However, given that there are many more software companies, evaluating this factor becomes a more difficult undertaking. Some of these companies consist of one full-time employee; others employ thousands. Microsoft Corporation, one of the world's largest software suppliers, has tens of thousands of support staff employees. As with many acquisitions, it is important to know with whom you are dealing, particularly if you expect to establish a long-term relationship. In an industry as dynamic as software development, those companies with proven track records should be considered over other companies that may be here today and gone tomorrow.

Track record cannot be considered in isolation, however, because many software companies specialize and develop expertise in limited applications. Companies that are the leaders in administrative software such as databases or spreadsheets may have very little expertise in instructional software such as simulations or interactive video programs. As a result, the evaluation of software vendors may require some in-depth exploration.

Software reviews, journal articles, and industry research services such as the Gartner Research Group (http://www.gartner.com/), CNET (http://news.cnet.com/), InfoWorld Test Center (http://www.infoworld.com/), and ZDNet (http://www.zdnet.com/) are all excellent sources of information regarding vendors. *Tech & Learning* (formerly *Classroom Computer Learning*) includes a software review column in each issue and devotes at least one issue to the best instructional software products of the year. Anyone involved with software evaluation, be they administrators or teachers, should use sources such as these to become familiar with the major software suppliers.

Cost

Costs for software vary significantly. On large computer systems, some comprehensive contracts—including software, certain levels of on-site support services, and training—can easily involve millions of dollars over several years. Integrated learning systems that combine software, hardware, and curriculum can easily cost in excess of a million dollars for a large school system. Some course management software (CMS) providers may charge a modest flat fee for the basic software license but might also require additional per-user (e.g., student) fees that can become quite expensive depending on the usage. In undertaking evaluations involving software of this magnitude, school districts must be careful and deliberate in making their selections.

On the other side of the spectrum, some instructional software programs for microcomputer applications cost less than $50. Where in the World Is Carmen Sandiego?, Broderbund Corporation's award-winning program, normally retails for $25 and on sale can be purchased for less than $20. Such inexpensive programs may be purchased simply for experimental purposes or as part of a software library without immediate application, which is desirable because it builds expertise and technical knowledge within a school. However, this approach should not constitute the modus operandi. Whether performed by an individual or, more desirably, by a team, software that is to be used regularly in a classroom should be reviewed and evaluated for both technical and instructional features. Simply because a software product might be inexpensive is not sufficient reason to relax or eliminate evaluation activities.

One of the most cost-effective approaches in acquiring software is the procurement of a site license. A site license allows the purchaser to use a software product for a number of users or computers. For example, Tom Snyder Productions sells its award-winning Science Court series for grades 4 through 6 science classes. A single copy of the entire series (12 programs) costs $799; 10 copies cost $4,000; and an unlimited site license cost $9,900. If a district planned to make extensive use of this program, the site license would be far more cost-effective than purchasing individual copies or even multiples of 10.

Chapter 13 provides a thorough treatment on finances and cost factors in acquiring technology. Readers are encouraged to review the material there.

ISSUES IN EVALUATING HARDWARE

In this section, several issues related to the evaluation of hardware in schools and school districts will be discussed. The purpose for presenting these issues is to make the reader aware of topics and trends in evaluating and acquiring hardware.

Evaluating Hardware for Administrative Applications

In evaluating hardware for administrative applications, several special considerations need to be mentioned. Because an objective of many administrative applications is developing information resources, certain hardware evaluation criteria such as compatibility and modularity/expandability become critical to ensuring that all equipment can contribute, connect, and grow together. Information needs to flow smoothly up, down, and across the school organization; any present or future incompatibility of hardware can seriously jeopardize this. As a result, school districts tend to establish central district control in developing hardware evaluation guidelines for administrative applications. In many cases, this might mean hardware standardization policies, district-wide procurement plans, or direct approval procedures by a district coordinator.

In school districts with large administrative computer operations, administrators generally do best by relying on their technical staffs. The technology for large systems is very sophisticated, and a trained staff is probably in the best position to conduct in-depth hardware evaluations and to recommend acquisition policies.

Administrative applications such as budgeting, personnel, and inventory control and the hardware used for them are almost identical to those in private industry and public agencies. Administrators and teachers involved with evaluating hardware for administrative applications should take advantage of the extensive data resources available in the private sector in addition to those in the educational sector.

Hardware manufacturers are increasingly designing all equipment to support and function in the client–server environment on which Internet technology is based. In large districts where schools are geographically dispersed, a wide area network likely is, or will be, put in place to integrate these schools and to connect the network to the Internet. Planning and upgrading data communications services to function effectively in the dynamic world of the Internet continues to be one of the more complex areas of technology. If necessary, consultants should be considered, especially when designing something new or making a major upgrade to an existing data communications system.

Evaluating Hardware for Instructional Applications

Evaluating hardware for instructional applications has evolved differently from administrative applications because many school districts have allowed more control and flexibility at the school level. To a degree, this is the result of differences in the hardware available for different subjects and grade levels. Hardware that is appropriate for teaching basic skills in the early grades may not have been appropriate for teaching business courses in the high schools or for doing desktop publishing. Districts will frequently provide guidelines for teachers to recommend equipment that they think will work best in their classrooms. As a result, some diversity of equipment, particularly with microcomputers, can be expected. However, administrators should also be careful to avoid a "technology of Babel" situation in which the district acquires many different machines that become difficult to maintain or worse yet be unable to communicate with one another.

Software availability is probably the most significant factor in evaluating hardware for instructional applications because, in many cases, teachers tend to identify software first and even consider it a far more important decision than the hardware. Teachers need to be aware of the hardware requirements of any software they are considering. All instructional software developers identify their products' hardware requirements. In addition, certain software packages used to control special-purpose devices such as voice synthesizers and scientific probes may work only with particular equipment.

Data communications capability has become increasingly more important as school districts seek to establish and maintain high-speed and reliable connections to the Internet. To plan for the development or expansion of a school district's data communications system to support instructional applications, a major hardware consideration is connecting local computer systems into local area (LAN) and wide area (WAN) networks first, and then connecting these to the Internet via a common communications interface. There can be many variations of this basic approach of computers connecting to LANs, LANs connecting to WANs, and WANs connecting to the Internet. Wireless networks (WLANs) also are becoming increasingly popular. Many benefits will derive from a well-planned network, but it is also a more complex technology than a stand-alone environment. If the expertise does not exist within a district, administrators should consider using consultant services in designing and evaluating the hardware required for a network.

Mainframes and Servers

The majority of the American public is familiar with acquiring microcomputer equipment. They shop in a local CompUSA or Best Buy store and have become familiar with acquiring computers and necessary components. Some of the experiences in acquiring computers for personal use are important when acquiring equipment for a school district or for a school. However, other classifications of computer equipment need more extensive technological experience. Through the 1980s, many organizations acquired large mainframe computers that formed the center or hub of most of their technological support. The large mainframe computers gave way to smaller microcomputers, and the era of the large mainframe computer was to come to an end. However, for large organizations including school districts, the end has not come yet. School districts in large cities with hundreds of thousands of students still maintain and acquire mainframe computers. IBM Corporation has the largest market share of the mainframe business and introduces new models every 2 or 3 years. Although the idea of a central computer center housing a large mainframe computer is understood in large urban school districts, it has little applicability in most school districts. However, even smaller school districts tend to have a central computer facility that houses servers rather than mainframe computers.

In Chapter 8, the concept of client–server architecture was presented as the fundamental underlying hardware system that characterizes most computer network environments, including the Internet and World Wide Web. In a client–server environment, the client, or end user of a computer, makes a request or query for data to a server. The server, performed by computer(s) sharing network control, processes the request and returns the results to the client. As a result, most organizations including school districts tend to maintain a center that houses the server or, in many cases, multiple servers that handle the requests for data from all of the microcomputers that are distributed throughout the school district in labs, classrooms, libraries, etc. Servers are essentially microcomputers that contain more-sophisticated software as well as specialized hardware capabilities that enable them to receive and send messages back and forth to the other microcomputers on the network and to other networks outside of the school or school district. Standard servers from companies such as Sun Microsystems or Hewlett-Packard cost from $2,000 to $5,000. However, more-sophisticated servers with the ability to control a large network of microcomputers can easily cost tens of thousands of dollars. A recent trend in the design of server hardware and software is to take on more functions that in years past were performed by mainframe computers (Vance, 2009). These functions include providing downloadable copies of the operating system, database programs, and other software packages that are being used throughout the organization. IBM, one of the largest manufacturers of mainframe computers, is presently in litigation with several companies over monopolistic practices involved with attempts to acquire companies that are developing servers that perform mainframe capabilities. What is important is not simply corporate strategy and competition but the trend for servers to take on more computing activity. In fact, an argument can be made that servers are evolving into the new mainframe computers but at much less cost.

Bulk Purchasing, State Contracts, and Life Cycles

The concept of bulk purchasing is well understood in many aspects of organizational procurement of equipment and supplies, that is, there are savings by buying a large number of units rather than one or two at a time. This is true of most computer hardware acquisitions, especially the standard microcomputer. School districts and state education departments have actively negotiated education discounts on computer equipment mainly to incur savings by providing pricing that school districts find attractive. As much as possible, school districts should take advantage of these discounts and procure multiple units once or twice a year, depending on the budget cycle.

The idea of bulk purchasing also has the benefit of standardizing hardware manufactured by one or two vendors rather than many vendors. This too is desirable in that maintenance and upgrades are easier if the technical support staff members are working with a fixed number of products and manufacturers.

Bulk purchasing and dealing with a limited number of manufacturers should also lead to desirable planning processes such as determining appropriate life cycles so that hardware is not simply being run until it no longer works or cannot be repaired. Earlier in this chapter, it was mentioned that most microcomputers have 4- to 7-year life cycles; that is, within 4 to 7 years, replacement for the equipment in question should be considered. Although 4 to 7 years is rather imprecise, how long a microcomputer or other piece of hardware might last depends on the amount and nature of the use it gets. For instance, a microcomputer on a secretary's desk is used day in and day out for hours on end in preparing memos and e-mail, doing database searches, and performing other computer-dependent activity. Computers in an instructional computer laboratory may get much less activity but are being used by many more individuals, some of whom might not be as careful in how the equipment is used. Buying in bulk once or twice a year to save on per-unit costs might also be beneficial in establishing a replacement life cycle system and ensuring that equipment throughout the school district is relatively current and in good working order.

ISSUES IN EVALUATING SOFTWARE

In this section, several issues related to the evaluation of software in schools and school districts will be discussed. The purpose of presenting these issues is to make the reader aware of topics and trends in evaluating and acquiring software.

Administrative Software Evaluation

Critical to software evaluation is a determination as to how well the software meets the specific needs of the application through the various features provided. Reviewing all the existing administrative applications software is not possible here, but Figures 10.4, 10.5, and 10.6 list some of the more important evaluation features for three popular applications: word processing, electronic spreadsheets, and databases. These features can be considered regardless of whether the specific software product is stand-alone or part of an integrated package such as Microsoft Office.

Microsoft Word is the most popular word-processing software package in use today. Originally developed for the DOS/Windows machines, versions are also available for Macintosh computers. Microsoft Word also measures up well against most of the features identified in Figure 10.4. Furthermore, it is regularly upgraded, with versions providing new features issued every year.

Figure 10.5 identifies some of the features to look for in electronic spreadsheet programs. Microsoft's Excel, Lotus 1-2-3, and Borland International's Quattro Pro are among the most popular packages. All of the products provide the standard spreadsheet cell and mathematical features. As spreadsheets advance in sophistication, more importance is being placed on graphics, charts, data presentation facilities, and integration with other software (word processing, database) applications.

The most important administrative software evaluation decision is the selection of a database management package (see Figure 10.6). Although it is not unusual to experiment with different word-processing and spreadsheet programs, most organizations, including schools, will standardize their database software and, once established, will be reluctant to change it. One of the most important features of database software relates to data and file sharing in both local and wide area networks. Given the inherent complexity of networked systems, administrators should rely on the expertise of the technical staff when evaluating the networking capabilities of database software. For many years, Ashton-Tate's dBASE had been the industry leader for database management software for microcomputer systems. However, other database products such as Access (Microsoft), Paradox (Borland), Approach (Lotus), FOCUS (Information Builders), and FileMaker Pro (FileMaker, Inc.) have become more popular. For mixed (mainframe and

Number and type of fonts

Number of type styles (boldface, underline, shadow, etc.)

Footnoting

Word wrap

Menu-driven

Lengthwise/Landscape printing

Print preview

Graphics integration

ASCII file conversion

Conversion of other word processing files

Multiple document processing (work on more than one document at a time)

Multiple column controls

Spelling checker (how many words?)

Thesaurus

Document security

Grammar checker

Web page interface

FIGURE 10.4   Features of Word Processing Software.

Number of rows and columns

Editing features

Copy features

Lengthwise/Landscape printing

Multiple spreadsheet processing

Menu-driven

Spreadsheet merging

Spreadsheet security

Graphics integration

Database integration

Types and dimensions of charts (line, bar, pie, etc.)

Types of statistical functions supported

Basic (summaries, averages, percentages)

Advanced (standard deviations, correlations, analysis of variance)

Web page interface

FIGURE 10.5   Features of Electronic Spreadsheet Software.

Database structure (relational, flat file, etc.)

File security

Report generator program features

Statistical reporting features

Query language capabilities

Database restructuring

Sort/merge

Speed

Sort options (ascending, descending, levels)

Data-sharing features

Conversion of other database files

File merge capabilities (electronic spreadsheet, word processing)

Internet access capabilities

FIGURE 10.6   Features of Database Software.

microcomputer) environments, products such as Oracle (Oracle, Inc.) and FOCUS (Information Builders) are often more appropriate.

Many school systems employ technical staff to develop customized programs for various administrative applications. Using high-level languages such as COBOL or PL/1, programming staffs have developed and continue to maintain extensive administrative applications for record keeping and data reporting. In these situations, school administrators make their most important decisions regarding technology when hiring their personnel and should defer to them on most matters of software development. Administrators should be involved in establishing major priorities and in ensuring that a good working relationship exists between the technical staff and the end users. Custom software developed by a district's staff should also be evaluated according to criteria established jointly by the technical staff and the end users. These criteria may vary significantly depending on the nature of the software; however, they should concentrate on the specific needs of the application.

Instructional Software Evaluation

Like their administrative counterparts, different instructional applications will have different needs and will require specific software features to meet these needs. As examples, a tutorial simulation program such as Tom Snyder Productions Science Court series would be evaluated differently from an instructional tool such as the Learning Company's Student Writing and Research Center. A programming language such as Logo would be evaluated differently from a desktop publishing program such as Adobe's PageMaker.

In a national survey, the U.S. Congress's Office of Technology Assessment identified more than 200 factors that could be used in evaluating instructional software. Many of these factors relate to pedagogical and instructional quality considerations (e.g., content, motivation, creativity). Some factors (e.g., simulations, probeware) relate only to a particular type of software. Other factors include the qualifying phrase "where appropriate" to signify that they are not always to be considered. Appendix C provides an extensive reference list of criteria for developing a software evaluation policy in a school district. Administrators and teachers should use these criteria as a reference with the goal of selecting a manageable number of criteria for their own evaluation policies.

Many school districts have adopted an instructional software evaluation form or checklist that highlights some of the more important criteria. The form approach does not necessarily provide the mechanism for a thorough evaluation and will not include the hundreds of factors identified. However, the form or checklist does have value; otherwise, it would not be employed in so many districts and schools. A software checklist, for instance, ensures a record of the opinions of the staff involved in doing the evaluation of some proposed software.

Because major software developers will provide preview copies of programs to a school free of charge and without any obligation to purchase, it is not necessary to purchase a product to do an evaluation. After previewing the software, the evaluators meet and discuss its strengths and weaknesses. Providing a common evaluation form helps focus the discussion.

The criteria can be identified in an open-ended or a check-off format. However, because the nature of these evaluations is subjective, the open-ended format may be more appropriate. It is also relatively simple to provide detailed explanations of the open-ended items in a supplementary manual of procedures for doing software evaluation. Figure 10.7 is an example of an evaluation form combining both the check-off and open-ended approaches. An evaluation form helps define the evaluation procedure itself, and administrators and teachers should work together to develop what they feel will work best in their schools.

The process of designing an instructional software evaluation form and procedure will provide many insights into the role of technology in the classroom and into many other curricular issues. Software evaluation should be a rigorous activity comparable to other important curricular and academic decisions. In addition to basic software evaluation criteria, the form in Figure 10.7 devotes an entire page to criteria associated with instructional quality.

Open Source Software

Open source software (OSS) refers to any software for which the source code is available to the general public and does not have licensing restrictions that limit use, modification, or redistribution. OSS is generally available free of license or other fees. The Linux operating system and the Mozilla Firefox Web browser are examples of popular OSS. Users who acquire OSS are free to modify, change, and upgrade it as they wish. OSS can be found for a wide variety of software tools. What is most attractive about OSS is the fact that an organization can realize considerable savings by acquiring OSS rather than comparable proprietary products.

The obvious question is: Why don't all organizations simply acquire OSS rather than pay a vendor for the comparable products. First, although OSS is available free of charge, it generally comes with minimal support services. The end user assumes responsibility for the stability and integrity of the OSS to perform accordingly. This is not an issue for simple or nonvital software tools but can be a problem for software packages on which organizations depend for delivery of their services. Organizations that acquire OSS critical to their operations generally are those that have competent and talented in-house computer programming staffs who develop knowledge about and are capable of insuring the stability of the OSS.

Second, related to the minimal support services is the fact that documentation for OSS is usually lacking or nonexistent. Many users have to rely on Frequently Asked Questions (FAQs) to determine how to best use some OSS packages.

Instructional Software Evaluation Form
North Central School District No. 1
Page 1 of 2

Title: _____

Company/vendor: _____

Subject matter: _____

Grade level: _____

Cost: _____
        (Attach additional supporting information if necessary)

Type: Simulation_____Tutorial_____Drill/practice_____Game_____
        Word processing_____Spreadsheet_____Database_____Other_____

Computer system: _____

Special hardware requirements: _____

Internet-based/enhanced: _____

Objectives:

Program description:

Evaluation (Grade 0=lowest; 9=highest
General characteristics

		Instructional quality	
Efficiency:	_____	Content:	_____
Documentation:	_____	Pedagogical features:	_____
Ease of use:	_____	Motivational:	_____
Company/vendor:	_____	Creativity:	_____
		Feedback:	_____
		Assessment:	_____
		Record keeping:	_____
		Graphics:	_____
		Flexibility:	_____
		Web interface:	_____

Overall rating: _____

Reviewer's Name: _____   Date: _____

(continued)

FIGURE 10.7   Instructional Software Evaluation Form.

```
┌────────────────────────────────────────────────────────────────────┐
│                   Instructional Software Evaluation Form             │
│                     North Central School District No. 1              │
│                              Page 2 of 2                             │
│                                                                      │
│  Comments Worksheet                                                  │
│                                                                      │
│  General characteristics                                            │
│    Efficiency:                                                       │
│    Documentation:                                                    │
│    Ease of use:                                                      │
│    Company/vendor:                                                   │
│                                                                      │
│                                                                      │
│  Instructional quality                                              │
│    Content:                                                          │
│    Pedagogical features:                                            │
│    Motivational:                                                     │
│    Creativity:                                                       │
│    Feedback:                                                         │
│    Assessment:                                                       │
│    Record keeping:                                                   │
│    Graphics:                                                         │
│    Flexibility:                                                      │
│    Web interface:                                                    │
└────────────────────────────────────────────────────────────────────┘
```

FIGURE 10.7   *(Continued)*

Third, even though licensing fees are not charged for OSS, there can be indirect costs associated with using them. Some companies that provide OSS packages have arrangements to provide support and/or consulting services for a fee. In addition, some popular "free" OSS packages have deluxe versions that have enhanced capabilities and are sold commercially. For example, a popular "free" OSS package is OpenOffice, which provides many of the same facilities as Microsoft Office. However, Sun Microsystems provides and supports a commercial version of OpenOffice called StarOffice that sells for about $60.

The open source movement is alive and well and offers attractive alternatives for schools and school districts to save software costs. However, school leaders should carefully evaluate the pros and cons of an OSS package especially when being considered for a major or vital school application or activity. For more information on the pros and cons of OSS, see several articles at Helium Publishing, a "knowledge" cooperative, at http://www.helium.com/knowledge/1620-the-pros-and-cons-of-open-source-software.

Software Life Cycles

There are two elements to a discussion of software life cycles: one is the fact that software tools and packages purchased by commercial vendors eventually will reach a point where support for "older" versions of the software is withdrawn; and second is the issue of applications software that has been developed in house by school district personnel, which continues to be used long after, in some cases, many years after its effective life cycle. For purposes of this discussion on issues associated with evaluating software, it is the former element that is more pertinent.

In years passed, software providers generally maintained a fairly long life cycle for their products. This was especially true if the software was bundled with hardware such as was the case with many of the large computer companies of the 1970s and 1980s. It was not uncommon for a company to maintain software support for as long as its hardware was under some type of maintenance contract. The typical life cycle for many large computer systems was 7 to 10 years. IBM, the largest provider of computer systems through the 1980s, owed part of its success to the fact that it had a fine reputation for maintaining its hardware and hence its software for many years. With the faster paced world of the Internet and World Wide Web, this is no longer the case. Much of the software is developed independently of the hardware. In addition, competition is incredibly keen. As a result, it is typical for software to have much shorter life cycles. For example, Microsoft's software life cycle policy states:

> Microsoft will offer Mainstream Support for either a minimum of 5 years from the date of a product's general availability, or for 2 years after the successor product (N+1) is released . . . Extended Support is not offered for Consumer, Hardware, and Multimedia products. Products that release new versions annually, such as . . . Microsoft Encarta, Microsoft Picture It!, . . . will receive a minimum of 3 years of Mainstream Support from the product's date of availability" (Microsoft Support Life Cycle Product, http://support.microsoft.com/gp/lifepolicy)

This puts an onus on the users to make sure that they keep updating their software on a regular basis. In evaluating and purchasing software, it becomes incumbent on school districts to make sure they know the vendors with whom they are dealing and their life cycle support policies.

CASE STUDY

Place: Cornwall School District   Year: 2010

Cornwall is a mid-size city in the southern part of the United States. Administered centrally by a city board of education, the Cornwall school district has a total enrollment of approximately 30,000 students and operates 15 elementary schools, 15 middle schools, and 8 high schools. Technology has always been seen as a priority at Cornwall. A comprehensive technology planning process was established in 2001 to ensure that teachers and students have access to computer equipment. The overall student-per-instructional-microcomputer ratio is 5.2 to 1. Every school has at least one central technology laboratory or media center as well as at least three microcomputers in each classroom.

In recent years, a number of high school students have been enrolling in online courses offered by the state virtual high school or by colleges in the state university system. In 2009, 350 students enrolled in online courses. The general opinion of these courses is that they offer students opportunities to take Advanced Placement and college-level courses that might otherwise not be offered in the Cornwall high schools. Recently, however, a number of the high school principals have also been enrolling more students for credit-recovery online courses to improve graduation rates. Most of these courses are offered by the state virtual school and by a for-profit online education provider. Cornwall pays for these students on a per seat basis. The feedback from students enrolled in these courses has been positive, but the principals have expressed concern about the costs. The principals of the eight high schools met recently and recommended to the district superintendent that consideration should be given to acquiring a course management software (CMS) system so that teachers could develop their own online course materials.

At the weekly meeting of her cabinet, the superintendent, Dr. Elaine Jensen, heard a number of concerns expressed regarding costs of acquiring and maintaining such a system as well as issues of instructional quality of online courses and the need for extensive professional development. James Bank, the district's assistant superintendent for administrative services, indicated that there are a variety of ways of acquiring a course management system, including leasing space and time on a host server provided by a commercial CMS provider, purchasing a server and CMS software for the district, and acquiring a server and an open source CMS that would be free of any licensing charges.

Discussion Questions

1. Assuming you are Dr. Jensen, what action(s) will you take?
2. What additional information do you need?
3. Is the issue here only about the cost of the course management software?

Summary

This chapter describes the major criteria used in evaluating hardware and software. Although hardware, with its color displays and lights, receives a lot of attention, many professionals consider software to be the most important component of a computer application because software directs or instructs the hardware.

The major criteria to be considered when acquiring computer hardware are performance, compatibility, modularity/expandability, ergonomics, software availability, vendor (support, maintenance, and industry position), and cost. Although some of these factors may be considered more important than others, none of them should be ignored when acquiring equipment.

Criteria for evaluating software were also discussed, including efficiency, ease of use, documentation, hardware requirements, vendor, and cost. Evaluators should also examine the specific features of software packages in terms of how well they meet the needs of the planned application.

Several major issues related to hardware evaluation were presented, including considerations of acquiring equipment for administrative and instructional applications, the emergence of multipurpose servers, the desirability of bulk purchasing, and equipment life cycles. Similarly, several major issues regarding software evaluation were discussed, including the differences for administrative and instructional applications. The chapter concluded with discussions of open source software and software life cycles.

Key Concepts and Questions

1. Many computer professionals think that software is where the action is. Why? Compared with hardware, which do you consider the more important component in planning and implementing computer applications? Why?

2. In evaluating hardware, the major factors are performance, compatibility, modularity/expandability, ergonomics, software availability, vendor (support, maintenance, and industry position), and cost. Are any of these factors more important than the others? Why? And under what conditions?

3. In evaluating software, the major factors are efficiency, ease of use, documentation, hardware requirements, vendor, and cost. Are any of these factors more important than the others? Why? And under what conditions?

4. Efficiency refers to how well a program is written. What are some of the specific efficiency measures used in evaluating software? How would you test some of these measures while doing an evaluation?

5. With the introduction of microcomputers, people are using equipment for a variety of applications. Because so many people have become familiar with computer equipment, has the need to produce software that is relatively easy to use been reduced or increased? Explain. Who are the best individuals in a school to determine whether a software package is user friendly?

6. Of the major software evaluation criteria, some computer professionals consider documentation the most important factor. What questions does the documentation have to answer? As a software evaluation factor, is documentation more or less important depending on the nature of the application or the type of equipment being used? Explain.

7. The relationship between hardware and software is critical in implementing computer applications. In terms of software evaluation, provide examples illustrating the importance of this relationship.

Suggested Activities

1. Review the policies (if they exist) for hardware acquisition in a school district. Evaluate these policies in light of the material in this chapter. Can you offer any suggestions for improving them?

2. Visit a Web site that provides computer hardware evaluation services—such as CNET (http://www.cnet.com) or ZDNet (http://www.zdnet.com)—and compare their evaluations of various types of equipment (such as microcomputers, handheld computers, and printers).

3. With three or four colleagues, select a software product (administrative or instructional) and review it using the software evaluation features identified in the chapter. Use the World Wide Web sources to gather data for your review.

4. Review the policies in a school district for evaluating and selecting instructional software. Can you offer any suggestions for improving them?

References

Baltimore County Public School District. (2009). Office of Instructional Technology Software Evaluation Form. Retrieved May 31, 2009, from http://www.bcps.org/offices/oit/software.asp

Vance, A. (2009, March 23). Rivals say I.B.M. stifles competition to mainframes. *New York Times.* Retrieved June 1, 2009, from http://www.nytimes.com/2009/03/23/technology/companies/23mainframe.html?_r=1&th&emc=th

Chapter 11

People, Technology, and Professional Development

An important ingredient for implementing change, improvement, and innovation in education is a knowledgeable and vibrant staff. Studies and research (Fullan & Pomfret, 1977; Huberman & Miles, 1984; Joyce, 1990; Joyce, Murphy, Showers, & Murphy, 1989; Joyce & Showers, 1988; Knapp & Glenn, 1996; Pink, 1989; Sheingold & Hadley, 1990; Cuban, 2001; Christensen, Horn, & Johnson, 2008) have consistently supported this concept. Regardless of the nature of change—whether it be introducing a new teaching technique or implementing a major new administrative policy—individuals involved must understand and to a degree accept what is expected and what is going to be done. Neglecting to develop this understanding among the people who ultimately will most influence success or failure will likely jeopardize the implementation of any new project.

In this chapter, the people element and the need for professional development are examined as they relate to implementing technology in our schools. Although all school personnel should be participating in professional development activities, particular emphasis is placed on teacher development, because using technology in the classroom has become and will continue to be a critical need in most schools.

A LONG WAY TO GO

All schools in the country have acquired some computer equipment, and every indication is that the hardware acquisition trend that began in the late 1970s and grew significantly in the 1980s and 1990s is continuing in the 21st century. Using surveys and field visits, governmental agencies, industry analysts, and academic researchers have monitored the number of computers purchased, the types of components acquired, and the dollars schools have expended (Becker, 1994; U.S. Congress, 1995; Quality Education Data, 1996; Fatemi, 1999; U.S. Department of Education, 2000; Park & Staresina, 2004). These activities have helped administrators make decisions to acquire equipment, develop facilities and infrastructure, and support technology services in their schools.

Data and surveys also report that this equipment is not being fully used. There have been anecdotes of microcomputers remaining unpacked in locked closets or sitting in the back of a classroom where they are rarely turned on because the teacher does not know how to use them. Studies and observations (Goodson, 1991; Becker, 1994; U.S Congress, 1995; Northrup & Little, 1996; Trotter, 1999; Cuban 2001; Park & Staresina, 2004; Christensen, Horn, & Johnson, 2008) consistently report that the majority of teachers are not making extensive use of technology. They suggest a situation in which hardware and software were being acquired at an escalating rate in the schools, and yet many teachers appeared not to know how to use or were otherwise not using them. In a national survey conducted for *Education Week* in 2004, many teachers considered themselves beginners in the use of technology in their classes. Furthermore, in a national survey of fourth-grade students, only 63% reported using a computer at least once a week in school. In eighth-grade mathematics courses, only 32% of the students reported using a computer at least once a week (Park & Staresina, 2004).

If administrators are to develop strategies for correcting a serious imbalance between computer acquisition and technical knowledge, some background information on the causes would be helpful. One fundamental reason for the imbalance is that some of today's teachers, especially those trained before the early 1990s and before the proliferation of microcomputers, were not exposed to technology as part of their preservice teacher training programs. As a result, they did not include it as part of their teaching repertoire and have been slow to do so. Schools of education as well as state education departments (which are responsible for certifying teachers) generally had not required competency in technology as part of a teacher certification program.

This situation began to change in the 1990s, and the problem is being alleviated as state agencies and schools of education come to recognize the importance of a technologically literate teacher corps. A majority of state education departments require technology training for certification of teachers (Park & Staresina, 2004). Most teacher preparation programs have developed and are requiring methods courses in educational technology in their programs. These courses typically include the following:

- Basic operations, including use of hardware, software, and simple programs such as word processing
- Information technology, including use of the Internet, database searching programs, and simple presentation authoring tools
- Evaluation of instructional software
- Pedagogical issues, such as integrating technology into the curriculum and lesson planning
- Values and ethical issues, such as appropriateness of information resources, copyright, censorship, and plagiarism

School administrators are finding that new teachers and recent graduates of teacher preparation programs are more familiar with technology but need ongoing training to keep their skills honed. A Metropolitan Life (2008) study of American teachers indicated that the value teachers place on technology varies by their generational cohort: 66% of those in Generation Y (30 years old or younger), 58% of those in Generation X (31- to 43-year-olds), and 49% of Baby Boomers (44-to 62-year-olds) strongly agree that technology enhances their ability to teach.

A more difficult problem is an attitudinal one. Many teachers are not convinced of the benefits of using computer technology. Some teachers feel threatened by technology and see it as impersonal and an infringement on their ability to maintain control of their classroom environments. Educators have observed that the natural evolution of technology is such that it changes the nature of teaching. In schools that use technology extensively, teachers, in addition to their teaching role, must also adopt a techno-managerial role in providing instruction. In environments where advanced computer-assisted instruction techniques such as integrated learning systems are in operation, teachers are required to spend more time monitoring student progress and prescribing appropriate curriculum materials rather than teaching the subject matter. In planning professional development activities, administrators should be prepared to deal with these attitudinal issues. Assuming that attitudinal concerns will go away simply by exposing teachers to the benefits of technology is a fallacy. Educators need to convey also that computer technology, although becoming an important tool in the teaching process, is not a substitute for caring, talented human beings.

One of the most important reasons that teachers do not use technology is that it is not always easy to implement in the regular classroom. In schools where teachers have received training, many other problems such as the lack of enough hardware, poor support services, or inappropriate software have hindered teachers' ability to use technology effectively in the classroom. Administrators and teachers find they spend a good deal of time on solving basic logistical and technological problems associated with implementing effective technology applications. Even in school districts where training and professional development activities are provided, teachers need to continue to invest time and effort to feel comfortable using computer technology routinely in their classrooms.

Sheingold and Hadley (1990), in a national study of teachers who were identified as experienced and accomplished in integrating technology into their teaching, found that it took several years of practice to master computer-based teaching approaches. Although these teachers were supportive of professional development programs that have enabled them to use computer technology, they also cautioned against one-shot approaches or quick fixes. A major recommendation of this study was that there should be ample support and time for teachers not only to learn how to use technology but also to plan carefully for its use in the classroom. This may even require fundamental changes in the way teachers teach.

THE PROFESSIONAL DEVELOPMENT PLANNING MODEL

Figure 11.1 is a schematic for a professional development planning model that can be integrated with the general planning for technology model discussed in Chapter 2. A basic assumption is that professional development is a product of the larger technology planning model. The major components of the professional development planning model consist of

- planning for professional development (integrating professional development with other planning activities),
- assessing needs (identifying the professional development needs of a district or school),
- designing a program that meets the needs of both district and school,
- providing incentives for staff to participate,
- implementing the program, and
- evaluating and reviewing the program.

This model forms the framework for most of the discussion in the remainder of this chapter.

WHO LEARNS?

In planning professional development activities, the critical question is: Who learns? The simplest and broadest answer is *everybody*—administrators, teachers, clerical staff, and so forth. However, a more specific answer to the question should be related directly to a district's planning objectives.

Assessing professional development needs is a logical outgrowth of the computer applications that a district or school wishes to implement. In addition to identifying hardware and software, planning computer applications should also inherently determine the users and developers of these applications and identify the targets for professional development. If a district is planning to implement a new financial management system, it would be appropriate to assess the needs of financial managers, accountants, and clerical staff in using databases, query languages, or electronic spreadsheet software packages. If a district is planning to begin using word processing as a tool for teaching writing in the elementary school curriculum, it should assess the needs of the elementary school teachers in using word-processing software. Once identified, the personnel (administrators, teachers, or clerical staff who will be using the actual applications)

FIGURE 11.1   Professional Development Planning Model.

should be included in the process of determining needs and designing appropriate professional development activities.

Professional development should relate to a planning objective and, in the case of technology, to a computer application. Although some school districts adopt professional development as a planning objective in and of itself, this should be the exception and not the rule. Planning that continually identifies professional development as an objective without relating it to an application is indicative of a planning integration problem and should be reviewed. Just as hardware and software should relate to the applications a district wishes to implement, the staff likewise should be trained to implement or use these same applications.

The importance of principals, superintendents, and other leaders participating in professional development activities should not be underestimated. The example set when a school leader participates in professional development or when she or he begins to use some new technology is extremely powerful. A clear and direct message that developing staff and implementing technology are important is sent, which will be picked up by staff and others.

High-level administrators who appear technologically illiterate or provide professional development activities for others but consistently avoid participation themselves send the opposite message. Many administrators rely heavily on some other person(s) to buffer them from technology. Such situations are very common and also unfortunate. These administrators would love to use the available technology but "just have not had enough time to learn it." In their schools, you will find that many of their teachers and other staff "have not had enough time to learn it," either. Readers may want to refer to Appendix B, which identifies the competencies required for educational administrators to be leaders in planning, developing, and implementing technology in their schools and districts. The International Society for Technology in Education NETS Project (http://www.iste.org/AM/Template.cfm?Section= NETS) also provides technology standards for teachers, students, administrators, and technology coordinators.

DIFFERENT ALTERNATIVES FOR DIFFERENT NEEDS

Designing a professional development program should be done in a systematic way so that the proposed program relates closely to the district's overall technology plan. Simply offering several workshops each year that may or may not be relevant to a district's goals and objectives will not be effective. A major requirement in planning a professional development program is conducting a needs analysis to identify what the district needs to do. If a district has not provided much professional development in the past, comprehensive analysis may be in order. If a district has been active in providing professional development and is experienced in using technology, then the analysis can be targeted to specific applications, educational objectives, or individuals.

Doing a comprehensive needs analysis for the purpose of designing a professional development program for technology requires an in-depth examination of all existing and proposed computer applications, both administrative and instructional, followed by an evaluation of all staff (administrative, teaching, clerical, etc.) in terms of their technical knowledge and their abilities to develop, implement, or use these applications. The needs that are identified become the targets of the professional development plan.

Although some districts are able to do comprehensive needs analyses, most limit them to specific school populations, categories of applications, or specific applications. For example, doing a needs analysis and designing a training program for all fourth- through sixth-grade school teachers in the use of digital video technology involves a category of application for a specific school population, whereas a needs analysis and training program for all 11th- and 12th-grade teachers in the use of the Blackboard course management system involves a specific application for a more-specific school population. Some districts may start with broad training of many teachers or staff and work to more specific applications; others might experiment with a smaller group and, if successful, expand the program for larger groups and categories of applications. Both approaches can and do work. Which approach should be taken is best determined by the district as part of its overall planning activities.

When identifying and targeting professional development to specific applications, planners should keep in mind that the common or unifying goal should always be to build and expand on the accumulated mass of technical knowledge and expertise (see Figure 11.2) in the district. As districts attempt to do more, a correspondingly larger accumulated mass of technical knowledge is required. An interesting characteristic of technical knowledge is that it grows almost naturally as a district implements more technology. Ravitch (1992) referred to this phenomenon by describing educational technology as difficult and costly to initiate, but once established it has a "relentless forward momentum" (p. 7). Therefore, the more teachers and other staff use technology, the more they learn and the more capable they become in expanding to newer technologies.

As a result of professional development, a threshold or level of technical confidence is reached in most organizations, which acts as a driving force from within for further technological enhancement and development. Many staff members will learn a great deal on their own through contacts with colleagues, both inside and outside the school or district. This is similar to the discussion in Chapter 5 of Wenger (1999) and a "community of practice" as a body of shared

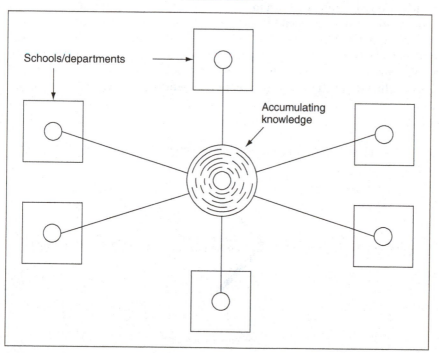

FIGURE 11.2   Accumulating Mass of Technical Knowledge/Expertise.

knowledge and resources, which enables community members to develop and grow for the good of the organization.

DESIGNING AND IMPLEMENTING EFFECTIVE PROFESSIONAL DEVELOPMENT PROGRAMS

Designing and putting into practice effective professional development programs is a complex undertaking. The input of the target groups is most important and will provide many suggestions for the nature of the development activities. As much as possible, programs should be designed such that they provide some variety of activities (lectures, demonstrations, discussions, hands-on workshops, Web-based activities, etc.) and that take place over an extended period of time to allow participants to practice and experiment. Professional development programs also require resources, and budgets need to be allocated as part of the design and implementation.

School districts use a wide-ranging assortment of professional development activities. Workshops (on- and off-site), large conferences, small seminars, World Wide Web courses, electronic bulletin boards, and user group activities abound. The most effective common elements (see Figure 11.3) for technology training are hands-on activities, one-on-one coaching, training the trainer, and equipment availability.

Hands-On Activities

A fundamental tenet of professional development for technology is the concept that you learn by doing; therefore, a portion of any technical training program should include hands-on activities. Participants can listen to and read about technology, but not until they use it will they develop an understanding. Consider how you learn to use a keyboard. A teacher may lecture on how to use a keyboard or a student can read about keyboarding, but until the student actually uses a keyboard, he or she really cannot develop the skill of keyboarding. The same is true with computer technology. To understand computer technology, you need to use hardware and to experiment with software, and the more you practice, the greater your proficiency. This holds true whether the target populations are high-level engineers and computer scientists, teachers, secretaries, students, or principals.

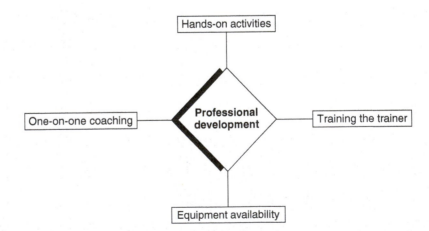

FIGURE 11.3 Elements of a Professional Development Program for Technology.

One-on-One Coaching

Individualized training or coaching is another characteristic of many professional development programs. If a district has support staff who can function as individualized trainers or coaches, they should be used. If not, then coaching should be provided by outside experts or consultants. Regardless of who provides the individualized training, short (1 or 2 hours), one-on-one coaching sessions are more effective than longer, large-group activities. A common format is a large-group, information delivery session followed by much smaller coaching sessions in which participants can practice or experiment with the assistance of a coach who customizes the training to individual needs. A variation of this format is to have participants enroll in a Web-based course, followed by smaller coaching sessions that are in person, made available through blogs or electronic bulletin boards, or a combination of both.

Another benefit of one-on-one coaching is that professional development activities can be customized to meet the individual needs of teachers. In education, a concept growing in popularity and acceptance is the need to differentiate instruction to meet the needs of individual students. The same concept can be applied to professional development for teachers. There is no reason to assume that all teachers are at the same level of technological expertise. One-on-one coaching might be beneficial in identifying and subsequently differentiating professional development to meet the needs of individual teachers.

Training the Trainer

A certain amount of outside expertise and consulting is required for many professional development activities, but relying extensively on external trainers can become costly over the long term. A popular approach is to have outside consultants train a cadre of trainers who in turn will train large numbers of the staff. This "train the trainer" approach can be most effective in developing a core group of in-house experts who become actively engaged in sharing their knowledge with others.

A cadre of trainers can be a critical component that drives the entire professional development activity for a school or district. Such a group can begin with technology teachers, media specialists, and representatives from every department or grade level, who have shown a particular interest in technology.

Deciding whether to convert numbers of present employees into full-time trainers depends on the size of the district and the number of people to be trained. Large districts with thousands of employees would probably find that a group of full-time trainers would be less expensive than the large-scale use of outside consultants. Small districts might make training a part-time or add-on responsibility (for extra compensation) for existing full-time staff who have an aptitude for technology training.

Using existing staff versus outside consultants for training can also provide many attitudinal benefits. Teachers, for instance, might relate better to colleagues who are a few steps ahead of them in using technology in the classroom. A sense of "If they can do it, so can I" frequently develops. This approach also can be effective in fostering a team or "we are in this together" attitude. It helps build an esprit de corps among the teaching staff that begins in the technology area and carries over into other areas of the school, such as implementing collaborative learning, reviewing a writing program, or expanding the teaching of process skills in science instruction. Given the many problems involved with integrating technology into the curriculum, training a group of trainers may be one of the most effective ways of resolving them.

Teachers Need Equipment, Too!

The design of a professional development program that includes hands-on activities implies that equipment, software, and other facilities are available for the participants' use. Along with other factors such as costs and travel arrangements, access to equipment becomes a critical consideration. Frequently, the number of participants may be limited by the availability of equipment.

Administrators understand the need to acquire equipment for instruction and student use, and providing this same equipment for teachers to learn and to use is also a necessity. Whereas secretaries and other administrative staff are routinely given equipment to take advantage of standard office automation applications such as e-mail, word processing, or electronic spreadsheets, teachers frequently are the last group to receive equipment from the district and in some cases are even expected to acquire it on their own. Given the premise that one learns technology by doing, attempts to integrate technology into the classroom are likely to fail if teachers are not able to practice, to experiment, and "to do technology."

The most common approach to resolving this problem is to set aside a teachers' area (laboratory, library, media center, lounge, study room, etc.) where equipment is provided exclusively for teachers' use. This approach is effective because it provides access to equipment and also allows for the informal exchange of information and ideas among peers. Teachers can work together on common computer applications, and a good deal of technology sharing can occur. For this reason, schools that have progressed and moved away from central computer laboratories and provide equipment for individual teacher use should also consider offering or maintaining a small central training area for teachers.

Some school districts have begun to adopt policies that aim at supplying every teacher with a portable laptop microcomputer. Though costly, this may be the best approach for providing teachers with access to equipment and ultimately for using technology in instruction. The Shoreline School District in Seattle, Washington, was among the first to adopt such a policy in 1989, providing a laptop for each of the district's 600 teachers (Schlumpf, 1991). Although the district owns the equipment, teachers are free to take the computers home. Administrators report that this approach not only has been effective in terms of professional development and the use of technology but also has unleashed a mass of creativity and has given the teachers a sense of technological empowerment. Other districts implementing a "computer for every teacher" policy have reported similar results (Buckley, 1995).

Before long, every teacher will likely have a computer on her or his desk or a laptop that she or he can take home. Some administrators and teachers have doubts that this will happen, but a simple look at the desks of stockbrokers, insurance salespersons, department store cashiers, attorneys, and others suggests otherwise.

Incentives

Professional development programs should also consider providing incentives for teachers and others to ensure active participation. Both intrinsic and extrinsic rewards need to be considered for staff who become substantially involved with developing other staff and implementing technology in their schools. Professional growth, stimulating involvement with instructional innovations, experimentation with different teaching styles, and other intrinsic rewards may be the most important reasons that teachers become involved with technology. However, because of the time and effort involved, particularly in districts that have fallen behind technologically, more extrinsic incentives such as extra compensation, release time, or gifts of equipment are also needed.

Staff should be compensated for attending workshops, seminars, and other activities conducted in the summer or on weekends. Tuition reimbursements or sabbatical leaves should be considered for teachers who upgrade their skills by taking college courses. Teachers who agree to be trainers should receive extra compensation for assuming additional responsibilities. Those involved with developing a major new curriculum using technology or some other innovation should be provided with release time to evaluate and plan their materials carefully. Faculty involved with evaluating software (which if done properly can take many hours of viewing, discussing, and reviewing) should be compensated. Recognizing faculty members who make a major contribution to professional development, in the form of a cash award or a gift of a laptop computer, can be a strong inducement for others to participate.

The possibilities for providing incentives are extensive, and administrators should be attuned to offering incentives that would be most appropriate for the staff involved and for the nature of the contribution. In developing an incentive program, administrators may have to conform to existing employee compensation policies within the district. Schools that have advanced technologically develop a culture that lends itself more to incentives involving recognition and professional acknowledgment. Schools that have to catch up with technology or are planning major leaps forward should consider more direct rewards such as extra compensation and release time. Regardless, administrators should be able to identify incentives to which a school staff will respond, and provisions for them should be made accordingly.

Evaluation and Review

As with any other technology planning activity, professional development should be evaluated and reviewed. Participants in workshops or demonstrations should evaluate the effectiveness of these activities and offer suggestions for improvements. Simple evaluation questionnaires distributed and collected at the end of a professional development activity are common practice. Depending on financial resources, external evaluators might also be considered. Because a major purpose of professional development is to have teachers and others using technology in their classrooms or offices, evaluation should also provide for some follow-up to determine whether participants have, in fact, been able to transfer their training to actual application.

Evaluation and review activities should not be considered the end of professional development. As with other planning activities, evaluation should naturally start the process of assessing needs and designing new professional development programs.

A Continuous Process

Planning a professional development program for technology should be a continuous process, primarily because technology is constantly changing and new equipment and software are regularly being introduced. Mechanisms should be in place for evaluating and sorting out new technology to determine appropriateness in a district. Some individuals must be provided with the resources to visit other schools or attend vendor meetings and specialized workshops that enable them to keep up with the technology. Determining who these individuals are is best decided as part of an overall planning activity. Obviously, technology coordinators and trainers are the most likely candidates; however, teachers who show an interest in or have an aptitude for technology should also be included.

The need for continual professional development will become apparent as planners review and evaluate their activities. Whether it be the evaluation of a single workshop or an entire year's program, the most common suggestions and requests from participants tend to be for additional professional development opportunities and activities. Besides the enjoyment they have in attending such activities, teachers and other staff members quickly recognize their need to learn and advance, advance and learn. As planners look at the broader professional development picture, they will see different individuals functioning at different levels along a skills or competencies continuum. The essence of their professional development planning will be to keep all these individuals moving along this continuum.

One inexpensive and effective approach to continuing professional development activities is to set up an electronic bulletin board or a blog. Such a bulletin board or blog is dedicated to initiating issues and questions regarding the use of technology in a school or district. Trainers and professional development participants can share their work, ideas, or techniques with others and solicit feedback. Electronic bulletin boards and blogs are most effective as vehicles for follow-up activities to a professional development program or activity. In certain situations where participants already possess a degree of technological skill, they can be used in place of face-to-face activities.

RESOURCES

Although the emphasis in this chapter has been on developing and using in-house staff as much as possible, outside expertise and consultants should also be considered, particularly if a new or inherently complex technology is being considered.

Consultants abound in every state and most urban centers because the need for technical training is broad-based and exists in all types of commercial enterprises and public agencies. Before contracting with any consultants—whether private individuals, state agencies, or divisions of large corporations—administrators should do a careful review of their expertise and track record in providing the type of training or development that the district or school is seeking. Local colleges and universities, particularly if they have a school of education, generally are helpful resources for providing professional development expertise. Professional organizations such as the International Society for Technology in Education (ISTE) and collective bargaining unions also provide assistance for setting up professional development programs aimed at the use of technology in schools. Most states fund some type of assistance to school districts in the use of technology. User groups based on vendor hardware, special interests, common software, or subject matter are excellent sources of information and can be extremely valuable in helping keep school personnel current on technological developments.

Vendors know their products better than anybody else, and if they provide training services, which in many cases may be free or at a discount for customers, school districts would be wise to take advantage of them. Major technology corporations such as Apple, Microsoft, and IBM provide a wide range of training services and facilities. Major educational software suppliers such as Broderbund and Tom Snyder Productions provide many excellent curriculum materials to help teachers use technology in the classroom. Vendors who specialize in particular products—such as Blackboard (course management systems) and Sun Microsystems (local area networks)—have extensive expertise that they routinely provide to their customers and potential customers. In acquiring computer products, a vendor's background and reputation regarding support services, including training, should always be considered. Additional cost may be warranted if the staff's ability to use the product is facilitated.

The National Staff Development Council (http://www.nsdc.org/) provides a wealth of information about standards and effective practices regarding professional development and is highly recommend for further references.

CASE STUDY

Place: Learning Town   **Year: 2008**

Learning Town is an urban school district in the farm belt. It has 41,100 students and operates 75 schools. The board of education created a planning committee in 1985 that regularly establishes a broad set of goals for the district. The planning committee relies heavily on subcommittees to study issues at length and make recommendations, most of which it accepts. In terms of instructional technology, the board of education has been supportive. In 1991, a major procurement was made to equip the schools with microcomputers. Since then, the board has regularly allocated funds to allow each school to make incremental improvements in equipment and software. As a result, all of the schools have computer laboratories, a variety of software, and at least one computer coordinator. The overall student-per-microcomputer ratio is 5:1. Most schools have placed equipment in individual classrooms; however, each school still maintains one or more centralized computer facilities.

Last year a proposal was made to the board of education by the chair of the Middle School Principals' Association that the district consider making a major new thrust in the use of technology as a teaching tool. She recommended that the district make an investment in digital video technology and that each classroom be equipped with a teacher workstation that would consist of a microcomputer, a DVD player, and a whiteboard. Such a workstation would allow teachers to take advantage of new multimedia materials combining sound, pictures, video, and the programming power of the computer. Teachers would be able to use authoring languages such as HyperStudio and PowerPoint to enhance classroom presentations. Each school would also acquire digital camera equipment so that teachers could make and edit their own instructional video materials. She concluded her presentation with the success stories of two of the schools in the district, which have begun using interactive digital video technology on a limited basis.

An ad hoc subcommittee of the district-wide planning committee has met six times in the past 5 months to study the feasibility of implementing this proposal. Members of the central administration have been supportive, providing a variety of data and analyses for the subcommittee members. Initial hardware costs for each workstation have been estimated at approximately $6,000. Costs for digital cameras, editing software, and supplies would vary depending on the size and level of the school.

The subcommittee appears split in terms of recommending this proposal to the planning committee. Whereas some members view interactive digital video as an exciting and stimulating instructional technology, others do not feel that the district should invest in it at this time. Specifically, some members are concerned that classroom instruction and effort would be better spent on basic subject matter and after-school tutoring sessions to ensure that students do well on state proficiency tests. The subcommittee has nearly completed its work for the year and would like to either recommend this proposal or table it for reconsideration next year. Also, the chairperson of the subcommittee has just received a memorandum from one of the committee members who represents the Teachers' Association. It indicates that the Teachers' Association discussed this proposal at its last two meetings and is very supportive. However, it stated that most of the teachers were not familiar with using digital video technology and would need training, especially in developing and editing their own video materials. The head of the subcommittee, a supporter of the proposal, has asked the superintendent to do a quick analysis of the training needs of the district regarding the proposal before the next, and last, meeting of the year, which will be in 2 weeks.

Discussion Questions

1. Analyze this case study assuming that you are the superintendent. What course of action will you take?
2. Although you respect the divergent opinions of the subcommittee members, you would like to see the subcommittee recommend the proposal to the planning committee rather than table it until next year. However, you also recognize that the Teachers' Association has raised an important issue, and you do not have any data at this time to provide to the subcommittee. If your decision is to do a quick analysis, what information would you need?

Summary

In this chapter, professional development is examined as a critical component for implementing technology in a school district. National estimates and other indications are that most schools have a long way to go to train their staffs, particularly teachers, in the use of technology. The reasons for this involve lack of preservice training, attitudinal concerns, and lack of support services, which together have made it difficult for many teachers to use technology effectively.

Planning a professional development program should be integrated with other planning activities and should relate to the objectives that a district hopes to achieve. The key elements of a professional development planning model include assessing needs, designing programs for specific applications, providing incentives, and doing a review and evaluation. In designing a program, a unifying goal is the expansion of the mass of technical knowledge and expertise that exists in a school district. Professional development techniques proving to be most successful include hands-on activities, one-on-one coaching, in-house trainers, and ready access to equipment. Because of the time and effort required to implement new technology, administrators should be prepared to provide incentives such as extra compensation, release time, and recognition awards for staff who actively participate and make significant contributions to professional development activities.

Professional development is a continuous process. Technology changes and so do the people who use it. Planning professional development requires a long-term commitment that aims to upgrade technical skills gradually and continually rather than on a short-term or one-shot basis.

Key Concepts and Questions

1. Professional development for technology has been a major issue in the nation's schools for many years. Why? What are the factors that have made professional development such an important issue? Is it likely to be resolved in the near future? Explain.
2. Professional development should be integrated with other planning activities. Why? What planning objectives should be considered in designing a professional development program for technology? Who are the personnel within a school district who should participate in professional development?
3. Identifying the needs of a school district for professional development should be a careful and well-planned activity. What are some of the critical questions to be answered in a needs analysis?
4. As a district develops its technical resources and capabilities, a mass of knowledge and expertise develops. How does this mass of technical knowledge relate to professional development?
5. Designing a professional development program for technology can consist of many different activities. What are some of the common characteristics of a professional development program? Why are they effective?
6. Equipment availability for participants in professional development is important for the success of a program. Why? What does it provide? Is it essentially a short-term or long-term requirement? Explain.
7. Professional development is described as a long-term, continuous process. If this is so, why do so many professional development activities consist of relatively brief workshops and seminars?

Suggested Activities

1. Review the planning that goes into professional development in a school district or school. What suggestions, if any, would you make for improving the planning? To get started, below are the URLs to several school district action plans that comment on or address professional development issues:

   http://www.pcssd.org/dept/account/districtactionplan.pdf
   http://www.episd.org/_district/docs/EPISD_Tech_Plan.pdf
   http://er.bhusd.org/pdf/ab1339-02_er.pdf

2. Review the incentives that are provided in a school for participating in professional development activities. Are the incentives intrinsic or extrinsic? Which do you think is the more effective?

3. School districts, schools of education, and professional organizations have begun to discuss developing a list of technology competencies that every teacher should have. Using the World Wide Web, search, find, and review three or more policy statements/lists of technology competencies for teachers. How are the competencies similar? Different?

References

Becker, H. J. (1994). *Analysis and trends of school use of new information technologies.* Irvine: University of California.

Buckley, R. B. (1995). What happens when funding is not an issue? *Educational Leadership, 53*(2), 64–66.

Christensen, C., Horn, M. B., & Johnson, C. W. (2008). *Disrupting class: How disrupted innovation will change the way the world learns.* New York: McGraw-Hill.

Cuban, L. (2001). *Oversold & underused: Computers in the classroom.* Cambridge, MA: Harvard University Press.

Fatemi, E. (1999). Building the digital curriculum. *Education Week, 19*(4), 5–8.

Fullan, M., & Pomfret, A. (1977). Research on curriculum and instruction implementation. *Review of Educational Research, 47*(5), 335–397.

Goodson, B. (Ed.). (1991). *Teachers and technology: Staff development for tomorrow's schools.* Alexandria, VA: National School Boards Association.

Huberman, M. & Miles, M. (1984). Innovation up close. New York: Plenum.

Joyce, B. (Ed.). (1990). *Changing school culture through staff development.* Alexandria, VA: Association for Supervision and Curriculum Development.

Joyce, B., Murphy, C., Showers, B., & Murphy, J. (1989, March). *Reconstructing the workplace: School renewal as cultural change.* Paper presented at the annual meeting of the American Educational Research Association, San Francisco.

Joyce, B., & Showers, B. (1988). *Student achievement through staff development.* New York: Longman.

Knapp, L. R., & Glenn, A. D. (1996). *Restructuring schools with technology.* Boston: Allyn & Bacon.

Metropolitan Life. (2008). *The 25th Metlife survey of the American teacher: Past, present and future.* New York: Metropolitan Life Insurance Inc.

Northrup, P. T., & Little, W. (1996). Establishing instructional technology benchmarks for teacher preparation programs. *Journal of Teacher Education, 47*(3), 213–222.

Park, J., & Staresina, L. (2004, May 6). Tracking U.S. trends. *Education Week, 23*(35), 64–67.

Pink, W. (1989, March). *Effective development for urban school improvement.* Paper presented at the annual meeting of the American Educational Research Association, San Francisco.

Quality Education Data. (1996). *Education market guide & mailing list catalog, 1996 & 1997.* Denver: Quality Education Data.

Ravitch, D. (1992). TECHNOS interview. *TECHNOS Quarterly for Education and Technology, 1*(3), 4–7.

Schlumpf, J. F. (1991). Empowering K–12 teachers. *Technological Horizons in Education Journal, 18*(9), 81–82.

Sheingold, K., & Hadley, M. (1990). *Accomplished teachers: Integrating computers into classroom practice.* New York: Bank Street College of Education, Center for Technology in Education.

Trotter, A. (1999). Preparing teachers for the digital age. *Education Week, 19*(4), 37–46.

U.S. Congress, Office of Technology Assessment. (1995). *Teachers and technology making the connection* (Report No. OTA-EHR-616). Washington, DC: U.S. Government Printing Office.

U.S. Department of Education, National Center for Education Statistics. (2000). *Internet access in U.S. public schools and classrooms: 1994–99,* NCES 2000–086. Washington, DC: U.S. Department of Education, National Center for Education Statistics.

Wenger, E. (1999). *Communities of practice: Learning, meaning, and identity.* Cambridge, UK: Cambridge University Press.

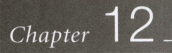

Chapter 12

Facilities, Policies, and Procedures

An important aspect of planning for and implementing technology is the establishment and management of facilities, an area that generally did not receive enough attention in the early days of computer acquisition. Schools purchased equipment and housed it as best they could. Classrooms were converted into laboratories overnight by simply putting microcomputers on available desks, running additional electrical cables, and assigning release time to one of the teachers (whoever was most interested in technology) to "manage" the facility. This approach enabled schools to get their programs started, but soon they ran into many problems as computer acquisitions increased, more space was needed, and the management of equipment, software, and training became a full-time job. This chapter examines the planning and management of technology facilities, including issues related to infrastructure, space utilization, personnel, policies, procedures, and security.

GETTING BIGGER

As late as the 1930s, airplanes were regarded with a certain awe, much the same way people view a space shuttle today. However, now airplane travel is routine and among the safest ways to travel. In the next 20 or so years, space travel, maybe as provided by a space shuttle or its successor, will also become more routine, and its mystique will disappear. So too with computers; the mystique behind computer technology is gone because computer equipment has become so commonplace. The days of huge blue and gray boxes in temperature-controlled computer centers have given way to the nearly ubiquitous presence of microcomputers. Cash machines, personal digital assistants (PDAs), checkout counters, exercise equipment, and video games are some examples of computers that we see and use in everyday life. In schools, too, we are beginning to come across computers just about everywhere: in laboratories, classrooms, and libraries; on the desks of secretaries and administrators; and in student book bags.

Because of their convenient size and propensity to become smaller, microcomputers are fitting into almost any available space. However, although computer equipment has become remarkably smaller in the past 30 years, the number of machines has increased dramatically, and so has the job of managing them. School administrators should be planning for computers to exist nearly anywhere in their buildings. At the same time, they need to be aware of the infrastructure, policies, and support services to make sure the technology is used effectively.

STAFFING AND ADMINISTRATION

Though getting easier to use, computer technology will require more management in the foreseeable future for both administrative and instructional applications. More resources and support will likely be needed to help in planning hardware, software, physical environments, and infrastructure; to provide maintenance; to establish data communications systems; to distribute and maintain documentation; and to assist in training. This will be true regardless of where equipment is located. However, the nature of the resources and support will change depending on the applications and the location of equipment.

For administrative applications, the need to establish highly efficient information systems tends to support a strong centralized approach. Major databases are implemented and maintained centrally by well-trained technical staff and distributed as needed throughout the district. This operation is housed in a central computer facility whose size depends on the size of the district in terms of both enrollment and geography. The informational resources are distributed throughout the district through a data communications network. Secretaries and administrators use microcomputers both to access database information and to perform tool applications such as word processing, e-mail, and electronic spreadsheets. This approach is not unique to schools but is common in businesses and governmental agencies and has been evolving over the past 50 years.

The staff requirements to manage these applications depend on the size and geographic distribution of a district. Larger districts with tens of thousands of students will need larger and more technically sophisticated staffs to develop and maintain systems and to distribute them over data communications networks than will smaller districts with 2,000 or 3,000 students. The staffing for administrative applications in schools has been evolving similarly to other noneducational environments such as private businesses and governmental agencies. Typically, a staff of computer programmers, computer operators, data communications specialists, and other technicians is established at a central location. In districts governed by municipalities, a certain amount of support may be provided by local governments, particularly for financial and payroll applications. The staffing and management for administrative applications is better understood and in many districts has matured as the applications have developed.

For instructional applications, the use of computing technology is still an evolving phenomenon, becoming more widely used in the early 1980s as microcomputer technology became available and again in the 1990s as the Internet grew in popularity. The nature of instructional applications is somewhat different from administrative applications. Whereas administrators need efficient and accurate information flow, teachers and students need variety, stimulation, and ease of use in their applications. Administrators find rewards in using computers because they reduce manual efforts and produce accurate and timely reports for use inside and outside the school. Teachers and students, on the other hand, require pedagogically appropriate software designed more to meet individual needs. The applications needed for language arts, for example, are frequently different from those needed for science and mathematics or the fine arts.

These requirements tend to support a more decentralized environment unique to educational institutions. The staff to support these applications needs to be not only technically knowledgeable but also pedagogically knowledgeable. The key to effectiveness is being able to integrate technology into the regular curriculum with its diversity of subject matter and content. In the 1980s, schools generally established centralized laboratories mainly because of the limited amount of equipment on hand and because there was a tendency to follow the administrative approach with which most district administrators were more familiar. Centralized facilities will continue to play an important role in supporting instructional applications, but the general thinking is that more equipment has to be placed in the regular classrooms to be effective. The staff needed to support these facilities includes technology teachers who have received both pedagogical and technical training. In addition to teaching responsibilities, they also frequently function as coordinators for technology in each school and work with regular classroom teachers. Their main roles are to help other teachers use technology and provide basic technology instruction for the students. As equipment continues to be acquired for instruction, schools increasingly will need at least one staff member who will serve to coordinate technology activities. Schools with an extensive amount of equipment (e.g., several thousand microcomputers) may have a number of staff members coordinating activities.

To manage technology facilities throughout the district, school superintendents must decide on an appropriate administrative structure. Two common organizational models (see Figure 12.1) for managing administrative and instructional technology are (a) one central administration managing both activities (Model A in the figure) or (b) separate administrations for administrative and instructional technology (Model B). Either model works.

The single administration model (Model A) can provide significant economies in terms of technical knowledge and maintenance services. Certain applications that require good student

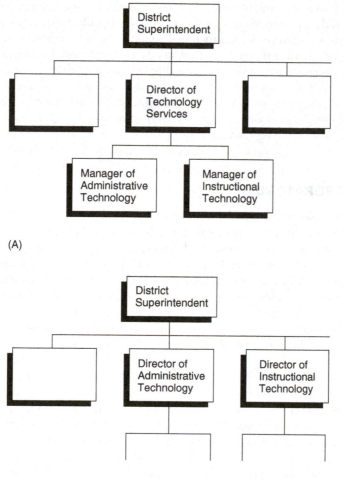

(A)

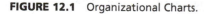

(B)

FIGURE 12.1   Organizational Charts.

record keeping, such as data-driven decision making and computer-managed instruction, might be easier to establish if both administrative and instructional technology report through the same administrator. Data communications systems for applications such as Internet access also are better planned and implemented from a single administrative source. However, the director in this model needs to make sure that both administrative and instructional technology are equitably provided for in terms of philosophy and share of resources. Hardware, software, and training decisions may be very different for administrative and instructional applications, and an effective administrator has to develop different procedures and processes for the two areas.

Organizational Model B, which separates the administration of services into two separate entities, generally will produce more philosophically appropriate applications and will ensure a more equitable distribution of resources. On the other hand, certain economies may not be realized, particularly for basic hardware acquisitions and maintenance. Regardless of the model being used, a district administrator or superintendent will attempt to make sure that economies are realized where appropriate while allowing differences in philosophy, staffing, and approaches to occur. Planning and policy committees for the two activities would remain separate and have different participants. Committees for instructional applications need to have greater participation at the building level to ensure that various academic departments and disciplines are represented. Committees for administrative applications need to involve administrative and clerical staff for analyzing the system and for using the centralized applications effectively. Budgeting for the two areas should be kept separate mainly because the sources of funds generally are quite different. Administrative technology usually relies on the local school district operating budget for funds, whereas instructional technology can pursue a variety of funding sources including not only the operating budget but also gifts and grants, special state appropriations, and so forth.

CENTRAL LABORATORIES

A major issue in facilities planning and management is the establishment of centralized laboratories for instructional applications. If a school district had the funds to purchase an unlimited amount of equipment, make it available throughout the day, and provide assistance to and train all the teachers, such a district would locate technology where learning occurs—in the classrooms. Computers would routinely be available as tools to be used as needed by teachers and students. The "one laptop per child" philosophy exemplifies this approach. However, school districts do not have unlimited funds; therefore, alternative locations for computer equipment must be considered.

Centralizing computers is appropriate when the supply of equipment and the supply of technically trained teachers are limited. The familiar approach of moving students to a central laboratory for several periods per week is effective given limited resources, but it is not ideal. In addition to disrupting the schedules of both students and teachers, a central facility tends to separate computers from the learning that goes on in the regular classroom. On the other hand, many teachers are not yet able to use computer equipment effectively in their instruction. In this case, the centralization at least guarantees that students will have some computer experience, and it especially benefits those students who are more interested in or better able to use computer technology. The solution is to compromise and provide for some mix of centralized and decentralized facilities depending on the amount of equipment available and the technical training of the teaching staff.

The location of central computer facilities can be a significant decision. The choices are typically between developing a dedicated central computer laboratory or becoming part of another centralized instructional support center such as a library or media facility. Either approach works and essentially depends on the skills and knowledge of the personnel supervising the areas. If library and media staff are knowledgeable about the technology, then housing a computer facility as part of these centers is appropriate. If they are not knowledgeable, then the tendency has been to set up a separate computer laboratory.

Other organizations such as colleges and universities have had to make similar decisions. The major tendency there has been to establish dedicated computer centers, either separated from or integrated in a library or other instructional support activity. Instructional computing in colleges evolved differently from that in primary and secondary schools. Higher education, particularly research universities and schools of engineering, were at the forefront in the early years of computing in the 1950s and 1960s when computer centers were all centralized and staffed by highly trained technicians and faculty from the science and technology departments. Primary and secondary schools did not become involved with computing until the late 1970s and 1980s with the introduction of microcomputers, which physically did not require a central facility and could be housed almost anyplace. These could be operated by most teachers interested enough in using the equipment in their lessons. Colleges in the past 10 years have been making major strides in distributing equipment throughout their campuses, and microcomputers can now be seen in dormitories, libraries, and hallways as well as in classrooms. In the 1990s, colleges and universities started examining the organizational structure of information services. Computer centers, library services, and media services in particular are now being examined in terms of greater organizational integration.

Primary and secondary schools, likewise, should be focusing on how to distribute and integrate computers into everyday instruction by physically locating equipment where teaching and learning occur. Where centralization is necessary because of equipment or staff limitations, locating computers where staff can assist teachers and students makes good sense. However, an increasingly popular alternative to the central computer facility is the mobile/portable laboratory or central lab on wheels. A cart equipped with slots for up to 30 laptop computers can be wheeled almost anyplace in the school building. This eliminates the need to move the children to the lab and brings the technology to them in the classroom. These carts are also equipped with wireless communications devices so that all of the laptops have immediate access to the Internet without a need to wire them individually to a local or wide area network. Most of the major computer manufacturers (e.g., Apple, Dell, Hewlett-Packard) market complete mobile labs that include the cart, laptop computers with wireless adaptor cards, and a wireless access point or transceiver.

PHYSICAL ENVIRONMENT

The physical environment in which computer equipment is located—regardless of whether it is centralized or not—is important and should be well planned. Ergonomics, floor layouts, furniture, electrical precautions, and security requirements are critical. School districts in which some degree of administrative computing exists probably have technical staff who can be helpful in planning the facilities. However, there are certain factors in designing space for children and learning, which are not the same as designing work spaces for adults.

Facilities for Administrative Applications

For administrative applications, expertise in designing the physical environments is frequently available both inside and outside the district. In establishing or expanding a central mainframe computer facility, the technical staff, with assistance from a computer vendor, is usually able to design an efficient and pleasant work environment.

In facilities for office staff, computer workstations should be comfortable and blend into the office environment. Desks and chairs with adjustable heights are readily available and help make it easier for staff to use their keyboards. Wall space should be used to reduce the amount of electrical cable and wires that have to be distributed onto areas where people walk. Even when covered by floor strips, cables can be serious tripping hazards. For administrators or secretaries who are expected to spend a great deal of time using a workstation, glare on a video screen can be annoying and lead to eyestrain. Situating workstations to minimize glare is a common practice, and using polarized video shields is also effective. Most districts may call on the expertise of their professional computer and architectural staffs to design pleasant and safe workstation layouts to provide comfortable work environments.

Modern administrative applications (office automation, database, Internet access, etc.) are increasingly relying heavily on a high-speed data communications network. Careful planning should be done at the district level in developing the physical infrastructure requirements of such a network.

Facilities for Instructional Applications

For instructional applications, the physical layout should be conducive to learning and meet the needs of children of different ages, sizes, and understanding. For a central laboratory or a computer classroom, the location of workstations should be carefully evaluated.

Figures 12.2, 12.3, and 12.4 provide several floor plans for a 20-station computer facility. These figures assume that each station has at least a keyboard, mouse, and video monitor resting on top of the processor equipped with a disk drive, as is typical for many Apple Macintosh and DOS/Windows machines. Additional equipment, such as printers, DVDs, and CD-ROMs, can be added as needed. Most of these peripherals, especially printers, can also be shared to use the available space efficiently. Local area networks, either hardwired or wireless, also fit into this basic workstation configuration without any problem.

The row design (Figure 12.2) is a common layout for a computer facility and represents an efficient use of floor space. It is conducive to teaching, with the teacher in the front of the class delivering lessons and instructions. However, a drawback involves the distribution of electrical wires and computer cables, which can become tripping hazards if not hidden or entrenched in conduits. In computer instruction, students need a good deal of time for hands-on use of the equipment. Most teachers during this time move from workstation to workstation, providing advice and helping children with their computer work. Teachers may also encourage other students to look at what one of their peers has accomplished for both demonstration and recognition. This is especially true in the younger grades. For both teachers and students, this configuration tends to create barriers that inhibit free movement around the room.

Figure 12.3 illustrates a cluster design with four student workstations grouped together. It makes efficient use of available floor space and reduces some of the tripping and mobility problems by locating most of the computer cables in the back of the equipment away from where teachers or students might walk. The cluster design provides open spaces for teachers and students, which is effective for group and collaborative learning environments, especially if large tables are used for the workstations. If this floor plan is used in an instructional resource room

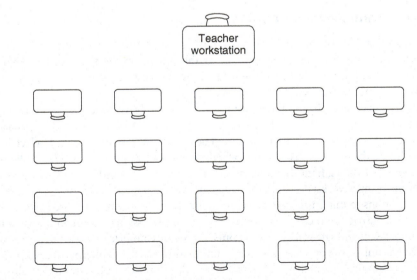

FIGURE 12.2 Floor Plan for 20 Workstations: Rows.

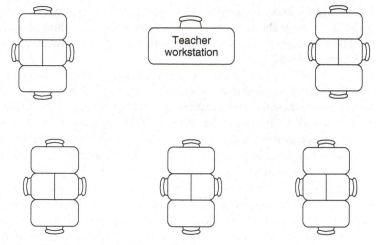

FIGURE 12.3   Floor Plan for 20 Workstations: Clusters.

where students are expected to work alone, a recommendation is that carrels be used for the workstations.

Figure 12.4 depicts a horseshoe design that places workstations along the walls of the room. This approach is the least efficient in terms of the use of floor space, but it may be the most conducive to teaching and encouraging free movement. In this configuration, all wiring and cables are located along walls, away from walking areas. Teachers can choose to be either in the front

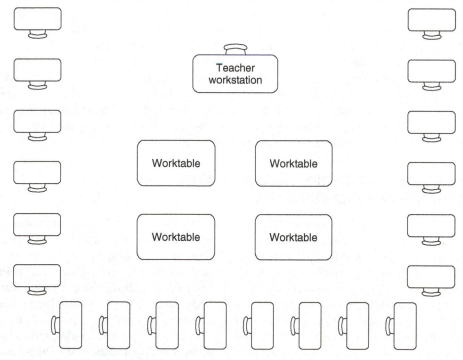

FIGURE 12.4   Floor Plan for 20 Workstations: Horseshoe.

or right in the middle of the class. Students will never have to have their backs to the teacher, and they can easily and safely move about the room. Variations of the horseshoe approach are used in some schools to allow students to work in teams, with each station providing equipment and chairs for two or more students.

Regardless of the configuration, some consideration should also be given to furniture that will be comfortable, useful, and conducive to learning. Large, open worktables allow for greater sharing and group activity, whereas carrels are more appropriate for individual activity. Light colors are more cheerful than dark colors and blend better with the equipment, most of which is beige, gray, or white. Glare, especially natural light coming in from windows, can be a serious distraction for students using video monitors. In planning the placement of monitors, some evaluation should be done as to whether certain stations would have a glare problem. One solution for this might be the installation of vertical blinds, which are very effective in shutting out natural light.

Physical planning for the teacher's workstation also requires special consideration and should be designed to maximize learning. Large monitors (e.g., 36 inches), video projection systems, and whiteboards (discussed in Chapter 7) are increasingly becoming the standard demonstration vehicles for computer-based lessons. Many products are available, and improvements in resolution and image quality are being made every day. In general, a large monitor provides better image quality than an overhead projection system, but it is also more expensive. Light switches or controls should allow teachers to dim all or part of the room so that students can view a monitor free from glare. If an instructor likes to move about a great deal while teaching, consideration should be given to situating the keyboard on a high stand rather than on a standard-height desk, so that commands and other keyboard operations can be executed while standing up rather than bending over. Simple overhead projectors and whiteboards using dry markers should be provided rather than chalkboards that generate dust—a potential problem for the equipment.

In designing spaces for standard classrooms where only a limited amount of equipment is provided, many of the considerations mentioned still are appropriate. If two to five workstations are to be provided, consider setting them up in a computer corner to take advantage of the wall space for wiring and cables. In classrooms with only one computer, give consideration to providing a large monitor so that several children can participate and view what is happening. This can be especially effective when used in conjunction with group or cooperative learning exercises where the large images can make an activity come to life. For readers wishing additional information on teaching with limited equipment in a classroom, *Great Teaching in the One-Computer Classroom* (Dockterman, 1998) provides many useful suggestions.

DATA COMMUNICATIONS FACILITIES AND INFORMATION INFRASTRUCTURE

As discussed in Chapter 8, technology is becoming increasingly dependent on data communications facilities for teaching and learning. Internet access, local area networks (LANs), wireless local area networks (WLANS), and wide area networks (WANs) are becoming common wherever computing is taking place. As a result, administrators should consider developing an overall planning and support mechanism for providing "connectivity" throughout a district for both administrative and instructional applications. Such plans should consider not only the local school needs but also the larger community's or municipality's planning and requirements. These plans can take into consideration all aspects of information processing, including telephone, fax, video, and computer. Other key factors such as the geographic distribution, the size of population, and the reliance on public or private telephone and cable systems should be evaluated and understood.

Of all the areas of information technology, planning and implementing a data communications network combining computer, telephone, and video technology is probably the most complex. Even districts with experienced staff frequently require the services of consultants in planning a new data communications system or making major revisions to an existing one. Investing funds to hire a good consultant for this planning is generally very worthwhile. Such planning can take into consideration the cooperation of local utilities and businesses, especially telephone, cable television, and other technology-based enterprises.

In the 1980s, planning and implementing communications systems usually focused on the wiring of buildings and rooms to be able to receive digital transmissions. Modern communications systems require a far more careful analysis and design. Carlitz, Lentz, and MacIlroy (1995) recommend a "layered" approach that considers data communications networks in three basic layers:

1. The physical layer
2. The protocol layer
3. The application layer

The physical layer contains all aspects of the media and devices through which data or signals will pass. Discussions regarding physical transmissions using copper wire, fiber optics, or wireless transmission are critical. Whereas school districts can control to some degree the physical medium within their buildings and campuses, outside connections are totally dependent on local utility providers—hence the need to involve these providers in planning this aspect of the system.

An example of an issue discussed within this layer would be bandwidth. The frequency with which signals can be transmitted and received directly affects the speed of a network and is dependent on the medium. Lower bandwidth, as is available over standard telephone lines, is fine for simple data transmission, and many existing networks use telephone lines for their outside connections. However, applications requiring high speeds, such as video transmission, will need much larger bandwidth than that provided through standard telephone connections. Identifying how higher bandwidth can be provided at a reasonable cost is a serious issue that is and will continue to be discussed in many school districts and communities.

The protocol layer refers to the rules or standards that enable one device to send signals to other devices on a network and to receive signals from them. Although the Internet has provided an overall standard protocol (see Chapter 8), most LANs and WANs are using machine and/or manufacturer-designed protocols for local signal processing. In the past, planning the protocol layer would involve determining whether and how the protocol from one LAN or WAN would interact with the protocol from another LAN or WAN. This has begun to change as more schools adopt the Internet and its derivative protocols as the standard for their networks, especially for WANs. Schools are developing Internet-based protocol networks—or intranets—within their districts. If a school district has existing communications systems that use several different protocols in place, it would be wise to begin the planning process of replacing these different systems with a standard Internet-based protocol.

The application layer refers to all the existing and foreseeable applications that are expected to run on computers connected to the networks. At this third layer, it is especially important to identify how data are to be transferred from one network to another and from one program to another. School districts might adopt basic tool applications (e.g., word processing, e-mail, spreadsheet, virus protection, database) and may establish popular software packages such as Microsoft Office as the district standards for use on the network, thereby ensuring easy transfer of data. Some applications, however, such as multimedia and digital video, are still evolving as software technologies and generally accepted standard packages and formats are more difficult to establish throughout a district.

Because of the phenomenal growth of the Internet in the 1990s, all organizations, including school districts, are rethinking their data communications systems. Schools, private corporations, and government agencies at all levels are examining their information infrastructures to determine whether they are poised to use the evolving resources on the Internet. This type of facilities planning will be the focus of district-wide planning discussions for many years to come.

The vast majority of all data communications systems in schools rely extensively on cables or hard wires to connect computing equipment in LANs and WANs. However, in the past few years, many schools have begun to invest in wireless local area networks or WLANs (Park & Staresina, 2004). Conceptually, a WLAN is the same as a LAN without the connecting cables or wires (see Figure 12.5) and instead uses high-frequency radio waves to send and receive data signals.

Although there are several variations, in a typical WLAN configuration, a transceiver device, called an *access point,* connects to the school's wired network backbone from a fixed location using standard cabling. A *backbone* is a large data transmission line that carries data gathered from smaller lines that interconnect with it. Generally all LANs are connected to a network backbone in order to access the Internet and other wide area networks. The access point receives and transmits data between the WLAN and the wired network backbone. A single access point can support a number of users. Users access the wireless LAN through WLAN adapters, installed as PC cards in laptop or desktop computers or integrated within personal digital assistants (PDAs) and other handheld devices.

The benefits of WLANs are their flexibility, mobility, and ease of use. They also may be especially cost-effective in older school buildings where coaxial cables or fiber optics are not available or may be expensive to install. WLANs also will increase in importance as school districts establish policies and decide how to support mobile digital devices (laptops, intelligent PDAs) brought to school by students. The drawbacks of WLANs are that they are not as fast, secure, or reliable as cable LANs. Also there are no communications or signal standards for WLANs although Wi-Fi—Institute of Electrical and Electronics Engineers (IEEE) Wireless Standard 802.11b—is emerging as the most commonly used. In planning data communications infrastructure, school administrators should be considering both cable and wireless options.

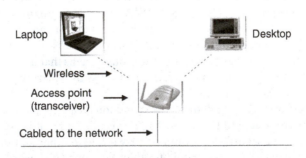

FIGURE 12.5 Wireless Local Area Network.

HARDWARE MAINTENANCE

As more equipment is acquired, maintaining it in good working order becomes a bigger and more complex job. The three major components of hardware maintenance are repairs, preventive maintenance, and upgrading.

Making Repairs

Computer hardware, because it has mostly electronic components rather than mechanical parts, is not prone to breakdowns. This is especially true of the main processor components but less true of printer and disk devices, which do have mechanical and moving parts. However, when repairs are needed they have to be performed by someone with the appropriate knowledge and training. For mainframe computer systems and large server systems, a district should have a comprehensive service contract with an outside vendor that provides for quick response by field engineers to correct any hardware problems. Generally these contracts also offer a certain number of preventive maintenance visits involving testing, cleaning, and making minor repairs to the equipment. Most major mainframe and large server manufacturers are responsive in accordance with the stipulations of their service contracts and do a good job of keeping their equipment functioning.

Also available are third-party repair companies whose service contracts are usually less expensive than those provided by the manufacturer. The services from these companies vary significantly. Before entering into a contract with a third-party vendor, carefully evaluate the company's service record, particularly with other organizations in the immediate geographic area. The qualifications of local repair personnel, response times, the availability of parts, and attention to preventive maintenance schedules are critical evaluation criteria.

Large mainframe computer systems and servers that are providing networking services throughout a school district are expected to be functioning every day. Administrators, teachers, and other staff who use such systems expect them to always be available; when they are not, the day's planned activities can be seriously disrupted. Extensive downtime due to repairs can be costly in terms of human resources, and good operations management should be able to keep it to a minimum.

For microcomputer systems, several options for handling repairs are available. First, service contracts similar to those used for large mainframe computers are available from both manufacturers and third-party vendors. This tends to be the most reliable, but also the most costly, approach.

Second, because microcomputer systems are much simpler in their design than large mainframe computers, school districts are also developing their own hardware maintenance staffs. The size of these staffs depends on the number of machines that need to be maintained. Major manufacturers such as Dell, Compaq, and Apple will train staff and provide various diagnostic tools to help identify and locate hardware problems. Less-expensive parts can be kept on hand to make repairs, and more-expensive parts can be ordered and generally received within 24 to 48 hours from manufacturers. A modest number of backup computers can also be kept on hand and substituted during repairs. Serious problems beyond the skills of a district's staff may require packing the problem computer and bringing it to a manufacturer's local outlet for repairs. As more and more microcomputers are being acquired, the trend in school districts is increasingly to do their own repairs.

A third alternative is a combination of the two options already cited, with the district handling certain (usually simpler) repairs and an outside service company, either the manufacturer or an independent, addressing more complex problems.

Providing Preventive Maintenance

Regardless of the approach a district takes in handling repairs, attention should always be given to preventive maintenance. The old adage that an ounce of prevention is worth a pound of cure is appropriate for computer hardware. Documented procedures should be in place for equipment maintenance. These include daily routines and periodic examinations.

Students should be taught to respect the equipment and should be involved with its care. Basic rules such as no eating or drinking anywhere around computer equipment should be strictly enforced. Dust covers should be used and kept in place, especially for equipment such as printers with mechanical and moving parts. School districts may draw on their own high school students to help in doing repairs and in providing periodic preventive maintenance services such as cleaning and testing equipment. This is especially true if the school district has vocational programs in electrical or mechanical technology.

Upgrading

Hardware upgrades and replacement plans are also important as school districts become more dependent on computer technology. After a while, computer equipment needs to be replaced because of extensive repairs or obsolescence. Hardware replacement plans should be in place that assume a 4- to 7-year life cycle for equipment, depending on use and function (see Chapter 10). For mainframe computer systems that are critical to administrative functioning, upgrades are especially necessary to keep up with current software and available technology. Microcomputer systems, especially those used by students, may need to be replaced because of wear and tear and accidents that can occur in an instructional environment.

Regardless, equipment will need to be replaced on some regular basis. Administrators need to be aware of the replacement schedule so that budgets and resources can be secured and disruption of services minimized.

SOFTWARE MAINTENANCE AND DISTRIBUTION

Computer software, like hardware, needs to be maintained. Depending on the nature of the computer applications, the manner in which software maintenance is provided can vary significantly. Large administrative software systems require a great deal of maintenance. In large administrative computer centers, a substantial portion of the programming staff will be dedicated to software system maintenance. Studies indicate that the human resources devoted to software maintenance exceed those devoted to new software development.

Maintenance involves correcting problems, modifying the software because of changes in policies or procedures, or upgrading it to take advantage of newer technology. School districts are particularly cognizant of making modifications due to changes in policies because they are dependent on various governmental bodies for funding. These bodies tend to increase their demands for data and accountability as they establish new programs or make additional budget allocations.

A current trend in instructional software is to acquire proprietary products—from companies such as Blackboard, Broderbund, and Tom Snyder Productions—that cannot be modified by teachers or academic support staff. Assuming users know how to run the programs, most instructional software will operate without problems, and generally it is not subject to changes in policies or procedures.

When software manufacturers do upgrade their software, they will generally supply a completely new version of the package to replace the old, either free of charge or for a reduced fee. However, distributing the new version requires increased attention as software packages are used by more and more students and teachers. Questions of centralization and decentralization arise. Some control may be maintained by having a central software library that might be located in the school's library; software may be borrowed in the same fashion as books. In addition, a central software library can provide basic services such as testing newly acquired software; cataloging, securing, or making backup copies; and establishing standard software documentation manuals. Because so much instructional software is customized for specific subjects, departments will also acquire it for the use of their own teachers and students. This reduces the amount of software that can be shared throughout a school and leaves most of the responsibility for software maintenance to the individual departments.

Both centralized and decentralized approaches are used in the schools. As with hardware, the trend is to adopt a decentralized approach, with departments and teachers acquiring software specifically for their classes much like other instructional supplies and materials. A compromise approach may be to have a central library for software that can be distributed throughout the school while allowing departments to keep a limited number of specialized packages.

Particularly effective in solving software distribution problems is the use of networks (LANs or WANs) in which a software library is kept on a central file server (with high-capacity disk equipment), with users throughout a school or district being able to access the software they need through the network. This is a major benefit of using networking to distribute computer services, both hardware and software, throughout a school.

In managing software distribution, school districts should adopt certain policies to protect their software and ensure compliance with vendor contracts and other legal stipulations. Software and files that are used regularly need to have current backup copies. For administrative software, this should be done routinely on a cyclical basis (daily, weekly, etc.), with backup copies kept in protected areas such as a magnetic tape or disk vault. Instructional software likewise should be backed up if the vendor allows copying the software. In many cases, this is not true, and a backup copy of the software needs to be purchased, usually at a nominal price.

There is a temptation to make copies or at least to try to make copies of software even when a vendor prohibits it. This is against the law and should not be encouraged. Federal laws and regulations afford considerable protection to software vendors for their products. School district administrators should acknowledge these regulations and should make sure that their students, teachers, and other staff are aware of them by prominently posting notices in computer areas against illegally making copies of software.

As mentioned in Chapter 10, software vendors generally will make available site licensing arrangements or quantity discounts to address the need for additional copies. Site licenses allow customers to make unlimited copies of packages. Modified site licenses allow customers to make some specified number of backup copies. Generally, they are attractively priced, and school districts intending to use a particular software package extensively should acquire a site license.

Some vendors do not provide site licenses but instead offer quantity discounts in the form of "lab packs." These are discounts for purchases of certain quantities, usually the number that would be needed for a single class. In addition to price discounts, vendors such as Tom Snyder Productions and Logo Computer Systems encourage the acquisition of lab packs by including curricular material that may be helpful to teachers in preparing their lessons.

POLICIES, PROCEDURES, AND DOCUMENTATION

Written policies, procedures, and documentation are critical to the effective use of computer technology. Unfortunately, too often their importance is realized only when a problem, breach, or violation has occurred that forces administrators to wonder why a policy did not exist for the situation.

Policies

As technology expands in schools, policies related to its use have emerged, covering a wide range of ethical, legal, social, and education issues. A number of these issues have been raised throughout this book. For example, in Chapter 3, policy issues regarding equity such as gender, student access, and special education populations were discussed; in Chapter 7, copyright issues were presented in the context of multimedia; and in Chapter 8, there was a discussion on policy responsibilities of school districts in protecting students from prurient and other undesirable material on the World Wide Web. Almost any aspect of technology can generate important policy issues that administrators should carefully consider and especially, if anything, can be done in the school. Daniel Domenech, executive director of the American Association of School Administrators, in response to a question regarding what actions school should take regarding young people displaying nude pictures of themselves or other students on the Internet or on cell phones, remarked that these types of activities clearly involve "major legal issues, policy issues and educational issues . . . and the easiest for [schools] to deal with are the educational issues" (Manzo, 2009). Domenech's response implies that although schools need to do something, the larger society also bears responsibility for helping students see the dangers of these types of activities. It is not the intent here to cover policy issues in depth, mainly because they can be lengthy discussions with many ramifications depending on local situations, societal issues, culture, and mores. However, some of the major technology policy issues that school districts should be considering include the following:

- Equity issues (gender, socioeconomics, and special education)
- Student access to technology at school, especially after school hours
- Student home use of technology
- Student use of mobile digital devices (e.g., cell phones, PDAs) in school
- Cyber bullying
- Loaning of equipment (e.g., laptop computers) and loaner responsibilities
- Use of school technology resources for personal activities
- Internet etiquette
- Appropriate use of school e-mail systems
- Protecting students from questionable material (pornography, hate-group activity) on the World Wide Web
- Ethical issues (plagiarism and the World Wide Web)
- Copyright and fair use
- Intellectual property
- Hardware standardization
- Access to student records (grades, addresses, telephone)
- Access to personnel records (salaries, addresses, e-mail)
- Freedom of Information Act policies

For readers wishing more information on policy issues, the following Web sites may be helpful:

- Edvancenet, a partnership formed by the Consortium for School Networking (CoSN), the National School Boards Foundation, and MCI WorldCom that was created to address education technology in the context of major policy issues
- Responsible Netizen, an initiative of the Center for Safe and Responsible Internet Use, aimed at assisting schools and other organizations to develop policies with regard to the "safe, responsible, legal, and ethical" uses of the Internet and other information technologies
- Stanford University Libraries' Web site on copyright and fair use, a most useful and up-to-date resource on this very complex issue

Once a school has developed new policies or revised existing ones, disseminating them becomes paramount. Posting them in public places such as libraries and computer laboratories is helpful. Establishing a Web site with an updated collection of technology (and other school district), policies can be a most effective form of communication.

Procedures

Procedures are the overall manner of doing things. They are frequently developed in conjunction with policies and form the framework within which an organizational entity operates. Procedures should be developed for all the basic operations that can occur in a computer facility. Examples of procedures include activities such as the following:

- Backing up files and software
- Using facilities (access, hours of operation, and priorities)
- Scheduling preventive maintenance
- Evaluating software
- Testing software
- Distributing and lending software
- Distributing and lending hardware

Procedures should be well communicated so that everyone using the facilities knows them. A procedures manual or Web site that is regularly updated, reviewed, and distributed to users of computer facilities can be very effective in this regard.

Documentation

Documentation refers to applications and describes how to use specific computer programs or sets of programs. All applications, administrative and instructional, require some documentation. Organizations that do not devote enough attention to documentation are vulnerable if key staff persons who know a great deal about the software applications leave. Written documentation must be maintained and made easily accessible for every program used in a school. For simple instructional software packages, it may consist only of the documentation that the vendor supplies. Teachers who use computers occasionally need documentation to understand how to use the software. The best software packages will not result in the best applications if teachers do not understand how to use them. The reverse is also sometimes true; that is, some mediocre software packages result in successful applications mainly because good documentation was provided and teachers understood how to use them.

For complex administrative applications, the standard operating procedure should require up-to-date, detailed descriptions and maintenance histories of all the programs that comprise the software system. For major administrative applications, the basic documentation for each program should include the following:

- Program specifications and design
- Program description
- Logic flowcharts
- Operations documentation
- Samples of output and input formats
- Maintenance documentation and history

In addition, user manuals for the overall application have to be developed for administrators and staff who are expected to maintain and use it. User manuals may be supplemented by online Help facilities that assist users in "navigating" through a computer application. Online Help is useful but should not replace a written document; it may be stored in a text editor file.

School administrators should not underestimate the importance of documentation when dealing with computer technology. Computer center staffs are more conscientious in developing documentation than are other departments, mainly because of their training and because they understand the vulnerability should key staff persons who know a software application leave. However, technical staff will also admit that more documentation is needed. In decentralized environments, procedures for monitoring documentation are rare and difficult to implement. Furthermore, with instructional applications, the wide variety of available software packages from many different sources makes it difficult to require documentation standards. As a result, documentation tends to be inconsistent and, in some cases, poorly done or nonexistent. Regardless of the degree of centralization or decentralization in a district or school, administrators should develop a minimum documentation standard and require it for all computer applications.

SECURITY

Computer security refers to procedures for protecting software and sensitive data files. Issues of security are of growing importance to schools as well as many other organizations. In corporate America, there have been many cases of unauthorized access via computer to customer bases, research and development test results, and financial accounts. Two well-publicized cases (O'Brien, 1989) involved major thefts from Wells Fargo ($21 million) and Security Pacific Bank ($10.2 million). Federal laws such as the Computer Fraud and Abuse Act of 1986 provide severe penalties for persons convicted of computer crime.

Schools do not maintain data subject to regular, high-volume financial transaction processing as is common in banks and brokerage houses. However, a school's payroll or accounts payable files can be vulnerable to abuse if security procedures are lax. Other files, such as student records, must also be protected. They contain sensitive information about individuals and must not be readily available except as needed for legitimate educational purposes.

Data security minimally involves establishing password protection to access a computer system. Additionally, it entails devising access codes that allow certain individuals to access particular files and data. All commercially available database management software packages routinely provide password and access code protection and should be used as standard operating procedures. Written policies should be developed, citing which offices and individuals have the authority or need to access specific data. These policies also establish the degree of access—that is, whether an individual can simply view data or change or update data.

In developing and monitoring data security, school administrators should be particularly concerned with students. Although a more common problem at the college level, there have been many cases of high school computer hackers with the talent to break through a password system to access student data such as grades and test scores. Just one or two such individuals can cause havoc to the integrity of data files. A solitary breach of the security system may require major review and verification of the violated data files to determine the extent of the damage. This process can take a great deal of staff time; more important, it can also leave users feeling insecure and wondering about the integrity of the data files.

In recent years, another form of unauthorized access to data files has emerged in the form of computer "viruses" that are designed to spread from one central processing unit to another. Whereas some viruses are harmless and simply generate annoying messages on a video screen, others are destructive and designed to erase data files, especially disk directories and operating system files. Computer viruses technically only refer to programs that copy themselves and infect computers without the permission or knowledge of the owners. However, the term *computer virus* also generically refers to a host of software intrusions (also referred to as malware), some of which are destructive and some of which are annoying. Trojan horses, worms, and spyware are some of the forms of malware or software that is unwanted and potentially destructive.

The concern for the destructive power of a computer virus was evident a few years ago, when headlines worldwide reported the spread of the *Michelangelo* virus designed to attack on the anniversary of Michelangelo's birth (March 6). Since then every few months computer viruses (e.g., Storm, Sasser, Conficker) are regularly reported in the news media. There are thousands of known computer viruses floating around the Internet, and school administrators would be wise to make sure that a district has established policies and have taken some steps to protect the school technology resources from attacks.

To protect against viruses, software products—referred to as "antiviruses" or "vaccines"— are available that will scan incoming e-mail, file transfers, and secondary storage devices. Antivirus software is a prudent investment for all computer operations but especially in network environments in which viruses can easily spread from one computer to another. The Norton AntiVirus from Symantec and Virex from Microcom are two popular products.

In addition to data security, some schools, especially those in high-crime areas, should plan to expend resources on physically securing computer equipment and protecting it from theft and vandalism. As computer equipment becomes smaller, lighter, and more easily disposed of, this need increases. A variety of measures can be taken to secure computer equipment. Anchor pads, which bolt the main computer components to a desk or table, are commonly used and are effective in most areas. Electronic security systems for doors and windows can also be used in centralized computer facilities and likewise are effective.

Security also becomes a more serious problem when distributing equipment throughout a school and into the classrooms. Anchor pads should be used in the classrooms; they may be the most cost-effective security measure. Electronic security systems can become expensive depending on the physical distribution of equipment and the accesses to a school building, which for fire code and ergonomic reasons tend to have many more doors and windows than other facilities.

In planning computer facilities, security issues should not be underestimated. To ignore them leaves a school or district vulnerable and subject to major setbacks in computer development should a breach in security occur.

THE HELPING PLACE

One of the most important responsibilities for those who manage computer facilities is to develop the proper schoolwide attitude to technology. The external elements (e.g., hardware maintenance, room organization, security), if done well, will contribute to a school's overall success in using technology.

Critical to this success will be the development of a positive attitude or a computer culture that is supportive and nonthreatening to the teachers and staff who are expected to use the technology.

The concept is not a new one and should be familiar to many administrators and teachers. In some schools, "helping places" have been established to provide support services to students. They may be extensions of a guidance office or a tutoring program and are usually friendly places staffed by teachers who smile easily, have positive dispositions, and will go out of their way to help a student with a problem. Computer facilities likewise should be helping places. In addition to the popular "What if?" questions, staff should be available to answer the "What happened?" and "How can I do it?" questions. Given the wide disparity in training and understanding that exists regarding computer technology, computer center staff members need to be oriented to respond to simple as well as complex questions.

Technology educators (Sheingold, 1991) have espoused establishing computer environments in which children have free and open access to equipment so that it becomes a basic and routinely used tool for learning. This concept also applies to teachers, secretaries, and clerical staff who are called on to use technology systems. Furthermore, they need access not only to equipment but, just as important, to the expertise and knowledge necessary to use it. Managers of computer facilities need to provide both equipment and expertise in a friendly, helpful manner.

Formal staff training sessions are a good beginning, but continuous, ongoing support services are what will make for a positive technology culture. Hotlines, help desks, and help phones, staffed by knowledgeable personnel, are extremely effective for answering questions. User groups that meet regularly in person or on electronic bulletin boards are helpful in establishing relationships among users and technical staff. Newsletters providing suggestions and hints for using hardware and software are effective communication vehicles for keeping staff informed. These are all excellent examples of ways to establish a positive computer culture in a school or district. In the final analysis, however, the most important element for building such a culture will be the positive attitude of the people providing these services.

CASE STUDY

Reread the section titled The Anatomy of a Survey about Richter Park High School in Chapter 5, and review carefully the recommendations made by the committee of teachers and parents.

Discussion Questions

1. Assume you are an assistant to the superintendent at Richter Park, and you need to write a position paper on these recommendations expanding on their implications for the district. Classify your paper in terms of their implications for changes/additions to district facilities, policies, and/or procedures.
2. Include in this position paper a preliminary cost analysis for funding the recommendations.

Summary

This chapter presents the basic elements of planning and managing computer facilities. Space utilization, personnel considerations, security, and hardware and software maintenance are examined.

As more and more equipment is acquired, the task of managing it grows too. Increasingly, school districts are establishing larger technical support groups to support technology in their schools.

Several major issues such as the centralization and locations of computer support facilities are examined. The evolution of the Internet and the demand for more extensive data communications systems is specifically identified as a major issue in facilities planning.

Documentation and security are also discussed. The chapter concludes with a call for establishing a positive computer culture in the school, directed not just to students but to teachers and other staff as well.

Key Concepts and Questions

1. Computer equipment is becoming increasingly easy to use, but managing computer facilities in schools is becoming more complex. Is this situation likely to change in the near future? Does it depend on the nature of the applications? Explain.

2. Various organizational models exist in school districts for managing computer facilities. Which model do you think is most appropriate? Why?

3. Centralized computer facilities are common in many schools. What are some of the major considerations in managing centralized versus decentralized facilities?

4. Ergonomic factors in the design of computer facilities are critical for the comfort and safety of users (teachers, students, and staff) in schools. What do you consider some of the most important ergonomic considerations? Do they change depending on the users? Explain.

5. With the proliferation of technology throughout the schools, maintenance of hardware and software is becoming more difficult. Why? Is it simply a matter of more equipment and software requiring more maintenance? Explain.

6. The concept of developing a positive culture in a school or any organization is a recurring theme in many discussions about leadership and administrative style. Borrowing from this theme, what are some of the techniques that can be developed to promote a positive technology culture in a school?

Suggested Activities

1. Identify the organizational structure for managing computer facilities in a school district and in a school. Evaluate the effectiveness of the structure(s). What suggestions, if any, do you have for improvement?

2. Evaluate the computer culture that has evolved in a school. What factors do you feel have contributed to this culture?

3. Review the technology plan of a school district and compare it to other school districts. Review, specifically, the goals and objectives related to physical facilities or infrastructure. Are there similarities? Differences? To help in this comparison, feel free to use the two Web sites whose addresses are below; they show the technology plans for two school districts:

Bellingham (Washington) Public Schools http://www.bham.wednet.edu/technology/technology.htm

Quincy (Washington) District Technology Plan http://www.qsd.wednet.edu/qsdtechplan.htm

References

Carlitz, R. D., Lentz, M., & MacIlroy, A. (1995). Standards for school networking. *Technological Horizons in Education Journal, 22*(9), 71–74.

Dockterman, D. A. (1998). *Great teaching in the one-computer classroom* (5th ed.). Cambridge, MA: Tom Snyder Productions.

Manzo, K. (2009, June 17). Administrators confront student 'sexthing'. *Education Week, 28*(35), 8.

O'Brien, J. A. (1989). *Computer concepts and applications.* Homewood, IL: Irwin.

Park, J., & Staresina, L. (2004, May 6). Tracking U.S. trends. *Education Week, 23*(35), 64–67.

Sheingold, K. (1991). Restructuring for learning with technology: The potential for synergy. *Phi Delta Kappan, 73*(1), 17–27.

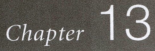

Chapter 13

Financial Planning for Technology

Previous chapters of Section III emphasized the need for planning the hardware, software, and people components of proposals to implement technology programs in a school or district. However, proposals cannot become realities without the financial resources necessary to initiate them and maintain them. This chapter examines the financial side of planning, with emphasis on evaluating costs for technology and on seeking funds to support it. Several of the ideas and approaches discussed in previous chapters are considered again from a cost perspective.

TECHNOLOGY CAN BE EXPENSIVE

As late as 1980, the spending for computer technology in education was negligible. Becker (1994) was among the first researchers to track the acquisition of technology in K–12 education. He conducted a series of national surveys in the 1980s and early 1990s and concluded that America's schools were acquiring approximately 300,000 to 400,000 microcomputers per year. Becker predicted that this trend would maintain itself, if not accelerate, well into the 21st century. Several years earlier, the U.S. Congress's Office of Technology Assessment (OTA) issued a comprehensive report estimating that as much as 32% of the average school district's instructional materials budget would be devoted to computer technology by the year 2000 (U.S. Congress, 1988). This represented an expenditure of approximately $4 billion per year for the country's 15,000-plus school districts. Quality Education Data (QED) (1991) supported the OTA estimate. Based on actual 1990 expenditures of $1.4 billion for instructional technology, QED projected an increase of $800 million through the 1994–1995 school year, or $2.2 billion. A further projection of the QED figures through the year 2000 would generate estimated expenditures of almost $4.5 billion. These estimates all have proven to be too low. QED (1996) later reported that the actual expenditures for instructional technology by the nation's schools had already exceeded $4 billion by 1995. School expenditures for technology for the year 2001–2002 have been estimated at close to $6 billion (McCabe & Skinner, 2003). Later estimates forecast the total K–12 education technology market hovering around $7 billion for fiscal year 2006 and slightly higher in 2007, with growth ultimately reaching $10 billion in spending by fiscal year 2010 (McEachern, 2005).

These computer expenditures are based on what has been occurring rather than what is needed. In fact, the case has been made that schools are not investing enough in technology. The President's Committee of Advisors on Science and Technology (PCAST) Panel on Education recently recommended that $13 billion annually should be used for instructional technology if education is to catch up with other segments of the country (American Geological Institute, 2009).

School administrators will need to plan wisely to meet the funding requirements for technology and to make sure that they have the resources to maintain technology-based programs. In some years, they may "hold the line" or reduce expenditures because of some budgetary problems, but these measures tend to be temporary, and the long-range, overall pattern is to increase funding. This pattern of increased expenditures for technology is not unique to the field of education. It is typical in private corporations, governmental agencies, and most other organizations that have been using technology since the 1960s, well before technology became popular in schools. Once a technology-based program is established, the normal cycle has been to expand and provide additional services and to upgrade it with newer technology when necessary.

THE COST-EFFECTIVENESS OF TECHNOLOGY

A common assumption is that computers can be cost-effective and save money in the long run. This complicated issue greatly interests many people, including administrators, school board members, teachers, union representatives, and taxpayers. The simple and popular notion that machines can replace people and thereby save money in an instructional setting, however, is yet to be proved. In other human endeavors, this concept was often promulgated by technology salespersons as a marketing or sales strategy. In the automobile industry, telephone communications, banking, and printing, without a doubt jobs have been lost to automation. It is likely that savings can be achieved in educational administration, school district communication, and record-keeping applications; however, cases in which technology has replaced teachers or significantly reduced instructional expenditures are rare.

Many teachers and administrators do see the computer as making them more effective in their daily activities. Albert Shanker, the late president of the American Federation of Teachers, spoke and wrote extensively on the potential benefits of computer technology in the classroom and saw it as a tool to be integrated into the learning process by the teacher. Early on, he indicated that the installation of computer equipment in the nation's classrooms should be education's top priority (Shanker, 1989). The National Education Association (NEA) regularly releases reports and statements declaring that computer technology holds great promise for enriching classroom instruction and management. As early as 1989, the NEA recommended that a computer be installed on the desk of every teacher (National Education Association, 1989). This has not happened yet, but the recommendation indicated the positive attitude of the nation's major teacher organization to technology in the classroom.

Although many educators are enthusiastic about the technology, the cost-effectiveness is open to debate. The basic question is: Are the funds expended on technology worth the improvement in learning when compared to costs of other types of instructional delivery? Research on the beneficial effects of technology on learning has been mixed, as already discussed in Chapter 6. Although a number of studies and reports have found that technology can have a beneficial effect on student achievement (Archer, 1998; Educational Testing Service, 1999; Schacter, 1999; Shaw, 1997; U.S. Congress, 1988; Waxman, Connell, & Gray, 2002; Wenglinsky, 1998), other studies (see Dynarski et al., 2007, and Campuzano, Dynarski, Agodini, & Rall, 2009) concluded that there were few significant learning differences between students who used the technology and those taught using other methods. However, reports or studies that examine the cost of technology as compared to other instructional costs and student achievement are quite rare. One example was a series of studies conducted by Levin and Meister (1986) comparing four cost-effective strategies: computer-assisted instruction, peer tutoring, increased instructional time, and reduced class size. They concluded that peer tutoring was the most cost-effective approach in terms of improved reading and mathematics scores on standardized tests. Computer-assisted instruction was the second most cost-effective strategy, followed by reduced class size, and increased instructional time. These studies were challenged by Niemiec, Blackwell, and Walberg (1986), who in reviewing Levin and Meister's methodology concluded that computer-assisted instruction was more cost-effective than peer tutoring. A group of superintendents and secondary school educators gathered recently to discuss how online courses might help offset budget cuts. Although officials from some states (Maryland and Florida) indicated that their virtual Advanced Placement classes are a cost-effective way to get high-quality coursework to more students, others were not in agreement (Ash, 2009). However, there was some agreement that depending on the circumstances, online courses could be cost effective. Picciano and Seaman (2007, 2009) in national surveys of school district leaders found that for many small rural schools, online courses provided cost-effective mechanisms for offering courses that otherwise would require hiring teachers, many of whom would be uncertified in their subject areas and who would not have enough students to justify their salaries.

The debate on the cost-effectiveness of technology will continue for some time. Technology is used mainly as an enhancement to existing instructional delivery rather than as a replacement. Even in large-scale deployment of instructional technology, such as an integrated learning system (ILS), teachers are still needed to manage the environment. As a result, technology has in fact been adding to instructional costs in most cases. The methodological control and rigor in cost–benefit studies needed to isolate technology costs and at the same time control other costs in determining the effects of each on student outcomes is very difficult to achieve, so this issue will continue to be discussed and debated for quite some time.

A TIME LINE FOR FINANCIAL PLANNING

With the introduction of microcomputers in the late 1970s, a major breakthrough was realized in the costs for computer technology, comparable to the introduction of the Model T automobile by Henry Ford, which made a car affordable for practically every American family. Before the Model T, cars were viewed mainly as luxury items affordable only to somewhat wealthy people. Within a few decades after its introduction, and even with the depression of the 1930s and World War II in the 1940s, cars became indispensable, and the multicar family has now become commonplace. We now see the same situation with microcomputers.

The major catalyst for this phenomenon originally was the cost, not the need. In the 1960s and 1970s, computers were not items that the average person felt he needed in order to live from day to day. As late as 1977, Ken Olsen, the president of Digital Equipment Corporation, the leading manufacturer of minicomputers, stated publicly that there was no need for any individual to have a microcomputer in his or her home (Stoll, 1995). As a matter of fact, with the exception of some video games and very rudimentary home applications such as balancing a checkbook, calculating mortgage payments, and estimating a grocery bill, there were very few applications for the average person. In the late 1970s, most people purchased microcomputers because the cost, typically about $1,000, was attractive. Large quantities of computers were purchased, and this trend has continued into the present. In the meantime, computer vendors and software firms caught up with the availability of hardware by developing tens of thousands of computer programs to meet all kinds of interests and needs. Although basic applications such as word processing, e-mail, Internet access, social networking, and electronic games tend to be the most common home uses today, microcomputers routinely touch our daily lives in the form of cash machines, checkout counters, and telephone information services.

Primary and secondary schools were among the last organizations to become dependent on computer technology. With the introduction of microcomputers, this began to change, mostly because schools were able to afford to purchase this equipment. Furthermore, the trend is clear: computer equipment is becoming indispensable for administrative applications in many schools, just as it has in many other individual and organizational activities. Educational applications have been developed and will continue to be developed to meet the demands of the education market. Administrators will be devoting more and more of their budgets to computer technology even though the unit cost of a microcomputer has been decreasing.

To understand this situation better, review Table 13.1, which provides a time line of the trends in digital technology with their respective costs from 1940 through the early 21st century. In the second half of the 20th century, digital computing steadily progressed by providing greater capacity at lower cost and in smaller sizes. As a result, more and more people have been able to

TABLE 13.1 Digital Technology Time Line, 1940–2010

	1940→ 1950→	1960→	1970→ 1980→	1990→	2000→ 2015→
	Premainframe	**Mainframe**	**Minicomputer**	**Microcomputer**	**Post-microcomputer**
Machine	Experimental machines such as ENIAC	IBM 700, 360, 4300 Series	Digital Equipment PDP Series	PC Macintosh	Digital information appliances
Cost	Unaffordable	Affordable to large businesses	Affordable to large and small businesses	Affordable to individuals	Inexpensive—individuals will own several
Size	Large room	Room	Large desk	Desktop laptop	Palm-size
Distribution	One in existence	Thousands sold	Hundreds of thousands sold	Hundreds of millions sold	Billions will be sold

acquire computing equipment. In the 21st century, this progression has culminated in relatively inexpensive, palm-sized information appliances that use wireless communications (satellite transmissions) to allow anyone, anywhere, to look up a bank statement, compose and forward e-mail, view a television program, or call mom. Furthermore, these devices are so inexpensive that most households own several. If there is any doubt, just consider how Americans have moved from one telephone on the wall to a telephone in every room, a portable for the patio, and a cellular in the car or in a pocketbook. Handheld information appliances such as the BlackBerry Storm or the Palm Pre smartphones are now commonplace.

The convergence of computer, communications, and audio/video technologies resulting in inexpensive, portable information devices is having a major impact on all aspects of information-related activities, including education. Communication at all levels will be more convenient and will allow teachers to teach and students to learn via technology more gracefully than ever before.

In examining costs, computing equipment has evolved from the expensive mainframe computers of the 1960s to the minicomputers of the 1970s to the relatively inexpensive microcomputers of the 1990s as characterized by Macintosh and DOS/Windows machines. The 1990s also saw the introduction of handheld data organizers and other super-lightweight microcomputers. Through the early part of the 21st century, microcomputers have continued to evolve, especially with advances in data storage capabilities and developments in optical disc and DVD technologies that provide virtually unlimited online storage with both read and write features. Digital video delivered on the Internet is beginning to compete with television as the primary visual mass medium. Internet access and networking capability via high-speed modems had phenomenal growth in the 1990s and continues to increase. Educational workstations that combine computing, video, and networking are commonplace, and all components (computer, video, and data communications) are available from a single manufacturer. A majority of students either own their own digital appliances and/or have access to a microcomputer in their homes. American society is moving in the direction that everyone will have access to a computer device.

In terms of cost, the unit price of computer hardware has fallen dramatically from the typical $1 million large mainframe systems of the 1960s to the under-$1,000 microcomputer systems of today. Although unit prices of microcomputers were stable—even decreasing—throughout the 1980s and 1990s, performance (speed, primary storage, and secondary storage capacities) continued to expand and improve. In the 1990s, the typical microcomputer system ranged between $1,000 and $2,500 depending on options such as CD-ROMS, printers, and other peripheral equipment. Handheld and other limited application microcomputers that sold for as little as $300 were introduced. By 2010, small, portable digital appliances using wireless communications have come to dominate the market. The cellular phone, a BlackBerry, or Palm PDA with Internet access are provided on a single device that cost under $200 or, in some cases, are given away for free as part of the incentive for contracting with communications service providers.

The cost for software has also begun to decrease, with many basic packages available for free on the Internet. Educational software will range from $20 for simple programs to as much as hundreds of thousands of dollars for integrated learning systems and course management systems. The Internet continues to grow as the major source of software and media. Interactive video packages, introduced in the late 1980s, are easier to use and more generally available, especially if the cost for producing these materials can be reduced.

The people needed to support technology continue to be the crucial factor in providing technology-based education in the schools. The highly paid programmers of the 1980s and 1990s are increasingly being replaced by computer networking engineers whose main jobs are to install and maintain data communications facilities in classrooms, administrative offices, libraries, and so forth. Teacher education programs in colleges have expanded and increasingly are providing specializations in computer education that combine technical training with teaching and learning. Many teacher education programs and state certification agencies have begun to require all new teachers to be technologically literate and to take course work in educational technology. Presently, practically all schools depend on technology teachers to assist regular teachers, the majority of whom already have a basic proficiency in using technology. Regardless, staff development continues to be needed to maintain technology skills and to integrate new software products into everyday teaching and learning.

With the time line in Table 13.1 providing the necessary background and a glimpse of the costs for technology, let us consider a budgeting process for funding technology.

THE BUDGET WORKSHEET

Financial planning supports the overall planning processes of a school district. It should not dominate the process but be integrated as needed. As with many aspects of administration, a proper balance must be achieved so that those doing the educational planning are not stifled by budget considerations—and at the same time are cognizant of the costs of what they are proposing to do.

In planning for technology, the first step is to develop a planning process that yields worthwhile proposals for possible implementation. Each of these proposals should include a budget worksheet identifying the major costs associated with the application (see Figure 13.1). Information is required for the major components (hardware, software, personnel, etc.) of each technology planning proposal.

This worksheet serves several purposes. First, it requires those making a proposal to identify the necessary costs for implementation. Although this may be a routine procedure in some schools, administrators frequently face situations in which the cost of a project or proposal has not been carefully determined. A common example in many technology proposals is that emphasis is placed on hardware costs alone, which frequently may account for only a fraction of the total cost. The use of a budget worksheet requires an examination of all the costs associated with the proposal.

North Central School District No. 1

Please complete all sections as best as you can. Include the costs for consultants within the categories of hardware, software, personnel, and so forth. Attach additional pages if necessary. If you need help in completing this worksheet, feel free to contact Jane Dawson (Technology Coordinator) at 916-443-8445.

Name: _____

Department: _____

School: _____

Description of the project

-

-

Hardware (Identify the type of equipment and its cost.)   Subtotal $ _____

-

-

Software (Identify the software needed and its cost.)   Subtotal $ _____

-

-

Personnel (Identify any staff requirements including   Subtotal $ _____

training and release time for curriculum development.)

-

-

Repairs/upgrades (Estimate any projected costs for repairs   Subtotal $ _____

and upgrades to equipment.)

-

-

Supplies (Estimate the annual costs for supplies.)   Subtotal $ _____

-

-

Facilities (Identify where equipment is to be located and   Subtotal $ _____

any special requirements for electricity, security, etc.

Also include any requests for new furniture.)

-

-

                                                                 Grand Total $ _____

FIGURE 13.1   One-Year Budget Worksheet for a Technology-Related Proposal.

Second, the worksheet initiates important information-gathering activity for those making a proposal. Collecting information on costs requires administrators, teachers, library media personnel, and other staff to seek out vendors, salespersons, suppliers, and others who can provide important information not only about costs but also about new models of hardware, educational discounts, and demonstration opportunities. The inclusion on the budget worksheet of the name of a person in the district who functions as a technology coordinator is also very helpful. Such a person can be an important source of information about what already exists in the district and can bring together individuals who may have common purposes—which is especially effective in larger school districts where interaction between schools may be limited. Such an individual can also be effective in encouraging teachers and other staff to share equipment and facilities.

Third, the use of a budget worksheet makes it easier to coordinate the costs of all proposals into one overall financial plan. With the cost information readily available, summarizing and approximating all costs is much easier for determining the total budget request. This, in turn, can be compared to the existing or projected availability of funds, and the process of evaluating funding can begin.

A BUDGET MODEL AND TOTAL COST OF OWNERSHIP

In developing an overall financial plan, much time is spent in determining the component costs of the various proposals. The budget worksheet is helpful in providing the approximate costs for all the requests. However, administrators will need to refine these requests because rarely are there enough resources to fund all proposals. As part of this refinement, administrators will ask teachers and administrators to reduce or, sometimes, to expand their requests and very frequently to pool or share resources. With technology, the pooling of resources to acquire hardware, software, supplies, and so forth can result in substantial economies. Essentially, this was one of the most important reasons that schools centralized rather than decentralized computer facilities when they first began new computer-based education programs.

In developing the overall financial plan, administrators should make sure the proposals presented have accurately projected all the various costs for implementing a plan and have considered sharing and other means to achieve the greatest benefit from available resources. For applications that may be implemented over several years, the costs should be projected accordingly (see Figure 13.2).

Table 13.2 illustrates a budget model of an overall financial plan that might be used to fund a school technology program. The major cost categories of hardware, software, and personnel comprise 67% of the total, with other items such as staff training, repairs/upgrades, supplies/furniture, and miscellaneous categories accounting for the remaining 33%. These percentages are meant to provide a general direction and can vary depending on the computer applications being supported and other local conditions.

An important element of Table 13.2 is the fact that budgets for all costs, not just hardware, are clearly identified. This is a major issue for which many administrators do not plan. In an article titled "Technology's Real Costs," Fitzgerald (1999) suggested that schools use a total cost of ownership (TCO) approach. TCO is commonly used in the business sector to represent the total cost of installing, operating, and maintaining technology. Essentially, a yearly calculation is made per hardware unit (computer workstation) for all of the costs (software, support, repairs, upgrades, etc.). Fitzgerald (1999) referred to one study of 400 school districts, which calculated the TCO for a school with 75 networked computer workstations as $2,251 per workstation per year. This is more than double the purchase price (approximately $1,000) of each workstation.

North Central School District No. 1

Please complete all sections as best as you can. Include the costs for consultants within the categories of hardware, software, personnel, and so forth. Attach additional pages if necessary. If you need help in completing this worksheet, feel free to contact Jane Dawson (Technology Coordinator) at 916-443-8445.

Name: _____

Department: _____

School: _____

Description of the Project
-
-

	Year 1	Year 2	Year 3
Hardware (Identify the type of equipment and its cost.)	Subtotal $ _____	Subtotal $ _____	Subtotal $ _____
•			
•			
Software (Identify software needed and its cost.)	Subtotal $ _____	Subtotal $ _____	Subtotal $ _____
•			
•			
Personnel (Identify any staff requirements including training and release time for curriculum development.)	Subtotal $ _____	Subtotal $ _____	Subtotal $ _____
•			
•			
Repairs/upgrades (Estimate any projected costs for repairs and upgrades to equipment.)	Subtotal $ _____	Subtotal $ _____	Subtotal $ _____
•			
•			
Supplies (Estimate the annual cost for supplies.)	Subtotal $ _____	Subtotal $ _____	Subtotal $ _____
•			
•			
Facilities (Identify where equipment is to be located and any special requirements for electricity, security, etc. Also include any requests for new furniture.)	Subtotal $ _____	Subtotal $ _____	Subtotal $ _____
•			
Year Totals	Total $ _____	Total $ _____	Total $ _____

Grand Total (All Years) $ _____

FIGURE 13.2 Three-Year Budget Worksheet for a Technology-Related Proposal.

TABLE 13.2 Budget Model for a School Technology Program	
Component	**Percentage**
Hardware	30
Software	10
Personnel	27
Training	12
Repairs/upgrades	9
Supplies/furniture	6
Miscellaneous	6
Total	**100%**

One might ask: How can the yearly cost be so much more? When one calculates the cost for supplies, repairs, upgrades, and so forth, the TCO becomes obvious. Let's take the case of a simple printer.

Hewlett-Packard makes an excellent Officejet (6110) printer that sells for under $100 on sale. The black ink cartridge it uses costs $24 and prints good quality for approximately 500 pages. Each ream (500 pages) of paper costs $5. In a school where this printer would use a ream of paper every 2 weeks requiring replacement of the print cartridge and a ream of paper 26 times a year would incur supply costs of (26 weeks x $29 for cartridge and paper) or approximately $750 per year for just this one printer that was purchased for less than $100. Just imagine the potential TCO for hundreds of microcomputers. In a *New York Times* article entitled "Seeing No Progress, Some Schools Drop Laptops," Hu (2007) reported that a number of schools in New York, Virginia, Massachusetts, California, and Florida were giving up on their "one laptop per child" programs because of modest academic performance and also because of the cost of maintaining hundreds of computers. One chief information officer stated that the "yearly costs were prohibitive." (Hu, 2007, A1) At Liverpool High School (near Syracuse, New York), a room that used to be the meeting place for the yearbook club was converted hastily into the laptop repair shop for the "80 to 100 machines that broke each month." (Hu, 2007, B1) These schools might have been better prepared if they had taken a TCO approach when planning and budgeting for these programs.

SPECIAL CONSIDERATIONS OF BUDGETING FOR COMPUTER APPLICATIONS

Although budgeting for computer applications, whether administrative or instructional, is similar to other budgeting exercises, administrators should be aware of several special considerations unique to technology.

Opting for Centralized or Decentralized Computer Facilities

The decision to centralize or decentralize computer facilities has significant budgetary ramifications. As discussed in Chapter 12, a centralized computer laboratory can be far more efficient than decentralized facilities. Sharing technical support—whether it be the expertise of laboratory personnel, backup maintenance equipment, or a software library—is much easier to accomplish in a central facility. Other considerations such as physical security, accidental breakage, making facilities available for after-school hours, and renovation costs also contribute to the efficiency of central facilities.

On the other hand, the trend has been toward decentralization, with more and more equipment being acquired and placed where the activity occurs. For administrative applications, microcomputers are placed on the desks of administrators and secretaries. Likewise, for instructional applications, microcomputers are more and more often being placed on the desks of students and teachers. Decentralization is desirable to resolve problems of ready access to the equipment, to integrate computing with other instructional activities, and to avoid the logistics of scheduling and moving children to the central laboratories. Administrators should be planning for a more decentralized computing environment than presently exists in most schools.

That is not to say that the concept of sharing resources should be entirely abandoned. A common hardware maintenance contract for all equipment is far more economical than having each computer location handle repairs on an individual or as-needed basis. The sharing of software through site licenses is very cost effective. The use of networks at the building level to share software, data, and documentation can also be efficient. Some centralization also can and should continue to exist for certain applications, and the movement toward decentralization should not be viewed as completely incompatible with centralized facilities. Such a combination of centralized and decentralized facilities sharing certain resources is commonly described as a *distributed system*. Schools are moving in the direction of distributed systems. Typically, they are centrally coordinated, and hardware and software are shared via computer networks.

Hiring a Consultant

Routinely used in the field of education, consultants are readily available for assisting in the design or implementation of technology applications. School districts that have been late in developing technology programs, and are just beginning to invest significant resources, should consider the use of consultants to help avoid common pitfalls and costly mistakes. In the budget model provided, consultant costs are not specifically identified but should be included within specific budget categories such as hardware, software, and personnel.

Technical expertise is becoming more specialized, so a consultant who is effective in recommending and guiding a district in one aspect of technology may not be as effective in another. For example, an expert in the hardware and data communications requirements of a wireless local area network may not be effective in helping launch a comprehensive teacher training program. As districts or schools do more, internal expertise develops and accumulates, which lessens the need for outside consultants.

However, even in districts where a good deal of expertise exists, administrators should not rule out the need for consulting services, particularly if considering some new or inherently complex technology. For example, integrating voice and data communications in a wide area network is not a simple task, and many school districts, regardless of their staffs' expertise, would probably seek outside technical advice to help them plan and implement such a project. In some states such as California, Kentucky, Minnesota, New York, and Texas, educational cooperatives and technical centers are supported by the state education departments and may be good starting points for seeking assistance.

Standardizing on a Common Vendor

The question of standardizing on some common hardware vendor and thereby realizing efficiencies in terms of quantity acquisitions, software development, hardware maintenance, or staff training should be addressed. Before the microcomputer explosion, school districts and most other organizations attempted to standardize on a common hardware vendor for these purposes. However, with the advent of microcomputer technology, this has changed. For administrative applications, the tendency is still to acquire compatible equipment, if not a common vendor. The use of common hardware will allow for the sharing of software and, most importantly, the sharing of common databases (e.g., student, personnel, scheduling) for various administrative applications within the school. In addition, in large urban school districts and districts governed by municipalities, schools may have to acquire equipment that is compatible with the local government's administrative systems so that common data systems such as financial accounting, census, and payroll can easily be used.

For instructional applications, this is not necessarily the trend. A variety of equipment is being used in the classrooms, and every indication is that this will continue in the future. Apple Computer, Dell, and Compaq, among other firms, are all providing excellent pieces of equipment. School administrators should allow for variety as long as it can be justified because of the needs of the proposed application. If the proposed application requires specialized software that is only available for a particular model of computer, then this might be a justifiable reason for acquiring that equipment. For instance, some excellent educational software packages using digital video are written in specific authoring languages that are only available on Apple Macintosh computers. The school should be able to get this software and the requisite Macintosh hardware even though the standard in the building or district happens to be DOS/Windows computers.

Hardware First, Other Needs Later?

A common practice in acquiring computer equipment is to buy as much hardware as possible up front and plan to take care of the other costs later on. This approach is becoming more common as competition among hardware vendors grows, and significant savings may be realized by taking advantage of bulk purchases or special, limited-time discounts. Buying equipment first is acceptable as long as the equipment meets the needs of an overall plan, and funds for the other costs will be provided. However, given the up-and-down budget cycles in some states and school districts, this is not always the case. Unfortunately, some administrators find themselves with equipment that is not fully used because the proper software is not available, teachers have not been trained, or electrical upgrades in the computer facilities have not been completed. The recommended planning approach for an application should include all the component costs, not just hardware.

Choosing a Purchasing Plan

Purchasing plans vary with the vendor and type of equipment. The choice of a plan was much more significant before the introduction of microcomputers, when the purchase prices of large mainframe and minicomputers were substantial. School districts and most other organizations wanted to spread out costs over a period of time. Spreading costs through a lease–purchase agreement rather than paying full price, for example, is still recommended for districts making large acquisitions such as installing a new data communications system, deploying a large-scale integrated learning system, or purchasing high-end servers.

The main reason for this approach is to reduce the budget impact in any one given year and to spread out the costs over several fiscal years. Another reason to build a base budget is that it will be much easier to replace or upgrade equipment without having to request funds for a major new acquisition every 4 to 7 years. The yearly lease–purchase allocation can simply be continued with small percentage increases for upgrading or adding on to the original configuration. Regarding the acquisition of microcomputers, the vast majority of educational users purchase this equipment outright. However, administrators should also build an equipment replacement plan into their base budget to make sure that they can replace units that will become damaged or obsolete. This is generally referred to as life cycle planning. Readers may wish to review the material in Chapter 10 on life cycles of hardware and software.

SOURCES OF FUNDS

Once a number of worthwhile planning proposals have been received and consolidated into an overall financial plan, an examination of the sources that will finance the plan is now required. The four major funding sources are the school district budget, bond issues, governmental entities, and gifts and grants.

The School District Budget

The school district budget, generally, is the primary source of funds for implementing technology applications. If not already in place, two base budgets for technology need to be established: one that will support administrative applications and a second that will support instructional applications.

Administrative applications are almost always supported entirely by a school district's tax levy budget. In general, boards of education are cognizant of the need for timely and accurate data and the efficiency of office operations utilizing basic computer technology; hence, they tend to be supportive of providing funds for administrative applications. School boards also tend to be very demanding in terms of receiving data about their school districts, and they are receptive to technology that improves their information delivery systems. In some cases, other governmental agencies may provide the impetus if not the funding because of a special initiative (e.g., the U.S. government's E-Rate program) or a mandatory reporting requirement that exists outside the school. One result of No Child Left Behind was requirements on the part of state education departments and school districts to provide more timely and accurate data (e.g., school report cards) on schools, especially regarding student achievement.

Instructional applications, on the other hand, because there are perceptions that funds can be provided from a variety of other sources, may require more negotiation and justification to be funded fully by the school district's tax levy budget. This situation varies significantly depending on the wealth, tax base, and financial personality of a district.

Both budgets, administrative and instructional, should have an established minimum base within the district's budget because all technology applications require some ongoing cost items such as maintenance, supplies, and upgrades. How much is needed for a base budget depends entirely on the goals and objectives that a district has identified in an overall technology plan. There are no fixed percentages of a total budget for funding technology-related programs. Estimates indicate that the average school district is devoting about one third of its instructional materials budget for technology-related items such as hardware, software, and direct computer repairs. This will likely increase, and recommendations/projections are that they will at least double (Shaw, 1997). Besides the basic material costs (hardware, software, and supplies), additional budget allocations will be needed for personnel costs, training, facilities, and infrastructure.

In seeking funds from boards of education for instructional applications, school administrators should consider drawing support from parents, many of whom want their children to learn about and use computer technology. Many parents use technology in their jobs and see technological literacy and competence as important for career success. They can be very helpful in securing budgetary approvals from elected school officials.

Bond Issues

Bond issues for the purpose of some major capital improvement, such as the construction or renovation of a school building, can be an important source of funds, because equipping and furnishing the building is generally an accepted part of the project. These funds, sometimes quite substantial, provide a school district with an infusion of dollars to launch major new technology programs. Of course, many districts are not necessarily building new facilities, and capital construction funds may not be available. If this is the case, administrators might ask the board of education or the governing board of the municipality to consider a special bond issue for developing a new information infrastructure, making major equipment purchases and upgrades for the entire district—including those schools that are not targeted for any capital improvements in the near future.

If a school district does acquire a significant amount of new equipment as a result of a bond issue, the necessary funds to maintain this equipment in the future should immediately be built into the operating budget (total cost of ownership or TCO principle discussed earlier). The understanding should be that bond or capital funds will be used for significant and not simply incremental acquisitions. In general, a school district should not rely on bonds for equipment and other needs that normally should be provided for in an operating budget.

Governmental Entities

Governmental entities at the federal, state, and local levels may also be the source of funds for instructional computing programs. Although subject to changing political and financial climates, various governmental agencies have demonstrated interest in technology and responded accordingly. State education departments throughout the country are increasingly providing support for technological improvements. Federal programs administered by the U.S. Department of Education and the National Science Foundation have provided funds to acquire computer equipment for educational programs, usually directed for specific populations and purposes. The Elementary and Secondary Education Act, reauthorized as No Child Left Behind, has had several provisions for assisting schools to acquire technology. The E-Rate is a federally managed program that provides significant discounts on telecommunications technologies to schools in low-income areas. Discounts of as much as 90% are available based on the percentage of students in a school who participate in the federal school lunch program. The E-Rate is administered through the Universal Service Fund, which is funded by fees charged to all telephone users.

All levels of government are aware of pressure from the business community, which has been influential in calling attention to the need for a well-educated and well-trained workforce. All over the country there have been calls for developing 21st century job skills that will allow future workers to compete effectively in the global economy. Organizations such as the Southern

Regional Education Board (SREB), the New York City Partnership, and the Delta Regional Authority have promoted the need for schools to provide more resources for the development of technology and information skills of their students. The Partnership for 21st Century Schools (see http://www.21stcenturyskills.org/index.php) was founded in 2002 by the U.S. Department of Education and a number of corporate partners to serve as a catalyst to position 21st century skills at the center of American K–12 education by building collaborative partnerships among education, business, community, and government leaders.

Two excellent sources of information regarding federal grants and funding are

- The Federal Register, Office of the Federal Register, National Archives and Records Administration, Washington, DC 20408 (http://www.gpoaccess.gov/fr/), and
- The Benton Foundation (http://www.benton.org/), which has an excellent Web site for information on the U.S. government's E-Rate program.

Gifts and Grants

Gifts and grants can also be a significant source of funds to implement computer applications. A certain aggressiveness on the part of administrators is required to seek out potential donors, foundations, and other grant agencies, but the rewards can be quite substantial. Individuals, parent–teacher organizations, small local businesses, and international corporations contribute hundreds of millions of dollars each year for improvements in schools, and technology has particularly benefited from this generosity.

One of the first substantial gifts for technology occurred in the state of Mississippi in 1990 when two businessmen—Richard Riordan and Richard Dowling—donated $7 million for a 5-year program to improve reading and writing skills. The gift required that the state contribute $6 million to the program, which entailed establishing IBM's Writing to Read computer program in kindergartens and first grades in all public schools.

This gift exemplified several common characteristics of gift giving and grantsmanship directed to education. First, the gift required a matching contribution. Many donors—individuals as well as foundations—prefer to give to those who are willing to invest some of their own resources in a project as evidence of its need and validity. Second, the gift required that a certain program be implemented. Attaching certain conditions to a gift or grant is not uncommon. Third, the donation was targeted specifically for technology, which is indicative of the belief by an increasing number of businesspeople in the benefits of technology.

In recent years, several major foundations have concentrated on supporting large-scale education projects with technology as their central theme. The Bill and Melinda Gates Foundation, the Carnegie Foundation, and the Open Society Institute awarded $30 million in grants in December 2000 to improve New York City high schools. Smaller schools and instructional technology were integral components of these grants. In November 2000, the Bill and Melinda Gates Foundation awarded $36.9 million to California, part of which was used to create small, high-tech high schools. The Bill and Melinda Gates Foundation has also had a special focus on school leadership and the use of technology. The following are major grants this foundation has awarded in this area:

New Jersey: $5.1 million to upgrade the technology skills of principals and supervisors

Mississippi: $1.1 million to establish a Technology Academy for School Leaders

Illinois: $2.25 million to bring technology into the mainstream of school administration

Texas Association of School Administrators: $6.25 million to broaden its Technology Leadership Academy

At the time of this writing, the Bill and Melinda Gates Foundation was developing a new funding initiative for greater integration/cooperation between K–12 and higher education. It is likely that technology will have a major role in this initiative. Further information is available at the Bill and Melinda Gates Foundation Web site (http://www.gatesfoundation.org/Pages/home.aspx).

Although not all donors are willing to give millions of dollars to education, many business-people are willing to make more modest donations to their school districts or localities. Banks, insurance companies, and department stores are enormous users of computer information systems and need to employ local people to operate these systems. They may be willing to make donations to ensure that their future employees are familiar with technology. Three excellent sources for information on grants from private corporations and foundations are

- The Foundation Center, 79 Fifth Ave., Third Floor, New York, NY 10003-3076 (http://foundationcenter.org/);
- The Grantsmanship Center, P.O. Box 17220, Los Angeles, CA 90017-0220 (http://www.tgci.com/); and
- Education World Grants Center (http://www.education-world.com/a_admin/archives/grants.shtml).

No discussion of gifts and grants to schools would be complete without mention of the work and generosity of parent–teacher associations (PTAs) throughout the country. PTAs and their volunteering efforts have made significant contributions to American education. In the area of technology, many school districts have received gifts of computer equipment from these associations. Imaginative fund-raisers such as bake sales, craft fairs, and collecting grocery market receipts have been used to acquire modest amounts of equipment. Administrators should encourage these activities because, in addition to acquiring funds, they also generate interest and enthusiasm for computer education.

CASE STUDY

Place: Watson Middle School   Year: 2011

The Watson Middle School offers an alternative program for bilingual students. It shares facilities with an elementary school located in an inner-city neighborhood in a large metropolitan center. The program was started in 1996 with 100 students. It has grown consistently and is regarded as a major success in the district. The current population is 300 students.

Watson is administered by a director, Marion Halo, who reports directly to a district superintendent. Fourteen teachers are assigned to the school. Ms. Halo, who started the school, feels very strongly that the success of the program can be attributed to its small size. Though supportive of the district establishing similar programs in other schools, she does not feel the program should grow any further at Watson.

Ms. Halo has been supportive of technology and established a central computer laboratory when the school first opened. Presently it houses 20 microcomputers. A high-speed Internet connection was added to the lab in 1999. One teacher who previously taught mathematics has served as the computer coordinator and has done an excellent job. In 2003, as part of a capital project, the central laboratory was renovated and re-equipped with new computers, and additional computers were acquired and distributed into individual classrooms. The entire building (including the classrooms) was rewired for high-speed Internet connections. Each classroom has at least three computers with several (e.g., science) classrooms having as many as five. Most, but not all, teachers make good use of the available technology.

During the last 3 years, funds for technology have been scarce; however, a special budget allocation has been made for next year. The district superintendent contacted Ms. Halo and asked for a proposal for $50,000 by June 1, 2011, for upgrading Watson's technology facilities. To prepare the proposal, Ms. Halo has met several times with the technology coordinator as well as with her teaching staff to discuss possibilities. Her coordinator has presented her with a $50,000 proposal to replace all existing computers that are 6 years old or older. This would entail replacing the 20 computers in the central lab and 24 of the 46 computers that are in individual classrooms. The coordinator also indicated that he had other needs regarding maintenance of the central computer lab, including a new security system and air-conditioning. In meetings with the teachers, there appears to be a mix of interests including replacing older computer equipment, purchasing whiteboards, and upgrading the software library. Ms. Halo has also attended three meetings called by the superintendent, where technology proposals were discussed. At these discussions, the superintendent appeared to be particularly supportive of several of her colleagues' (principals and directors at other schools) interest in acquiring whiteboards for their classrooms. The superintendent also indicated, that in preliminary discussions with a vendor of the whiteboards, that if the district purchased 100 or more, a substantial discount could be realized reducing the price of each whiteboard to approximately $3,000.

In sum, Ms. Halo has two proposals in front of her, each of which appear worthy:

1. Replace the older equipment in the school and improve the security and air-conditioning in the central lab;
2. Equip each of the 14 classrooms with whiteboard projection systems.

Discussion Questions

1. It is May 1, 2011. Assume that you are Ms. Halo; which of these options would you like to support based on the merits of the proposals?
2. Do a cost analysis of each of the proposals to determine how you can maximize the $50,000 budget allocation.
3. Are there any other alternatives that you might want to pursue?

Summary

This chapter presents the background and several issues associated with financial planning for computer applications. Technology can be expensive, and even more so if not planned properly. Cost considerations for an entire technology application should be identified and go well beyond the direct hardware and software costs. Trend data indicate that although the unit cost for computer technology has decreased, the overall expenditure for computer technology is increasing each year in both primary and secondary schools.

A review of the literature on the cost-effectiveness of computer-based education leads to inconclusive results. Most of the major reviews of the effectiveness of computer technology in education tend to ignore the questions of cost. Regardless, schools are well on their way to implementing new systems and expanding existing ones.

A procedure for gathering budget information using a budget worksheet should be integrated into the overall computer technology planning process within a school district. A composite funding model suggesting percentage distributions of the various costs associated with computer applications has been presented. However, school districts will likely fund according to their own goals and financial abilities. Several major issues associated with computer technology costs such as total cost of ownership, centralization, shared resources, single vendor procurement, and use of consultants are presented, with suggestions for possible courses of action.

In funding computer technology, school districts should establish base budgets and seek the support of their boards of education. Administrators should also be aggressive in seeking funds from other sources such as local businesses, governmental agencies, parent–teacher groups, and individuals who might be interested in providing funds for computer technology.

Key Concepts and Questions

1. Financial planning for technology requires an understanding of changes in component costs that have occurred over time. Identify some of these changes, explaining how they have affected financial planning for educational technology.
2. Financial planning for technology requires a consideration of all the component costs of an application. What are the major component costs of a computer application? Are some more important than others? Explain.
3. Centralization and decentralization of computer resources is a recurring issue in education. Review this issue from a financial perspective for administrative applications. Do the same for instructional applications.
4. School administrators have been struggling with the standardization of hardware for many years. What are some of the factors that administrators should consider when establishing a policy regarding hardware standardization?
5. Securing resources for technology is a critical part of financial planning. What are some of the common sources of funds? On which should an administrator most rely? Why?
6. Financial planning, like planning in general, is an ongoing activity requiring a good deal of careful analysis. How might an administrator involve others, including teachers, in financial planning for technology?

Suggested Activities

1. Review the financial expenditures/budgets for computer technology in a school or district for the past 3 years or more, if data are available. Try to isolate different component (hardware, software, maintenance) costs. Can you identify any clear trends?
2. Identify the policies in a school or district regarding standardization of computer hardware. Have these policies been formalized, or is there an informal understanding? Do you have any suggestions for improving them?
3. Do a search of the World Wide Web and gather information on the U.S. federal government's E-Rate program (start with the Benton Foundation Web site mentioned earlier in this chapter). Assume you are an administrator in a school district, and prepare a position paper on whether and how your district should apply for the E-Rate discount.

References

American Geological Institute. (2009). *Report to the president on the use of technology to strengthen K–12 education in the United States.* Retrieved June 15, 2009, from http://www.agiweb.org/hearings/pcastedu.tml

Archer, J. (1998). The link to higher scores. *Education Week, 18*(5), 10–21.

Ash, K. (2009, March 18). Experts debate cost savings of virtual ed. *Education Week, 28*(25), 1, 9.

Becker, H. J. (1994). *Analysis and trends of school use of new information technologies.* Irvine: Department of Education, University of California.

Campuzano, L., Dynarski, M., Agodini, R., & Rall, K. (2009). *Effectiveness of reading and mathematics software products: Findings from two student cohorts* (NCEE 2009-4041). Washington, DC: National Center for Education Evaluation and Regional Assistance, Institute of Education Sciences, U.S. Department of Education.

Dynarski, M., Agodini, R., Heaviside, S., Novak, T., Carey, T., Campuzano, L., Means, B., Murphy, R., Penuel, W., Javitz, H., Emery, D., & Sussex, W. (2007). Effectiveness of reading and mathematics software products: Findings from the first student cohort. Washington, DC: U.S. Department of Education, Institute of Education Sciences.

Educational Testing Service. (1999). *Computers and classrooms: The status of technology in U.S. schools.* Retrieved January 30, 2005, from http://www.ets.org/pub/res/compclss.pdf

Fitzgerald, S. (1999, September). Technology's real costs. *Electronic School.* Retrieved June 17, 2009 from http://www.electronic-school.com/199909/0999sbot.html

Hu, W. (2007, May 4). Seeing no progress, some schools drop laptops. *New York Times,* p. A1, B4.

Levin, H., & Meister, G. (1986). Is CAI cost-effective? *Phi Delta Kappan, 67*(10), 745–749.

McCabe, M., & Skinner, R. A. (2003, May 8). Analyzing the tech effect. *Education Week, 22*(35), 50–52.

McEachern, C. (2005, September 15). Education spending slows. *Channel News.* Retrieved June 15, 2009, from http://www.crn.com/government/170703644;jsessionid=XMAQWM5XY4F5YQSNDLPCKH0CJUNN2JVN

National Education Association. (1989, July). *Report of the NEA special committee on educational technology.* Paper presented at the 127th annual meeting of the National Education Association, Washington, DC.

Niemiec, R., Blackwell, M., & Walberg, H. (1986). CAI can be doubly effective. *Phi Delta Kappan, 67*(10), 750–751.

Picciano, A. G., & Seaman, J. (2007). *K–12 online learning: A survey of school district administrators.* Needham, MA: The Sloan Consortium.

Picciano, A. G., & Seaman, J. (2009). *K–12 online learning: A 2008 follow up of the survey of U.S. school district administrators.* Needham, MA: The Sloan Consortium.

Quality Education Data. (1991). *Technology in the schools: 1990–1991 school year.* Denver: Author.

Quality Education Data. (1996). *Education market guide and mailing list catalog, 1996–1997.* Denver: Author.

Schacter, J. (1999). *The impact of technology on student achievement.* Santa Monica, CA: Milken Exchange on Education Technology. Retrieved January 30, 2005, from http://www.mff.org/pubs/ME161.pdf

Shanker, A. (1989, December 24). Technology holds the key. *New York Times,* p. E7.

Shaw, D. E. (1997). *Report to the president on the use of technology to strengthen K–12 education in the United States.* Washington, DC: Panel on Educational Technology. Retrieved June 20, 2009 from http://www.ostp.gov/PCAST/k-12ed.html

Stoll, C. (1995). *Silicon snake oil: Second thoughts on the information superhighway.* New York: Doubleday.

U.S. Congress, Office of Technology Assessment. (1988). *Power on! New tools for teaching and learning* (Report No. OTA-SET-379). Washington, DC: U.S. Government Printing Office.

Waxman, H. C., Connell, M. L., & Gray, J. (2002). *A quantitative synthesis of recent research on the effects of teaching and learning with technology on student outcomes.* Naperville, IL: North Central Regional Educational Laboratory. Retrieved June 13, 2009 from http://www.ncrel.org/tech/effects/

Wenglinsky, H. (1998). *Does it compute? Policy information report of the Educational Testing Service.* Princeton, NJ: Educational Testing Service. Retrieved January 30, 2005, from http://ftp.ets.org/pub/res/technolog.pdf

EPILOGUE

At a national computing conference held in June 1992, Dr. Robert D. Ballard, a senior scientist at the Woods Hole Oceanographic Institution, delivered a paper titled "Living the Dream," in which he described the development of a new project that he termed "telepresence." Using computers, satellite telecommunications, fiber optics, and robotics, this project allowed scientists on land to experience deep-sea explorations by manipulating a robotic system, named the ARGO/JASON, by remote control. Using deep-sea image technology, scientists in their offices and laboratories saw everything that they could see if they were actually on the ocean floor (Ballard, 2000).

Ballard compared it to other events in his life, which included substantiating theories involving plate tectonics and continental drift, discovering mountains higher than Mt. Everest, seeing canyons deeper than the Grand Canyon, and locating the RMS Titanic located 12,460 feet deep in the North Atlantic Ocean. Ballard also stated that one of his major goals was to share these experiences with children. Through an initial series of "downlink" sites across the United States, in the most ambitious ARGO/JASON undertaking ever, 600,000 students were able to watch a deep-sea exploration of active volcanoes just off the Galápagos Islands. Ballard indicated that the highlight of this event was when young children at the remote sites actually took turns steering and manipulating the arms of the deep-sea robots. He said that seeing the expressions of wonder and excitement on the faces of these children was a joy incomparable to any other (Ballard, 1992).

What started as an experiment in 1989 has reached several million children, and Ballard has received national awards for his innovative approach to bringing "real-life" science into classrooms around the world. When asked about the future of his work, Ballard quoted his grandmother, who told him, "Great is the person who plants a tree, not knowing whether he will sit in its shade." (Ballard, 1992) When he started, he was not sure whether the JASON project would be a success but was willing to take a chance on something in which he believed. He was confident, however, that through hard work and by assembling good people who shared in his dream, the JASON project would touch the lives of children for many years to come.

Planning for technology has been the basic emphasis of this book, and fundamental to planning is thinking about and developing strategies for the future based on an understanding of the past and the present. The background, history, and current issues associated with the developments in the use of technology in education have been examined and discussed. With 100,000 schools in the United States at various stages of technological development, one school's present might be another's future—or, conversely, one school's present might be another's past. Planning for the future, therefore, may mean different things to different readers. What is important is that the women and men of vision in our schools think about, plan for, and take chances to develop and implement programs that will touch the lives of their children for years to come. In this new millennium, regardless of one's political, sociological, or educational philosophy, technology should not be something separate from but should be a part of every school leader's vision. It need not be the centerpiece of that vision, but it undoubtedly has a role to play in the future of every school.

References

Ballard, R. D. (1992, June). *Living the dream*. Paper presented at the IBM Academic Computing Conference, San Diego, CA.

Ballard, R. D., & Hively, W. (2000). *The eternal darkness: A personal history of deep-sea exploration*. Princeton, NJ: Princeton University Press.

APPENDIX A

Basic Concepts of Computer Technology

Computer science, like other disciplines, has developed a language of its own. *Hardware, software, client-server, icons, LAN, WLAN, bytes, blogs, wikis, DVDs, modems, RAMs,* and *ROMs* are just some of the terms that are heard in everyday school affairs. These are common words for the technologically trained but can evoke insecurity and frustration among even the most experienced school administrators. When faced with making major decisions such as purchasing new computer equipment for the science laboratories, upgrading Internet access in a library, implementing a new data-driven decision-making program, or acquiring a database management system for student records, administrators must quickly learn as much of the technology as they can, relying extensively on the advice and recommendations of others. An administrator should not become the top technician in a school to manage technology. However, an acquaintance with commonly used terms as well as an overall conceptual understanding of computer systems will help administrators plan for and incorporate technology into schools.

THE CONCEPT OF SYSTEM AS A STARTING POINT

The starting point for the conceptual understanding of computer technology is that it is a system. A *system* is defined as a group of interrelated parts that are assembled to achieve some common goal or end. The three basic parts of any system are input, process, and output (see Figure A.1). Specifically, a computer is a system of interrelated input, processing, and output devices, which are assembled for the processing of data (characters and numbers). This is true whether we are talking about a single microcomputer located on a secretary's desk or a national network of large mainframe computers that might consist of thousands of devices connected by telephones or satellites. The major difference is in the number of devices, not the basic operating concept.

The minimum configuration of a computer system is best exemplified by the common microcomputer, which consists of at least a keyboard or mouse for input, a central processing unit for process, and a video monitor or printer for output. In addition, it usually has a secondary storage device such as a magnetic or optical disk drive for storing data and instructions and a single communications interface or modem for establishing a telephone link (see Figure A.2). Larger computer systems are simply variations of this same basic microcomputer configuration. The major differences are that the larger systems are capable of having many input and output devices,

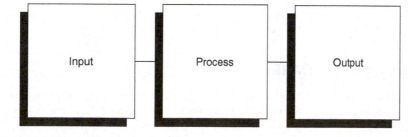

FIGURE A.1 Basic System Design.

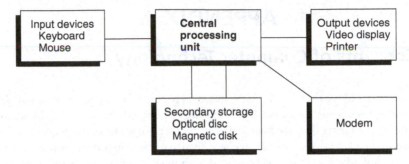

FIGURE A.2 Microcomputer System Configuration.

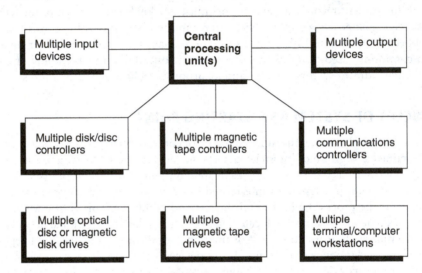

FIGURE A.3 Large Computer System Configuration.

multiple processors, and several additional secondary storage and other special-function devices (see Figure A.3).

An important characteristic of systems is that multiple systems can interact with one another. Some systems can function within other systems as subsystems. This interactive quality also applies to computer technology. A microcomputer on a secretary's desk is a system unto itself with input, processing, and output devices, and it can also be used to connect to a larger computer system that, for example, might be housed at a district office. Under this circumstance, the microcomputer functions as a part of the larger system or as a subsystem.

HARDWARE AND SOFTWARE

In the preceding discussion, the references are to the physical devices that comprise a basic part of any computer system. However, all computer systems must include two fundamental components: hardware and software. Hardware is the physical component—such as keyboards, video monitors, and disk drives. It also includes the wiring, circuit boards, and cabinetry that we can see and touch.

Software is the nonphysical component or instructional component that directs the hardware. It consists of computer programs or sets of instructions communicated to the physical devices via electronic media such as CD-ROMS, disks, and tapes. Critical to an understanding of computer technology is the fact that the physical devices are unable to perform any task without being directed to do so by software (computer programs).

The nonphysical aspect of software is sometimes difficult to understand for people who are not technically trained. Even trained technicians tend to refer to the computer as making the decisions and generating instructions. This is not the case.

To clarify this point, a comparison may be helpful. Imagine one person giving another person directions on how to get to the Grand Canyon from Chicago. The basic instructions might go something like this:

Take airport car service to O'Hare International Airport.

Board American Airlines flight 999.

Fly to Phoenix.

Rent a car.

Drive north on Route 17.

Decide to go to either the North or the South Rim of the Grand Canyon.

If going to the South Rim, drive north on Route 64.

Check in at the Bright Angel Lodge.

Enjoy!

To make sure that the traveler does not get lost or forget a point, the directions might be written on a piece of paper. In this example, the plane, car, and roads represent the computer hardware; they are the physical things that enable the traveler to get from one place to another. The directions are similar to computer software; they instruct the traveler in using the hardware to get to a destination—in this case, the Grand Canyon. These directions are not something physical; they are a logical plan of instructions that provide guidance to the traveler. Computer software is composed of the many logical plans of instructions called computer programs that guide physical devices to achieve a desired result. The piece of paper on which the directions to the Grand Canyon are written is similar to computer media such as CD-ROMs that are used to communicate with the physical devices. The piece of paper can be referred to or read over and over again, as can computer media.

It is easy to understand how one person communicates with another person as long as they both speak the same language, but it is difficult to understand how the software communicates with the hardware. Does the hardware actually interpret and understand instructions? The answer is that it does so electronically.

THE CENTRAL PROCESSING UNIT

The most important piece of hardware in any computer system is the central processing unit (CPU). This unit is composed of vastly sophisticated, high-speed circuits that are capable of transmitting electronic impulses at speeds measured in nanoseconds (billionths of a second) and picoseconds (trillionths of a second). The exact nature of these circuits differs from one computer manufacturer to another, and one would need several courses in electrical engineering to comprehend the finer points of modern CPUs.

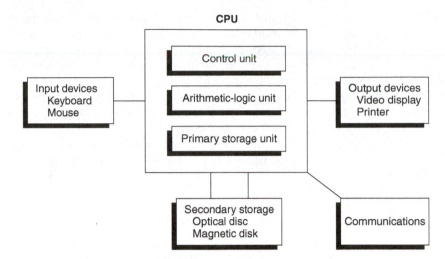

FIGURE A.4 Conceptual Design of a Central Processing Unit.

Central processing units generally consist of three basic subunits: a control unit (CU), an arithmetic-logic unit (ALU), and a primary storage unit (PSU) (see Figure A.4). Each of these subunits has a specific function and purpose. The CU interprets instructions and directs the processing of the other physical devices. The ALU performs all arithmetic operations, including comparisons. The PSU stores instructions and data. Physically, these subunits can be either separate components or integrated. Many computers use an integrated circuit or microprocessor that combines the control unit and the arithmetic-logic unit on a common *chip,* which is a thin wafer of silicon or other type of semiconductor material. The primary storage units generally are separate components within the CPU, which can be replaced and enhanced as needed.

The control unit is the most sophisticated component of the CPU. It is capable of interpreting instructions that have been converted into electronic impulses or codes and directing the physical operations of all the other devices in the computer hardware system. The control unit alone determines the sequence of tasks performed by the physical equipment. Before assigning new tasks, it verifies that the preceding tasks have been satisfactorily completed.

The arithmetic-logic unit performs all arithmetic operations such as addition, subtraction, multiplication, and division. It can do this because all data are converted into numeric codes in the CPU before they are received by the ALU. Data used in computer systems consist of all the letters of the alphabet, the digits 0 through 9, and special characters such as commas, periods, exclamation marks, and so forth. Each of these has a unique numeric code that enables the arithmetic-logic unit to manipulate them as numbers. Because all characters are converted into numeric codes, operations that usually might not be considered as arithmetic, such as alphabetizing or sorting a list of names, becomes an arithmetic operation in a CPU. Alphabetizing or sorting actually becomes a series of "less than/greater than" or subtraction operations.

The primary storage unit stores instructions and data; thus, it is also referred to as the memory unit. There are generally two types of PSUs: random-access memory (RAM) and read-only memory (ROM). Random-access memory stores instructions and data temporarily as needed to perform a specific computer operation. It is used to store instructions (portions of computer programs) at the time they are to be processed by the control unit. It is never used to store instructions or data permanently. Read-only memory is used to permanently store a set of instructions that are to be used over and over again. Once a set of instructions has been stored on a ROM, it generally cannot be changed—hence the term *read only*. Special versions of ROM do exist that can be changed but are not regularly used in computer systems. Programmable read-only memory (PROM) and erasable programmable read-only memory (EPROM) are examples. All CPUs must have RAM for the temporary storage of instructions and data. Those that have only RAM store the instructions and data permanently on other non-CPU storage devices such as magnetic or optical disks.

The primary storage or memory capacity of a CPU is measured in terms of characters or bytes. A byte is the minimum amount of memory needed to store a character of information and is made up of binary digits or bits. A bit is a single electronic circuit capable of being in either the "on" or "off" position, conceptually similar to an ordinary light switch. When it is on, the electrical current is flowing; when it is off, the electrical current is stopped. Eight of these bits comprise a single byte or the amount of memory needed to store one character of data (i.e., one letter of the alphabet, one digit 0 through 9, or one special character).

An important characteristic of all CPUs is the memory capacity of the primary storage unit. The earliest computers in the 1950s had memory capacities measured in thousands of bytes. Modern computers are measured in millions of bytes. Most microcomputers purchased today will have a minimum of 128 million bytes of primary storage. Large-capacity mainframe computers may have many millions of bytes of primary storage.

The number of bytes of primary storage available in a CPU determines the size and the number of computer programs that can be resident (running) at any one time. Therefore, the larger the primary storage capacity, the more computer programs that can be running and hence the more computer processing that can be performed. Although not as critical on microcomputers, which usually run several programs (e.g., Internet browser, word processing, database management, e-mail, electronic spreadsheet) at a time, memory size is very critical on mainframe computers, which are designed to run hundreds of programs simultaneously.

A brief introduction to data representation may be helpful for visualizing how characters are actually stored in the primary storage unit of the CPU. The two basic coding schemes for storing characters are American Standard Code for Information Interchange or ASCII (pronounced "as-key"), and Extended Binary Coded Decimal Interchange Code, or EBCDIC (pronounced "ebb-sih-dick"). Table A.1 provides the actual coding schemes used in primary storage units. Note that each individual character code is eight binary digits (bits) long or the length of a single byte. These bits represent individual circuits that can be turned "on" or "off." A bit turned on is represented by a 1, and a bit turned off is denoted by a 0. For example, the ASCII codes for the first three letters of the alphabet are as follows:

A = 0100 0001

B = 0100 0010

C = 0100 0011

The vast majority (99.9%) of people who use computers do not need to know these codes. However, knowing that they exist provides a broader understanding of how computers operate. A fundamental characteristic of all digital computer systems is that data must be converted into a series of bit patterns or codes to be processed. The frequently used term *digital*, as applied to computer systems, means the numerical representation of data in bit format.

The control unit interprets instructions that have been converted into electronic impulses or codes. As with data, the various instructions that a computer can execute, such as reading a file from an input device or displaying a data record on a video monitor, are coded as a series of bit

TABLE A.1 ASCII and EBCDIC Data Codes		
Character	**ASCII**	**EBCDIC**
0	0011 0000	1111 0000
1	0011 0001	1111 0001
2	0011 0010	1111 0010
3	0011 0011	1111 0011
4	0011 0100	1111 0100
5	0011 0101	1111 0101
6	0011 0110	1111 0110
7	0011 0111	1111 0111
8	0011 1000	1111 1000
9	0011 1001	1111 1001
A	0100 0001	1100 0001
B	0100 0010	1100 0010
C	0100 0011	1100 0011
D	0100 0100	1100 0100
E	0100 0101	1100 0101
F	0100 0110	1100 0110
G	0100 0111	1100 0111
H	0100 1000	1100 1000
I	0100 1001	1100 1001
J	0100 1010	1101 0001
K	0100 1011	1101 0010
L	0100 1100	1101 0011
M	0100 1101	1101 0100
N	0100 1110	1101 0101
O	0100 1111	1101 0110
P	0101 0000	1101 0111
Q	0101 0001	1101 1000
R	0101 0010	1101 1001
S	0101 0011	1110 0010
T	0101 0100	1110 0011
U	0101 0101	1110 0100
V	0101 0110	1110 0101
W	0101 0111	1110 0110
X	0101 1000	1110 0111
Y	0101 1001	1110 1000
Z	0101 1010	1110 1001

patterns referred to as the instruction set. The instruction set for each manufacturer's central processing unit is different, and there are no generally accepted standards. Like data, every single instruction has to be converted into an appropriate bit code before being interpreted by the control unit.

INPUT DEVICES

The central processing units of all computers receive instructions and data through input devices. The keyboard and the mouse are probably the most familiar. However, in the past 15 years, an assortment of other input devices (touch-sensitive screens, light pens, Koala pads, joysticks, etc.)

have evolved that are appropriate for educational applications. They may be a bit more expensive now or require special software, but they will likely play a more significant role in the years to come.

The basic input device for computers is the *keyboard,* which has been the mainstay for all types of computer systems since the 1950s and continues to be so today. Whether used for developing software, maintaining records, or doing word processing, the keyboard is the essential input device for computer systems. The key arrangement is the same as that of a typewriter keyboard. When a key is depressed, an electronic signal is sent to the CPU with the code of the respective letter, number, or special character. In addition, keyboards have special function keys that can be programmed to perform certain tasks automatically, such as transferring the contents of a video screen to a printer or saving a file on a disk. Many keyboards will also have a number pad, which simulates a calculator and is an important time-saver for users such as accountants, bank tellers, and bookkeepers.

Standard on microcomputers, the *mouse* is a handheld input device electronically connected to a video screen. The user uses the mouse to position a pointer on the screen and then presses a button to select options depending on the software used. For example, Macintosh and Windows-based microcomputers allow users to choose basic computer operations, such as shutting the computer down, formatting a new disk, or discarding an old file, simply by pointing the mouse to the desired option and clicking. For young children, the mouse is an especially attractive input device and easier to use than a keyboard.

A *touch-sensitive screen* performs the same function as a mouse but allows users to point to one of the options provided on the video screen. Although similar to a mouse, a touch-sensitive screen provides a more natural connection between the person and the machine. However, the options provided must be displayed in areas large enough to be easily discriminated by the size of a person's finger. For this reason, the mouse may be more appropriate for certain applications because it allows for very small objects to be available for selection. A touch-sensitive screen is also more expensive than a mouse and requires a special monitor.

Light-sensitive pens likewise can be used to point to options provided on a video screen. They are versatile, allowing for a great deal of interaction between the user and machine. Of all the various input devices, light-sensitive pens permit the greatest accuracy when pointing or selecting an option. They also may be used for painting or drawing on a screen and so have significant potential in educational applications. They require special software that may be expensive depending on the application.

Graphics tablets such as *Koala pads* are electronic surfaces connected to a CPU and include software that allows instant display of the surface on the video monitor. They come with a pen, stylus, or arm that is used to manipulate or alter the image on the tablet and simultaneously on the monitor. Depending on the accompanying software, they can also perform other functions. They are popular for electronic drawing applications and are easy to use. They are also used by teachers who like to correct papers by writing notes and suggestions in the margins. Graphics tablets are becoming common on handheld microcomputers and information appliances.

Joysticks, trackballs, and *game paddles* are commonly used input devices for computer and video games. They allow for faster manipulation of the pointer and other objects on the video screen. Trackballs, in particular, became popular in the 1990s and are being supplied as standard input devices on several popular laptop computers.

Voice recognition devices allow users to input data or instructions by speaking into microphones that convert human speech into electronic impulses. Although getting off to a slow start by not living up to its original promises, this technology has now gotten to the point where useful education applications are available. Because speech is the most natural way for people to communicate, it is likely that voice recognition devices will eventually be the major way of communicating with computer systems. Various voice recognition devices are on the market and working well in limited applications. Generally, these devices need a good software package to be used effectively. Nuance Communications markets its Dragon Naturally Speaking software package that is being used in a number of instructional applications especially in bilingual education and in special education classes whose students may have limited hand dexterity.

Optical scanning devices—which include optical mark recognition (OMR), optical character recognition (OCR), handheld wands, and digitizers—have been available as special-purpose input devices for many years. They are used for scoring tests, reading bar codes on labels, and converting paper images into digital form. A number of machines have come on the market in recent years, securing the future of optical scanners as important input devices because they can be significant time-savers in converting printed and graphic materials into digital form, which thereby obviates the need to manually key in extensive amounts of data.

OUTPUT DEVICES

The major purpose of most computer systems is to produce various types of output so that users can see or read the results of their input and computer applications. The two basic output devices are video displays and printers.

Up until a few years ago, *cathode ray tubes* (CRTs) were the most common type of video displays. They generally used an electron gun to generate a light beam that can be scanned across a video screen. However, *liquid crystal displays* (LCDs) or flat-panel displays have become by far the most popular type of computer monitor. Originally used in watches, LCDs have evolved to the point where the quality of screen images is as good as a CRT. Because of their slimness, LCDs are much lighter and easier to situate on a desk. They have also become standard on all types of portable electronic devices, including laptop and handheld computers. In addition to CRT and LCD displays, there are *plasma displays* that use neon and argon gas to produce a high-quality and bright image.

Video monitors display all images as a series of picture elements, also known as pixels that appear as single dots of light in horizontal and vertical patterns. A pixel (derived from the words *picture* and *element*) is very small. For example, on a medium-resolution video monitor, 128 pixels are needed to display a single character of data. Generally, the quality of a picture on a video display is directly related to its *resolution,* which is the number of pixels that can be displayed on the screen. The resolution of video monitors ranges from tens of thousands to more than a million pixels per screen. In addition to the number of pixels, the number of colors that can be displayed is also a significant factor in terms of image quality. For example, an image displayed on a video monitor with 300,000 pixels and 16 colors will not necessarily look as sharp as the same image displayed on a monitor with 60,000 pixels and 256 colors. The reason for this is that the large array of available colors can refine the image quality and make up for less resolution or a smaller number of pixels.

The tendency in education is to acquire color monitors to take advantage of the vast array of graphics software that is available. In evaluating color monitors, the choices are extensive, and options include standard color, RGB (red, green, blue), CGA (color graphics adapter), EGA (extended graphics adapter), PGA (professional graphics adapter), and VGA (video graphics adapter). These options all refer to the resolution and number of colors available. For most student uses, a standard color monitor is sufficient. For classroom presentations, the higher quality color monitors should be considered. This is especially the case for any monitors that are to be used for classroom presentations such as with an electronic whiteboard.

Computers' ability to generate paper has become legendary. Stories abound about reams of computer-generated reports "drowning" their users in paper. Despite the jokes, the popularity of printed material in computer technology and the importance of printer output devices cannot be denied. Many types of printers are available, differentiated by the technology used to generate characters and images on a page. For microcomputers, the basic types are ink-jet, laser, dot-matrix, and daisy-wheel printers. For large mainframe computers, the basic types are laser and line printers.

Dot-matrix printers are the least expensive and are most commonly used with microcomputer systems. They generate a series of small dots to form images and characters. The quality of images produced on dot-matrix printers ranges from poor to letter quality.

Ink-jet printers use tiny droplets of ink sprayed from a nozzle to produce images. They are considered letter quality, are very quiet, and are capable of producing color. If an application requires good color output, ink-jet printers are probably the best solution.

Laser printers are letter-quality printers that use laser technology to produce whole images on a page similar to a photocopying machine. The fact that they are page printers is an important distinction from the other printers that produce one character at a time along a print line. An important feature of some laser printers is their ability to be programmed to produce different size and style images including print fonts. For this reason, they are extremely popular with desktop publishing applications. Because of their advanced technology, laser printers are also more expensive than other printers. However, as the technology improves and production becomes cheaper, they are becoming less expensive. Laser printers for microcomputers can range from several hundred to several thousand dollars, depending on their features and options. For large mainframe computers, they can easily cost tens of thousands of dollars.

Line printers are used on large mainframe computers. They are very high-speed devices, printing at speeds in excess of 3,000 lines per minute. They print a line at a time using little hammers to strike characters through a ribbon onto continuous sheets of paper. Although associated with the early days of computing, line printers are still in use but will likely disappear in the not-too-distant future.

Plotters are a special type of printer designed to draw graphic displays on paper. Plotters are available for all types of computers (micros, minis, and mainframes). They are extremely useful for applications in art and drafting for which high-quality and color images need to be produced.

Voice output or *audio-response units* use speech synthesis to replicate the human voice. Most examples of voice output are for special and limited-purpose applications such as toys, games, and telephone answering systems. Like voice recognition units, which are input devices, they represent the most natural way for humans to communicate. Because of this, their future as an important part of computer technology is ensured. However, the technology is still evolving and needs to improve to be used routinely and to become a standard component of most computer systems. In education, their application in special education classes, especially those for the visually impaired, shows great promise.

SECONDARY STORAGE DEVICES

Secondary storage devices are used to store data and instructions permanently or at least until the application no longer needs them. They are called secondary storage devices to distinguish them from the primary storage devices that are part of the central processing unit. They are also referred to as input/output (I/O) devices because they are capable of reading data and instructions (input) and writing them (output). The major types of secondary storage devices are magnetic disks, magnetic tape, and optical discs.*

Magnetic disks were for many years the most basic type of secondary storage devices and include floppy disks, hard disks, and fixed-head disks. They all use a similar technology that stores

*According to the *Microsoft Press Computer Dictionary* (2002), "It is now standard practice to use the spelling *disc* for optical disc and the spelling *disk* in all other computer contexts (p. 1009). This approach is used throughout this book.

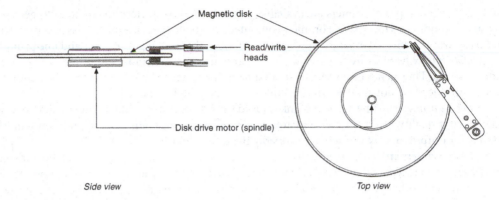

FIGURE A.5 Magnetic Disk Drive Operation.

characters of data or instructions electromagnetically on disks or platters. These disks can be hard or rigid (i.e., composed of a metallic material) or soft or "floppy" (i.e., composed of a plastic material).

The disk drives (see Figure A.5) on which the disks rotate are spindles similar to a phonograph player. They use microscopic read/write heads, rather than a stylus (phonograph needle), that are capable of electromagnetically decoding and encoding data in digital format (bit patterns) on the disk's surface. These read/write heads are mounted on an extension arm that can extend itself across the radius (from the center to the outer edge) of the rotating disk. Data and instructions are stored on the disk in a series of concentric circles called tracks. Through software instructions, the read/write heads can move across the rotating disks and directly access any information stored on the disk. For this reason, magnetic disks are also referred to as *direct access storage devices* or DASD (pronounced "dazz-dee"). The fact that the read/write heads actually move or extend themselves has led to their being called *moving-head disks.*

Another type of magnetic disk has a series of stationary read/write heads, one for each of the tracks on a disk. Because the heads do not have to move to access any of the information stored on the disk, these disks are referred to as *fixed-head disks.* Their major advantage over moving-head disks is that they save time by not having to extend the read/write heads across the radius of a rotating disk. But because they have a read/write head for each track (as many as 200), they are much more expensive than the single, moving-head disk drive. However, some extremely high-volume, high-speed applications required the additional speed, which made these disks worth the additional cost.

An important characteristic of magnetic disks is their storage capacity. The smallest disks can store 1.5 million bytes of data. These are the 3.5-inch floppy disks that were commonly available on microcomputer systems. Hard disks may be as large as 14 inches in diameter and can store from millions (megabytes) to billions of bytes (gigabytes) of data. Most mainframe computers use disk drives that can operate on a number or "pack" of disks stacked one on top of another. A stack of disks used for this purpose is referred to as a *disk pack.* On most microcomputers, there is a limit as to how many hard disk drives can be attached to a CPU. On large mainframe computers, many disk drives can be attached, which thereby increases a computer system's storage capacity to billions and trillions of bytes (terabytes).

Magnetic tape drives were the original secondary storage devices used on all computer systems. They operate similarly to a tape recorder; that is, a length of tape passes through an electromagnetic read/write (playback/record) head as it moves between two reels. Magnetic tapes were the major secondary storage devices used on large mainframe computers through the early 1970s.

However, as magnetic disk technology developed with faster and greater direct access capability, magnetic tape (a device requiring the physical reading of all data records in sequence to reach the desired record) became too slow for many high-volume computer applications. As a result, the computer industry gradually moved to the use of disk equipment for most secondary storage needs. Magnetic tape is now used primarily to back up (make copies of) disk files and to transport large data files from one location to another.

The newest and, increasingly, the most popular type of secondary storage is the *optical disc.* The term *optical* is used because the technology depends on laser light for reading data from the disc surfaces. CD-ROM (compact disc read-only memory), WORM (write once, read many) discs, rewritable or erasable optical discs, DVD (digital versatile disc), and videodiscs are examples of the variety of devices available using laser technology for storing data. An important distinction among these different devices is the method of encoding data. They use either digital format— that is, bit patterns (on/off or 1 and 0) similar to all other digital computing equipment—or analog format similar to a series of video frames and sound tracks. Digital format can be directly accessed by CPUs and easily manipulated. Analog format cannot be directly accessed by CPUs and must pass through an analog to a digital converter or a video digitizer.

Optical discs that use digital format are already having a significant impact on secondary storage technology and are replacing the older magnetic disk devices. Devices such as CD-ROMs are common on microcomputer systems. Although read-only, they are relatively inexpensive and capable of high storage capacities. They look alike and are similar in size (4.75 inches) to CDs used for audio players. Compared with other secondary storage devices, they have high storage capacity for their size. For example, a CD-ROM can hold as much data as 400 of the original floppy disks (3.5-inch floppy disk with a storage capacity of 1.5 million bytes). Presently, a wide variety of computer applications are used with CD-ROM equipment—including reference works, software documentation, training manuals, and textbooks. WORM devices were the first attempt to develop a writing capability for optical discs. They have high capacity and are similar in appearance to CD-ROMs. However, they provide the user with the ability to record or write data once on a disc surface. Data can then be accessed or read over and over again but can never be erased from the disc.

Erasable optical discs are also available. Their potential is significant—so much so that they have become the dominant secondary storage devices used on all computer systems. Erasable optical discs are also used to manufacture the popular portable flash drives that are used to transfer, store, and back up data files.

Digital versatile (or video) disc (DVD) is a form of optical disc technology that uses a small plastic disc used for the storage of digital data and is the successor to the compact disc (CD-ROM). A DVD may have as much as 26 times the storage capacity of a CD-ROM; it also has better graphics and greater resolution. A DVD stores digital data as a series of microscopic pits on an otherwise polished surface. The disc is covered with a protective transparent coating so that it can be read by a laser beam. The playback or record heads never touch the encoded portion, and the DVD is not worn out by the playing process. Because DVD players are backward-compatible to existing optical technologies, they can play CD-ROM discs; however, CD-ROM players cannot play DVD discs.

At the time of this writing, a standard DVD format had not been established. DVDs can hold data in a number of evolving formats depending on the application. DVD formats include DVD-Video (often simply called DVD), DVD-ROM, and DVD-Audio. DVD-Video discs hold digitized movies or video programs and are played using a DVD player connected to a standard television monitor. DVD-ROM (read-only memory) discs hold computer data and are read by a

DVD-ROM drive hooked up to a computer. DVDs also include recordable variations. DVD-R (Recordable) discs can be written to sequentially but only once. DVD-RAM (random-access memory), DVD-RW, and DVD+RW (ReWritable) discs can be written to thousands of times.

The amount of content available in DVD format is growing significantly, especially for entertainment purposes. Educational content has begun to be developed and it is likely that this will grow significantly also. For example, Microsoft offered its Encarta Electronic Encyclopedia on one DVD—it used to require five CD-ROMs. Microcomputer manufacturers have also made DVD drives their standard equipment replacing the earlier generation CD-ROM drives. Because of the backward compatibility mentioned earlier, most buyers are naturally opting for the newer DVD technology. All of this bodes well for the future of DVD.

DATA COMMUNICATIONS

Although the integration of computer technology and video technology is a relatively new development, computers have been routinely integrated with communications technology since the 1960s to provide an array of applications that transcend physical distance. The term *data communications* refers to the transfer of data between two or more digital devices over some physical distance. This distance may be several feet or thousands of miles.

The interconnection or "connectivity" of computer equipment transferring the data is called a *data communications network*. The most common interconnections use cable for short distances and telecommunications (i.e., telephone) for longer distances, although telephone systems can also be used for short-distance communications. Interconnecting computer equipment over some limited distance such as a room, building, or campus is commonly referred to as a *local area network* (LAN). Interconnecting equipment over longer distances such as throughout a large city, across a state, or spanning a nation or continent is called a *wide area network* (WAN). The 1990s saw the phenomenal growth of the Internet, which is the epitome of a wide area network.

Usually, LANs use coaxial cable to connect various computer devices together, especially when confined to a single room, floor, or building. In addition to connecting the equipment physically, LANs also require specialized software to handle the transferring of data from one device to another. The sophistication of the software needed to control the network depends on how much interaction is required between the various devices.

Along with the number and type of devices, the amount of data to be transferred and the speed needed for transferring data are important factors in determining the software requirements. Central computer laboratories in many schools use a LAN to distribute instructional software. A typical network might consist of 20 or 30 microcomputers in a single room, with one microcomputer functioning as the central file server for the other microcomputers. The central file server usually has added hard disk storage so that it can contain a library of all the various software programs acquired by the school. Teachers or students using the other microcomputers access the central file server directly to select the individual program(s) needed. The central file server then downloads or sends a copy of the program over the network to the microcomputer that requested the program.

In the past few years, schools have begun to invest in *wireless local area networks* or WLANs. Conceptually, a WLAN is the same as a LAN without the connecting cables or wires but instead uses high-frequency radio waves to send and receive data signals. Although there are several variations, in a typical WLAN configuration a transceiver device, called an access point, connects to the school's wired network backbone from a fixed location using standard cabling. A backbone is a large data transmission line that carries data gathered from smaller lines that interconnect with it. Generally, all LANs are connected to a network backbone in order to access the Internet and other wide area networks. The access point receives and transmits data between the WLAN and the wired network backbone. A single access point can support a number of users. Users access the wireless LAN through WLAN adapters, installed as PC cards in laptop, desktop, or portable (handheld) computers.

Although conceptually similar, WANs are more sophisticated networks than LANs because of the distances involved, the number of users, and the large amounts of data that can be transferred. However, the most important difference between WANs and LANs is that WANs require telecommunications facilities to connect the various devices on the network. In a LAN environment using coaxial cable, all the data transferred are in digital (bit pattern) format, and conversions are not required as the data pass from one device to another. In a WAN environment using telephone lines, this is not possible because telephone communications are not in digital but in analog frequency format. This analog frequency format is a varying electric current that is generated from or converted into sound (i.e., human voice) by telephone transmitters or receivers, respectively. For computer equipment to use a telephone line, the computer's digital format must be converted into a frequency format and vice versa. To do this conversion, special equipment called *modulator-demodulators*, or *modems*, are needed. These are relatively inexpensive devices when used to connect a simple computing device such as a microcomputer, and most microcomputer manufacturers are now providing modems as standard devices. For larger computing systems, modems may be combined with other communications control equipment such as multiplexors, routers, and communications controllers, which in addition to modulating and demodulating signals are also able to perform complex message handling, protocol, and queuing operations.

The speed of modems as measured in bits per second (bps) varies significantly. Most microcomputers are being equipped with modems in the range of 56,000 bps. Modems for larger computer systems are usually measured in millions of bits per second. The growth of the Internet has generated a good deal of research and development in improving the speed of modems and other data communications devices. Broadband technology, for instance, which allows a single transmission circuit to carry millions of bits of data, is becoming more commonly available via cable modems, digital subscriber lines (DSL), and integrated services digital networks (ISDN). The costs for these broadband services have also been reduced dramatically so that many people can now afford them in their homes. Although WANs were originally designed and used by large corporations and public agencies for long-distance transaction processing such as making airline reservations and transferring funds, they are increasingly being used by everyone for a host of services. National networks such as Facebook, MySpace, Travelocity, and America Online provide a host of social networking, shopping, reference, and financial services for little or no fees to the general public. Many state education departments and large school districts have established WANs for record keeping and other administrative services such as reporting attendance, purchasing, and making library exchanges.

In view of the proliferation of the Internet, the telecommunications industry recognized the need for facilitating the integration with computing equipment and has moved rapidly to provide several high-speed digital data services, including wireless communication via satellite technology and fiber-optic cable-based services. The Internet established a standard protocol so that networks throughout the world could communicate with one another. As a result, the Internet has evolved to be the major source of all digital information. Additional information on data communications technologies as applied to education is available in Chapters 8 and 9.

COMPUTER SOFTWARE

Computer software is the instruction component of a computer system that directs the physical devices (hardware). Sets of instructions are called computer programs. These instructions may be communicated to the CPU through input devices such as a keyboard or a mouse, whereas instructions and programs that are executed over and over again are usually stored on storage devices such as magnetic disks or optical discs.

There are two broad categories of software: system software and application software. *System software* directs, supervises, and supports the computer hardware system and all the tasks that are to be executed on it. *Application software* consists of all the computer programs "applied" to specific computer user activities such as word processing, record keeping, e-mail, computer-assisted instruction, and so forth.

The relationship between system software and application software is an important one for understanding how computers perform tasks. For clarification, compare two components of an automobile assembly-line plant. In the plant, the people who work directly on the assembly line are actually accomplishing the task of building cars. This is the application. However, for the assembly-line workers to complete their task, other workers must supervise and coordinate activities such as making sure that resources (e.g., raw materials) are available in sufficient quantities, that basic utilities (e.g., electricity) are functioning, and that certain tasks (e.g., quality control) are completed satisfactorily before commencing a new task. These activities are comparable to system software functions.

SYSTEM SOFTWARE

The most common example of system software is the *operating system,* which is a set of programs that all computer manufacturers provide for their computer systems. The operating system supervises and controls the activities of the physical devices and the application software. It is the master control program on which all computer processing depends. On larger mainframe computers, the operating systems are the most complex and sophisticated software programs being used, and the computer programmers who develop and maintain them are generally the most talented people on the technical staff.

Computer manufacturers and software developers have in the past named their operating systems as *master control programs* or MCPs. IBM has used names such as OS (operating system), DOS (disk operating system), and VS (virtual system). Apple Inc. uses Mac OS (operating system). Microsoft uses Windows because all the commands can be executed by opening up a window. One of the most powerful, and one of the few machine-independent, operating systems is UNIX, developed by AT&T's Bell Laboratories in the 1970s. The UNIX operating system has proven to be especially effective in network environments and functioning as the server in client–server applications that are common on the Internet. A variation or hybrid of UNIX is an operating system named Linux, which was developed by Linus Torvalds in 1991. (Linux gets its name by combining *Linus* and *UNIX*.) Linux is a open source software (OSS) that aims to be a viable alternative to proprietary operating systems.

On microcomputers, the operating systems are complex yet much easier to use and understand. Examples include Microsoft (MS)-DOS, Linux, OS/2, and Microsoft-Windows. Apple Inc. with its Macintosh OS popularized the concept of windows or a menu-driven operating system on its Macintosh computers. The menu can be displayed as small pictures or icons representing the available programs. Using a mouse, users click on the icon of the program or command they wish to execute.

TABLE A.2 Basic Functions of Operating Systems

Supervisor Programs	Utility Programs	Language Processors
Job management	Execute a program	Assembler
Resource management	Disk copy	C
Data management	File copy	BASIC
	Sort files	COBOL
	Merge files	FORTRAN
	Disk format	PL/1

Although operating systems differ in some features, almost all provide several fundamental programs or commands (see Table A.2). The three most important features of most operating systems are supervisor programs, utility programs, and language translator programs.

Supervisor programs include job management, resource management, and data management programs. Job management programs allow users to execute their programs or tasks. They set job priorities and queues when there are multiple requests. Such ordering is critical, especially on mainframe computers capable of executing hundreds or thousands of programs simultaneously. Resource management programs allocate physical resources (devices) to programs and determine whether they are available. Computer systems with numerous physical devices require sophisticated resource management programs to control them. Data management programs allocate and retrieve data and programs on input/output devices such as optical discs or magnetic disks. Because a major function of computer systems is to store data and programs, data management is critical on all computer systems. *Utility programs* that are used repeatedly are generally supplied in the operating system. Examples include programs for copying data files from one storage area to another, sorting data into alphabetical or numerical order, making backup copies of storage media such as magnetic disks, and preparing (formatting) new disks to store data.

Language translators, also referred to as *compilers* or *interpreters,* are programs that convert or translate commands into machine-readable or bit-pattern instructions. Hundreds of programming languages are being used today. However, to use a particular language on a particular computer, a language translator program must be part of the operating system to convert instructions into a form that can be interpreted by the control unit of the CPU. Examples of language translator programs include the following:

BASIC (Beginner's All-Purpose Symbolic Instruction Code): The most commonly used programming language available on microcomputers; developed by John Kemeny at Dartmouth University.

C: A machine-independent language developed by Dennis Ritchie at Bell Laboratories in 1972. Because of its close association with the UNIX operating system, C has been especially popular in microcomputer-based networking environments. *C++* is an object-oriented version of C.

COBOL (Common Business-Oriented Language): One of the first languages to use words (English) as the primary method of providing commands; the most commonly used language for business applications.

FORTRAN (Formula Translation): One of the oldest programming languages, used mostly for scientific and mathematical applications; replaced by BASIC as the most commonly used programming language.

Logo: A language designed for teaching young children how to program a computer; developed by Seymour Papert at MIT.

PL/1 (Programming Language 1): A language originally designed to provide the best features of COBOL and FORTRAN.

Most of these languages use English-like words or commands such as *print, read, input,* and so forth, or arithmetic operators such as "+" (for addition) to provide instructions. These words, commands, or operators must be converted into a series of bit patterns (on/off codes) similar to the ASCII codes, discussed earlier, in order for them to be executed by the control unit. Simple programs may consist of several hundred instructions; more complex programs may consist of tens of thousands of instructions, all of which are translated before they are executed. The 1980s saw the introduction of object-oriented programming languages such as C++. These languages use a series of discrete objects that can be invoked to generate a series of commands or command structures. Object-oriented languages simplify programming by making commonly used tasks available at the click of a mouse. In all likelihood, the days of command-driven language translator programs may be numbered as object-oriented languages take their place.

DOS, MACINTOSH, AND WINDOWS

DOS was probably the most widely used operating system ever developed. Most users of microcomputers, especially those that had Microsoft Windows, would question this statement. However, through the year 2000, Windows was basically a graphical interface for DOS on Intel-based microcomputers. So, every microcomputer that used Windows also used DOS. Developed for IBM machines by Microsoft, DOS originally was referred to as *PC-DOS* when used on IBM PC/PS microcomputers and as *MS-DOS* (the "MS" stands for Microsoft) when used on IBM-compatible computers. It was considered the standard operating system for all Intel-based microcomputers through the 1980s and 1990s, and many other manufacturers besides IBM used it or something similar on their own equipment.

DOS was a command-driven operating system, which means the user keys in a command on the keyboard to invoke a particular function. For example, the user would key in the command "Copy" to copy a disk file. Users are expected to commit these commands to memory or at least be able to look them up in a user's manual.

The Macintosh OS operating system, developed in the mid-1980s, is radically different from DOS and is patterned after operating system models developed in the 1970s at Xerox's Palo Alto Research Center (PARC). Though performing most of the same functions, the Macintosh OS is a menu-driven operating system that provides the user with a series of window selections from which a particular function can be invoked. Rather than key in a command on a keyboard, the user employs a mouse to select or click on a selection on a menu by pointing to it. The Macintosh operating system also introduced the extensive use of picture representations or icons to represent functions, files, and other system facilities rather than words or file names. The use of icons and menus that open as electronic windows is also referred to as a *graphical user interface* or GUI (pronounced "gooey"). Other microcomputer operating systems have begun to move to the GUI style. The popular Microsoft's *Windows* operating system, for example, uses the GUI style as an interface for DOS. Because of this design, Windows has evolved to become probably the best-known operating system ever developed. Starting in 2000, Microsoft stopped using DOS as the underlying operating system for Windows.

In terms of the future, a new type of operating system that moves much of the work that computers do to online environments is evolving. Google, in particular, has developed what it calls its *Chrome* operating system that transfers many of the tasks that are performed on a personal computer to online activities on the Internet. So, rather than running programs and storing data files on individual computers, the program's operations and data are stored online someplace else available in any place, at any time, and by any type of Internet device (computer, laptop, netbook, cell phone, and so forth). This type of technology is referred to as "cloud" computing because everything is stored "out there in the clouds." This approach makes a good deal of sense in terms of efficiency and ease of access, but it is not clear that everyone is willing to entrust all of their computer operations and data files to some other online entity. Regardless, education leaders and technology planners should be aware of cloud computing and operating systems such as *Chrome*.

APPLICATION SOFTWARE

Application software includes the programs that actually perform the specific user tasks for which the computer system was acquired. In a bank, they would involve the financial record-keeping applications. In a hospital, medical record keeping and patient monitoring would be common applications. In a school, administrative and instructional applications are the two major categories; Chapters 4 through 9 in this book are devoted entirely to the nature of these applications.

Summary

This appendix introduces the basic concepts of computer systems. Covering the entire field of computer science is not possible here; only the major concepts and developments in hardware and software important to school administrators are included.

In terms of hardware, the computer system is made up of input, processing, output, and storage devices. The central processing unit (CPU)—which includes the control, arithmetic-logic, and primary storage units—is the fundamental hardware component of every computer system. Input devices such as keyboards provide data and instructions to the CPU. Output devices such as printers receive data and instructions from the CPU. Storage devices such as magnetic disk drives provide data and instructions and receive them from the CPU. All of these physical devices work together as a common hardware system to provide computer services to users. These are sometimes connected through data communications systems called wide area networks (WANs) and local area networks (LANs).

The physical devices or hardware can respond only to instructions that have been provided in the form of a computer program. Computer programs, developed by people, are communicated to the CPU by way of keyboards, magnetic disks, and other computer media. The two broad categories of computer software are system software and application software. System software includes all the programs and instructions that control, supervise, and coordinate the physical devices and the application software programs. Application software includes all the other programs that actually accomplish the specific tasks for which the computer is being used. In schools, the two major categories of application software are administrative applications and instructional applications.

Key Concepts and Questions

1. A computer system is made up of interrelated hardware and software components. How do you distinguish hardware from software? What are some of the major hardware components? Are they essentially the same in all computer systems? Explain.

2. The central processing unit (CPU) conceptually is divided into three subunits: control, arithmetic-logic, and primary storage. How do these subunits differ? What is a microprocessor, and what is its relationship to the CPU? What is the difference between primary and secondary storage?

3. Computer systems can include a variety of different input and output devices. Identify those devices that are appropriate only for specialized applications. Which are common to all applications?

4. Secondary storage devices have advanced significantly during the past 30 years. In particular, storage technology has favored direct access processing such as that provided by magnetic disks and optical discs. Why is direct access processing beneficial? What types of applications are dependent on it? What is sequential processing? Which secondary storage device is most associated with it? What does the future hold for secondary storage technology?

5. Computer software is categorized as system software and application software. How do they differ? Is one dependent on the other? Explain. Are they different depending on the type of computer equipment being used? Explain.

APPENDIX B

Educational Leader Competencies

This appendix attempts to identify some of the competencies required for educational administrators to be leaders in planning, developing, and implementing technology in their schools and districts. A more extensive set of National Educational Technology Standards (NETS) for administrators, teachers, students, and technology facilitators has been developed by the International Society for Technology in Education (ISTE) and can be found at www.iste.org.

Basic Technology

1. Educational leaders have an understanding of the principles of a digital computer system and other communication and media technologies used in schools and school districts.
2. Educational leaders have an understanding of the use of basic software applications (e.g., word processing, spreadsheet, office automation applications, and Internet tools).
3. Educational leaders have had experience in making efficient and effective use of complex electronic information resources (e.g., databases) to support administrative and instructional decisions.
4. Educational leaders understand the power of data communications networks and are able to use these networks to facilitate communications and professional growth (e.g., e-mail, electronic bulletin boards, Internet/World Wide Web resources, and social networking).
5. Educational leaders understand the benefits of multimedia, presentation, and distance learning technologies for communication, teaching, and learning.

Planning, Developing, and Implementing Technology

1. Educational leaders model the effective use of technology in support of teaching, learning, and administrative functions in their professional activities.
2. Educational leaders are competent in leading and managing systemic change processes at the school building and/or district levels.
3. Educational leaders are able to initiate and support professional development processes and programs that respect the concerns of adult learners.
4. Educational leaders develop and maintain knowledge of the current applications of technology related to administration, teaching, and learning.
5. Educational leaders are able to identify and establish the hardware, software, and people infrastructure to provide for the technological needs of students, teachers, and administrators in their school buildings and/or districts.
6. Educational leaders are proactive in initiating policies and procedures related to technology and its use in their school buildings and/or districts.
7. Educational leaders are able to identify and maintain the financial resources needed to support technology applications at the school building and/or district levels.

8. Educational leaders are aware of the ethical, social, and equity issues related to technology (e.g., equitable access, fair use, copyright, free speech).
9. Educational leaders are aware of a variety of strategies and techniques for evaluating the outcomes of technology-related initiatives and projects.
10. Educational leaders understand the importance of integrating technology into an overall school building and/or district planning process.

APPENDIX C

Instructional Software Evaluation Factors

General

Program is useful in a school setting.

Program avoids controversial teaching methodologies.

Program allows completion of lesson in one class period.

Instruction is integrated with previous student experience.

Program is likely to save time when compared with other means of presentation.

An electronic (CD-ROM, Web site, or DVD) tutorial for the program's command structure is provided.

Content

Content is appropriate for intended student population.

Content is accurate.

Content is current.

Content breadth is reasonable.

The processes and information learned are useful in domains other than the subject area of the program.

Content is free of any bias or stereotyping.

Content supports the school curriculum.

Content is relevant to the subject field.

Definitions are provided when necessary.

There is continuity between the information presented and prerequisite skills required.

Content avoids taking a side on controversial moral or social issues.

There is a need for better than the standard treatment of this topic in the curriculum.

Appropriateness

Application is well suited to computer use.

Pedagogic approach is superior to what is available elsewhere.

Readability level is appropriate for the intended student population.

Tone of address is appropriate for the intended student population.

Means of response is appropriate for the intended student population.

Prerequisite skills required are appropriate for the intended population.

Time required for use by a typical student does not exceed the attention span of that student.

Multiple levels of instruction are available.

Difficulty levels are based on discernible logic.

Sufficient exposure and practice are provided to master skills.

Sufficient information is presented for intended learning to occur.

Questioning Techniques

Questions are appropriate to the content and effectively measure student mastery of the content.

Questions incorrectly answered can be repeated later in the lesson/exercise.

Number of trials is reasonable and appropriate.

Calculation can be accomplished easily on-screen when appropriate.

Approach/Motivation

Approach is appropriate for the intended student population.

Format is varied.

Overall tenor of interaction is helpful.

Student is an active participant in the learning process.

Evaluator's Field Test Results

Student understands on-screen presentation and is not confused.

Student enjoys using the program.

Student retains a positive attitude about using the program.

Student maintains the desire to use the program again.

Student has the desire to pursue the topic in other ways.

Program involves students in competition in a positive way.

Program fosters cooperation among students.

Creativity

Program challenges and stimulates creativity.

Pedagogy is innovative.

Program allows the student as many decisions as possible.

Program provides opportunities to answer open-ended questions and supplies evaluative criteria to assess responses.

Program demonstrates a creative way of using knowledge.

Program challenges the student to change an underlying model or design an alternative model.

Learner Control

Learner can alter program sequence and pace.

Learner can review instructions and previous frames.

Learner can end activity any time and return to main menu.

Learner can enter program at different points.

Learner can stop in the middle of an activity and at a later session begin at that stopping point with the previous record of progress intact.

Help is available at likely points of need.

Learning Objectives, Goals, and Outcomes

Learner objectives are stated, and purpose is well defined.

Steps taken to make learning generalizable to other situations.

For programs requiring use over several days, learning outcomes are worth the time invested.

Feedback

Feedback is positive.

Feedback is appropriate to the intended student population.

Feedback does not threaten or reward incorrect responses.

Feedback is relevant to student responses.

Feedback is timely.

Feedback is informative.

Feedback is corrective when appropriate.

Feedback remedies and/or explains when appropriate.

Feedback employs a variety of responses and avoids being boring.

Feedback remains on the screen for the appropriate amount of time.

Branching is used effectively to remediate.

Program uses branching to automatically adjust difficulty levels or sequence according to student performance.

Simulations

Simulation model is valid and neither too complex nor too simple for intended student population.

Variables used in the simulation are the most relevant.

Assumptions are adequately identified.

Program simulates activities that can be too difficult to demonstrate in reality.

Time needed to complete both a step and the entire simulation is reasonable and effective.

Program encourages decision making or calculation rather than guessing.

Teacher Modifiability

Teacher can easily change or add content.

Teacher can easily regulate parameters for each class.

Teacher can easily regulate parameters for each student.

Parameter setups can be bypassed.

Evaluation and Record Keeping

Program provides an adequate means of evaluating mastery of the content.

If tests are included, criteria for success are appropriate for the ability/skills of the intended student population.

If tests are included, content accurately reflects the material presented.

Score keeping and performance reports are provided when appropriate.

Useful information about student performance is stored for future retrieval.

Useful diagnostic pretest or placement test is provided, where appropriate.

Useful diagnostic or prescriptive analysis of student performance is available to the teacher, when appropriate.

Student performance information is easily accessible to the teacher.

Management system includes adequate security.

Program allows printout and screen display of student records.

Program can hold multiple performance records of a single class.

Program can hold multiple performance records of several classes.

Documentation and Support Material

Quality of packaging is durable and appropriate for student use.

Student, parent, or teacher guides and materials are clearly identified.

Technical and operational explanations for implementation are clear and complete.

If appropriate, "quick start-up" section is included.

Useful, reproducible student worksheets are provided.

Other valuable support materials are supplied.

Sample screen-by-screen printouts of the program are provided.

Teacher support materials can be separated from student materials.

Useful suggestions are offered for introductory classroom activities.

Useful suggestions are provided for classroom activities during the use of the program, where necessary or helpful.

Useful suggestions are given for classroom logistics in a variety of hardware situations and student groupings.

Useful suggestions are provided on how to integrate program with the regular curriculum.

If the program is open-ended, subject-specific suggestions are included.

Clear explanations of the differences between the various difficulty levels are provided.

Prerequisite skills are clearly stated.

Accurate and clear descriptions of content topics are made.

Accurate and clear descriptions of instructional activities are given.

Where appropriate, how material correlates to standard textbook series is described.

Necessary information can be found quickly and easily.

Quick reference card for program use is included where appropriate.

Printed text is clear and readable.

Printed graphics are clear and readable.

Printed text is free of errors in spelling, grammar, punctuation, and usage.

Technical Quality

Audio can be adjusted.

Audio is clear and used effectively.

Character sets used in text display are clear, appropriate, and visually interesting.

Graphics are acceptable on a monochrome monitor.

Graphics are clear and easily interpreted.

Program is "crash-proof."

Program runs without undue delays.

Program runs consistently under all normal conditions.

Transitions between screen displays are effective.

Program guards against multiple key presses advancing the student past the next screen.

Program avoids unnecessary or inappropriate moving back and forth between screens.

Special features (e.g., flash, scrolling, split screen) are used effectively.

Program requires a minimal amount of typing.

Random generation is used when appropriate.

Program judges responses accurately and accounts for minor variations in input format.

Program allows user to correct answer before being accepted by the program.

Program is capable of accepting partial answers when appropriate.

Where students must input responses, inappropriate keys are disabled.

Control keys are used consistently.

Students require a minimum amount of teacher supervision while using the program.

Computer operation does not interfere with concentration on activity.

Program makes effective use of peripheral devices.

Program considers a previously unexplored potential of the computer.

Program uses other technologies (e.g., audio, video) to enhance learning.

Printing is easy to accomplish.

Procedural and instructional statements are clear.

On-screen prompts clearly indicate where the user should focus attention.

Frame formatting is clear, uncluttered, and consistent from screen to screen.

Presentation of each discrete content topic is logical.

Sequence of content topics and instruction is logical.

Sequence of menu items is logical.

Prompts and cues are clear and consistently and logically applied.

Hints are clear and not misleading.

Demonstrations and examples are clear and available when appropriate.

Interface is simple enough to be used with little or no reading of the documentation.

Program makes clear where the user is in the program.

User–computer communication is consistent and logical.

Prompts to save work are given when appropriate.

Start-Up and Implementation

Software code modifications or unusual manipulations of disks are not required.

Start-up time for teacher implementation is not excessive.

Teacher needs a minimum of computer competencies to operate the program.

Start-up time for student implementation is brief enough to permit completion of a lesson.

Students need a minimum of computer competencies to operate the program.

Graphics and Audio

Graphics and audio are used to motivate.

Graphics and audio are appropriate for the intended student population.

Graphics, audio, and color enhance the instructional process.

Graphics help focus attention to appropriate content without being distracting.

Probeware and Peripherals Included in the Software Package

Probes or peripherals are durable.

Probes or peripherals are sensitive.

Audio and/or graphic quality is effective.

Probes or peripherals are easy to install.

Calibration is accurate and easy.

Data displays are flexible.

Data analysis is useful.

Hardware and Marketing Issues

Potential usefulness of the program justifies its price.

Peripherals that are difficult to acquire or inappropriately expensive are not required.

Producer field test data are available.

Field test data indicate that students learned more or better as a result of using the program.

Preview copies are available.

Backup copies are provided.

Adequate warranty is provided.

Telephone support is available.

Assistance is available on the World Wide Web.

If allowable, multiple loading is possible.

Site license is available.

Network versions are available.

Multiple-copies discount is available.

GLOSSARY

access point A transceiver device that connects to the school's wired network backbone from a fixed location using standard cabling. It is used in wireless data communications.

access time The time required to fetch data from a source once a request has been made. It is most commonly used to refer to accessing data from a primary or secondary storage device.

Advanced Research and Projects Administration Network (ARPANET) A worldwide data communications network established by the U.S. Department of Defense in the 1960s, which evolved into the Internet.

ALN *See* asynchronous learning network.

ALU *See* arithmetic-logic unit.

analog A general term used to refer to a continuous physical property such as voltage, current, fluid pressure, rotation, and so on.

application software Programs that "apply" the computer to perform specific tasks or solve specific problems. Examples include word processing, electronic spreadsheets, and graphics programs.

arithmetic-logic unit (ALU) The part of the central processing unit that performs all arithmetic operations, including comparisons.

ARPANET *See* Advanced Research and Projects Administration Network.

ASCII An acronym for American Standard Code for Information Interchange, a coding scheme that represents letters of the alphabet, numerals, and special characters as a series of binary digits or numbers.

asynchronous Happening at different times. Asynchronous communication, for instance, is characterized by time-independence; that is, the sender and receiver do not communicate at the same time. An example is electronic mail.

asynchronous learning network (ALN) A form of distance learning that uses computer networking technology—especially the Internet—for instructional activities.

audio response unit Any device that produces a spoken word from a computer in response to a question or command.

authoring language A user-friendly programming language used to develop specific applications such as teaching presentations, computer-assisted instruction, and multimedia. Examples include PowerPoint, HyperCard, HyperStudio, and ToolBook.

authoring system *See* authoring language.

backbone A large data transmission line that carries data gathered from smaller lines that interconnect with it.

bandwidth In communications, the frequencies within which signals can be transmitted and received. Bandwidth directly relates to data transfer speed. The greater the bandwidth, the faster the data transmission speed.

BASIC An acronym for Beginners' All-Purpose Symbolic Instruction Code, a high-level computer programming language developed by John Kemeny and Thomas Kurtz at Dartmouth University in the 1960s. Because of its general availability on most microcomputers in the 1970s and 1980s, BASIC became one of the most popular high-level language ever developed.

benchmark A test used to measure the performance (e.g., speed or accuracy) of computer hardware or software.

binary digit In the binary number system, either 0 or 1. *See also* bit.

bit A binary digit. In the binary number system, the bit is either 0 or 1. In electronic storage, it represents the smallest unit of data and is characterized as being either "on" or "off." Groups of eight bits are combined to represent characters of data that are referred to as bytes.

blog An abbreviation for the term *Weblog* that refers to a Web site that can easily be updated and edited with entries or postings that appear in reverse chronological order. Most blogs provide facilities for posting text, images, and increasingly sound and video clips.

broadband A high-capacity communications circuit that is capable of transmitting data at high speed, up to millions of bits per second.

browser software (Web browser) Software that provides facilities for accessing uniform resource locators (URLs) on the World Wide Web. Examples of Web browsers include Firefox Mozilla and Internet Explorer.

bug An error or problem in software or hardware.

byte The minimum amount of primary storage or memory needed to store a character (letter, numeral, special character, etc.) of information. It is usually eight binary digits or bits.

C A programming language developed at Bell Laboratories in 1972. Designed originally to work with the UNIX operating system, it has become widely popular on many microcomputers.

C++ An object-oriented version of the C programming language.

CAI *See* computer-assisted instruction.

CAL Acronym for computer-assisted learning or computer-augmented learning. *See* computer-assisted instruction.

cathode-ray tube (CRT) A common type of video display screen. It uses an electron gun to generate a light beam that is scanned across a screen.

CBE *See* computer-based education.

CBT *See* computer-based teaching.

CD-ROM An acronym for compact disc read-only memory. It is a form of high-capacity optical storage that uses laser technology.

central file server The central or host computer in a network that provides files and programs to other computers.

central processing unit (CPU) The part of a computer hardware system that directs all processing activities. It consists of electronic circuitry and includes a control unit, an arithmetic-logic unit, and a primary storage or memory unit. On large computers, the term is used to refer to the entire main computer console. On some microcomputers, it refers only to the control unit and the arithmetic-logic unit.

character A letter, numeral, or special character such as a comma or exclamation point that can be represented by one byte.

client–server system A distributed data communications system in which computers perform two important functions as either "clients" or "servers." The client function makes requests for data (e.g., files) from the server, which locates the data on the data communications system and processes the request for the client.

clip media Digital files or libraries containing images, video, sounds, and other media, which can readily be incorporated into a multimedia program.

cloud computing A type of technology that depends on executing all computer activities and storing all data online or "out there in the clouds" rather than on personal computers. The term *cloud* really is a metaphor for the Internet.

CMI *See* computer-managed instruction.

CMS *See* course management software.

COBOL An acronym for Common Business-Oriented Language, a high-level programming language developed in 1959 that uses English-like commands. It became popular for business applications.

communications controller A data communications device that is used to send and receive messages from multiple sources. A multiplexor is an example of a communications controller. In some networks, communications controlling is performed by computer programs that are also referred to as communications controllers.

communications control program *See* communications controller.

computer An electronic device that accepts input, processes it according to a set of instructions, and produces the results as output. Computers can be classified as supercomputers, mainframes, minicomputers, microcomputers, laptop computers, and so forth, depending on physical size, speed, and peripheral devices.

computer-assisted instruction (CAI) The use of the computer to assist in the instructional process. One of the earliest used terms to generically refer to computer applications in education, it is used now to refer to tutor-type applications such as drill and practice and tutorials.

computer-assisted learning *See* computer-assisted instruction.

computer-augmented learning *See* computer-assisted instruction.

computer-based education (CBE) A generic term used to refer to the broad array of instructional computer applications.

computer-based teaching (CBT) A generic term used to refer to the use of a computer by teachers as part of an instructional presentation such as an interactive video.

computer chip *See* integrated circuit.

computer hack *See* hacker.

computer-managed instruction (CMI) The use of the computer in an instructional process in which student progress is monitored and recorded for subsequent instructions and review. Most CMI applications are also able to adjust material to each individual student's level of understanding.

computer program A set of instructions to direct physical devices to perform some task.

constructivism Theory of learning that stresses the importance of experiences, experimentation, problem solving, and the construction of knowledge.

control unit (CU) The part of the central processing unit that interprets instructions and directs the processing of the other physical devices.

course management software (CMS) A set of computer software tools designed to enable users to create Web-based courses. Examples include Blackboard, WebCT, Sakai, and Desire2Learn.

CPU *See* central processing unit.

CU *See* control unit.

cyberspace Descriptive term for the Internet.

daisy-wheel printer An impact printer that uses a daisy-wheel-type element to strike a character through an inked ribbon onto a sheet of paper.

DASD *See* direct access storage device.

database A collection of data files and records.

database management system (DBMS) A package of computer programs that allow users to create, maintain, and access the data on a database.

data communications The methods and media used to transfer data from one computer device to another. Common data communications media include coaxial cable, telephone, fiber optics, and satellite systems.

data disaggregation The use of software tools to break down data files into various characteristics. An example might be using a software program to select student performance data on a standardized test by gender, by class, by ethnicity, or by other definable characteristics.

data-driven decision making Using data analysis to inform when determining courses of action involving policy and procedures. An important aspect of this definition is that data analysis is used *to inform* and does not replace the experience, expertise, intuition, judgment, and acumen of competent educators.

data element A grouping of characters (letters of the alphabet, numerals, and special characters) to represent some specific data characteristics of a person, place, or thing. Examples include a person's name, street address, and gender. Also referred to as a data field or data item.

data element dictionary A table used to identify the content and coding schemes used for all the data elements in a database. Can also refer to a document that identifies the content, definitions, and coding schemes used for all data elements in a database.

data field *See* data element.

data file A collection of related data records. Examples include a personnel file of all personnel records or a student file of all student records.

data item *See* data element.

data mining A frequently used term in research and statistics that refers to searching or "digging into" a data file for information to better understand a particular phenomenon.

data processing A general term used for the systematic processing (storing, manipulating, sorting, etc.) of data on computer systems.

data record A grouping of related data elements for a single entity such as a person, place, or thing. Examples include a personnel record, inventory record, and financial record.

data structure The method by which data are organized in a database.

data warehousing A computerized database information system that is capable of storing and maintaining data *longitudinally* over a period of time.

DBMS *See* database management system.

desktop publishing The use of computer equipment to develop text and graphics. It usually refers to software that provides enhanced facilities for displaying characters, pictures, and color.

digital Related to digits. Computers are considered digital because all data and instructions are represented as binary digits.

digital versatile disc (DVD) A small plastic disc used for high-capacity optical storage of digital data that uses laser technology. Same as digital video disc.

digital video disc *See* digital versatile disc.

digitizer Any device used to convert analog (continuous physical property such as voltage or current) signals into binary or digital format.

direct access storage device (DASD) Any secondary storage device, such as a magnetic disk or optical disc, that allows users to access data in a direct or nonsequential manner.

directory A grouping or catalog of filenames that reside on a secondary storage device such as a disk. On some operating systems, a directory is referred to as a folder.

disk operating system A generic term used to refer to any operating system that resides on a disk device and is loaded as needed into primary storage.

Disk Operating System *See* DOS.

distance learning A term for the physical separation of teachers and learners that has become popular in recent years, particularly in the United States. Although used interchangeably with distance education, distance learning puts the emphasis on the "learner" and is especially appropriate when students take on greater responsibility for their learning, as is frequently the case when doing so from a distance.

distributed system A form of computer processing that distributes and links hardware over some geographic area as in a network. It assumes that the local hardware can perform some tasks and expand its capabilities by connecting to other hardware.

DOS An acronym for Disk Operating System, the most popular operating system for Intel-based (i.e., IBM PC and PC-compatible) microcomputers. It is also referred to as Microsoft or MS-DOS after the company that developed it.

dot-matrix printer An impact printer that forms text and images as a pattern of dots.

downlink The transmission of data from a communications satellite to an earth station.

download In a computer network, the process of transferring a copy of a file from one computer, generally referred to as a central file server, to another, requesting computer.

drill and practice A form of tutor software used to reinforce a lesson or material that has already been presented to a student. It is characterized by repetitive questioning or drills.

DVD *See* digital versatile disc.

EBCDIC An acronym for Extended Binary Coded Decimal Interchange Code, a coding scheme developed by IBM for use on mainframe and minicomputer systems, which represents letters of the alphabet, numerals, and special characters as a series of binary digits or numbers.

electronic bulletin board A group e-mail or mailing list that allows all participants to post and read messages.

electronic mail (e-mail) The transmission of messages over a data communications network.

electronic spreadsheet Application programming software that provides the user with an electronic grid of rows and columns similar to a ledger worksheet. It is used extensively for budgeting, forecasting, projections, and other number-based applications. Examples include Excel and Lotus 1-2-3.

e-mail *See* electronic mail.

environmental scanning A term used in planning that means engaging in activities to provide information outside of an organization or on the external environment.

EPROM An acronym for erasable programmable read-only memory, which is a type of read-only memory that can be programmed or rewritten to.

E-Rate A U.S. government-managed program that provides discounts on telecommunications technologies to schools. Discounts are based on the percentage of students in a school participating in the federal free lunch program.

ergonomics The study and design of people in work environments. The objective is to develop comfortable and safe conditions so as to improve worker morale and efficiency. Ergonomics is especially important in designing computer hardware such as keyboards and video display devices.

Facebook A free social networking Web site that provides users with a host of services including personal profiles, blogs, and user groups.

fiber optics The method of transmitting and receiving light beams along an optical fiber that is usually made of a thin strand of glass. Fiber optics are destined to radically change the speed and nature of communications throughout the world.

file transfer protocol (FTP) A popular protocol used for transferring data files on the World Wide Web.

floppy disk *See* magnetic disk.

folder A grouping or cataloging of filenames that reside on a secondary storage device such as a disk. It is similar to a directory on DOS (disk operating system) computers.

FORTRAN An acronym for Formula Translation, a high-level programming language developed in 1954. Although originally developed for scientific and engineering applications, it established several programming concepts such as variables, subroutines, input/output formats, and so forth, which have formed the basis for many other programming languages.

frame rate The number of frames or images per second displayed on a video device. Thirty frames per second is the full-motion video standard.

FTP *See* file transfer protocol.

gigabyte One billion bytes.

gopher A database communications protocol used for locating data files on the World Wide Web.

graphical user interface (GUI) The graphic display of software options in the form of icons and pictures that can be selected, usually by a pointing device such as a mouse. It is considered a feature of user-friendly software such as that provided with the Macintosh operating system, Microsoft Windows, and many application software packages.

graphics tablet An electronic surface connected to a central processing unit. It comes with a pen, arm, or stylus to draw images that are automatically transferred to the CPU.

GUI *See* graphical user interface.

hacker Someone who seems overly involved with computer hardware and software. Also refers to people who gain unauthorized access to computer networks and databases.

handheld computer A small portable computer capable of being used (held) in one hand.

hard disk *See* magnetic disk.

hardware The physical components of a computer system, such as the central processing unit, printer, keyboard, and so on.

high-level language A programming language that uses common words and symbols that are translated into computer machine language instructions by way of a compiler or interpreter. Examples include FORTRAN, BASIC, COBOL, and Pascal.

HTML *See* hypertext markup language.

http *See* hypertext transfer protocol.

HyperCard An authoring language designed for the Apple Macintosh microcomputer. It established several important new concepts—such as fields, buttons, and stacks—that have been copied by other authoring languages.

hypermedia A computer-based information retrieval system for accessing sound, text, images, graphics, or video in a nonsequential or nonlinear format.

hypertext A computer-based text and document retrieval system that can be accessed in a nonsequential or nonlinear format.

hypertext markup language (HTML) Software language used to establish data files for access on the World Wide Web.

hypertext transfer protocol (http) The most commonly used protocol on the World Wide Web. It runs in conjunction with TCP/IP.

ICAI *See* intelligent computer-assisted instruction.

icon A graphic image displayed on a video screen, representing an object—usually a file or command that can be referenced or executed by a user. Icons are common features of user-friendly software referred to as graphical user interfaces.

IIS An acronym for integrated instructional system. *See* integrated learning system.

ILS *See* integrated learning system.

information superhighway Descriptive term for the Internet.

ink-jet printer A nonimpact printer that uses droplets of ink sprayed from a tiny nozzle.

input device Any device that is used to enter or bring data to a central processing unit.

input/output device (I/O device) Any device that can be used to enter data to or receive data from a central processing unit.

instruction set The set of machine instructions that the control unit of a central processor recognizes and can execute.

integrated circuit Circuit that combines two or more electronic circuits (transistors, resistors, etc.) onto a thin wafer of silicon or other type of semiconductor material. A microprocessor is an integrated circuit that usually combines a control unit or circuit and an arithmetic-logic unit or circuit. Same as a computer chip.

integrated instructional system (IIS) *See* integrated learning system.

integrated learning system (ILS) A single computer package for delivering instruction that combines hardware, software, curriculum, and management components. It is usually supplied by a single vendor.

Integrated Services Digital Network (ISDN) A high-speed (128 kilobits per second) data communications network evolving from existing telephone services.

integrated software package A software package that integrates several programs into a single comprehensive program. An example is Microsoft Office, which combines word processing, spreadsheet, database, communications, and graphics.

intelligent computer-assisted instruction (ICAI) Similar to CAI but also uses a substantial database of information for presenting material and selecting instructional paths.

intelligent whiteboard An electronic presentation system that usually consists of a large interactive display screen that can be used to integrate a range of digital software tools for presenting digitally formatted information, be it text, images, sound, or video. An intelligent whiteboard usually comes with interactive features so that teachers and students can manipulate the displayed information. SMART Technologies Inc. manufactures intelligent whiteboards under the product name SMART Board.

interactive Operating in a back-and-forth mode. It refers to user and machine dialogue or interaction in which both are active participants in a process.

interactive video Combining computer and video technologies to provide an active video environment in which users can control and select options based on a given application. Interactive video is a major advancement over other video technologies such as film and television, which are considered "passive."

interface The point at which two components meet. With computers, it is used for both hardware (when two physical devices connect to one another) and software (when two programs work with one another). It is also used to refer to points at which people connect to computer devices such as with graphical user interfaces.

Internet The network of networks that provides the basic protocol standard for allowing data communications systems to link themselves together throughout the world.

Internet Relay Chat (IRC) Computer software that allows multiple parties to participate in synchronous (same time) communications on the Internet.

intranet In data communications, the adoption of the standard Internet protocol and software tools for a local network or for establishing a mini-Internet within a local system.

ISDN *See* Integrated Services Digital Network.

Java An object-oriented programming language that attempts to operate across software platforms.

JavaScript A programming language similar to Java that generally operates with World Wide Web browser software.

joystick An input device popular with computer games and used to point to objects on a video screen.

kilobyte (KB) One thousand bytes.

Koala pad A form of graphics tablet or electronic surface connected to a central processing unit. It comes with a pen, arm, or stylus used to draw images on the tablet that are automatically transferred to the CPU.

LAN *See* local area network.

laptop A type of portable computer that can easily be used by resting it on one's lap.

laserdisc An optical disc used to store video images and associated audio or sound information in analog format. Same as a videodisc.

laser printer A nonimpact printer that uses laser technology to produce a high-quality image on a page.

light pen An input device that allows the user to point to objects on a screen with a pen-shaped wand. It can also be used for drawing and designing shapes and figures.

line printer An impact printer that prints one line at a time.

Linux A variation of UNIX that is an open source operating system developed by Linus Torvalds in 1991.

liquid crystal display (LCD) A flat-panel video display that uses electroluminescent (liquid crystal) material to produce a light image. In the past few years, LCDs have bypassed CRTs as the most popular video plays used on computer systems.

LISP An acronym for list processing. It is a high-level programming language developed in 1959 and used extensively in artificial intelligence applications.

local area network (LAN) Connecting computer equipment using data communications over a limited geographic area such as a room, building, or campus.

Logo A high-level programming language developed by Seymour Papert in 1968; a very popular programming language for teaching young children to use a computer.

machine cycle The time required for a central processing unit to perform its fastest operation as determined by its internal clock.

machine language Instructions that are represented in binary form (1s and 0s). All computer instructions must be converted or reduced to machine language instructions for the central processing unit to execute them.

magnetic disk A form of secondary computer storage that uses electromagnetic technology to store data. A magnetic disk can be made of metallic (hard disk) or plastic (floppy disk) substances. Because the read/write head on a magnetic disk drive can move across the surface of a disk, this technology is used for direct or random processing. A magnetic disk is the actual platter on which data reside. The device that stores and retrieves data on magnetic disk is a disk drive.

magnetic disk drive *See* magnetic disk.

magnetic tape A form of secondary computer storage that uses Mylar tape to store data. Because the tape passes through a stationary read/write head, this technology is used strictly for sequential processing. Magnetic tape is the actual reel of tape on which data reside. The device that stores and retrieves data on magnetic tape is a tape drive.

magnetic tape drive *See* magnetic tape.

mainframe Large computer systems capable of processing extensive amounts of data and controlling many peripheral devices. IBM and Hitachi are the major manufacturers of mainframe computer equipment.

media distribution system A computer-based system that integrates several media sources (videotape, videodisc, computer, camera, etc.) and is able to distribute them to selected output devices.

megabyte (MB) One million bytes.

megaflops (MFLOP) One million arithmetic operations per second.

megahertz (MHz) One million machine cycles per second.

memory *See* primary storage unit.

menu A presentation of options available that a user can select or request from a program. Menu-driven software anticipates user options and presents them in the form of lists or icons.

microcomputer A small computer system that usually uses one central processing unit. Apple, COMPAQ, Dell, Gateway, IBM, and Sony are among the most popular manufacturers of microcomputers.

microprocessor A central processing unit used for most microcomputer systems capable of being integrated on a single chip. *See* integrated circuit.

microsecond One millionth of a second.

millisecond One thousandth of a second.

minicomputer A computer system, midrange between a large mainframe and microcomputer. Minicomputers are highly effective in network environments where they are used to control microcomputers and other minicomputers. Digital Equipment Corporation (now a part of COMPAQ) and Sun Microsystems are among the leading manufacturers of minicomputers.

MIP An acronym for million instructions per second. Similar to megaflop.

modem *See* modulator-demodulator.

modulator-demodulator (modem) A data communications device used to convert computer digital signals into a telephone frequency or analog signal and vice versa.

monochrome A video monitor that displays images in one color.

morphing Relating to form or structure. Morphing software is designed to edit and manipulate graphics such as images and video.

mouse A handheld input device that is electronically connected to a video screen and is used to position a pointer to make software selections by pressing a button.

multimedia Combining sound, text, images, animation, and video. With computers, it refers to a variety of applications that utilize CD-ROM, videodisc, and audio equipment.

multiplexor A data communications device used to control many messages by funneling them into a smaller number of communication lines or ports.

MySpace A free social networking Web site that provides users with a host of services including personal profiles, blogs, and user groups.

nanosecond One billionth of a second.

narrowband A low-capacity communications circuit that is capable of transmitting data at speeds of up to 56 thousand bits per second.

network A group of computer devices connected by a data communications system. Two major types of networks are local area networks (LANs) and wide area networks (WANs).

notebook A very lightweight, portable computer, usually weighing less than 10 pounds, that can be easily carried under one's arm.

office automation The use of computer and data communications equipment to perform office functions electronically rather than manually. Examples of office automation applications include word processing, electronic mail, and desktop publishing.

open source software Refers to any program in which the source code is available to the general public for use and/or modification from its original design free of charge. Linux is an example of open source software.

open system architecture A term used to refer to any computer or hardware device that has published design specifications so that other (third party) manufacturers can develop compatible hardware components.

operating system A type of system software that acts as a master control program and directs the processing of all physical devices and application programs. Examples of operating systems include DOS (Disk Operating System), Windows, and the Macintosh operating system.

optical character reader (OCR) *See* optical scanning device.

optical disc A secondary storage device that utilizes laser technology for storing data. CD-ROM and DVD are forms of optical disc.

optical mark reader (OMR) *See* optical scanning device.

optical scanning device An input device that uses light sensors to scan paper documents and convert images into digital format. Optical mark readers and optical character readers are types of optical scanning devices.

output device Any device that receives data from a central processing unit.

Pascal A highly structured, procedural programming language developed by Nicholas Wirth in 1967. It is very popular for teaching structured programming techniques to beginning programmers.

PC An acronym for personal computer. *See* personal computer.

PDA *See* Personal Digital Assistant.

peripheral Any hardware device—such as a printer, keyboard, magnetic disk, magnetic tape, and so on—that connects to a central processing unit.

personal computer A generic term used for any microcomputer that is used by one person. It is also the model name (Personal Computer or PC) that IBM adopted for its microcomputers.

personal digital assistant (PDA) A handheld computer that provides a variety of services including mobile telephone, e-mail, Web browsing, and other digital services.

picosecond One trillionth of a second.

pixel Short for picture element. A point on a grid such as a video screen that represents a single dot of light. Text and images are developed by manipulating many pixels.

plasma display A flat-panel video display that uses neon or argon gas to produce a light image. Also referred to as a gas-discharge display.

platform The foundation hardware and operating system software technology of a computer system. Examples include Motorola/Macintosh and Intel/DOS/Windows platforms. The term *software platform* is also used to refer to only the basic operating system software.

PL/1 An acronym for Programming Language I. It is a high-level programming language developed in 1964, designed to combine the best features of FORTRAN and COBOL.

plotter An output device used to draw charts, maps, diagrams, and other line-based graphics.

plug-in A dynamic computer code module that performs a specific task, which generally is made available or functions with World Wide Web browser software.

portable computer Any computer designed to be carried and moved about. Laptop, notebook, and handheld computers are examples of portable computers.

portal A main point of entry to the Internet that provides a full range of Internet services such as e-mail, search engines, access to databases, and useful links to other Web sites.

primary storage unit (PSU) The part of the central processing unit that stores instructions and data. Also referred to as memory.

probeware Hardware and software used to conduct experiments of physical properties such as temperature, light, and humidity. Probeware is characterized by the use of probes to measure physical surroundings.

PROM An acronym for programmable read-only memory, which is a type of read-only memory that can be programmed or written to once.

protocol A general term for a set of rules, procedures, or standards used to exchange information in data communications. Examples include a code or signal indicating the beginning of a message, a code or signal indicating the end of a message, or a code or signal indicating that a device is busy with another task. Computer manufacturers have established various protocols for exchanging information on their equipment.

PSU *See* primary storage unit.

query language A user-friendly language that enables users to retrieve and display data from a database.

RAM An acronym for random-access memory. A type of primary storage that can have data and instructions read from and written to it by a central processing unit. Also referred to as volatile memory because it can keep changing.

read/write head The read and write or playback and record mechanism on secondary storage devices such as magnetic disk and tape drives.

relational database A database structure that uses a table to relate or link one data element with another data element.

resolution Clarity of detail available on a video monitor or printer.

response time The time required for an operation to be performed once a request has been made. It generally refers to software but can also refer to hardware.

ROM An acronym for read-only memory. A type of primary storage from which data and instructions can be read by a central processing unit. Because ROM is read-only, data and instructions on it can never be changed.

router An intermediary device on a communications network that accepts and routes messages from one link (e.g., LAN) on the network to other links.

sampling rate The rate, as measured in kilohertz (KHz), at which sound can be recorded and played back.

search engine Software that provides keyword and other search facilities for locating information on the World Wide Web. Examples include Yahoo!, Google, Lycos, and Alta Vista.

secondary storage Input/output devices, other than the primary storage unit, that are used to store data and instructions. Common examples include magnetic disk, magnetic tape, and optical disc.

semiconductor Any substance between a full conductor and a nonconductor of electricity. In computer electronics, silicon and germanium are the most common semiconductor materials used for manufacturing microprocessors.

simulation A form of tutor software used to represent a real-life situation on a computer.

SMART Board See intelligent whiteboard.

social networks Electronic networks such as MySpace, Facebook, Twitter, and YouTube that provide various services for people to communicate and contact one another.

software Computer programs and instructions that direct the physical components (hardware) of a computer system to perform tasks.

software platform *See* platform.

sound board A CPU component capable of generating and synthesizing sound.

sound capture Term used for converting analog sound into a digital file.

speech synthesis Producing spoken words from computer-generated or controlled equipment.

spyware Software that collects information, without a user's knowledge, about computer use habits and then uses the information for marketing purposes.

supercomputer The largest, fastest, most expensive computers manufactured. They are used to process extensive amounts of data and to make very precise mathematical calculations. Cray XMP systems are examples of supercomputers.

synchronous Happening at the same time. Synchronous communication, for instance, is characterized by time-dependence; that is, the sender and receiver communicate at the same time. An example is a telephone conversation.

system A group of interrelated parts assembled to achieve some common goal or end. The three major components of most systems are input, process, and output. Examples of systems include computer systems, ecological systems, economic systems, political systems, and school systems.

system software Programs that direct, supervise, and support the computer hardware system and all the tasks that are to be performed on it. An operating system is an example of system software.

TCO *See* total cost of ownership.

TCP/IP *See* transmission control protocol/Internet protocol.

terabtye One trillion bytes.

T1 A dedicated digital circuit that uses broadband data communications to provide high-speed transmissions of data at the rate of up to 1.5 million bits per second.

tool software One of the classifications of instructional software established by Robert Taylor. It assumes that the computer is used to assist in a learning activity. Examples include word processing, spreadsheet, database, and graphics software.

total cost of ownership (TCO) A yearly calculation used to represent the total cost of installing, operating, and maintaining hardware such as a computer workstation.

touch-sensitive screen A video screen designed to recognize the location of touch on its surface. It allows users to use a finger to point to options provided on the screen by software. Also referred to as a touch screen.

trackball An input device that functions similarly to a mouse and is used for pointing to objects on a video screen.

train the trainer An approach to staff development that relies on developing a cadre of well-trained individuals in an organization who train other staff.

transfer rate The time it takes to transfer data from one location (device) to another. In computer hardware evaluation, transfer rate would be used to measure the performance of input and output devices.

transmission control protocol/Internet protocol (TCP/IP) The standard protocol used on the Internet. Originally developed by the U.S. Department of Defense for ARPANET.

Trojan horse A form of computer virus that appears to be a program or file that might be of use on a computer but when opened actually can be destructive. Some Trojan horses are designed to be more annoying than malicious; others

can cause serious damage by deleting files and destroying information on the system.

tutee software One of the classifications of instructional software established by Robert Taylor. It assumes that the student possesses the necessary information and controls the learning environment. Examples include programming languages such as Logo, BASIC, and Pascal.

tutorial A form of tutor software similar in style and appearance to drill-and-practice software. However, tutorials are designed to teach new material, whereas drill-and-practice programs are designed to reinforce material already learned.

tutor software One of the classifications of instructional software established by Robert Taylor. It assumes that the computer possesses the necessary information and controls the learning environment. Examples include drill-and-practice programs, tutorials, simulations, and educational games.

Twitter A social networking and micro-blogging service that enables users to send and receive messages known as *tweets*.

uniform resource locator (URL) An electronic address that identifies a unique location of a data file on the World Wide Web.

UNIX A powerful multitasking operating system developed at Bell Laboratories in 1969 and written in the C programming language. Variations of UNIX enable it to run on IBM, Apple, and other manufacturers' computers. The UNIX operating system is especially popular for supporting the "server" function in client–server environments such as the Internet.

uplink The transmission of data from an earth station to a communications satellite.

upload In a computer network, the process of transmitting a copy of a file from a computer to a central file server.

URL *See* uniform resource locator.

video board A CPU component capable of accepting and generating video.

video capture Term used for converting analog video into a digital video file.

videoconferencing The use of analog or digital video technology to connect multiple parties simultaneously in a conference where participants can see and hear each other. Point-to-point video conferencing refers to a two-party conference. Multipoint videoconferencing refers to a multiple (more than two) party conference.

videodisc An optical disc used to store video images and associated audio or sound information in analog format. Same as a laserdisc.

video display device An output device capable of displaying text or images on a video screen.

virus A computer program designed to reproduce (infect) as it is used in computer networks and copy programs. Some viruses are merely nuisances; others are designed to damage files or programs. *See also* Trojan horse, worm, and spyware.

voice output unit Any device that produces spoken words from a computer. *See* speech synthesis; audio response unit.

voice recognition device Any device that can be used to recognize and record sounds. Frequently used with a digitizer to convert sounds into digital format.

WAN *See* wide area network.

wave format Digital file format used to store sounds as a pattern of oscillatory periodic electronic signals.

Web browser *See* browser software.

Weblog *See* blog.

whiteboard *See* intelligent whiteboard.

wide area network (WAN) Connecting computer equipment using data communications over a widespread geographic area such as a town, city, or country.

Wi-Fi A communications or signal standard for WLANs based on the Institute of Electrical and Electronics Engineers (IEEE) Wireless Standard 802.11b.

wiki Derived from a Hawaiian term meaning "quick", a wiki is a Web site that facilitates the creation and editing of content on a Web page or other electronic document. It is especially useful in collaborative work and learning environments.

wireless local area network (WLAN) A form of a local area network that uses high-frequency radio waves to send and receive data signals.

WLAN *See* wireless local area network.

word processing The use of computer equipment for entering and editing text. Popular word processing programs include WordPerfect, WordStar, and Microsoft Word.

World Wide Web The protocol and file format software incorporating hypertext and multimedia capabilities for use on the Internet.

WORM An acronym for write once, read many. It is a type of optical disc that allows the recording or writing of data once, which can then be accessed or read many times.

worm The name for a type of computer virus that spreads from computer to computer. A worm takes advantage of file or information transport features on your system, which allows it to travel unaided.

WWW *See* World Wide Web.

YouTube A free social networking Web site that allows users to upload and share *Flash*-formatted videos.

INDEX